D1712866

LANGUAGE AND LOGIC IN THE
POST-MEDIEVAL PERIOD

SYNTHESE HISTORICAL LIBRARY

TEXTS AND STUDIES IN THE HISTORY OF

LOGIC AND PHILOSOPHY

VOLUME 12

E. J. ASHWORTH

LANGUAGE AND LOGIC
IN THE
POST-MEDIEVAL PERIOD

D. REIDEL PUBLISHING COMPANY

DORDRECHT-HOLLAND / BOSTON-U.S.A.

Library of Congress Catalog Card Number 74–76478

ISBN 90 277 0464 3

Published by D. Reidel Publishing Company,
P.O. Box 17, Dordrecht, Holland

Sold and distributed in the U.S.A., Canada, and Mexico
by D. Reidel Publishing Company, Inc.
306 Dartmouth Street, Boston,
Mass. 02116, U.S.A.

Printed in The Netherlands by D. Reidel, Dordrecht

TABLE OF CONTENTS

PREFACE

Keckermann remarked of the sixteenth century, "never from the beginning of the world was there a period so keen on logic, or in which more books on logic were produced and studies of logic flourished more abundantly than the period in which we live." [1] But despite the great profusion of books to which he refers, and despite the dominant position occupied by logic in the educational system of the fifteenth, sixteenth and seventeenth centuries, very little work has been done on the logic of the post-medieval period. The only complete study is that of Risse, whose account, while historically exhaustive, pays little attention to the actual logical doctrines discussed. [2] Otherwise, one can turn to Vasoli for a study of humanism, to Muñoz Delgado for scholastic logic in Spain, and to Gilbert and Randall for scientific method, but this still leaves vast areas untouched. In this book I cannot hope to remedy all the deficiencies of previous studies, for to survey the literature alone would take a life-time. As a result I have limited myself in various ways. In the first place, I concentrate only on those matters which are of particular interest to me, namely theories of meaning and reference, and formal logic. For discussions of such matters as demonstration, the logic of scientific method, the categories, the topics, informal fallacies, humanist logic, Ramist logic, and the whole range of commentaries on Aristotle, the reader will have to look elsewhere. However, in my first chapter, which I must confess to be based largely on secondary sources, I attempt to give an overall picture of the period, so that the reader can assess the place of the people and the theories I discuss in a wider context.

In the second place, although I make extensive references to one or two medieval logicians, particularly Peter of Ailly, whose work was still widely read and discussed in the post-medieval period, I have made no attempt to fill in the medieval background, or to trace the historical antecedents of every doctrine I mention. There are two reasons for this deficiency. One lies in my original purpose, which was simply to describe just what logic a well-read man of the sixteenth or seventeenth century would have been acquainted with. The other, and most important, reason lies in the monumental nature of such a task. An adequate treatment of the historical antecedents would not only double the size of my book, but would quadruple the number of footnotes, as well as taking many years to accomplish. Fortunately medieval logic has been by no means as thoroughly neglected as post-medieval logic, and a very good idea of its scope and achievements can be obtained from the following works, which themselves contain extensive bibliographies:

Nuchelmans, G., *Theories of the Proposition. Ancient and Medieval Conceptions of the Bearers of Truth and Falsity*, Amsterdam, 1973.

Pinborg, J., *Logik und Semantik im Mittelalter. Ein Überblick*, Stuttgart-Bad Cannstatt, 1972.

Rijk, L. M. de, *Logica Modernorum, Vol. I, On the Twelfth Century Theories of Fallacy*, Assen, 1962.

Rijk, L. M. de, *Logica Modernorum, Vol. II, The Origin and Early Development of the Theory of Supposition*, Assen, 1967. This volume is in two parts, the second of which contains texts and indices.

In the third place, I have found myself unable to shed very much light on the historical relations between many of the authors whom I discuss. So far as those from whom I most frequently quote are concerned, there is little problem. The bulk of my references are to Caubraith, Celaya, Clichtoveus, Enzinas, Pardo, de Soto and Tartaretus, all of whom studied and/or taught at the University of Paris in the first years of the sixteenth century, or earlier in the case of Tartaretus. Needless to say, these men were acquainted with each other's works. Many other references are to Hieronymus of St. Mark of whom I know only that he studied at Oxford and that he frequently quotes from the work of Pardo; and to the Germans, Trutvetter, Gebwiler and Eckius, who are of the same period and who obviously knew the works of the Parisian logicians as well as the works of Ockham, Buridan, Marsilius of Inghen and Albert of Saxony. The only later sixteenth century author of whom I make much use is Fonseca, and the only seventeenth century author of whom I make much use is John of St. Thomas. The influences on these men have been comprehensively described in the works of Muñoz Delgado, and they stem back to early sixteenth century Paris. However, once one strays outside Spain and the Paris of the early sixteenth century, a number of obstacles to historical understanding immediately appear. Despite Risse's efforts, we still do not know exactly how many logic texts were published, where they were written, or when their first edition appeared. The books themselves usually contain neither biographical nor bibliographical information. Authors not only used each other's work without acknowledgement, but they also criticized each other's work without giving more specific references than "a certain doctor said". Little is known about the curricula of most sixteenth and seventeenth century universities. Moreover, there is a tremendous amount of sameness about the contents of logical textbooks, particularly in the later period. They can be roughly categorized as Philippist, Ramist, Philippo-Ramist, Aristotelian, or eclectic, but finer distinctions are hard to draw. Even when an author cites his sources, this may be of little help. For instance, we know that Joachim Jungius told Rhenius that he based his logic text upon the works of Dietericus and Johann Kirchmann,[3] but his work bears little obvious relation to that of Dietericus, and I have been unable to see a copy of Kirchmann. In any case, the first edition of Kirchmann listed by Risse appeared in 1638, the very year of the *Logica Hamburgensis*.

On the whole, I think that I will be content to leave the task of unraveling all the relationships between logicians of the later period to the intellectual historian. It is true that a number of medieval doctrines were preserved into the seventeenth century, much later than such authors as Boehner had supposed, and it is true that some new work was done, particularly with respect to the fourth figure of the syllogism, but generally speaking, nothing of interest to the logician was said after 1550 at the very latest. Indeed, now that I have written this book, I have compiled a large list of logic texts from the period 1550–1650 which I shall be happy never to open again. On the other hand, an enormous amount of interesting work remains to be done for the period 1450–1550, and I very much hope that my own research will provide a useful starting-point for research by others.

NOTES

[1] Keckermann, *Praecogniti*, 109f.
[2] For titles, see the bibliography.
[3] Jungius, editor's introduction, xx.

NOTE ABOUT ABBREVIATIONS

In order to simplify the footnotes, I give just the author's name when the title of the book appears in the bibliography. If he wrote more than one book or article, I have adopted the following conventions:

(1) For primary sources I give a short title which is listed in the bibliography.

(2) For secondary sources I give the author's name, followed by A, B, C etc. for the first and subsequent books cited, or by 1, 2, 3 etc. for the first and subsequent articles cited. The order is chronological.

I do not use *'ibid.'*, *'op. cit.'* or *'loc. cit.'* for any work which appears in the bibliography.

When a book or article does not make a significant contribution to the study of logic after 1429, I omit it from the bibliography and give the complete reference in the footnote. Any subsequent reference to such a work will include the words *'op. cit.'* My criteria here are, of course, those of subject matter, not of quality.

When an author's name appears in the text, but his only work is unpaginated, I omit footnote references.

I follow the Oxford University Press in using, e.g., '2 f.' to refer to page 2 and the one following, and '2 ff.' to refer to page 2 and more than one of the following pages. If I write '2–3' this means that the pages are only numbered on one side and I am referring to pages 2 (or 2 recto or 2a), 2vo (or 2 verso or 2b) and 3.

ACKNOWLEDGEMENTS

I would like to thank N. Kretzmann and J. Narveson for their helpful comments on the text; the staff of Inter-Library Loan at the University of Waterloo for finding even the most obscure secondary sources; and both the University of Waterloo and the Canada Council for the generous financial aid which made the research for this book possible.

I would also like to thank the editors of the *American Philosophical Quarterly* and the *Notre Dame Journal of Formal Logic* for permission to use material from the following articles:

'The Treatment of Semantic Paradoxes from 1400 to 1700', *Notre Dame Journal of Formal Logic* **13** (1972) 34–52;

'Strict and Material Implication in the Early Sixteenth Century', *Notre Dame Journal of Formal Logic* **13** (1972) 556–560;

'Andreas Kesler and the Later Theory of Consequence', *Notre Dame Journal of Formal Logic* **14** (1973) 205–214;

'The Theory of Consequence in the Late Fifteenth and Early Sixteenth Centuries', *Notre Dame Journal of Formal Logic* **14** (1973) 289–315;

'Existential Assumptions in Late Medieval Logic', *American Philosophical Quarterly* **10** (1973) 205–214.

CHAPTER I

HISTORICAL INTRODUCTION

Although many of the details of the development of logic in the Middle Ages remain to be filled in, it is well known that between the time of Peter of Spain (d. 1277) and Paul of Venice (d. 1429), a high level of sophistication and formalism was reached. The theory of consequences or valid inference forms, which involved a recognition of the place and value of propositional logic, was of particular importance, but supposition theory, which included an analysis of meaning and reference, as well as complicated quantificational inferences, and the study of logical paradoxes under the title of *insolubilia*, were also significant. Perhaps the most outstanding figures in these departures from the syllogistic logic of Aristotle were Ockham, Buridan and Burleigh, who all worked in the first half of the fourteenth century, but such followers as Albert of Saxony and Marsilius of Inghen, and such lesser figures as Strode and Heytesbury, should not be overlooked. An encyclopedic account of his predecessors' work was given by Paul of Venice in his *Logica Magna*, showing that formal logic was alive and well at the beginning of the fifteenth century, but hitherto no one has been able to give a clear answer to the question of what happened next. Many opinions have been offered, of course. Typical is that of Father Boehner, who claimed that at the end of the fifteenth century logic entered upon a period of unchecked regression, during which it became an insignificant preparatory study, diluted with extralogical elements; and the insights of such men as Burleigh into the crucial importance of propositional logic as a foundation for logic as a whole were lost.[1] His judgement is supported by studies of humanism and of Ramism, which, by concentrating upon schools little interested in formal logic, reinforce the impression that formal logic was very sick, if not dead. Nor has the focusing of attention upon isolated figures helped. John of St. Thomas, Joachim Jungius, and the authors of the Port-Royal logic have all been the subjects of discussion and study in recent years;[2] yet someone who is acquainted only with the works of these men will have a very poor grasp of what actually happened in the post-medieval period.

1. THE PUBLICATION OF MEDIEVAL WORKS

Before I attempt to answer the question of what happened to formal logic
after the death of Paul of Venice by examining the patterns of writing and
teaching, it is appropriate to consider the extent to which medieval authors were published once printing became the major means of com-
munication. The most important figure for investigation is Peter of Spain,
for his *Summulae Logicales* provided the core of most first-year university courses. Mullally tells us that the works of Peter of Spain were taught
at the universities of Paris, Vienna, Cologne, Freiburg, Leipzig, Ingolstadt and Tübingen; and that the *Summulae Logicales*, in the company
of various treatises attributed to Peter of Spain, appeared in no less than
one hundred and sixty-six printed editions during the period I am con-
sidering.[3] However, the picture is altered considerably when one looks
at dates and places of publication. If one looks up "Petrus Hispanus" in
Risse's invaluable *Bibliographia Logica*, one finds that no editions appeared in Spain or England, a few in Paris, some in Germany, Poland,
the Netherlands and Belgium. Deventer leads with sixteen editions between 1485 and 1528. After 1528 there are only seven editions, the last
in 1639, and *all* were printed in Venice. Turning to the commentators
who, of course, normally included the text in their work, one finds that
Versor, the fifteenth century Thomist is the most popular, having been
printed twenty-three times. Five editions appeared at Cologne before
1500, but otherwise the places of publication are scattered, including
Lyons, Basel, Nuremberg, Hagenau, Seville and Mantua. All nine editions between 1503 and 1639 were in Venice, except for one published at
Naples in 1577. George of Brussels was next in popularity, but all the
editions of his work appeared in France, eleven of them at Lyons, and
the last in 1515. The third most popular was Tartaretus. At the beginning
his work was published in Freiburg, Paris, Lyons and Basel, but between
1515 and 1621 the only editions came from Venice; Cologne was a favourite centre of publication for commentaries by less popular figures;
but printing houses in such diverse places as Cracow, Augsburg, Valencia, Seville, Florence, Salamanca, Leipzig, Vienna, Caen, Frankfurt,
Heidelberg and Tübingen did their share of the work. The commentary
of Alphonso de Veracruz was even published in Mexico in 1554, although
the three subsequent editions appeared in Salamanca. The latest written

commentary seems to have been that of Thomas de Mercado, published in Seville in 1571. The overall picture is clear. By the 1520s there was a sharp decline of interest in Peter of Spain which was only arrested in Spain to a limited extent, and in Italy to a surprisingly greater extent, given that Italy was the home of both humanism and Aristotelianism.

So far as other medieval writers are concerned, the publishing history is equally revealing. Paul of Venice apparently met with the steadiest demand, for in Venice alone sixteen editions of his *Logica Parva* were produced, six of them between 1525 and 1580. The *Logica Magna* appeared only in one edition, in Venice. Duns Scotus was also moderately popular. Various commentaries of his were published before 1512, and between 1586 and 1639 his works received five editions, three of which came from Venice. Albert of Saxony's *Sophismata* was popular in Paris, but the *Perutilis Logica* appeared only once, in Venice in 1522. Buridan's *Sophismata* and *Consequentiae* appeared in Paris, and his *Summulae* was printed three times, the last being at Lyons in 1510. Dorp's commentary on the latter work appeared in Lyons four times before 1500 and once in Paris, in 1504. Burleigh's *Super artem veterem expositio* appeared thirteen times in Paris between 1476 and 1541. Ockham's *Summa totius logicae* appeared three times in the sixteenth century in Venice, in 1508, 1522 and 1591, and in Oxford in 1675, but he certainly does not seem to have been a best seller. Strode's *Consequentiae* appeared seven times before 1507, once in Pavia, but otherwise in Venice. None of these men were published in such places as Deventer and Cologne, which had busy printing houses of their own. Even though books seem to have circulated quite widely in Europe, wherever they were printed, it does not seem that those interested in the logic of their medieval predecessors would have found it easy to acquaint themselves with their work.

While the history of publication gives some idea of what medieval texts were available, it is the history of new logical writings and of the content of teaching in the university that is of major importance for the purpose of establishing the status of formal logic from the fifteenth to the seventeenth centuries. The period is lengthy, and it is one of great diversity and change politically, economically and intellectually, as is reflected by the diversity of logical schools which developed, and by the complexity of their interactions with one another. Scholasticism, by which I mean the type of logical doctrine associated with the late medieval period, was joined by humanism, by Aristotelianism, by Ramism and by an eclecticism which borrowed doctrines from various schools and thrust them into convenient text-book form. Before I consider the developments which were peculiar to the period, I shall examine scholasticism in Italy, France and Spain, in order to assess how far medieval logic remained part of a living tradition.

2. Scholasticism in Italy and Germany

Fifteenth century Italy is usually thought of as the home of humanism, and hence of a complete reaction against scholastic logic, but in fact the teaching of logic remained very much the province of scholastics, while the new humanists took over the teaching of moral philosophy.[4] At the end of the fourteenth century, the works of the English logicians Ockham, Strode and Ferrybridge became very popular, along with those by other representatives of the nominalist school, such as Buridan. In Florence, for instance, the monk Giovanni di Baldassare acquired books by Buridan, Albert of Saxony, Marsilius of Inghen and Heytesbury, as well as unspecified *Sophismata, Insolubilia* and *Obligationes*;[5] and the interests revealed by this list were to characterize many Italians, at least until the end of the fifteenth century. Paul of Venice had spent time in both Oxford and Paris, and he taught what he had learned there at Padua. His pupil, Paul of Pergula, who died in 1451, continued this tradition at Padua and himself wrote *Dubia* on the *Consequentiae* of Strode. Cajetan of Thiene (1387–1465) who taught logic at Padua from 1422 to 1433 also wrote on Strode, as well as on Heytesbury and Ferrybridge, all of whom formed part of the standard logic curriculum at Padua, along with Aristotle.[6] Nor did this state of affairs undergo rapid change after the deaths of Cajetan and Paul of Pergula, for in 1496 a statute of the arts faculty assigned Strode and Heytesbury, Paul of Venice and the *Dubia* of Paul of Pergula.

What happened to scholastic logic in Italy during the sixteenth century is not so clear. Nominalism does not seem to have flourished, a state of affairs which is obviously connected with the absence of Italians from the University of Paris at the beginning of the sixteenth century. Instead, we find evidence of both Scotism and Thomism, although it must be pointed out that there was little practical difference between the three ways so far as formal logic is concerned. Niphus (d. 1546?) followed Pseudo-Scotus very closely in his remarks on consequences; and Bologna was the home of two Thomists, Silvester de Priero (1456–1523) and Chrysostom Javellus (d.c. 1538), a Dominican whose popular logical works still contained most of the scholastic doctrines. Ludovicus Carbo, of whom little is known save that he is not identical with the fifteenth century humanist, wrote on consequences, supposition and insolubles in a book first published in 1589; and in the seventeenth century supposition and consequences are mentioned by Thomas Campanella (1568–1639), a Dominican who spent a large part of his life in prison on heresy charges. The continued popularity of the commentaries of the Thomist Versor and the Scotist Tartaretus also serves as evidence for the climate of opinion in Italy at this time.

Before I turn to France and Spain, something must be said of the other European countries. Despite her glorious logical past, England was not worthy of much comment in this period. The beginning of the sixteenth century was marked mainly by the publication of the undistinguished *Libellus Sophistarum*, a logic text for the use of students at Oxford and Cambridge. Poland produced John of Glogovia (c. 1445–1597), who taught in Cracow for nearly forty years, and wrote a commentary on Peter of Spain. Only in Germany was there much new writing going on. At Leipzig we find both Gregorius Breitkopf, who produced editions of Horace and Petrarch as well as his logical works, and Konrad von Buchen [Wimpina] (1465?–1531) who was a Thomist, and became Rector of Frankfurt in 1505. At Erfurt there were the Nominalists Bartholomaeus of Usingen (d. 1532) and Jodocus Trutvetter (d. 1519), who moved to Wittenberg in 1507. Both of them taught Luther. The most prolific writer was Johannes Eckius (1486–1543), who was a humanist and theologian as well as a writer of traditional logical commentaries, and who ended a varied academic career at the University of Ingolstadt. The logic curricula at all these universities were of a standard type. Marsilius of Inghen was particularly popular; [8] and various commentaries on Peter of Spain were circulated.

3. SCHOLASTICISM IN FRANCE AND SPAIN

The University of Paris was the outstanding centre for scholastic logic in Europe, and a good deal is known both about the curriculum and the men who taught there.[9] The arts faculty was by far the largest, having, according to one source, between four and five thousand students at the beginning of the sixteenth century,[10] and it was here that the study of logic was carried out. All arts students devoted two years to logic, and a third year to the physics, metaphysics and ethics of Aristotle.[11] The teaching of logic fell into two parts, which gave rise to two distinct types of logical literature.[12] In the first year, the students studied Peter of Spain and such topics as exponibles, consequences and insolubles. In their second year they were faced with Porphyry's *Isagoge* and Aristotle himself; and various metaphysical questions were raised in addition to the logical ones.[13] The majority of the students following this course of study were young boys in their early teens, and the majority of the teachers in the various colleges were themselves not much older, despite a statute forbidding anyone to act as master before the age of twenty.[14] It was customary for a man to fulfil his arts teaching requirements before going on to the study of theology or law, so that there was a constant flow of lecturers in logic, most of whom presumably merely passed on what they themselves had been taught so recently. The schedule followed was a very heavy one for staff and students alike. The first class met at 4.00 a.m. and the last interrogation was at 7.00 p.m., with scarcely a break in between.[15]

Paris had early come under the influence of nominalist logic, for Peter of Ailly (1350–1420) who became chancellor of the university in the early fifteenth century, was a follower of Ockham and Buridan. In 1474 the king decreed that nominalism should not be taught any longer, but that instead the university should devote itself to the works of Aristotle and the commentaries of Averroes, Albertus Magnus, Aquinas, Scotus, Bonaventure, Alexander of Hales and Aegidius Romanus.[16] So far from being crushed, the nominalists leaped to their own defence, claiming that they did not multiply entities, and that they paid attention to the properties of terms, unlike the realists, who "neglected and scorned these matters, saying 'we go to the things and do not care about terms' ".[17] There was a sudden rise in the popularity of Ockham, Buridan, Albert of Saxony, Marsilius of Inghen, Peter of Ailly and Johannes Dorp, who commented on Buridan, and the decree was rescinded in 1481. Between that year and about 1520 Paris was a centre of tremendous logical activity, and the best logicians to be found in the entire period with which I am dealing spent some, if not all, of their active life in that city.

The earliest figures of note were George of Brussels, about whom almost nothing is known; Martinus de Magistris (1432–1482) who taught at Sainte-Barbe college and was the principal defender of Ockham after the decree of 1474; and Thomas Bricot, who worked with George of Brussels, but died as late as 1516. He was responsible for bringing Peter of Spain into a prominent position; he edited Buridan's versions of Aristotle; and he made Buridan's *Summulae* the basis of his own logic teaching.[18] Another leading nominalist was Jean Raulin, who became a Benedictine in 1497, and died in 1514. Peter Tartaretus was the single Scotist of note. He was Rector of the university in 1490, but later became a Franciscan and turned to theological studies. After the turn of the century the leading figure was John Major (1469–1550) who was himself a pupil of George of Brussels and Bricot,[19] and who taught at Paris from 1505 until 1517, when he returned to his native Scotland to take up the first chair of philosophy and theology at Glasgow. He did return to Paris, but never repeated his early days of glory when he gathered around himself at the college of Montaigu a brilliant and diverse group of men. The group included Pierre Crockaert, who later became a Thomist, and was from Brussels, and John Dullaert (c. 1470–1513) who was from Ghent. From Scotland came George Lokert (d. 1547), David Cranston (d. 1512), and Robert Caubraith. Jacques Almain (d. 1515) was a Frenchman. Gaspar Lax (1487–1560), Antonio Coronel and his brother Luis, Juan de Celaya and Domingo de Soto were all Spaniards. Other notable Spaniards in Paris during this period included Hieronymus Pardo (d. 1505), Juan Dolz at the college of Lyons, and Fernando de Enzinas at the college of Beauvais. Never again was scholastic logic to be the focus of so much attention from such an able group of men. I say nothing here of their works, as they will be amply discussed in the succeeding chapters.

It is not surprising that the Spanish universities were heavily influenced by the logical teachings of Paris, for most of those Spaniards who studied in Paris returned to their homeland as teachers, and according to Father Muñoz Delgado, who has made a number of excellent and detailed studies, nominalism was to flourish there until at least 1540, twenty years after it had died out at the University of Paris.[20] Alcalá, where Bartolus de Castro and Fernando de Enzinas both taught, was the first centre of nominalism, but Salamanca, not wishing to be outdone by Paris and Alcalá, opened its doors to nominalists in 1509,[21] and thereafter they flourished at both universities. The pattern of teaching was the same as at Paris, with a two year logic course of which the first year was devoted to Peter of Spain and ancillary matters.[22] According to the statutes of Salamanca in 1538, terms were to be studied from St. Luke to St. Andrew,[23] the first tract of Peter of Spain and the *Parva logicalia* (or treatises devoted to such matters as supposition and appellation) until mid-May, syllogisms until mid-July and exponibles, insolubles and obligations until vacation time.[24] The texts used were Paris-oriented. For instance, Christobal de Medina used works by John Major, Celaya, Dullaert and Enzinas.[25]

4. HUMANISM

But even Spain was to be affected in its turn by humanism, a movement which had its origin in late fourteenth and fifteenth century Italy; and it is to one aspect of this that I now turn. The revival of classical scholarship and the turning away from the old style of education led to at least two different approaches among those concerned with logic. Some men concentrated on a return to the pure Aristotle, freed from medieval accretions and misinterpretations; and some turned to a logic which was heavily tinged with rhetoric. I wish to examine the rhetorical logicians here; and I shall refer to them as 'humanists', bearing in mind that others also deserve this title. The humanists were frequently in close alliance with the seekers after a pure Aristotle, but unlike the latter, they did not produce lengthy and detailed commentaries on the original text, since they were also inspired by a desire to simplify for pedagogical purposes. Scholastic logic was thought to be too subtle and too complicated to be taught usefully to students, even when it was not condemned as empty and trifling. There was also a strong feeling that the scholastics had sinned in departing too far from ordinary language, or rather, ordinary Latin. Their contortions of language and their invented vocabulary struck the humanists as barbarous and to be avoided at all costs.

These emphases on a simplified Latin and on pedagogical ease were to shadow the subsequent history of logic. Not only the humanists but also Melanchthon, Ramus, the Jesuits, those who produced the *Cursus Artium* in places like Coimbra and Alcalá, and those who wrote the systematic text-books in seventeenth century Germany were preoccupied with teaching the rudiments of logic in as simple and effective a manner and in as ordinary a language as possible. These aims perverted the purpose of scholastic logic, which was also to teach, but to teach a developed formal logic rather than the art of thinking clearly. Much trouble would have been avoided had a symbolic language been developed by the scholastics so that, for example, the difference between examining an editorial for the cogency of its arguments and working out a problem in the first-order quantificational calculus could have been made clear. The scholastics were often concerned with the latter type of activity, but since they described what they were doing in Latin they gave the humanists the impression that they were merely perverting language. On the other hand, the humanists were preoccupied with ways of thinking clearly, but by keeping at least the apparatus of the categorical syllogism they gave the scholastics the impression that they were merely misusing formal systems.

One of the first to inveigh against scholastic logic was Petrarch, who felt that logic was merely a propaedeutic discipline, not to be lingered over, and certainly not to be encumbered by the inane questions raised by the English logicians whose works were flooding into Italy.[26] This theme was picked up at the beginning of the fifteenth century by Leonardo Bruni, who accused the scholastics or *barbari* of being ignorant of the value and human sense of language;[27] and who remarked of the English logicians that even their names were to be shuddered at.[28] However, Bruni offered no positive suggestion as to the way he would like logic to be; and Lorenzo Valla was the first to combine criticisms of scholasticism with the elaboration of a doctrine which was faithful to his aim of fostering a single art which would be of use to the human sciences of medicine, law, politics, poetry and history.[29] In his *Dialecticae Disputationes* he attacked the Aristotelian categories on the grounds that they were too many and too metaphysical, proposing instead just three fundamental notions, *substantia*, *qualitas*, and *actio*. He attacked the Aristotelian account of the relations between propositions, saying, for instance, that it was ridiculous to speak of two propositions which can both be false but cannot both be true, for if the first situation is possible the second must also be possible. Finally, he attacked the syllogism itself as giving scope to *cavillatores*. The five indirect modes of the first figure were dismissed, although not on logical grounds; and the third figure was dismissed because "it has no sanity but is entirely insane."[30] He was then left with the eight modes which in his view were truly convenient and useful. Throughout his work he emphasized the close links between grammar, logic and rhetoric, which cooperate towards the single end of providing clear and persuasive arguments.

Another influential figure who must be mentioned is George of Trebizond (1395–1484), a Byzantine scholar who settled in Italy in about 1430 and who probably wrote his *Dialectica* at the same time as Valla was working on his *Dialecticae Disputationes*.[31] George of Trebizond's book was first printed in 1470, and enjoyed a great vogue. It was marked by its simplicity and clarity, by its insistence on examples from orators and poets, and by its relative neglect of formal logic, although he did include some propositional logic in addition to the syllogism. Other humanist figures include Joannes Argyropulis; his pupil Poliziano, who strove to get back to the original Aristotelian doctrines and went through the *Organon* while teaching in Florence from 1491 to 1494;[32] and Giorgio Valla (d. 1500) who taught at Padua, Pavia, and Venice, and who laid great stress on the topics, on invention, and on rhetoric.[33]

Italian humanism was not without its effect on the University of Paris, even at the time when scholasticism was at the height of its powers, for the college of Cardinal Lemoine was the home of men who accused their colleagues of using words barbarously and of betraying Aristotle's teaching. The main figure was Jacques Lefèvre d'Etaples (1450?–1536) who visited Italy in 1491, before taking up a chair of philosophy at the college of Cardinal Lemoine.[34] He produced a commentary and paraphrase of Aristotle's *Organon*, and was also responsible for the publication in Paris of George of Trebizond's *Dialectica* in 1508. In his own logical work, the *Introductiones Artificiales*, he demonstrated his desire to combine clarity of expression and faithfulness to Aristotle with a recognition of the importance of scholastic insights into such matters as supposition and insolubles. His Flemish disciple and friend, Jodocus Clichtoveus (1472–1543) wrote a commentary on the *Introductiones Artificiales* which contains one of the most elegant expositions of these doctrines available to us. Unlike the Italians whom they admired, the Parisian humanists seem to have been clearly aware of the nature and place of semantical investigations and of formal logic.

5. RUDOLPH AGRICOLA AND HIS INFLUENCE

Neither the Italian humanists nor their Parisian followers can be credited with spreading rhetorical logic throughout Europe, for this honour belongs to Rudolph Agricola (1444–1485).[35] He was born in the Netherlands, studied in Erfurt, Louvain, Cologne and Paris, but was most influenced by the education he received in Italy where he went in about 1469. He had intended to study law, but turned instead to classical language and literature; and while in Italy he began to write *De Inventione Dialectica*, which was not actually printed until 1515, but which circulated in manuscript for many years before that. This book, one of the most popular of the sixteenth century, was chiefly devoted to the logical topics and their use. Although Agricola claimed to have a great respect for Aristotle,[36] he felt that the latter had left many logical matters unmentioned or undiscovered; and his own purpose was to fill in some of these gaps, with particular reference to the works of Cicero and Themistius. Like Cicero, he divided logic into two parts, invention and judgement, and in accordance with this division, his first Book dealt with the invention or finding of the logical topics, while the second dealt with their use in argumentation. In this second Book, Agricola discussed the nature of logic and of its instruments, which are the parts of speech and the four forms of argumentation, two perfect, the syllogism and enumeration or induction, and two imperfect, enthymeme and example. His treatment of the syllogism is the only directly logical part of the *De Inventione Dialectica*, but he confined himself to listing names for the three terms and the three propositions involved, and to giving a few examples. The latter are not even of syllogisms in the strictest sense, for he included proper names. Agricola claimed that logic was very closely allied to rhetoric, which had the function of expressing and ornamenting the products of logic,[37] and his orientation throughout tended to be rhetorical rather than logical. The third Book, in fact, is devoted to the art of influencing, and to the disposition of arguments, both subjects belonging to rhetoric, not logic.

That Agricola should have written a treatise which was largely devoted to rhetorical matters was perfectly legitimate, and would be unremarkable were it not for the fact that the *De Inventione Dialectica* was regarded as a logical treatise and influenced not only rhetoricians but those who claimed to be logicians. The prevailing attitude to his work is neatly illustrated by a prefatory epistle written by Johannes Matthaeus Phrissemius. It is a tedious piece of polemic, but its general theme is significant.

Phrissemius imagines readers asking "Why should we prefer this book to the *Summulae Logicales* of Peter of Spain?" and he replies that Agricola teaches the finding and using of arguments, a subject barely touched upon by Peter of Spain. Moreover, he says, when one compares the neatness, elegance, reason and clarity of Agricola to the barbarisms and solecisms of Peter of Spain, one realizes that looking for Agricola's virtues in the latter is like trying to obtain wool from an ass or water from a stone. The implication is that the well-rounded man need only read Agricola, and may safely disregard Peter of Spain.

Agricola's work raised questions which were of great importance to the sixteenth century, namely the place of the topics in logic and the relationship of logic to rhetoric. Topics, or the ways of dealing with and classifying those arguments which were not thought to be susceptible to formal treatment, since they depended for their effectiveness upon the meaning and type of terms involved, had always been regarded as part of logic. The early middle ages knew Boethius's *De Differentiis Topicis*, and Aristotle's *Topics* was included in the *logica nova*.[38] A section on the topics appeared somewhere after the treatment of the syllogism in any treatise which was intended to be comprehensive, including the *Summulae logicales* of Peter of Spain. Topics were also an integral part of rhetoric, which, although part of the trivium along with grammar and logic, was usually seen as subordinate to logic. After the *logica nova* appeared, the standard division of logic was into three parts, demonstration, which dealt with certainties, dialectic, which dealt with probabilities, and sophistic, which dealt with fallacies. Rhetoric was usually classed as a subdivision of dialectic, although as McKeon points out, some theologians did exalt rhetoric above logic.[39] The traditional parts of rhetoric were *inventio*, *dispositio* or *iudicium, pronuntiatio, elocutio* and *memoria*. The revolution introduced by Agricola, and taken up by Ramus among others, involved assigning *inventio* and *dispositio* or *iudicium* to logic, dropping *memoria*, and confining rhetoric to *pronuntiatio* and *elocutio*. This meant that the topics were no longer discussed twice, by both logicians and rhetoricians, and it also meant that they were placed before the syllogism, in a place of honour. Rhetoric was now seen as superior to logic, in the sense that the effective presentation of arguments was not just an optional extra, but essential to the process of persuasion. Validity was not enough; logic must be used, it must be seen to work, and for this one needed the skills provided by rhetoric. Such an attitude toward rhetoric had its roots in the writings of the Italian humanists, of course; but they had not taken the step of emphasizing the topics and the place of *inventio* in logic. That was Agricola's own contribution.

One of those whom Agricola influenced was Philip Melanchthon, the *Praeceptor Germaniae*, who must be discussed here even though he was not primarily a logician, and has no claim to originality in this field. Apart from his activities as a leader of the Lutheran reformation, Melanchthon's main importance was as an educationalist, since both through his encouragement of new schools and through the series of text-books he wrote, it was his image which was most firmly stamped upon German protestant education. His confessed aim was to encourage the study of the original works of Aristotle, freed from medieval accretions, for he felt that they contained the formal method which alone could save the young church from intellectual confusion. As a result, the scheme of learning he imposed upon the schools was the study of Aristotelian logic, physics, and ethics; and this curriculum remained basically unchanged until the influx of Ramism in the latter part of the sixteenth century. Melanchthon's influence as a logician, then, was a part of his wider influence, and the *Dialectices libri IIII*, first published in 1527 but many times revised, was but one of the widely used text-books which came from his pen.

One must not be misled by Melanchthon's support of Aristotle into supposing that the contents of the *Dialectica* were a direct restatement of the Organon, for Melanchthon was also a humanist. His book reads rather like a literary essay, and there are constant references to Demosthenes, Cicero, Virgil, Horace and Agricola, as well as to Aristotle himself. Like Agricola, he placed continued emphasis on the close relationship between logic and rhetoric, which adds "living colours" to the basic arguments of logic;[40] and he took the division of logic into invention and judgement as standard, although the three books of *dialectica judicativa* precede the one on *dialectica inventiva*. Book I is devoted to the five predicables, the ten categories, definition and division, and Book II to a brief discussion of propositions and their relationship. Melanchthon did not go into much detail over these matters. He referred the reader to Aristotle if he should require further information about modal propositions;[41] and he remarked that he felt conversion to be more a matter for grammar than for logic.[42] Book III is devoted to the four forms of argumentation, syllogism, induction, enthymeme and example; but although Melanchthon included the main points of traditional teaching, his discussion was not very detailed and tended to be discursive. For instance, when dismissing the reduction of the figures of the syllogism as unnecessary, he included a short diatribe against "those unskilled men, unlearned in eloquence and with no claim to style" who had up till then been teaching boys logic; and he claimed that he himself was presenting only what was really necessary and useful for writing and disputing about weighty matters [*de gravibus rebus*].[43] Much space, moreover, was devoted to quotations from Demosthenes, Cicero and other classical authors. Book IV first gave an account of the topics, which echoed Agricola's teaching, then finished with a section on fallacies. The 1537 edition of the *Dialectica* is remarkable for adding his first reference to method; and a whole section was included on this subject in his last logical work, the *Erotemata Dialectices*.[44] He was one of the earliest to introduce a theme which dominated much of later logical writing.

Neither Italy nor Spain, to which I shall return later, was much affected by Agricola, but England and France were in a different situation. A royal injunction given to Cambridge University in 1535 demanded that students should read Agricola together with Aristotle, George of Trebizond and Melanchthon, instead of the "frivolous questions and obscure glosses of Scotus, Burleigh, Anthony Trombet, Bricot, Bruliferius etc.";[45] while the faculty of theology in Paris complained in 1530 that the faculty of arts studied Agricola more than Aristotle.[46] It had taken some time for Agricola to gain a foothold in Paris, for at first even the humanists there were not sympathetic to his rhetorical style of logic; but gradually he did so through the efforts of Sturm, Caesarius, and Latomus.[47] Bartholomaeus Latomus (1485–1570) taught at Freiburg and Cologne before going to Paris, and was the author of an epitome of Agricola's work. Johannes Caesarius (1460–1551) was another German who migrated to Paris, and his *Dialectica*, published in 1532, showed the influence of Agricola although it was conventional in tone. The Alsatian Johann Sturm (d. 1587), who ended his career at Strassburg, was probably responsible for introducing Agricola to Paris in 1529, when two editions of the *De Inventione Dialectica* were published there.[48] He was also one of the first to discuss the question of method.

6. PETRUS RAMUS AND HIS INFLUENCE

The most famous of those who followed Agricola at Paris, and perhaps the most famous of all the sixteenth century logicians, was Petrus Ramus or Pierre de la Ramée (1515–1572). Much has been written about him, so I will not dwell upon his career, which took place at the University of Paris and was successful, if stormy. He was forbidden to teach in 1544 because of his outspoken denunciations of Aristotle, but soon returned to favour, and became a regius professor in 1551. He retained royal favour despite his conversion to protestantism, and it seems that his death in the Massacre of St. Bartholomew's Day had not been intended by those in authority. His *Dialectique*, first published in 1555 and whose Latin version, *Dialecticae libri duo*, appeared the following year, was constantly revised and re-edited during his lifetime, and constantly reprinted after his death. Ong lists two hundred and sixty-two editions, one hundred and fifty-one of which appeared in Germany.[49] The work is divided into two Books, one on invention or the finding of arguments, and one on judgement or the disposition of arguments. In the latter he put forward new theories both of the syllogism[50] and of method which he took to be the most important part of judgement, thus differing from Melanchthon and Sturm, who had classed it with invention. His treatment of the problem was very straightforward. He wrote that method was simply the disposition by which, of a number of ideas, the first was placed in the first place, the second in the second, and so on. Method began with the clearest and most general ideas, and moved towards the most obscure and most particular.[51] An essential feature of method, as exemplified by Ramus's own writings, was classification by dichotomy; and this was one of the aspects seized upon most eagerly by his followers. The whole discussion is notable for the fact that it takes place in a kind of logical vacuum; no reference is made to any discipline, especially any scientific discipline. Ramus even omitted the brief treatment of induction which was customary in logical texts.

If one compares the writings of Ramus on method with those of his near contemporary, Zabarella, it becomes clear how lacking in breadth and perception they were. The principles he laid down are not invalid, but they are exceedingly limited. They offer nothing to the scientist, and they would serve only to bolster the dogmatism of a mind already convinced that it perceived the truth in an orderly manner. Nor is the *Dialectique* taken as a whole any more remarkable. Ramus made certain changes in terminology; he made some notable omissions, such as the square of opposition and the categories; and he attempted to refurbish the syllogism. Basically, however, he said nothing new; and a list of the argument forms he actually discussed would occupy a very small space. There is even less logical substance in the *Dialectique* than in the work of Melanchthon. Yet, despite all its glaring faults, it is not difficult to see why this rather messy little book became as popular as it did. If logic had to be learned at school or university, far better from the student's point of view to learn it from a book written in a lively manner with a minimum of technical jargon and, indeed, a minimum of logic. Moreover, it was a book which by its very simplification and reliance on self-evident axioms seemed to promise a short cut to the mastery of argumentation. Ramus appealed both to dogmatists and to those who wished to attain intellectual eminence fast.

However, it must not be denied that many sober and well-intentioned logicians also adopted the tenets of Ramism, not so much in France as in Germany. Ramus's books came flooding into that country after his death, and many schools there began to teach his logic in preference to any other; although he was not so popular in university circles, owing to his intellectual insufficiencies.[52] Numbers of books were written in his defence, including the *Logicae Rameae Triumphus* of Thomas Neigius, a professor at Altdorf, who published his book at Basel in 1583. But Ramism did not have it all its own way, despite the support of most Calvinists, for almost at once it came into violent conflict with Melanchthon's Aristotelianism, or Philippism as it was called, which continued to be championed by the majority of Lutherans. Melanchthon's doctrines remained triumphant in various places, but especially at Leipzig, where Ramus was banned in 1592,[53] and at Tübingen where both Johann Weldelius (d. 1612) and Jacob Schegk (d. 1587) were carrying on the fight for Aristotle. Indeed, the confrontation between Philippism and Ramism led in many respects to an even closer adherence to the *Organon* of Aristotle than had been evident in the writings of Melanchthon himself.[54]

The struggle between the two movements was eventually to be resolved in the more eclectic text-books of the seventeenth century, which had their origin in a third school, that of the Semi-Ramists, or Philippo-Ramists, which appeared in the 1590s and which had the aim of taking the best points from both sides and bringing them together in a unified work. Especially at the beginning, this attempted unification was generally effected by first enumerating the categories and then proceeding serenely with the Ramist scheme,[55] as is shown by the *Institutiones Logicae* of the lexicographer, Rudolph Goclenius the Elder (d. 1628). The *Logicae libri duo* of Amandus Polanus, published in 1590, and one of the most important Philippo-Ramist texts, is similar; but the *Institutiones Dialecticae* of Conrad Dietericus, another important work, which appeared in 1613, is more complex. Dietericus stated that he had adopted a way of handing on precepts which was not purely Aristotelian, nor purely Ramist, but mixed.[56] He did, it was true, divide his logic into two parts, invention and judgement, in defiance of the Aristotelian three-fold division into simple terms, enunciation, and *Dianoia*, or syllogistic and method; but, he claimed, Ramists include the last two under judgement, while the first corresponds to invention.[57] The first Book was outwardly Ramist, but contained a discussion of the categories, while the second was less Ramist even outwardly, since there were chapters on the equivalence, conversion and opposition of propositions. He gave a traditional account of the syllogism; he mentioned demonstration and induction; and his account of method, unlike that of Ramus, included a discussion of the difference between analytic and synthetic method.[58]

7. SEVENTEENTH CENTURY LOGIC: ECLECTICISM

A number of other German logicians of the same period are worthy of some mention. There are, for instance, Bartholomaeus Keckermann (1571–1609), who taught Hebrew at Heidelberg and philosophy at Danzig, and wrote systems of politics, mathematics, ethics and theology as well as logic; and J. H. Alsted (1588–1638), a protestant theologian who taught at Herborn. However, the most interesting is Joachim Jungius (1597–1657), who made contributions to such varied disciplines as theology, physics, mineralogy, botany and educational theory. He studied medicine at Padua, and taught in various German cities before becoming Rector of the two classical schools in Hamburg in 1629, a position which he held until his death. His boys learned mathematics with unusual thoroughness, and were introduced to various scientific subjects, although complaints were made that Jungius neglected the teaching of religion; and it was for them that he wrote the *Logica Hamburgensis*, first published in 1638. In outline, the book was a standard one, for the six parts were devoted respectively to the categories and allied matters, to propositions, to argumentation, to demonstration, to topics, and to fallacies. None of the specifically scholastic doctrines appear, but the book is nevertheless of some logical importance, and details will be discussed in subsequent chapters.

In other European countries, as in Germany, the seventeenth century was rather a humdrum period. Ramism was important for a while in the Netherlands, but in 1635 the Estates ordered all schools to use the *Institutionum Logicarum libri duo* of Franco Burgersdijck (1590–1636), which included the standard Aristotelian subjects, although the author also discussed demonstration and method in a way which showed the influence of Zabarella. Three writers associated with Louvain were A. Hunnaeus, (1521–1578); Philippe Du Trieu, who gave up a chair of philosophy there in order to become a Jesuit; and A. Geulincx (1623–1670), who became a Calvinist in 1638. Pierre Du Moulin (1600–1684) was a reformed theologian who studied at Leiden. D. Derodon, another French protestant, taught in France for a while, then went to Geneva, where he died in 1664. The *Port-Royal Logic*, written by A. Arnauld and first published in 1662, contains an unusually clear discussion of the syllogism, but it is set apart from other logic texts of the period by its debt to Descartes and its emphasis on epistemological issues.

In England, Ramism met with some temporary enthusiasm, especially at Cambridge, but the standard works were far more orthodox. The set text in Cambridge for some while was written by John Seton (d. 1567), a Cambridge man who died in exile as a Roman Catholic priest, as did another Cambridge man, John Sanderson (d. 1602). At Oxford, the authors read by John Locke's students included Du Trieu, Burgersdijck, Robert Sanderson, Zabarella, and other late sixteenth or seventeenth century figures, both English and foreign.[59] Direct acquaintance with Aristotle was probably minimal; and no logical writing of any real interest was done until Henry Aldrich (1647–1710) published his *Artis Logicae Compendium* in 1691. Even he did not go far beyond the syllogism, although he mentioned *insolubilia*.

8. HUMANISM AND LATE SCHOLASTICISM IN SPAIN

Spain has not been mentioned since my discussion of scholastic logic, and it is now time to return to that country. It was by no means immune from the forces operating on the rest of Europe, and in J. L. Vives had produced an aggressive young humanist of its own. He had been taught at Paris by Dullaert and Lax, and said "I have often heard them complaining with the greatest grief that they had expended so many years on a thing [scholastic logic] so empty and futile,"[60] a sentiment which presumably belonged more to Vives than to his teachers. Fernando Alonso de Herrera commented on George of Trebizond and L. Valla, while Narciso Gregorio of Salamanca followed Agricola.[61] Even Ramus had some limited influence in Spain. Nevertheless, Father Muñoz Delgado estimates that what he calls 'Renaissance logic' was only of importance between 1540 and 1570, and that Spanish logicians then returned to a modified scholasticism,[62] if indeed they had ever left it. An early reformer of scholastic logic was Domingo de Soto (d. 1560), a Dominican who had studied at Montaigu and taught at Burgos and Salamanca. He felt that too much time was devoted to the *Summulae Logicales*, that too many metaphysical and theological questions were included, and that doctrines which were difficult or which were already clearly expressed by Aristotle should be omitted. His own commentary on Peter of Spain reflected these beliefs, particularly in the second edition, and, according to Father Muñoz Delgado, he began the movement whereby Peter of Spain was dethroned and the *Summulae* became just an easy and useful introduction to Aristotle,[63] though still retaining a good deal of scholastic doctrine even in their rewritten form. The movement was continued by such men as Domingo Bañes (1528–1604), a Dominican who, like Domingo de Soto, is better known as a theologian; Thomas de Mercado (d. 1575) a Dominican who taught in Mexico; and Pedro de Oña (d. 1626). Gaspar Cardillo de Villalpandeo (1527–1581), who edited commentaries on Aristotle, wanted the *Summulae Logicales* suppressed altogether, but nevertheless wrote the *Summa Summae Summularum* which itself contains much discussion of scholastic doctrines. The most outstanding figure of the later period was Petrus Fonseca (1528–1599), a Portuguese Jesuit who taught at Coimbra, and whose *Institutionum Logicarum libri octo* was known throughout Europe, partly because it appeared on the

Jesuit *ratio studiorum* of 1595 as one of the two books to be used for
explaining logic in the first term of the first year. The other was by
Toletus. Fonseca's book received at least fifty three editions, the first in
Lisbon in 1564 and the last in Lyons in 1625.[64] Only two logicians are
worthy of note in the seventeenth century: John of St. Thomas (1589–
1644), another Dominican; and J. Caramuel Lobkowitz (1606–1682), a
Cistercian who was at one time Archbishop of Prague. The doctrines of
all these men will be discussed in subsequent chapters.

9. Other schools of logic

To conclude this general survey of logic and logicians, those schools
with which I have no direct concern should be mentioned. A few followers of Ramon Lull were to be found throughout the period, but their
work seems to offer nothing to those interested in formal logic, semantics, or scientific method.[65] Italy, however, was the home of two schools
which are of genuine interest and value, though I regret that I will be
unable to discuss them in this book. The first, like rhetorical logic, was
the product of humanism, and it involved the study of the Greek text of
Aristotle, together with the commentaries of such Greek logicians as
Alexander of Aphrodisias, Philoponus, Ammonius and Themistius.
Many Latin translations of these men were published during the sixteenth century, almost exclusively done by Italian scholars;[66] while such
authors as Augustinus Niphus and J. F. Burana produced their own
commentaries on works of Aristotle. They emphasized that there were
three parts to Aristotle's logic, and they spoke of demonstrative, dialecti-
cal and sophistic syllogisms, in a way which was to annoy such men as
Ramus for seeming to detract from the unitary nature of logic.[67] The
other school, that of the so-called Averroists,[68] who concentrated upon
scientific method and the doctrines of the *Analytica Posteriora*, had its
roots as far back as the twelfth century, and was centred on Padua.[69]
The university of Padua was especially renowned for its medical school,
and Aristotle was taught there with a markedly secular emphasis, as an
introduction to medicine rather than theology. As a result much attention was paid to Aristotle's physical writings, to natural history, and the
work of the *medici* or medical professors who set Galen up against Aristotle as the authority on logic and methodology, and who wrote com-

mentaries on the *Ars Medica* which included much discussion of scientific method.[70] The most eminent figure in the Paduan tradition was Jacobus Zabarella (1538–1589). His longest treatise was a commentary on the *Analytica Posteriora*, but he also wrote on method, on the nature of logic, and on the fourth figure of the syllogism, a matter which was apparently discussed by the *medici*. Zabarella was well-known outside Italy, especially in Germany, where his collected writings were first published in 1594.

As will become apparent from succeeding chapters, if it is not already clear, the most interesting work of the period under consideration was done at the end of the fifteenth century and the beginning of the sixteenth century, mainly in Paris. Those working in the scholastic tradition, especially in Spain, retained some of the concern with semantics and formal logic in general that had characterized the earlier period, but otherwise later logicians were either, as Zabarella was, devoted to what are from my present point of view peripheral concerns, or they were concerned only with Aristotelian syllogistic, a subject which they did not always manage to present clearly. It is not easy to explain why this should be so. It is not sufficient to blame Italian humanism, especially when one considers that Venice throughout the sixteenth century continued to print some of the best of the medieval texts, and that the best work in the logic of scientific method was done in Italy. One cannot blame the overthrow of logic as a university subject, for it was not overthrown during this period. Nor can one say simply that because of changing interests the brightest young men turned to other topics, for it had always been the case that logic was a young man's subject, to be studied and taught before one turned to more serious matters, such as theology. However, a recent study by Terrence Heath [see bibliography] in which he investigates the grammatical training offered at three German universities, Freiburg, Ingolstadt, and Tübingen, at the end of the fifteenth century and the beginning of the sixteenth century, gives us a new and valuable clue to the reasons for the decline of logic. His argument is that the *Doctrinale* of Alexander of Villa-Dei, the basic book for the first year of university-level grammatical studies at the end of the fifteenth century, was peculiarly well-suited to prepare students for the intricacies of scholastic logic, and that the commentaries on it focused on material which was clearly preparatory for the courses in logic rather than for the study of literature. Humanist grammars, however, which gradually replaced the *Doctrinale* at German universities, severed the links with scholastic logic and philosophy. They prepared students for the study of Latin poets and orators, but not for the kind of rigorous language analysis which was essential to formal logic. Moreover, "the temporal sequence of the changeover to humanist grammar in the 1520s and to humanist dialectics in the 1530s and later indicates the prime importance of humanist work in grammar."[71] It seems highly probable that this changeover from scholastic to humanist grammar took place in other European universities, with results similar to those that Heath has documented for southern Germany. Thus humanism is the culprit, but because it rendered students unfit for the study of logic, rather than because of its more generally seductive properties.

10. A NOTE ON TERMINOLOGY

A note should perhaps be added here on the use of the terms *logica* and *dialectica*. *Dialectica* was the term used by such early writers as Martianus Capella to refer to logic, and this usage was predominant in the early middle ages.[72] By the thirteenth century the term *logica* was usually employed, except by Buridan and by such Oxford logicians as Grosseteste. Valla and other humanists brought the term *dialectica* back into general favour, and it was used not only by such men as Agricola, Melanchthon and Ramus, but by such later scholastics as Fonseca. *Logica* regained ground in the seventeenth century. *Dialectica* was also the word used for probable arguments, or the logic of the topics, as opposed to demonstrative and sophistic arguments, but Dorp, for instance, warned the reader not to confuse this narrow sense with the wide sense in which dialectic and logic are the same. Some attempts were made to make the use of the term *dialectica* a matter of dispute; and Ramus chided Aristotle, "or, more accurately, his followers", for their desire to make two arts out of disputation and reasoning, one for science called 'logic' and one for opinion called 'dialectic'. This was a grave error, he said, for logic and dialectic are the same thing and the same rules apply to both science and opinion.[73] On the whole, however, no important issues were involved, and the term employed was a matter for taste and custom.

NOTES

[1] P. Boehner, 'Bemerkungen zur Geschichte der De Morganschen Gesetze in der Scholastik', *Archiv für Philosophie* 4 (1951) 145.

[2] For editions and translations see the bibliography. For judgements on the importance of the Port-Royal Logic and of Jungius, see I. M. Bocheński, *History of Formal Logic* (trans. and ed. by Ivo Thomas), Notre Dame, Indiana, 1961, 257; W. and M. Kneale, *The Development of Logic*, Oxford 1962, 313; and H. Scholz, *Geschichte der Logik*, Berlin 1931, 41f.

[3] J. P. Mullally, *The Summulae Logicales of Peter of Spain*, Notre Dame, Indiana, 1945, lxxviiif.

[4] J. E. Seigel, *Rhetoric and Philosophy in Renaissance Humanism: The Union of Eloquence and Wisdom*, Princeton 1968, 227.

[5] E. Garin, 'La cultura fiorentina nella seconda metà del '300 e i 'barbari brittani'', *La Rassegna della Letteratura Italiana* 64 (1960) 183.

[6] Silvestro da Valsanzibio, 8.

[7] Silvestro da Valsanzibio, 8.

[8] G. Ritter, *Marsilius von Inghen und die Okkamistische Schule in Deutschland, Sitzungsberichte der Heidelberger Akademie der Wissenschaften, Phil.-hist. Klasse*, 1921, Abh. 4, 45f.

[9] See Elie; Muñoz Delgado[5]; Renaudet; Villoslada.

[10] Villoslada, n. 27, 39f. The number was as high as ten thousand under Peter of Ailly, it is claimed.

[11] Villoslada, 42. Cf. Muñoz Delgado[4], 163.

[12] Muñoz Delgado[3], 435.

[13] Muñoz Delgado[3], 435.

[14] Ong[A], 137.

[15] Villoslada, 44.

[16] See Villoslada, 53f., for the text of the decree.

[17] Villoslada, 89f. The document quoted dates from 1473, the year before the decree was actually issued.

[18] Elie, 198f.

[19] Renaudet, 464.

[20] Muñoz Delgado[3], 436.

[21] Muñoz Delgado[2], 175.

[22] Muñoz Delgado[3], 435.

[23] According to Sánchez Ciruelo, Peter of Ailly was the first to write an introduction to terms; then the subject was taken up by Major, and by subsequent authors. See Muñoz Delgado[2], n. 6, 174.

[24] Muñoz Delgado[1], 154.

[25] Muñoz Delgado[2], n. 13, 181.

[26] Vasoli[A], 10.

[27] Vasoli[3], 412.

[28] Garin, *op. cit.*, 187. "Quid cum Brittanis, quorum nomina ipso sono horrenda sunt."

[29] For a discussion of Valla's work, see Vasoli[3].

[30] "... nihil se habet sanitas, sed tot plane insana est": Valla, xxxvii. The other references are to Valla, xiif.; xxvi[vo]; and xxxvi.

[31] See Vasoli[5].

[32] See Vasoli[2].

[33] See Vasoli[6].

[34] See Vasoli[4].

[35] See Vasoli[1].

[36] Agricola, *De Inventione*, 452ff.

[37] Agricola, *De Inventione*, 538ff.

[38] The *logica nova* consists of those treatises which became known only in the twelfth century, i.e. Aristotle's *Analytica Priora, Analytica Posteriora, Topica* and *De Sophisticis Elenchis*. The *logica vetus* included the *Categoriae* and *De Interpretatione*, together with works by Boethius, Porphyry and Apuleius. The *logica vetus* and the *logica nova* together are referred to as the *logica antiqua* when they are contrasted with the *logica moderna*, or treatises on such non-Aristotelian matters as supposition.

[39] For an excellent discussion of the relationship between rhetoric and dialectic, see R. McKeon, 'Rhetoric in the Middle Ages', *Speculum* **17** (1942) 1–32. Another valuable study concerns Zabarella's traditionalist views on the place of rhetoric: see Edwards.

[40] Melanchthon, *Dialectica*, 7. "... Rhetorica addit vivos colores."

[41] Melanchthon, *Dialectica*, 65.

[42] Melanchthon, *Dialectica*, 65.

[43] Melanchthon, *Dialectica*, 86–87.

[44] Vasoli[8], II. The whole article is devoted to Melanchthon.

[45] Ong[A], 94.

[46] Ong[A], 95.

[47] See Vasoli[8], III.

[48] Ong[A], 96.

[49] Ong[A], 296. Ong gives an interesting table of the places of publication of both the *Dialectica* and *Rhetorica* of Ramus.

[50] For details, see Chapter Four.

[51] Ramus, *Dialectique*[2], 55.

[52] Ong[A], 299.

[53] Ong[A], 299.

[54] Max Wundt, *Die deutsche Schulmetaphysik des 17. Jahrhunderts*, Tübingen, 1939, 50.

[55] Miller, 248.

[56] Dietericus, Introduction, 10.

[57] Dietericus, 37.

[58] Dieterius, 360.

[59] Kenney, 32, 61.

[60] Vives, 63. For an account of Vives's doctrines, which seem to be remarkably similar to those of the Italian humanists, see Vasoli[7].

[61] Muñoz Delgado[3], 440.

[62] Muñoz Delgado[3], 436.

[63] Muñoz Delgado[1], 152f.

[64] Ferreira Gomez, 633.

[65] Further information on the followers of Lull can be found in Risse[A], 532–560; and in Rossi[A].

[66] Gilbert, 165.

[67] Risse[1], 17.

[68] Risse[1], *passim*; and P. O. Kristeller, 'Paduan Averroism and Alexandrinism in the Light of Recent Studies', *Atti del XII Congresso internazionale di filosofia. IX*, Firenze, 1960, 147–155. Kristeller argues (152f.) that 'Averroist' may mean simply a secular Aristotelian, and 'Alexandrinist', one who uses the Greek commentators on Aristotle.

[69] See Randall for a complete account. Cf. Gilbert.

[70] See W. F. Edwards, 'The Averroism of Jacopo Zabarella (1535–1589)', *Atti del XII*

Congresso internazionale di filosofia, IX, Firenze, 1960, 102–103.

[71] Heath, 64.

[72] See P. Michaud-Quantin, 'L'emploi des termes *logica* et *dialectica* au moyen-âge', *Arts libéraux et philosophie au moyen-âge*, Montréal-Paris, 1969, 855–862.

[73] Ramus, *Dialectique*[2], 2f.

MEANING AND REFERENCE

SECTION I

THE NATURE OF LOGIC

1. THE CONTENTS OF LOGICAL TEXT-BOOKS

The purpose of this second chapter is to examine theories about the nature of language and about the conditions determining the meaning, reference and truth of propositions. By no means all logicians even mentioned such matters, let alone discussed them in detail, but the assumptions they obviously started with are indispensable for an understanding of the nature and scope of their investigations. Without exception they were concerned with an ordinary language, particularly Latin, whose units were meaningful, and whose indicative sentences were normally known to be either true or false. They did not start with an artificial language which could be viewed either as an uninterpreted or as an interpreted system, and no preliminary lines were drawn between syntactical and semantical questions. The results of this choice of starting point are clear. In the first place, normal semantic assumptions placed a constraint upon the kind of rules which were offered. Prior beliefs about the cases in which true premises lead to a true conclusion determined the types of transformation and deduction which were allowed, and there was no suggestion that one could vary one's interpretation in order to accommodate a different set of rules. There were, of course, such cases as those of propositions with non-referring subjects where no prior intuition could be appealed to, and these were decided in such a way as to avoid invalidating otherwise desirable rules. In the second place, no axiomatization took place. Since ordinary language as a whole was the basis for discussion, and no neater sub-system was ever isolated, no attempt was made to present a complete set of rules, or to treat one group of rules as axioms from which the rest could be derived. Obviously it was realized that the rules given had to be consistent with one another, and that some of them were clearly derivable from others, but no further steps toward a formal system were taken. In the third place, only very rough and ready distinctions were drawn between the various types of inference which are possible in even a moderately flexible and sophisticated ordinary language. Propositional inferences, syllogisms, and those inferences whose validity can only be demonstrated in a calculus with modal or temporal operators, were discussed in different places, but more on grounds of convenience than for any theoretical reasons. This is not surprising, for these inferences are normally distinguished precisely on the grounds that they are shown to be valid within different formal systems.

A corollary of the approach to the study of valid inferences through ordinary language rather than formal systems was the inclusion, or possible inclusion, of a range of such interesting matters as the detailed analysis of sentences containing such exclusive and exceptive terms as 'only' and 'except';[1] and the discussion of inferences whose validity or invalidity depended on the category or meaning of the terms involved rather than on the formal properties of the premisses and conclusion.[2] On the other hand, there was a corresponding temptation to include matters which are more properly viewed as belonging to the province of metaphysics or epistemology. The number and nature of categories, the existence of universals, the nature of beings of reason, the ways in which concepts are acquired and organized, were all questions which were raised in the context of logical investigations, but which might be thought to have no direct bearing upon the study of inference. However, it should be pointed out that those who devoted most time to such matters, such as Smiglecius and the writers at Coimbra and Alcalá, were clearly aware that they were discussing what might be called philosophical logic, and were doing so out of interest rather than because they were in the grip of some misapprehension.

So far as the majority of authors is concerned, it is not clear whether they were prepared to offer theoretical justification for their choice of contents or not. The humanists and Ramists were only too eager to explain why they excluded many of the traditionally accepted doctrines, but their opponents were more reticent about what they included. It is quite possible that tradition and precedent were the determining factors. If one were writing a commentary on Peter of Spain, the order of contents had already been chosen. Equally, if one were writing a text-book, one could very easily follow the pattern of the *Organon*, and many did. Even if one were striving for independence, there were standard doc-

trines to be covered. The undoubted differences in content and organization between texts do not usually seem to mirror any corresponding
differences of view about the nature and scope of logic itself, but rather
differing opinions as to what was pedagogically useful or necessary. An
author might very well have chosen to discuss supposition but to omit
semantic paradoxes just because he felt that problems of meaning and
reference in general are more easily seen to be important than problems
of self-reference in particular, or he might have chosen to omit these
matters altogether and concentrate upon syllogistic just because that was
generally taken to be the one part of logic essential to the training of
young men. If there was more at stake than this kind of consideration,
they did not bother to write about it. It may be added that the polemic
of the humanists and Ramists suggests that they themselves had nothing
more profound in mind.

The most explicit attempt at an explanation of the contents of a logic
text is to be found in the thirteenth century logicians. They are echoed
by St. Thomas Aquinas, who held that the *Organon*, and hence logic as
a whole, was organized according to the three operations of the human
mind. The *Isagoge* of Porphyry and the *Categories* correspond to the
apprehension of simples, the *De Interpretatione* to composition and division, and the rest to ratiocination. More simply, we have a division into
three operations which produce in turn concepts, propositions and arguments. Many people, including such disparate seventeenth century figures as John of St. Thomas, Joachim Jungius and Henry Aldrich, followed Aquinas in this, but it is doubtful whether any more than organizational significance should be attached to such an arrangement. One
can accuse all these people of psychologism, but this accusation does not
seem to be justified. If one believes, however erroneously, that there is a
neat correspondence between the operations of the mind and the stages
of logical investigation, then one is not culpable for stating this. If the
study of the latter is said to involve an investigation of actual mental
operations, then the cry of psychologism can indeed be raised; but this
was never the case with the authors I am concerned with.

Curiously enough, the only figure who repays attention to his organization and choice of contents is Andreas Kesler, a Protestant theologian
who was born at Coburg in 1595, educated in Jena and Wittenberg, and
died in 1643 after a long career in education. In 1623 he published a book

entitled *De Consequentia Tractatus logicae* which is unique in that it explicitly subsumes the whole of formal logic under the theory of consequence or inference. The laws of opposition and conversion, the categorical and hypothetical syllogism, were all seen as different types of consequence. Moreover, no extraneous material was included. Instead of starting with the categories, as did the Aristotelians, or with the invention of arguments, as did the Ramists, he devoted his first chapter to the definition of consequence. Topics, informal fallacies, and other such subjects found no place, whereas some of the more rarely discussed matters such as exclusive propositions and the modal syllogism did appear. But despite his clear stand with respect to the nature of logic, Kesler took the details of particular doctrines straight from Fonseca, or, occasionally, from Regius. It was only with respect to organization that he was original.

2. The definition of logic

It should not be supposed that no attempts were made to define logic, but these attempts were either too general to be of help in deciding what should properly be discussed, or went into details which were irrelevant to this particular question. Most popularly, logic was said to be the art of discoursing or reasoning well, but various elaborations were possible. Some said that logic teaches us to define, divide and argue, and to distinguish the true from the false by means of reasons,[3] while others isolated the latter claim and said that logic was the art of directing the operations of the mind to discern the true from the false,[4] or, more accurately, the valid from the invalid. Occasionally it was said that logic is the art leading the mind to the knowledge of things,[5] but this suggestion was not developed. Presumably logic was seen as leading to knowledge only in so far as correct deduction is a necessary part of the acquisition of knowledge, for text-books exhibiting this definition contained no more epistemology than other text-books. In any case, the usual next step after the preliminary definition was to plunge into the study of logic as if everyone knew what was involved. Apart from Zabarella, who devoted a whole treatise to the subject, only those who wrote commentaries on Peter of Spain or on Aristotle investigated the matter in depth.

Among those who did discuss the nature of logic, it was agreed that there were different kinds of logic. The first distinction was between

natural logic, or the ways in which people do in fact argue, and artificial
logic, which results from a reflection upon and formalization of natural
logic.[6] Logicians were taken to be concerned with the latter, although
occasional appeals were made to the former in order to reject ways of
argument, such as the fourth figure, which were found to be distasteful.
Artificial logic was again divided into *logica utens*, or logic as used in
various disciplines, and *logica docens*, or logic as taught by the logician
for its own sake.[7]

The chief question raised about *logica docens* was whether it was an
art or a science. It is not possible here to go into the often elaborate discussions of what constitutes an art as opposed to a science, so I will
merely give a brief summary of the conclusions to which people came.[8]
Smiglecius, the seventeenth century Jesuit, wrote that there were five
possible views: logic is both an art and a science, it is an art alone, a
science alone, a faculty, or an instrumental habit.[9] The first view is found
preeminently in Peter of Spain, who wrote that logic is the "art of arts
and science of sciences, having the road leading to the principles of all
methods."[10] Many later logicians, including John of St. Thomas, accepted this view without much comment;[11] although Dorp had argued
that the inclusion of science made the statement redundant, if one took
science in the broad sense of the word as a discipline whose conclusions
are reached through demonstration, since any art was a science in this
sense. Alternatively, if one took science in the narrow sense of the word
as involving theoretical demonstrations, the statement would be false,
for logic is practical. However, the repetition is not useless or super-
fluous, he added. The chief exponents of the view that logic is an art were
found, not among the scholastic commentators, but among the humanists, including Melanchthon and Ramus. Scotists in particular held to
the view that logic was just a science, though there was disagreement as
to whether it was speculative or practical. Nominalists tended to say that
it was practical, as did the later writers of Coimbra.[12] Tartaretus, Domingo de Soto and the later writers of Alcalá, thought it was speculative.[13] Others, including those who saw logic as more than just a science,
took a wider view. John of St. Thomas, for instance, saw it as having
both speculative and practical elements.[14] It is, he agreed, essentially
theoretical, but "shares in the style of practical thought, inasmuch as it
supplies rules and direction to speculation itself."

The last two classifications of logic were less common. Smiglecius attributed the view that logic is a faculty to Aristotle, but did not dwell on it. The final view, with which both he and Robertis agreed,[15] comes from Zabarella, who wrote a whole book on the nature of logic. In it he denied that logic was an art, since it was not directed toward some external end; and he also denied that it was a science, since it had no independently necessary subject matter, but was concerned only with second intentions [*secundae notiones*], or such concepts as those of genus, species and syllogism, which were contingent.[16] His view of logic was two-fold. In so far as it was applied to natural things, for example, it became natural philosophy, for natural philosophy was merely the product of the many propositions, inductions, and syllogisms applied to natural things.[17] Logic as such, he said, was an instrumental intellectual discipline, arising from the philosopher's practice of philosophizing or forming secondary notions which can be instruments to tell the true from the false.[18]

Zabarella's view of the relationship of logic to other sciences was not radically different from that of other writers. The second part of Peter of Spain's definition, that logic is "the road leading to the principles of all methods," had inspired a fair amount of comment. Dorp, like Tartaretus after him, had pointed out that logic does not lead to the principles of all sciences in the sense that it proves them, but only in the sense that arguments in any field presuppose the principles of logic.[19] Indeed, in the same way that logic can show other disciplines how to form arguments out of their peculiar principles, it can teach the formation of arguments out of its own principles. A fifteenth century commentator had elaborated on this.[20] He listed the principles of logic, such as "Every argument is either valid or invalid" and "Every proposition is either true or false," and said that all arguments are logical in the sense that they are in accordance with logical rules, but not in the sense that they are fabricated out of logical principles and terms. The idea that logic was in some way necessary to other sciences continued to be mentioned into the seventeenth century. For instance, John Case made the *opponens* in a dialogue claim that although Hippocrates could cure people without logic and Euclid draw lines, neither could prove any precepts without it.[21]

Questions were raised about the status of grammar in this context, for grammar too is a science, but without a prior grasp of significant and well-formed utterances one would not be able to do logic. The answer given by such men as Versor and Eckius was that grammar had two aspects, the natural, whereby we learn to handle language by experience or on the authority of a schoolmaster,[22] and the scientific, which involves grammar as a body of rules and demonstrations.[23] Natural grammar is necessary for the learning of logic, but logic is in turn necessary for the development of scientific grammar.

3. The Object of Logic

Potentially the most important question raised about the nature of logic concerned its object, and in particular whether it was concerned with language or not. The view that logic was a *scientia sermocinalis*, or linguistic in nature, was apparently standard in the early middle ages, and William of Sherwood put it succinctly when he wrote that this science has three parts: "grammar, which teaches one to speak correctly, rhetoric, which teaches one to speak elegantly, and logic, which teaches one how to speak truly."[24] However, by the later middle ages another doctrine had become current, namely that logic was a *scientia rationalis*, concerned with beings of reason rather than with linguistic entities. Various versions of this view were possible, so that logicians of the early sixteenth century were faced with a large range of alternatives. Indeed, Domingo de Soto said that there were as many views about the object of logic as there were heads.[25]

The first main candidate was the nominalist view that logic was a *scientia sermocinalis*, and that its objects were such terms as *terminus* and *argumentatio*.[26] The logician was taken to concern himself with the various properties of terms, propositions and arguments, such as being affirmative, being negative, concluding directly, concluding indirectly, being a syllogism and so on.[27] This view was not altogether popular. Domingo de Soto thought it as stupid to suppose that the object of logic was an actual term as to suppose that the object of theology was the word 'God' rather than God himself, or that the object of physics was the phrase 'natural being', rather than natural beings.[28] In the seventeenth century, Isendoorn argued that words could not be the proper object of logic because if they were so regarded it could only be because of their sound, because of their signification, or in so far as they were signs which manifested concepts.[29] In the first case, words are the proper object not of logic but of physics; in the second case, words are the proper object not of logic but of grammar; and in the third case words are the object not only of logic but also of physics, metaphysics and mathematics. More importantly, words have to be subordinated to concepts in order to be meaningful, and hence they should not be given priority over concepts.[30]

It was not only the nominalists who saw logic as essentially linguistic, for the humanists took up the Ciceronian definition whereby logic is the *ars disserendi* or art of discoursing.[31] Ramus himself hedged. In 1555 he called logic the *'art de bien disputer'* and in 1576 he called it *'l'art de bien raisonner'*, so that both definitions could appear in his followers.[32] A number of people, Ramist and non-Ramist alike, preferred the second version, which is more akin to that of Thomas Aquinas.[33] Fonseca, who was neither a nominalist nor a humanist, seemed to regard logic as an *ars disserendi*, and he explained that *orationes* or sentences were the proper objects of logic.[34] Since they were involved in the three processes of logic, definition, division and argument, one should begin by discussing nouns and verbs, which are the constituent parts of *orationes*.[35]

The other main candidates for the object of logic arose from the belief that logic is not a *scientia sermocinalis* but a *scientia rationalis*. Avicenna and his followers claimed that logic was concerned with second intentions, that is, those second-order concepts such as 'noun' which are formulated in order to categorize first-order concepts, or concepts of objects, in various ways. Albertus Magnus and his followers claimed that logic was concerned with argumentation, i.e. the thing, not the word. The Scotists gave a special emphasis to one kind of argumentation, namely the syllogism "which is as it were the prince and head of all."[36] However, the most popular view was that of the Thomists who argued that logic was concerned with *entia rationis*, or, as Domingo de Soto put it, "a condition in things which belongs to them only by virtue of the operations of the intellect."[37] *Entia rationis* included both such abstract entities as species and genus and such features of things, when viewed as signs, as being a noun, a proposition, or a syllogism. Thus such terms as 'genus' can be the objects of logic, but not in the nominalist sense as beings in their own right. Rather they are the objects of logic because they are terms of second intention, said Domingo de Soto.

In the late fifteenth century Tartaretus had offered a compromise between the two main views. Although, he said, logic is concerned with some second intentions, it can be called a *scientia sermocinalis* because it teaches us to distinguish true and false utterances.[38] Indeed, it does seem that there was no radical difference between the two views so far as their practical implications were concerned. Whether one argued that logic was concerned with utterances or with second intentions; whether one said that the principal second intention was the notion of syllogism, of argumentation, or of demonstration,[39] or whether one held such second intentions to be of equal importance, it was still necessary to discuss terms, propositions and the various kinds of argumentation in order to give an adequate account of valid inference. Moreover, since both nominalists and their opponents believed firmly in the existence of three kinds of terms and propositions, mental, spoken and written, of which the mental ones were fundamental, the nominalists found themselves discussing concepts, just as the others found themselves discussing utterances.

A third candidate for the object of logic was put forward in the seventeenth century by Smiglecius who argued that logic was concerned with directing mental operations, in particular the processes of defining, dividing and arguing; and that although second intentions were involved, they could not properly be called the formal objects of logic. Rather these objects are the mental operations themselves.[40] This view was echoed by such men as Burgersdijck,[41] and Joachim Jungius, who argued that the primary proximate object of logic was the operations of the mind, the secondary proximate object was external speech, and the remote objects were the universal things with which both mental operations and speech were concerned.[42] Some people went so far as to say that the direct objects were things, whether universal or particular, but this view was never well-articulated.[43] At all events, neither Smiglecius nor Jungius nor any of the others included any new material because of their views on the object of logic, nor did they display any new approaches to the old material which could be attributed to this cause. Indeed, speculation about the nature of logic seems to have been relatively divorced from the conduct of logic, as was perhaps inevitable given the direction of their speculations and their initial starting point in ordinary language. Only when the possibility of different kinds of formal systems and different kinds of semantical interpretations is envisaged, can speculation about the nature of logic radically affect the type of logic produced.

NOTES

[1] Sentences needing analysis were discussed under the heading of *exponibilia* by a number of authors, including Celaya, Enzinas, Javellus, Lax, and Domingo de Soto. For fuller details, see Ashworth[4].

[2] See Chapter Three for a discussion of the distinction between formal and material consequences. See also the chapters on topics and informal fallacies in most logical text-books of the period.

[3] See Trutvetter, *Breviarium*: "Est scientia docens artificialiter definire, dividere, arguere et verum a falso per rationes discernere." Cf. George of Brussels, *Cursus*; Breitkopf, *Compendium*; Gebwiler; Melanchthon, *Erotemata*, 513; Trutvetter, *Summule*. Domingo de Soto, *Commentarii*, 3vo, correctly attributed this definition to Isidore of Seville.

[4] Jungius, 1, said: "Logica est ars mentis nostrae operationes dirigens ad verum à falso discernendo." Cf. *Commentum*.

[5] Keckermann, *Systema*, 1, said: "Logica est ars dirigendi mentem in cognitione rerum." Cf. Airay, 1; Burgersdijck, 5; Goclenius, *Institutiones*, 27; Newton, 3; Wendelin, 1.

[6] E.g. Granger, 2; Javellus, 11f.; John of St. Thomas, *Material Logic*, 4; Tartaretus, *Commentarii*, 2. For more references, see Muñoz Delgado^A, 35.

[7] Alcalá, 51; Burgersdijck, 5; Coimbra, I 28ff.; Isendoorn, 34; Javellus, 11vo; John of St. Thomas, *Material Logic*, 47–59; Tartaretus, *Commentarii*, 2.

[8] The interested reader will find a long discussion of the definition of logic in John of St. Thomas, *Material Logic*, 1–88. John of St. Thomas owed much to Domingo de Soto, whose own discussion is treated at length in Muñoz Delgado^A. Another good source is Zabarella's *De Natura Logicae*, in *Opera* 1–102. Cf. Rubius, 1–108; Regius, *Libri IV*, 1–87; Robertis *Pars Prima* 8–29; Derodon, 26–70.

[9] Smiglecius, I 163–165.

[10] Peter of Spain, *Summulae:* Bocheński, 1.01, 1; De Rijk, 1. "Dialectica est ars artium et scientia scientiarum ad omnium methodorum principia viam habens." De Rijk omits "et scientia scientiarum" from the main text, but this phrase was included in the early printed versions of the *Summulae* and was the subject of extensive commentary. Cf. Versor, 2vo.

[11] John of St. Thomas, *Material Logic*, 12; Case, 3.

[12] Coimbra, I, 41ff. Cf. Isendoorn, 47. Nominalist doctrines are compared with others by Domingo de Soto, *Commentarii*, 8vo.

[13] Alcalá, 60; Domingo de Soto, *Commentarii*, 8vo; Tartaretus, *Commentarii*, 5. Note that these three sources are widely separated in time.

[14] John of St. Thomas, *Material Logic*, 37. Cf. George of Brussels, *Cursus*; Bartolus de Castro, xviif. The latter attributed this view to the nominalists.

[15] Robertis, *Pars Prima*, 13.

[16] Zabarella, *De Natura Logicae*, 6, in *Opera*. See Smiglecius, I, 181.

[17] Zabarella *De Natura Logicae*, 11.

[18] Zabarella, *De Natura Logicae*, 52. "Est enim logica habitus intellectus instrumentalis, seu disciplina instrumentalis à Philosophis ex Philosophiae habitu genita, quae secundas notiones in conceptibus rerum fingit, & fabricat, ut sint instrumenta; quibus in omni re verum cognoscatur, & a falso discernatur."

[19] Dorp; Tartaretus, *Expositio*, 2vo.

[20] *Commentum*.

[21] Case, 2.

[22] The author of *Commentum* uses the example of a boy learning grammar by rote from a master.

[23] Versor, 4[vo]. Eckius, *Summulae*, iiii[vo].

[24] William of Sherwood, *Introduction to Logic*, translated by N. Kretzmann, Minneapolis, 1966, 21.

[25] Domingo de Soto, *Commentarii*, 9[vo].

[26] For an outline of this view and others, see Sbarroya, *Expositio primi*, iv[vo] and Domingo de Soto, *Commentarii*, 9–10.

[27] Castro, ix[vo].

[28] Domingo de Soto, *Commentarii*, 9[vo].

[29] Isendoorn, 52.

[30] Isendoorn, 52f.; Coimbra, I 49.

[31] E.g. Agricola, 288f.: "definita dialectica, ars probabiliter de qualibet re proposita disserendi." Cf. Granger, 2; Goclenius, *Institutiones*, 27.

[32] Ramus, *Dialectique*[1], 1; *Dialectique*[2], 1. Cf. Jungius, 2: "Ramei Logicam definiunt artem bene disserendi sive ratione utendi."

[33] Gassendi, *Institutio*, 91: "Logica est Ars bene cogitandi." Cf. Wallis, 1: "Logica est Ars (sive Peritia) Ratiocinandi (seu commode utendi Ratione)."

[34] Fonseca, I 22.

[35] Fonseca, I 30. He thus gave an answer to a question which had been debated in the sixteenth century, whether it was more proper to start with the nature of terms, or with the *modi sciendi*, definition, division and argument: See Muñoz Delgado[5], 229. Examples of both approaches are to be found. For instance, in the first edition of his work on the *Summulae*, Domingo de Soto had begun with the *modi sciendi*, but in the second edition he began with terms.

[36] Castro, viii[vo].

[37] Domingo de Soto, *Commentarii*, 9vo.

[38] Tartaretus, *Commentarii*, 2[vo]f.

[39] Alcalá, 50, chose demonstration; Coimbra, I 57, chose the syllogism. Cf. Smiglecius, I 98f.

[40] Smiglecius, I, *passim*, especially 98, 100, 135. Cf. Gabriel of St. Vincent, 2, who said that the *modi sciendi* are the proximate objects of logic, whereas the operations of the intellect are remote objects.

[41] Burgersdijck, 6. He said that *logica docens* is concerned with second intentions, whereas *logica utens* has the operations of the intellect as its proximate objects and things as its remote objects.

[42] Jungius, 4.

[43] Wallis, 1: "Logices Objectum (circa quod versatur) sunt Res omnes (sive Reales sive Imaginarie)," The view was rejected by Isendoorn, 53. Cf. Robertis, *Pars Prima*, 18vo: "Subjectum propriè sumptum in logica res omnes, sive eorem primos conceptus esse dicimus." On p. 21 he added: "Subjectum per metaphoram, idest à fine sumptum, non incommodè in Logica ponitur ens rationis, sive secundo intellecta, sive syllogismus, sive demonstratio."

PROBLEMS OF LANGUAGE

Problems of language were discussed in some detail by scholastic logicians, whether they believed that logic was a *scientia sermocinalis* or not;
although the subject tended to be ignored both by the humanists who
were interested only in the use of language, and by the other non-
scholastic groups. It was recognised that the basic unit from the logician's point of view is the proposition, for it is this which is true or false
and which enters into arguments, but despite this, propositions were
usually approached indirectly, via the study of terms or the smallest
meaningful units. One reason was probably that syllogistic demands
analyzed propositions, or propositions which are broken down into their
constituent parts; but a more important reason was that propositions
were viewed as being built up out of terms, so that in order to grasp their
meaning and reference one had first of all to make quite clear what was
the meaning and reference of the terms involved. These two aspects of
breaking down and building up were well expressed by John of St.
Thomas, who said "And since the term of resolution is the same as the
principle of composition, what would have been the ultimate element
into which logical composites are resolved will be said also to be the
first from which the rest are put together."[1] It must be emphasized that the
approach was not one of a simple-minded reductionism. The meaning
of a sentence was no simple function of the meaning of the constituent
parts, for these acted and reacted upon one another in accordance with
their type and order. The presence of such syncategorematic words as
'all' and 'some', the temporal variations of verbs, and the conjunction
of such nouns as 'man' with such restricting terms as 'white' or 'painted'
or 'dead' were among the crucial elements which determined the import
of a sentence. Moreover, some people did question whether the signification of a proposition was equivalent to the signification of the terms,
or whether a proposition involved something over and above its con-

stituent elements, and elaborate theories supporting the latter possibility were discussed in the early sixteenth century.

1. TERMS: THEIR DEFINITION AND THEIR MAIN DIVISIONS

There were two ways of approaching the discussion of terms, which seem to be related to the attitude taken towards logic as such. Those who saw logic as a *scientia sermocinalis* tended to follow Peter of Spain, and to approach terms through a consideration of sounds.[2] The reason given was that logic can be taken as largely concerned with disputation, disputation involves speech, speech is made up of *voces* or utterances, and these in turn are made up out of sounds. Not all sounds are utterances, of course. Utterances come from the mouth of an animal using natural instruments, whereas the tramp of feet or the noise of a tree falling is pure sound. Some interesting things were said about coughs, groans, barks and so on. A dog's bark is an utterance because those who know the dog are aware that he is animated by anger or joy, but a cough is not usually counted as an utterance because it is "as it were produced by an inanimate body," and it offers no clue to the mind of the person who coughs.[3] As a fifteenth century commentator said, there must be an intention to signify before a sound can count as an utterance. However, if this condition is present, even a cough may count as an utterance.[4]

Those who did not view logic as being primarily concerned with spoken language saw no reason to devote any particular attention to sounds or to utterances as such, and the majority of those who discussed terms simply began with an examination of various possible definitions of 'term'. The only author I know of who noted that a choice had to be made between two different approaches was Javellus. He said that he would begin with terms rather than sounds because most people did, and because this approach was not essentially inconsistent with the other.[5] He seemed to feel that it was a matter of taste, and involved no weighty issues.

The consensus of opinion was that a term was a constituent part of a proposition, or, as many people said, a sign which can be placed in a proposition [*Terminus est signum ponibile in propositione*].[6] There were a number of possible ways of expressing these notions, and Dolz offered nine alternatives, ranging from "A term is that into which a proposition is analyzed" to "A term is a sign which can be placed in a proposition as a subject, as a predicate, or as exercising a certain function." [7] What counted as a part of a proposition was a question which had yet to be settled. Everyone agreed that individual letters and, presumably, their vocal counterparts did not count as parts in the sense of the definition,[8] but this still left open a number of possibilities. John Major listed five: a term could be every sign, whether significant or not, which could appear in a proposition; it could be every significant sign, including such complexes as "a white man hearing mass"; it could be every non-complex significant sign; it could be every significant sign which can function as subject or predicate in a sentence with a personal verb which is not an infinitive; or it could be every non-complex significant sign which can function as subject or predicate in such a sentence.[9] Judging by the distinctions which formed the subject matter of treatises on terms, the first alternative was usually adopted.

There were two main divisions of terms. On the one hand they were divided into mental, spoken and written; and on the other hand they were divided into meaningful [*significativa*] and meaningless [*non-significativa*]. The first division was standard, and it will be given no special attention, since its force is best explicated through the examination of meaning. The second division was also standard, but its explication involves a number of complex notions and relationships. A term of any kind was said to be meaningful, or to signify, if it represented something or some things, or in some way to the understanding [*significare est representare potentie cognitive aliquid vel aliqua vel aliqualiter*];[10] where 'understanding' was taken to include the cognitive faculty of animals.[11]

A typical discussion of representation is contained in Celaya's *Dialecticae Introductiones*. He said that to represent formally is to be a concept [*noticia*] or an act of the understanding, and mental terms all represent formally. He added the phrase 'act of understanding' in order to allow for syncategorematic terms, which are meaningful, but are not concepts of anything. Spoken and written terms represent not formally but instrumentally, for they are the means whereby concepts or acts of the understanding are caused.[12] More accurately one might say 'brought to mind', for strictly speaking concepts were taken to be caused by experience, and the part played by linguistic experience was not made clear, at least by any of the logicians I have read. For a term to signify in some way [*aliqualiter*] was often said to be for it to exercise a function [*officium*] whereby other terms were confused, distributed and so on. He warned that this was an inadequate characterization of 'signifying in some way' since in his view, though not in the view of all, propositions could also be said to signify *aliqualiter* and it makes no sense to say that a proposition affects the terms in it. He therefore offered an alternative definition, saying that a term signifies *aliqualiter* if it denotes a thing or things to exist in some way [*taliter se habere*], or not to exist in some way, in the case of negation.[13]

So far as utterances or spoken terms were concerned, certain restrictions were placed upon the notion of instrumental representation. Any utterance represents itself, so that in one sense all utterances are meaningful.[14] Moreover, any utterance can be taken to represent the speaker, though Versor argued that here we are dealing with the relation of effect to cause rather than of sign to thing signified.[15] In any case, it was required that a significant utterance must represent something other than itself, those things similar to it, or its utterer; except in the special case of such words as 'Peter' when said by Peter.[16]

One problem to do with spoken and written terms was whether to class them as meaningful in the absence of an interpreter. Whether a recorded announcement which has no hearer would be considered as meaningful was not, of course, discussed, but some relevant points were made in the discussion of written words. Hieronymus of St. Mark took it that for a word in a closed book to be a term, or for a sequence of words to be a proposition, someone had to read that word or words with understanding, so that for him meaningfulness was presumably dependent upon actual apprehension.[17] This accords very well with the common view whereby a proposition was taken as an occurrent, a token rather than a type. However, most people did not agree with Hieronymus of St. Mark. It was more usually said that a term was meaningful just in case it would convey something if it were heard or read;[18] and as a result both the contents of closed books and of recorded announcements could be taken as meaningful.

Meaningless utterances included such words as 'phlam', 'phlew', 'twitle', 'twatle',[19] or the more common 'bu' and 'baf'; but Versor raised the important point that even these could be meaningful in a way.[20] One could use them to express indignation or derision, or as some kind of interjection: so that in order to lack meaning they must be uttered in no special manner, accompanied by no special corporeal gesture. Of course, even meaningless words could legitimately appear in a sentence while retaining their meaninglessness, but only under certain conditions. One can say that 'Blictri' is a word with two syllables, for one is speaking here of the word or sound. 'Blictri' is mentioned, not used. Similarly one can write "○ is a circle", for one means 'the figure 'O''.[21]

Usually it was assumed that all mental terms were meaningful;[22] although at the beginning of the seventeenth century Villalpandeus did argue that since to signify was to make known [*significare autem est facere cognoscere*] signification can strictly speaking only be a property of written or spoken terms, since we cannot perceive the thoughts and concepts of others.[23] A century earlier Enzinas said that taking all mental terms to be meaningful did seem to have one untoward consequence, namely that of two apparently synonymous terms one might be meaningful and the other not.[24] He had in mind the spoken term 'buf' and the mental term which is the concept of that spoken term, and which is significant in the sense that it has a referent. However, it is not clear why the spoken term and the concept of the spoken term should be taken to be synonymous.

There were said to be two kinds of meaning, natural, and *ad placitum*, or conventional. Some utterances, such as groans and laughs, are said to have natural meaning, because they convey grief and joy to all men, no matter what particular language they speak, and indeed, independently of any language; but they are. Versor said, ill-formed utterances. They are connected with the passions and governed by instinct, and they do not signify concepts.[25] In the seventeenth century, Smiglecius raised the question of whether other sounds could have natural meaning by virtue of some similarity.[26] Could *'tara tantara'* signify the sound of a trumpet, or *'coax'* the sound of a frog, for instance? He concluded that this was impossible, both because the similarity was not that marked, and because one would have to be told which among many utterances signified by virtue of their sound and which did not. Those terms which were truly possessed of natural meaning were mental terms, and it was through these that the conventional meaning possessed by other terms, both written and spoken, was achieved.

To talk of mental terms is to talk of concepts, acts of understanding, the apprehension of things and so on;[27] and the possession of mental terms was seen as fundamental to the exercise of any linguistic abilities. There was no hint of any belief that the acquisition of spoken language is a primary activity which somehow determines the range and nature of our concepts, or that to have a concept is to be able to use a word correctly. Rather, we must acquire concepts before we can acquire a language, for spoken language is developed in order that we may express our concepts.[28] These come to us through experience, and since men share a common experience, they also acquire much the same set of concepts. For instance, all men seeing a stone will have the same concept of a hard inflexible body;[29] and the possession of this concept has nothing to do with an arbitrary choice or decision on the part of the individual or any group of individuals. The case with a spoken term is very different. Different groups use different sounds to express their concept of a stone; and even if it were the case that all men used the same sound, this would not alter the fact that an act of *impositio* had taken place.[30] The sound 'stone' was deliberately invested with meaning; or so people tended to suggest. A fifteenth century commentator had objected to this kind of phrasing on the grounds that both the world and the Latin language might be eternal, which would leave no room for a primal act of giving meaning; and he preferred to speak of voluntary usage and custom.[31] On the other hand, Manderston said firmly that words had been given their meaning by Adam, who did it by pointing his finger at an object and uttering a sound. Manderston realized that syncategorematic words created a difficulty here, and said that the meaning of these words could only be conveyed by constant repetitions in the company of a categorematic word. A further complication was introduced by the distinction between *impositio autentica*, when a word is given meaning by the state [*a re publica*], or by one having authority; and non-authentic imposition, which occurs, for instance, in disputations when a letter of the alphabet is said to have a certain meaning.[32]

2. THE RELATIONSHIP BETWEEN MENTAL, SPOKEN AND WRITTEN TERMS

Spoken words were said to have meaning only if they were subordinated to a mental term. If a speaker utters a word, perhaps in some foreign language of which he is ignorant, without intending to express some concept, then the spoken word is strictly speaking meaningless. The question now raised was whether spoken words referred directly to objects or to the concepts from which they acquired their meaning. The view, current in the earlier middle ages, that words refer directly to concepts and only indirectly to things, was held by Versor, although he drew a distinction between speaker and hearer.[33] He said that the speaker is expressing his concepts by means of words, so that for him they primarily signify concepts, but for the hearer the words primarily signify the things conceived. In the seventeenth century John of St. Thomas, following Thomas Aquinas, also held that the immediate significate of a word is a concept, but he elaborated on this claim by saying that immediacy and importance were not to be confused, for the principal function of a word is to refer to things.[34] Words have a double function [*officium*] but not a double signification. They signify both concept and thing at once "just as the noun 'man' signifies not only human nature but also the individuals for which it supposes with the same signification."[35]

Other authors, such as Pardo in the early sixteenth century, the writers of Coimbra in the late sixteenth century and Smiglecius in the seventeenth century preferred to argue that words refer directly to things and only indirectly to concepts. Pardo raised the problem of supposition. If a spoken word refers immediately to a concept, then it can be taken as standing for that concept rather than a thing. He criticized such a view on the grounds that it would lead to an infinite regress.[36] A word signifies a thing by means of a concept; if it signifies a concept then there must be another concept by means of which the word signifies the first concept, and so on *ad infinitum*. The writers of Coimbra said that it would lead both to equivocation, since 'man' would refer both to men and to a concept, and to falsehood, since "Man is an animal" is true, but "The concept of a man is the concept of an animal" is not.[37] They also made use of the point that the hearer takes words to refer directly to things in order to support their conclusion that words signify things, and that they do so by means of concepts to which they do not refer.

Smiglecius raised the further question of whether the meaning of an utterance was determined by the concepts of the speaker or the concepts of the hearer.[38] Does a word mean what it is intended to mean, or what it is taken to mean? Smiglecius claimed that Ockham and Duns Scotus had both said that a speaker could use the word 'God' to express a confused and imperfect concept, and that if the hearer had a clearer concept of God, then the word 'God' would signify God more perfectly than the speaker had intended. Others denied this on the grounds that if the hearer had a clearer understanding than the speaker, this was not by virtue of the word he heard, and that he transcended the meaning of what he heard. Smiglecius agreed with this second group. He did not make it explicit whether he was thinking of some individual speaker, perhaps with a poor grasp of the language and a limited range of concepts, or whether he was thinking of a larger group of language users, but probably it was the latter, for he remarked that men in general have a confused concept of God. He went on to contrast the word 'sun' as used by a blind man with the word as used by normal men, who "give it a perfect meaning because they see the sun perfectly." This suggests that the same word or sentence will have different meanings according to who utters it. Presumably man's experience was taken to be sufficiently uniform for no practical problems to be raised by this, but it does mean that one is debarred from learning the precise meaning of a given utterance unless one is somehow acquainted with the speaker's intentions.

The status of written language was also discussed. Written terms were seen as subordinate to spoken, for, as Pardo argued, one can pick out words in Greek but unless one is acquainted with the appropriate utterances and unless these in turn are subordinated to the appropriate concepts, they will not signify anything.[39] Written words do not signify spoken words, they signify things. Nevertheless, spoken words play a part in the process just as concepts play a part in the reference of spoken words to things.[40] However, a few doubts were raised about this. If I read Aristotle, said Fonseca in the second half of the sixteenth century, I do not conceive three things, an utterance, a concept and a thing. My mind can leap straight to the thing, leaving out the intermediate stages.[41] Even if one does not pass them over, said Pardo, they are certainly imperceptible.[42]

Since spoken and written words were objects of experience just as much as trees and stones, a further problem was raised by the presence of the concepts which naturally signified them. These concepts or mental terms were assigned a special status. Peter of Ailly spoke of 'mental terms

improperly so-called' and others spoke of non-ultimate concepts.[43]
Fonseca, for instance, said that every time we hear an utterance or see a
written word two concepts are involved, the concept of the thing referred
to by the word, and the concept of the word itself, which is the non-
ultimate concept, or *conceptus medius* as Fonseca preferred to call it.[44]
Like Tartaretus he mentioned the view that these concepts can be said
to have conventional meaning on account of what they signify.[45] Peter
of Ailly had added that one can also have mental sentences improperly
so-called which are images of spoken or written sentences and hence are
not common to all, since these sentences are in a particular conventional
language.[46] One can speak 'in one's heart' with these sentences. He does
not tell us how speaking in one's heart relates to using mental language
proper, which is not bound by any conventional language.

Another problem involving the relationship which obtained among
spoken, written and mental terms was that of synonymy. Two words
were said to be synonymous when they signified "the same thing adequately and in the same manner."[47] Thus 'man' when written is synonymous with 'man' when spoken; and 'Marcus' is synonymous with 'Tullius'
since these are both names of Cicero. On the other hand, 'Peter' is not
synonymous with 'Peter' when two men have the same name, for diverse
concepts are involved.[48] Nor are 'being', 'one' and 'diverse' synonymous,
even though they refer to exactly the same range of objects, for they
refer to them in different ways and by means of different concepts.[49]
Moreover, for the nominalists such concrete and abstract terms as 'man'
and 'humanity', 'father' and 'paternity' were also synonymous, since they
did not believe in the existence of universal natures.[50]

3. OTHER DIVISIONS OF TERMS

After the division of terms into mental, spoken and written and into
meaningful and meaningless, the next most important distinction was that
drawn between categorematic terms such as 'man' and 'runs' and syncategorematic terms such as 'every' and 'none'. A categorematic term
signified something or some things; but a syncategorematic term could
be looked at in two ways.[51] From the point of view of meaning, it
signified *aliqualiter*, or as later authors tended to put it, it signified the

modes of things.[52] Some people said that it did not signify at all, unless
in conjunction with another term.[53] From the point of view of its function, it could never (unless mentioned rather than used) serve as the subject, predicate or copula of a sentence. Instead, it affected the other terms
by distributing them, negating them and so on. Hieronymus of St. Mark
claimed that personal pronouns were syncategorematic terms along with
logical connectives and quantifiers, though one has to go back to Dorp
for an explanation of why this should be, namely that they have the
function of showing whether the term to which they are joined should
be taken singularly or discretely. Dorp added that pronouns were not always pure, for in a phrase such as "I am a man", 'I' can be used
demonstratively instead of as a sign of the thing, John, which is pointed
to, or it can be used as both a demonstrative act and a sign of John. Some
authors added a special category of mixed terms, such as *nemo*.[54] These
were spoken or written terms which had to be analyzed by means of both
a categorematic and a syncategorematic term, in this case '*nullus*' and
'*homo*'.

The last distinction which was of importance to logicians was that
between terms of first and second intention. Terms of first intention
referred directly to objects, whether physical or abstract entities, and
terms of second intention referred to terms of first intention. They were
signs of signs, and they included both the terms of grammar, rhetoric and
logic, such as 'noun', 'exordium' and 'proposition', and abstract terms
such as 'species', 'genus', 'universal' and 'predicable';[55] though such
earlier logicians as Crab often gave only those examples such as 'proposition' and 'syllogism' which fitted the description of a second intention as
signifying things by virtue of their being propositional signs.[56] Such
medieval logicians as Ockham had distinguished between terms of first
and second intention, which were mental, and terms of first and second
imposition, which were written or spoken,[57] but while this distinction
was occasionally noted,[58] most logicians of our period who mentioned
the word 'imposition' did so only as an alternative to 'intention' without
remarking that it had once enjoyed a different usage.[59]

Various other distinctions were discussed, including those between
univocal and equivocal, abstract and concrete, finite and infinite,
positive and privative, complex and non-complex, singular and common
terms, but I shall pass over the details here.

4. SENSE AND REFERENCE

Kretzmann has claimed that in the medieval period there were two separate theories about the meaning of propositions, one a theory of reference which was developed through the analysis of terms, and one a theory of sense which was developed through the analysis of the *significatum* or *dictum* of propositions.[60] This division is also found in the post-medieval period, as can be seen from an examination of the contents of the various sections of this chapter. Before I turn to those texts which were devoted to the proposition as a whole rather than to its parts, it seems relevant to make a number of comments on the notion of meaning. In post-medieval texts one of the biggest barriers to the development of an adequate theory of meaning in general or of distinctions between sense and reference in particular, was the use of the word '*significare*' to convey all notions connected with meaning. Accordingly, there was a strong tendency to confuse what a proposition signified with what a term signified [see below], and to confuse the sense of a term (or proposition) with the reference of a term (or proposition).

So far as terms were concerned, the crudest forms of such a confusion were avoided. The account of meaning embraced syncategorematic words, which do not refer; and it was also recognized that to tie the meaningfulness of terms to actual reference would make nonsense of historical propositions.[61] However, a number of factors do serve to demonstrate the presence of the confusion in question. In the first place, proper names were assimilated to common nouns. Both are said to signify, although proper names signify one and only one object while common nouns signify a plurality of objects, at least potentially. 'Sun' and 'world' do in fact signify only one thing, but not by virtue of the properties of the terms involved. In the second place, what common nouns were said to signify was very frequently just their total denotation. For instance, the distinction between *significare* and *supponere* was often drawn explicitly in terms of different ranges of reference, rather than in terms of sense versus reference [see below]. In the third place, much space in the late fifteenth and early sixteenth century was devoted to the question of how to treat those terms which have no denotation. Terms which refer to past or future objects, and terms which refer to objects which are possible, although they never have existed and never will exist, were not thought to be problematic; but there was much discussion of such terms as 'chimera' and 'irrational man' whose objects were thought to be impossible. In some contexts, such as "'Chimera' signifies a chimera", imaginary objects were introduced into the domain of discourse [see below]. Generally speaking, however, the popular answer was that 'irrational man' signifies all men and all irrational things, and that 'chimera' in a way signifies all things in the world. Of course, it could not be used to refer to them. 'Chimera' signifies Socrates, among other things, but one cannot use 'chimera' to pick out Socrates, for one cannot truly say of him "This is a chimera".[62]

This view was rejected by Domingo de Soto.[63] A term can only signify those things of which it can consistently be predicated, he said, and if something is a chimera it cannot be a man or a horse. Moreover, the intellect does not form ideas of everything in the world when it is presented with the term 'chimera'. Instead, it just conceives a monster. He saw no need to ascribe any artificial denotation to such non-denoting terms. 'Chimera' signifies a chimera in the sense that it signifies everything of which, if it existed, the concept of a chimera would be the natural similitude.

Terms were not always taken to signify just their total denotation. One alternative which was occasionally mentioned was that terms referred to some kind of intermediate being, called non-complex signifiables. These were analogous to complex signifiables [see below] but they were signified by non-complex terms rather than by propositions. Something was said to be a non-complex signifiable in so far as it was known, and existing as known was taken to be compatible with a lack of real existence.[64] However, non-complex signifiables were mentioned only infrequently and in passing, so that the postulation of such entities did not play any important role in the explanation of how terms signified.

Another kind of being which a term could be said to signify was a universal or common nature. These were introduced in the context of the distinction between primary and secondary signification. A term such as 'man' was said to signify a universal or abstract entity such as humanity primarily or immediately, whereas it was said to signify such actual objects as men only secondarily or mediately.[65] This distinction is of little use in explaining the difference between what a term means and what it refers to, for even when a term is clearly employed in its primary sense (as in "Man is a species") it is taken to denote an object, albeit a special kind of object.

The closest that logicians came to drawing an explicit distinction between sense and reference was in their discussion of absolute and connotative terms, the latter being adjectival in nature. For instance, 'white' was usually classed as a connotative term, whereas 'man' was said to be absolute. Various views as to the kind of reference connotative terms involved were possible. One could say that 'white' connotes whiteness and signifies its subject, or one could say that it connotes its subject and signifies whiteness.[66] Another way of expressing this duality involved a distinction between material and formal significates. In the late fifteenth century, Fantinus wrote that the material significate of a term was the thing signified but the formal significate was the mode of being of the thing signified. A connotative term signifies that the material significate exists in some way [aliqualiter se habere], that is, that it has a certain kind of form.[67] Clearly an absolute term was thought to give a unique determination of a group of individuals such as men by means of the formal property (or cluster of formal properties) which they all shared, but a connotative term was thought to determine a random group of individuals such as men, flowers and swans, by means of some one common property, such as whiteness. How these distinctions were used will be examined below in more detail [see simple and personal supposition and appellation].

5. PROPOSITIONS AND THEIR PARTS

There was remarkable unanimity over the definition of a proposition, for in nearly every source a proposition is said to be an indicative sentence which signifies the true and the false.[68] Some allowance was made for grammatical variations, for in the discussion of inferences it was often remarked that the antecedent and consequent could be complexes which were equivalent to propositions.[69] They had in mind such phrases as "an ass were to fly" in "If an ass were to fly, an ass would have wings". Just as terms had been divided into mental, spoken and written, so were propositions, and just as spoken and written terms were meaningful only if they were subordinated to a mental term, so were spoken and written propositions meaningful only if they were subordinated to a men-

tal proposition.[70] One of the first problems to arise from this classification concerned the composition of propositions: Do mental propositions
have separate parts, and can one have a written or spoken proposition
which does not have separate parts?

Usually it was assumed that written and spoken propositions were
characterized in terms of their parts. A sentence was defined as a complex
unit whose parts were individually meaningful; and it was assumed that
a sentence in order to be a sentence had to have at least a noun and a verb.
Moreover, propositions or indicative sentences were divided into two
kinds, categorical, or propositions with subject, copula, and predicate,
and hypothetical, or propositions made up of two or more categorical
propositions joined by a propositional connective. They were also divided
into assertoric and modal; but in every case the divisions presupposed the
presence of distinguishable parts. Dorp in his commentary on Buridan
had, however, cast doubt upon this. He cited two cases, the circle outside the tavern which means "Wine is sold here" and the letter 'a', which
could be used instead of the sentence "Man is an animal". Whether one
accepts 'a' and the circle as propositions or not depends, he said, upon
whether one takes it that a proposition needs merely to be subordinated
to a mental proposition, or whether one takes it that it is also necessary
for a proposition to have parts which are subordinated. People agree
that the verb 'is' can correspond to a copula and a predicate, 'is existent',
so why should one not say that a single utterance corresponds to a whole
mental proposition? He tended therefore toward the first approach even
though it meant, as he pointed out, that one could have propositions
which, like the circle, were neither written, spoken nor mental. Manderston agreed with Dorp about both cases; and various others agreed about
the possibility of 'a' being used as a proposition.[71] It is likely, however,
that many people would have rejected the second example, since the
circle is not an utterance. Crab certainly used the circle as an example of
a sign which was not a propositional sign and hence could not be any
kind of term, since 'propositional sign' and 'term' were convertible.

The problem of whether, and how, mental propositions were composed
of parts, gave rise to a livelier debate than the problem of spoken and
written propositions. Peter of Ailly, despite his insistence that mental
terms were naturally nouns, verbs or adjectives, and that they naturally
had their own cases and moods, nevertheless also suggested that a cate-

gorical mental proposition was a single unit whose parts could not properly be distinguished. It was not essentially made up out of partial concepts [*ex pluribus partialibus noticiis*] of which one was subject, one predicate and one the copula. It could be called a complex by virtue of the fact that it affirmed or denied, but not by virtue of the fact that it was equivalent in meaning to a spoken proposition with parts, or because it signified a division of entities. He said that he would continue to talk about the parts of a mental proposition, but only for the sake of brevity and to conform to common usage. On the other hand, he allowed hypothetical propositions to have parts, since otherwise one would have to admit that a unified mental complex could include a contradiction, '$P. - P$', and he did not wish to accept that consequence. The debate was taken up by his successors. Hieronymus of St. Mark said that it was the view of many modern Scotists, among whom we find Stephanus de Monte and Tartaretus,[72] that a mental proposition was a complex formed out of various concepts and acts. "Man is an animal", for instance, is made up of two concepts and one syncategorematic act whereby they are brought together. He felt that the more plausible doctrine was that which held a mental proposition to be *una noticia simplex*. This was caused by a concept (or concepts) and a syncategorematic act (or acts) but it formed an integral whole which was an entity distinct from its parts. It was a new cognition [*noticia*]. On the whole it was said to be complex because it was equivalent in meaning to several words or concepts; but there were some propositions such as "Socrates is Socrates" which were not complex in this sense. The complexity of "Socrates is Socrates" arises from the fact that through it we know something in a way [*qualiter*] that we do not know it through the simple concept, 'Socrates'. Pardo presented very similar arguments; and he denied that even hypothetical mental propositions were aggregates of concepts.[73]

A comprehensive overview of the entire discussion was given by Antonius Coronel, in *Prima Pars Rosarii*. He said that there were three schools of thought. The first, that of Ockham and Holkot, maintained that mental propositions were composed of parts; whereas the second, that of Gregory of Rimini, denied this. The third school, that of Heytesbury, maintained a compromise position. Affirmative propositions had parts, though if the subject and predicate were synonymous there were only two such parts, one corresponding to the subject and the other to

the copula.[74] On the other hand, written and spoken negative propositions correspond to a mental proposition which is united by the syncategorematic act of negation. Coronel himself maintained the view that
affirmative categorical propositions, whether written or spoken, corresponded to two mental parts, one of which was the subject and the other
of which was the copula and predicate combined. Some years later
Sbarroya commented on these views.[75] He said that Coronel's position
was not acceptable, because there was no better reason for making the
division into subject and copula plus predicate than there was for making
the division into subject plus copula and predicate. Gregory of Rimini's
position was, he said, adopted by some Thomists, who drew the conclusion that mental propositions are "simple in being but multiple in
representing." The first position, which he ascribed to the nominalists,
was also, he said, adopted by some Thomists. Unlike other logicians I
know, Sbarroya also examined the problem of angels. He quoted
Aegidius Romanus and Duns Scotus to support the view that angels have
a direct understanding of the quiddity of objects. Hence, they do not go
through any mental processes of dividing or conjoining, and as a result,
do not form propositions or utterances in the true sense.

In his discussion, Coronel also made two further points about non-
ultimate mental propositions, or those mental propositions which are
images of spoken or written propositions, and hence are not common to
all men. If a written or spoken proposition is composed of parts, he said,
then the non-ultimate mental proposition will consist just of those parts.
However, if a written or spoken proposition has no parts, as when the
symbol 'a' is used to convey that man is an animal, the non-ultimate
mental proposition which corresponds to 'a' will have the parts of the
proposition which 'a' conveys. Presumably he believed that for such a
symbol to convey anything, it must be read in a certain way, and reading
in a certain way involves a specific language.

6. SENTENCE-TYPES AND SENTENCE-TOKENS

So far I have taken it for granted that we know what is meant by the word
'proposition', but this is notoriously a matter of dispute, and I shall now
turn to an examination of the way in which logicians of our period used
the word. In modern usage a proposition is often taken to be whatever

it is that is common to sentences in different languages or to different sentence-types in the same language, all of which refer to the same state of affairs. Some logicians did indeed hold a view which has a certain similarity to this one, but it was expressed as a theory about the semantic correlate of a *propositio* rather than as a theory about the nature of the *propositio* itself. A *propositio* was firmly identified with an indicative sentence; and instead of talking about several sentences expressing one proposition logicians preferred to speak of several propositions being synonymous with one another. Two mental sentences were synonymous if they referred to the same things in the same way, or were related to the same complex signifiable[76] [see below]; and two or more spoken or written sentences in any language were synonymous if they were subordinated to one mental proposition, or to synonymous mental propositions.[77] Similar sentences were not necessarily synonymous. "I am Hieronymus" written on a wall but read aloud by several people is a different proposition, with a different truth value, for each person.[78] Care had also to be taken to distinguish between equivalence in meaning and logical equivalence [*in inferendo*]. The propositions "It is not the case that all men are not animals" and "Some man is an animal" are logically equivalent, but not synonymous, because, Dorp explained, the mental propositions to which they are subordinated are differentiated by their syncategorematic terms (or acts).[79] Bartholomaeus de Usingen, however, did regard such examples as synonymous.

No care was taken to distinguish between sentence-types and sentence-tokens, but it seems that they regarded sentence-tokens as propositions. For instance, the inference "*P*, therefore *P*" was said to be an inference from synonyms to synonyms rather than the inference of a proposition from itself.[80] Thus, if I say "Mary has a little lamb" and then I repeat it, I have uttered two synonymous propositions, not two tokens or instances of one proposition-type. A corollary of this was an insistence upon the need for a proposition to exist as a mental, spoken or written occurrent before general claims could be made about its properties and relationships. The definition of a valid inference of one proposition from another in terms of the first proposition being true when the second proposition was false was often rejected on the grounds that one could have a true instance of the first proposition at a time when the second was not true because it did not exist.[81] In the discussion of semantic paradoxes, such as "Every proposition is false", an extra premiss, "This is a proposition" or "This proposition exists", was thought to be necessary before its falsity could be shown to follow.[82] Even the apparently harmless equivalence, "'P' is true if and only if P" was rejected on the grounds that 'P' must exist in order to have the label 'true' attached to it, and there is no guarantee that it does exist.[83] Moreover, since a written or spoken proposition was a set of sounds or marks bearing a conventional meaning, that meaning might be changed so that 'P' no longer meant P.[84] Of course, not all logicians found such objections cogent. Clichtoveus argued strongly for the truth of "$P \equiv T'P$'" without any restrictions.[85] He said that if "$P \supset T'P$'" did not hold, it could only be because there was a true antecedent and a false consequent. It would follow that "'P' is not true" was true and hence that 'P' is false. The antecedent has already been assumed to be true, so we get a situation in which the same proposition is both true and false, which is impossible. Equally, if "$T'P' \supset P$" does not hold, the antecedent is true and the consequent false. Hence the contradictory of the consequent, "$-P$" is true and we have the situation in which two contradictories are true, which is also impossible.

Although I have just remarked that a proposition was identified with a sentence-token rather than a sentence-type, some of the things which were said about the meaning and truth of a proposition make it seem as if a sentence-type is being spoken of. This was inevitable, for there are various circumstances in which it only makes sense to speak of types rather than tokens; for instance, when reference is made to logical rules, to necessary truths, or types all of whose tokens are true, and to the fact that the same sentence-type can have tokens whose truth values are different because each token is used to signify a different state of affairs. This last point was discussed to some extent in the context of the *propositio plures*, or such sentences as "*Canis currit*", where '*canis*' can mean a dog, a sea-creature, or a star. The notion of an ambiguous proposition was not normally taken to be problematic. Moreover, it was commonly held that the very same proposition could be both true and false, both possible and impossible. For instance, "*Homo est asinus*" could mean that man is an ass in Latin, and that man is an animal in Greek. Similarly, "I am Hieronymus" written on a wall could be true or false depending on who was reading it, presumably with self-referential intent. Pardo, however, noted that the common view was inconsistent with the usual doctrines about the nature of a proposition.[86] One must deal with all the above examples by saying that one and the same written or spoken sequence may be said to be various propositions according as it is subordinated to various mental propositions. Thus "*Canis currit*" can express three different propositions; "I am Hieronymus" can express as many different propositions as there are speakers; and "*Homo est asinus*" can express one Greek proposition and quite another Latin proposition. For Pardo, and for Hieronymus of St. Mark who followed him exactly on these points, a proposition remains identified with a token and not with a type.

7. COMPLEX SIGNIFIABLES AND TRUTH

The most interesting theoretical question to be raised in connection with propositions concerned the existence of the *complexe significabile*, a notion first introduced in the fourteenth century by Gregory of Rimini.[87] The phrase means "something which can be signified complexly (or by means of something complex)" but I shall speak of a 'complex signifiable' for the sake of brevity. The original motivation for discussion had been a concern with the objects of knowledge and belief especially with respect to theological knowledge but also with respect to the objects of scientific knowledge which were supposed to be unchanging and perfect. It was argued that to know a conclusion was to know not a proposition, or particular utterance, but a fact, and that knowing a fact and knowing a proposition to be true involved two different acts of mind. Facts, however, while different from propositions, could not be equated with things in the world, for these were impermanent and not fitted to be the objects of scientific knowledge. Hence an intermediate thing, the *complexe significabile*, had to be postulated. These epistemological concerns were not emphasized by the logicians whose work I am concerned with. Rather, the stage for their discussion of complex signifiables was set by two other considerations. Firstly, there was the question of the status of the *dictum* or infinitive phrase in the following sentence: "*Homo est animal significat hominem esse animal*", which I will translate as "'A man is an animal' signifies a-man-to-be-an-animal". Some people preferred to rephrase the whole sentence in such a way that the infinitive phrase was excluded. For instance, Enzinas wrote "'A man is an animal' signifies that a man is an animal", and he remarked that 'that' [*quod*] was

not part of the meaning of the proposition.[88] Others, however, focused
upon the *dictum* and asked what it referred to or signified. What is the
significatum, or the thing that is said to be signified by the original proposition? Secondly, there was the question of the true and the false which
were said to be signified by a proposition. What was the bearer of truth
or falsity to which a proposition referred? As we shall see, not everyone
accepted such questions as proper.

Hieronymus Pardo devoted the opening pages of his *Medulla Dyalectices* to the problem of complex signifiables, and I shall use his lengthy
and elaborate discussion as the basis for my own.[89] Like Hieronymus of
St. Mark, Pardo saw the main question as being whether the semantical
correlate of a proposition, its *significatum* or *complexe significabile*, was
to be distinguished from the semantical correlates of the terms or not.
Does a proposition refer to some special kind of being; or does it refer
to a state of affairs whose characteristics can be ascertained from an
examination of the meaning and supposition of the individual terms and
the ways in which they are related to one another? Bricot put his questions
in another way: is a complex signifiable an ordinary thing (or group of
things) which can be signified complexly and verbally by a proposition,
or is it a special kind of thing which is quite different from non-complex
beings? Is a signifiable (or thing which can be signified) complex because
it can be signified by something complex, or is it complex because it can
only primarily be signified by something complex? In the first sense,
Socrates is a complex signifiable because he can be signified by means of
a proposition, though he can also be signified by a non-complex name; in
the second sense only "A-man-to-be-an-animal" is a complex signifiable,
and whatever it is, it is not identifiable with existent men, animals or states
of affairs. Of course, "A-man-to-be-an-animal" could also be signified
by something non-complex, as when 'a' is taken as standing for the
sentence "A man is an animal", but this usage is secondary.

There were two predominant views in accordance with which all these
questions could be answered, the first being that of Gregory of Rimini
himself. Pardo saw Gregory of Rimini's view as having three main features. In the first place, any complex signifiable was said to be something
[*aliquid*] although it was not an existent in the strict sense. 'Being' can
be taken in three ways. In the broadest sense, it covers complex signifiables
which are true or false, possible or impossible; and Peter of Ailly added

that it also embraced non-complex signifiables. In the less broad sense it covers only true and possible signifiables; in the strictest sense, it includes only existent things, whether created or uncreated, substance or accident.[90] According to Gregory, then, something could be a being without being an existent; and Peter of Ailly remarked sourly that it was difficult to attack Gregory without begging the question on this point. Certainly Peter did not think it made any sense to speak of a non-existent being, something which was neither substance nor accident, which was eternal although it was not identified with God, and which had no location. Pardo himself mentioned a number of objections. One was that such words as 'same' and 'different' could not properly be applied to such beings, but Pardo felt that their use was licensed by the authority of St. Anselm, though he did not apply himself directly to the question of what criteria of identity could properly be appealed to. Another objection was attributed to Andreas de Novo Castro who had said that God-to-be either contains God or it does not.[91] If it does not, then one can understand God to be without understanding God; if it does, then a non-entity contains an entity. Presumably he took it that terms referred directly to things, and was worried by the relationship between these things and the complex signifiable which was said to be the referent of the proposition, itself composed out of terms. Pardo replied by introducing non-complex signifiables as the components of complex signifiables. These non-complex signifiables are related to actual things in a way in which complex signifiables are not, but they are not actual things. They are assimilated to second intentions and beings of reason, since they are founded on things as known, rather than things as real. He did not, however, wish to commit himself to this view.

Pardo said that there were an infinite number of signifiables, corresponding to the number of possible and actual propositions but it is not clear whether he was speaking of sentence-types or sentence-tokens here, for he went on to say that all synonymous propositions share the same complex signifiable [*omnium propositionum synonymarum est idem complexe significabile singulare*]. In his view, the second main feature of Gregory's doctrine was that every affirmative proposition whose subject and predicate refer to a complex signifiable is false unless the subject and predicate propositions are synonymous. Thus one can say "Marcus-to-run is Tullius-to-run" but not "A-man-to-be-an-animal is a-man-to-be-a-substance". Anyone who tries to argue that the latter is true is confusing equivalence of meaning with logical equivalence.

The third and final feature of Gregory's doctrine according to Pardo was the account it gave of truth, falsity, necessity and so on. A proposition was said to be true, false, necessary etc. because it signified a complex signifiable with just these properties. The clearest account of what it means to say that a complex signifiable has these properties was given by Bricot, to whom I now turn. He argued that there are three ways of explaining the truth of a complex signifiable. Firstly, one can say that it is true because it is or can be signified by a true proposition; but this way has two defects. It is circular, since a true proposition is defined in terms of a true complex signifiable; and it fails to account for such possible truths as "No creature exists" and "No proposition exists", which cannot be signified by actual propositions. Peter of Ailly derived much of his ammunition against Gregory of Rimini from the fact that he only considered this first approach to truth. Secondly, one can say that a complex signifiable is true because it is assented to by the First Truth, God.[92] This solves the problem of "No creature exists"; but it does not solve the problem of "The First Truth does not exist" which would be true just in case there were no God. Pardo dealt with this problem by saying that an impossible proposition such as "God does not exist" implies any other proposition, including "It is true that God does not exist";[93] but Bricot preferred the third way, whereby a complex signifiable is said to be true "because it is just as things are" [quia ipsum est taliter esse si sit affirmativa qualiter est]. For instance, "'A-man-to-be-an-animal' is true because a-man-to-be-an-animal is a-man-to-be-an-animal, and it is the case that a man is an animal" [et est quod homo est animal]. This view allows for the truth of all complexes which are true and for the possible truth of those which can be imagined to be true, such as "God does not exist". He examined four ways of judging a complex to be false, including the additional view that it was judged to be false by a First Falsity; and he proceeded in a similar manner for possible, impossible and necessary complexes. In every case, he came back to the way things were, or could be, or had to be, to find his answer. Pardo, however, felt that complexes were false (or possible, necessary or impossible) when they were so judged by the First Truth. He added that it was only insofar as they were said to be judged by God from eternity that complex signifiables were said to be

eternal, and thus they could not be viewed as eternal independent exis-
tents. In this way he avoided another of the usual objections to Gregory
of Rimini.[94]

According to Pardo, the fundamental feature of the main alternative
to Gregory of Rimini's doctrine was the claim that "Every complex or
aggregate of parts signifies that very thing which its parts separately
signify, so that if I want to know what some complex signifies, then I
must see what its parts separately signify." Thus the referent of "A-man-
to-be-an-animal" cannot be distinguished from men and animals, and the
dictum refers to man existing as an animal [*homo existens animal*]. The
general instructions for finding the referent of any *dictum* were to replace
the accusative with a nominative and the infinitive with a participle.[95]
The language used suggests that the semantical correlate of a proposition
was taken to be a state of affairs, as opposed to the view of Pseudo-Scotus
that the semantical correlate of a proposition (if any) is to be identified
with the referent of the subject term, or an existent; and Dolz did draw
an explicit distinction between the view that a proposition signified something [*aliquid*] and that it signified something in some way [*aliquid aliqualiter*].[96] He identified the 'something' of the first view with the
significate of either subject or predicate; and he pointed out that not all
propositions were said to have a significate in this sense. Impossible
propositions such as "A man is an ass", false propositions such as
"Antichrist exists", and some negative propositions such as "A man is
not an animal" all signified nothing.[97] He explained the second view as
claiming that a proposition signified that the subject was related in some
way to the predicate.[98] He also spoke of a third view to the effect that
propositions signified *aliqualiter*, or syncategorematically [see below].
However, other writers did not draw these initial distinctions, and one
can only sort out precisely what was being claimed by examining the text
in some detail.

On the one hand Pardo in his exposition of the second position
claimed, like Bricot, that "A-man-to-be-an-animal is a-man-to-be-white"
was true because a-man-being-an-animal can be a-man-being-white;
which supports the view that they were concerned with the identity between entities rather than between states of affairs.[99] Moreover they
both argued that the very same thing was both a non-complex signifiable
and a complex signifiable, for these were extrinsic denominations. Socra-

tes can be referred to by a name, which is not complex, or by a proposition, which is. Finally, Bricot listed as a corollary of the general view the claim that a-man-to-be-an-animal is nothing but a man [*hominem esse animal non est nisi homo*]; and Pardo listed as a corollary the claim that "A-man-to-be-an-animal is signified by this term 'man', since a-man-to-be-an-animal is a man." Similarly, Hieronymus of St. Mark said "'A man is an animal' signifies a-man-to-be-an-animal, a-man-to-be-an-animal is nothing other than a man existing as an animal, and a man existing as an animal is a man."

On the other hand, Pardo's discussion of impossible propositions suggests very clearly that he did in fact make a distinction between referring to a state of affairs and referring to an entity which could enter into different states of affairs. The example Pardo considered was "A man is an ass". He agreed with Bricot that "No man is an ass" refers to anything in the world, since of anything it is true to say "This is not a man being an ass", but he felt that the affirmative raised some problems even for the adherents of Gregory of Rimini. They could claim that there were impossible signifiables, but it was not altogether clear that the impossible could be signified or understood. Some people argued that it could not; others remarked simply that although the concepts of a chimera or a golden mountain were possible, what they were concepts of was not possible.[100] They were complex concepts whose parts referred to what could not in fact exist together in the world. Others discussed the matter with reference to propositions. For instance, Pardo argued that although impossible propositions, including '*P* and not *P*' and such examples as "A man is an ass" cannot be understood by a simple act of the intellect, what is being asserted and what things are being compared can indeed be understood.[101] Given the view opposed to Gregory of Rimini, Pardo felt that one must argue that "A man is an ass" signifies both men and asses, for "nothing terminates the act of judging beyond that thing which is a man and that thing which is an ass." He thus disagreed with Bricot who said that "A man is an ass" refers to nothing. He rejected the argument that his interpretation had the consequence that the proposition was true, since men and asses, although existent, do not have the relationship they are said to have. Similarly, he said, one cannot claim that "God exists" and "God does not exist" are both true on the grounds that (as was generally agreed) they signify the same being, for in one case God is signified affirmatively, in the other case, negatively. In other words, there is one entity but two states of affairs, and the two propositions have the same or different semantical correlates according as one is concerned with entities or with states of affairs.

As well as looking at impossible propositions, Pardo also had a few words to say about the consequences of the second view for false propositions. One of his examples was "Socrates runs". One can say, he remarked, that "A running Socrates is Socrates" is true if Socrates is running and it is false if Socrates is not running, because the subject lacks supposition. Hence one can argue that Socrates-to-run is Socrates if Socrates runs, and Socrates-to-run is not Socrates if Socrates does not run. Thus he again denies that the referent of a proposition is simply its subject, irrespective of the state of affairs involving that subject.

Some of these issues are also involved in Pardo's discussion of Peter of Ailly's objections to the second view. Peter had argued that the *dictum* does not refer to anything when it is taken significatively, or used rather than mentioned, because there is no reason why it should stand for one thing rather than another. "A-man-to-be-an-animal" could stand for a man, but it could also stand for an ass. His conclusions were that a proposition has no total and adequate significate, and that although what is signified by the whole proposition is signified by the parts, the whole signifies in a way that the parts do not. If Peter is saying that propositions, unlike their parts, do not name entities, his conclusion makes a good deal of sense; but Pardo said that the conclusion itself was difficult to sustain, independently of the way in which Peter arrived at it. His main argument against Peter was that we must distinguish between two senses of *adequatum significatum*: it could be all things referred to by the terms taken independently, or it could be that thing which the aggregate stands for, namely man. There is no reason to talk about asses, because the terms 'man' and 'animal' are mutually restrictive. 'Animal' does indeed denote asses, but not in this context. Pardo also quoted Peter's grammatical argument to the effect that although one can say "'A man is an animal' signifies a-man-to-be-an-animal" one cannot say "A-man-to-be-an-animal is signified by 'A man is an animal'", for the latter is ill-formed [*incongrua*]. This point was important to Peter, for he used it to back up his claim that the *dictum* has no supposition when taken significatively; but Hubert Elie was quite wrong when he claimed that this was the main criticism Peter had to offer against Gregory of Rimini, and that it led all subsequent authors to confuse the significate of a proposition with its verbal expression, the *dictum*.[102]

One final problem connected with the rejection of complex signifiables concerned the status of truths before the creation of the world. Major said firmly that there were no truths before the creation, since there were no spoken, written or mental propositions; but Bricot took up the view of Peter of Ailly to the effect that God is a proposition, although being uncreated, he lacks the normal properties of created propositions.[103] He is not categorical or hypothetical, affirmative or negative, universal or particular. He is, Bricot said, a proposition from eternity, since from eternity he has represented truly [*quia ab eterno deus fuit representans vere*]. One of the things he has truly represented is "The world will be created;" hence, we can explain how "The world will be created" was true before the world was created, without having to postulate some eternal entity which is separate from God.

8. OTHER APPROACHES TO TRUTH

I stated earlier that one of the reasons for introducing the notion of a complex signifiable was to explain how it was that a proposition signified the true or the false; but there were, of course, other ways of explicating the matter which did not involve so many complications. One approach was that of Enzinas, who drew a distinction between the categorematic and the syncategorematic use of the *dictum*.[104] He first posed the question whether a proposition signified truly or whether it signified the true, namely something [*aliquid*]; and he then examined the argument: "'A man is an animal' signifies a-man-to-be-an-animal, a-man-to-be-an-animal is something, therefore 'A man is an animal' signifies something." He said that in the second premiss "a-man-to-be-an-animal" is used categorematically, as if it is the name of an object; but that in the first premiss it is used syncategorematically. That is, it indicates in what way [*aliqualiter*] things are said to be. It should be regarded not as a name, but as a substitute for a 'that' clause, i.e. "'A man is an animal' signifies that a man is an animal". Domingo de Soto examined the same argument, substituting "Peter is a man" for "A man is an animal", but he said that he did not see why the use of the *dictum* was taken to be equivocal.[105] If "Peter-to-be-a-man" can be taken to stand for Peter in the second premiss, so it can in the first. Celaya accepted that the argument involved equivocation and concluded that no (true) proposition signified something or some things truly [*aliquod vel aliqua vere*] but only in some way truly [*aliqualiter vere*].[106]

Another method of approach was to draw a distinction between written and spoken propositions and mental propositions. The first group was taken to signify the true and the false, namely a true or false mental proposition, but mental propositions were said to signify truly or falsely [*vere vel false*].[107] Eckius rejected this outright;[108] and Gebwiler, while using the distinction, said that it was "a voluntary fiction", and had no authority, for the words *verum* and *vere* were usually used synonymously. Other people examined the various uses of the word 'true' in more detail in order to arrive at their solution.[109] They said that 'true' could be used in three ways. It can be used as a term of first intention, as referring to things which have their proper form, and in this sense everything in the world is true.[110] It can be used as a term of second intention, as referring to propositions and this is the normal logical use. Finally, it can be used as a substitute for the adverb 'truly'. Most people agreed that the third sense was the proper sense in the present context.[111] To say that a proposition signifies the true is not to say that it refers to a true thing or to say that it refers to a proposition which is true, but to say that it signifies truly.

It was not only the claim that a proposition signified the true or the false that led to complications; for there was also controversy about the significance of 'true' in the phrase 'a true proposition'. Two questions were asked: is it the same thing to talk about truth as it is to talk about a true proposition (in logical contexts, at least); and if it is not, is truth an ordinary property or a relational property of propositions? Trutvetter sided with Ockham and Holkot, whom he quoted as saying that *verum* and *veritas* were synonymous, and that there was no distinction between truth and a true proposition. He dismissed the views of the realists rather cursorily; but Celaya examined them with some care.[112] They held that truth was distinct from a true proposition, but were divided as to whether it was a relational characteristic or not; and if it were relational, whether it was an ideal or a real relation that was involved. They attempted to show that it was a relation by arguing that the intellect takes a mental proposition and compares that proposition with the state of affairs (or whatever is thought to be the *significatum*) signified. Truth is a relation of conformity, falsity a relation of non-conformity [*difformitas*] between the proposition and its *significatum*;[113] or between intellect and thing.[114] There were various objections to the realist view that truth was something added to a proposition: *"Aliqua parva entitas addita propositioni,"* as Stephanus de Monte put it. One was that an insect could cause something in the mind of an angel, for if the angel contemplated the proposition "An insect flies" the insect could cause this to be true or false, since it was in its power either to fly or not to fly. Presumably this involved a kind of *lèse majesté*. Another objection was that a paradox results if one takes the proposition "God causes nothing" as being written before an instant *b* in which God does cause nothing. If the proposition is true, God causes nothing at *b*, yet if truth is caused then how can the proposition be true at a time when God is causing nothing?[115] Celaya said that the realists countered this by claiming that "God causes nothing" cannot be true. One objection, offered by Peter of Ailly, was that if truth and a proposition were distinct, God would be able to destroy the truth of a proposition whilst leaving the proposition intact which is impossible. Domingo de Soto mentioned the controversy, but said that it was not for first year logic students [*summuliste*] to inquire into. It was a metaphysical question, like that of the *complexe significabile*.[116]

An interesting development of the theory that truth is a non-essential property of propositions is found in the work of John of St. Thomas, who also raised the question of the relationship between indicative sentences and assertions.[117] He began by distinguishing a judicative proposition from an enunciative proposition on the grounds that judgement is posterior to enunciation.[118] In other words, an indicative sentence must be formed before a judgement is made about its truth or falsity, or before assent is given to what it asserts. Indeed, one can utter a sentence without making a judgement or assertion at all; and he cited the example of "The treasure is in this place." Perhaps he had in mind someone reading it off a map. Truth is not a property of a proposition, but of a proposition and a judgement. He quoted Aquinas as saying that the essence of a proposition was not to signify truly or falsely, but solely to signify a complex object about which a true or false judgement can be made.[119] The utterance "Peter sits" can after all change from true to false as the facts change, yet the proposition is always the same because it "says and signifies" the same. A proposition essentially signifies a complex object, namely a predicate and subject united by a verbal copula, or two propositions united by a propositional connective, and it is about this that the judgement is made. Hence truth and falsity are accidental properties of the proposition. He could be interpreted as saying that what is true or false is the assertively uttered token of a sentence-type. The sentence-type is what he calls a proposition, but its own essential function is not to exhibit truth or falsity but to bear meaning.

The clearest comments on whether a proposition can be said to change its truth value were those of Derodon.[120] He argued that if one says "Peter is running at this hour" at a time when he is running and then at a time when he is not, it looks as if the proposition changes its value from true to false. However, there are in fact two propositions involved, one which affirms Peter to be running at hour one and one which affirms Peter to be running at hour two. From here it is but a short step to the concept of an eternal sentence, a sentence-type all of whose tokens are true (or false) because of its exact specification of time, place and so on.

Leaving these theoretical questions aside, a true proposition can be characterized fairly easily. It was, everyone agreed, a proposition which signified things to be as they in fact were,[121] with appropriate expansions to allow for temporal and other modalities.[122] Those who specified more precisely under what conditions a proposition could be said to be true usually laid down six criteria.[123] First, an affirmative proposition whose terms suppose for (refer to) the same things is true, except in certain cases. Insolubles, such as "This (very sentence) is false", sentences with quantified predicates, such as "A man is every man", sentences with divine terms, such as "The Father is the Son", and some modal propositions such as "God is contingently God" were all false, even though the referent of both subject and predicate was the same.[124] Secondly, a negative proposition whose terms suppose for the same thing is false. Thirdly, an affirmative proposition whose terms do not suppose for the same thing is false. Fourthly, a negative proposition whose terms do not suppose for the same thing is true. Fifthly, an affirmative proposition is false if either one or both of its terms has no supposition, or reference. "A chimera is a chimera" is false, despite Boethius's claim that "nothing is truer than a proposition in which the same is predicated of itself".[125] Later in the sixteenth century Acerbus qualified the fifth criterion by pointing out that sentences with a non-existent subject and an incompatible predicate such as "Troy is burnt" and "Aristotle is dead" may very well be true.[126] Finally, a negative proposition is true if either term does not suppose. For instance, both "A chimera is not an animal" and "A chimera is not a chimera" are true.[127] These decisions about the way to treat non-referring terms are of great importance for the development of syllogistic logic [see below].

Some logicians added a further point about truth in their discussion of valid consequences when they said that one could infer a proposition with more causes of truth from one with fewer.[128] Hieronymus of St. Mark explained this by saying that a proposition has as many causes of truth as there are propositions from which it follows. "Some man is running" follows from "This man is running" and "That man is running" and so on, but "All men are running" is only true in the one case when all its singulars are true, so it presumably follows only from the proposition "This man and that man and... are running" [see section on descent].

9. POSSIBILITY AND NECESSITY

Truth was not the only aspect of a proposition in which logicians were interested, for they were also concerned with the four modalities, necessity, possibility, contingency, and impossibility. Usually the specification of the conditions for these modalities was modelled on the conditions for truth.[129] That is, a proposition was said to be possible when it signified things to be as they possibly could be, necessary when it signified things to be as they necessarily were, and so on. These modalities are not, of course, to be confused with such modal operators as "It is necessary that". Instead, they are linked with what Peter of Spain (and subsequent commentators) had to say about 'the matter of propositions', which he divided into three kinds: natural, in which the predicate belonged essentially to the subject; contingent, in which it could both belong and not belong; and remote, in which the predicate was incompatible with the subject.[130] Some interesting points were made both about possibility and about necessity, though not in any one context. I shall not speak specifically of impossibility, as the accounts given were closely parallel to the accounts of necessity, as might be expected.

Of possibility both Tartaretus and Bricot said that a proposition is not called possible because it can exist, for any set of words can be uttered.[131] Nor is it called possible because it can be true, for "Man is an ass" can be true if given a new meaning. Nor is it called possible because it can be true without a new imposition of meaning, for such sentences as "No proposition is negative" can never be true. To be true they have to be uttered or written or thought, and the moment they exist they are false. A proposition is said to be possible just in case the state of affairs to which it refers is a possible one; and in this way such puzzling cases as "No proposition is negative" can be dealt with. We shall see the use made of these distinctions in the treatment of semantical paradoxes and the definition of valid inferences.

Necessity is a more complicated topic, for there are various senses in which a proposition is said to be necessary. Tartaretus said that a proposition was not said to be necessary because it could not be false, for it might be given a new meaning; or because it could not be false unless there were a new meaning, because then "This is not true" (pointing to "A man is an ass") would be a necessary proposition,[132] as would "Some proposition is affirmative." Rather, it was necessary because things could not be otherwise than they were signified to be. He then went on to distinguish between two kinds of necessary propositions. Some were necessary by virtue of their form, as was '$P \vee -P$', and some by virtue of their matter, or the terms involved. These were divided again into propositions necessary *simpliciter*, such as "God exists", and propositions necessary *secundum quid*, such as "Adam existed", which cannot now be false, though it could once have been, before the creation. Not all authors approached the matter in quite the same way. Trutvetter, for instance, distinguished between simply necessary propositions, in which category he included both "God exists" and any disjunction with contradictory parts, since these cannot be falsified by any power, given that the meaning of the terms is retained, and conditionally necessary propositions.[133] The latter could be explicated in two ways. Both Trutvetter and the Mainz commentators said that such propositions as "Man is an animal" were true on condition that the order of nature established by God remained, and they accused Aristotle of erring when he assumed that such propositions were simply necessary and eternally true. His fault arose from the assumption that the world and all species of things had existed from eternity, the Mainz commentators added. However, Trutvetter also mentioned the interpretation of such propositions as equivalent to a conditional whose antecedent asserted the existence of the subject class and whose consequent spelled out the connection between subject and predicate. Thus "A man is an animal" became "If a man exists, a man is an animal." John Major emphasized the existential import of both terms even more clearly when he rewrote the proposition in question as "If a man exists, an animal exists."[134]

This raises the difficult question of the relationship between necessary propositions and existence. It has already been said that it was usual to dismiss "A chimera is a chimera" as false, despite its analytic nature, on the grounds that the terms had no referents; and the question now arises whether the necessity of "A man is an animal", "A triangle has three angles equal to two right angles", and "Thunder is a sound" depends on the existence of the things referred to, or on something else. Trutvetter's answer was unequivocal: these propositions are true only on the condition that there are referents, and some, including the Mainz commentators agreed with him. But it was a matter on which there was disagreement. One usual move was to draw a preliminary distinction between two senses of 'is'. It could be taken as having some specific temporal reference, in which case the existence of the things denoted by the terms was certainly required, or it could be taken as absolved or abstracted from time. Many believed that in the latter case the subject need not exist, so that "A triangle has three angles equal to two right angles" is true even if there are no triangles,[135] but their explanation was not always satisfactory. They tended to say that the terms in such a proposition stand for all their significates, even if these do not exist. This has a paradoxical ring to it, especially when it was explicitly denied that perpetual essences were in question.[136]

Some attempts were made to clarify the situation. Enzinas attacked the problem by arguing that the notion of abstraction from time could be interpreted in two ways.[137] 'Is' can refer to no time at all, or it can refer to every time indifferently. People usually reject the first sense, although, Enzinas argued, it is quite acceptable. Normally verbs designate time by definition, but 'is' is being used philosophically here, to show that the thing signified by the subject is the same as that signified by the predicate. Not time, but duration, such as that attributed to God, is involved, he said. However, Enzinas did not succeed in getting away from an extensionalist interpretation of necessary propositions, and to that extent he failed to give a satisfactory account.

The fifteenth century Cologne commentators offered an intensionalist interpretation which is far more plausible, although their attempts to extend it to propositions with singular terms raise the problem of how far such terms can be said to have an intension. They distinguished three senses of 'is'.[138] It could indicate the essence or nature of the thing referred to; it could indicate actual existence; or it could indicate that the predicate was not incompatible with the concept of the subject. In a context such as "Adam is an animal", which they took to be a necessary truth, 'is' was used predicatively and indicated the composition of the terms. "This composition", they said, "is a certain accident of reason belonging to things conceived and not to things existing outside the mind." As a result, they rejected the 'modern' claim that 'is' meant 'exists [as]' in such a context;[139] and they also rejected the 'modern' claim that "Adam is an animal" was false because its subject did not refer.[140] Their doctrines do not seem to have been accepted by their contemporaries, and the closest parallel I have found is in the seventeenth century writer Smiglecius, who argued that 'is' can indicate an "essential connection of terms which however does not exist except in reason."[141] "A rose in winter is a flower" is false if 'is' is taken to mean real existence, but it is true if 'is' is taken to mean rational existence, since "the concept of flower is included in the concept of rose." Isendoorn used the same sort of terminology, and said that in "A goat-stag is an animal" the predicate is included in the concept of the subject.[142]

NOTES

[1] John of St. Thomas, *Formal Logic*, 29.

[2] See, e.g., Dorp; *Commentum*; and various commentaries on Peter of Spain.

[3] Versor, 6ᵛᵒ: "Ad quintum dicitur quod licet in tussi non sit percussio corporum inanimatorum secundum substantiam, eorum tamen sunt ibi corpora inanimata quantum ad modum operandi, quia non sit ibi aliqua formatio vocis secundum aliquam virtutem cognoscituram animae."

[4] *Commentum*: "Tussis non est vox quia non fit cum intentione significandi aliquid. Si autem fieret sic tunc esset vox."

[5] Javellus, 12ᵛᵒf.

[6] E.g. Lax, *Termini*; Crab; Angelus, xiii. Cf. Domingo de Soto, vii: "Terminus est signum propositionis categorice constitutivum."

[7] Dolz, *Termini*, vi[vo]. For the text, see appendix. Cf. Coronel, *Termini*; Hieronymus of St. Mark.

[8] Major, *Termini*, pointed out that single letters could occasionally count as parts. For instance, 'a' and 'e' are both used as propositions.

[9] Major, *Opera*, ii. For the text, see appendix. Cf. Crab.

[10] Celaya, *Dial. Introd.*; Cf. Clichtoveus, 8; Eckius, *Summulae*, v[vo]; Lax, *Termini*; Dolz, *Termini*, x. For a later writer, see Hunnaeus, 68.

[11] Hieronymus of St. Mark; Peter of Ailly; Domingo de Soto, v; Manderston.

[12] For references to the distinction between formal and instrumental see Crab; Domingo de Soto, v; Lax, *Termini*; Manderston; Dolz, *Termini*, ix[vo]f. For a later writer, see Fonseca, I 34–36.

[13] For the full text, see appendix.

[14] Tartaretus, *Expositio*, 3[vo]; Eckius, *Summulae*, v[vo].

[15] Versor, 7.

[16] Dorp; Tartaretus, *Expositio*, 3[vo]; Peter of Ailly; Major, *Termini*; Crab.

[17] Hieronymus of St. Mark, "... suppositio saltem pro denominato non est nisi terminus acceptus in propositione seu cognito. sed nullo intellectu advertente non est aliquis terminus neque cognito. ergo nec per consequens est suppositio. Et si dicas in libro clauso sunt propositiones. Nego. Immo dico quod secluso intellectu non est veritas neque falsitas." In his discussion of propositions, Menghus Blanchellus Faventinus, 12, drew a distinction: "Nota quod ly significans verum vel falsum: capitur pro esse significativum veri vel falsi: Nam significans proprie dicit actum: sed significativum dicit aptitudinem: modo propositio qui est in libro clauso est propositio: et tamen non significat verum nec falsum: sed significativa est veri vel falsi."

[18] Tartaretus, *Expositio*, 3[vo], "sufficit quod nata sit representare." Cf. Major, *Termini*; Dolz, *Termini*, viii[vo].

[19] J. Sanderson, 7.

[20] Versor, 7.

[21] Fonseca, I 52, 54. Cf. John of St. Thomas, *Cursus*, 92.

[22] E.g. Coronel, *Termini*.

[23] Villalpandeus, 34[vo].

[24] Enzinas, *Termini*.

[25] Versor, 7[vo]. Cf. Hieronymus of St. Mark; Eckius, *Summulae*, v[vo]; Javellus, 15[vo].

[26] Smiglecius, II 10. "Dicimus igitur tales proprietates non esse sufficientes ad exprimendas res naturaliter. Nam hae proprietates et paucae sunt in vocibus et non habent tantam proportionem ad res ut possint rerum naturas explicare ut vel ex eo patet, quod hactenus, ne ii quidem authores qui hoc tenent tales voces invenire potuerunt, ex quarum proprietatibus, res quam significant agnosci posset. Quare neque voces ab Adamo impositae eiusmodi fuerunt, ut naturas significarent, hae enim voces etiam nunc extant in lingua sancta, et tamen nullus unquam ex iis naturam illius rei cognovit, et nisi doceatur, quid vox quaelibet significet ex sono vocis scire non poterit significationem."

[27] Peter of Ailly wrote: "... terminus mentalis conceptus sive actus intelligendi et notitia rei apprehensiva idem sunt."

[28] Versor, 8.

[29] Campanella, 13f.

[30] Dorp.

[31] *Commentum*: The author said: "Debet ergo diffinitio sic intelligi. vox significativa ad

placitum est vox quae ad voluntatem primi instituentis id est ex impositione actu facta vel voluntario usu vel consuetudine significat aliquid...."

[32] Domingo de Soto, v^{vo}. Cf. Mercarius; Coronel, *Termini*; Sbarroya, *Dial. Introd.*, lxviii. A full discussion of non-authentic imposition and the problems it raises can be found in treatises on obligations.

[33] Versor, 8. "Quarto sciendum, quod cum res presentatur sensui, mediante sensu generat suam similitudinem in anima, & per illam similitudinem anima format intra se conceptum rei, quam postea vult exprimere, propter quod imponit vocem ad significandum talem conceptum, & mediante ipso rem conceptam, & ideo apud proferentem, vox primo significat conceptum, licet apud audientem primo repraesentat rem conceptam. unde ipsa non significat conceptum tantum nec rem tantum, sed rem sub conceptus." See Boehner, 242f., for an account of the medieval background.

[34] John of St. Thomas, *Cursus*, 105ff.

[35] John of St. Thomas, *Cursus*, 105.

[36] Pardo, cxlix^{vo}f.

[37] Coimbra, II 34. Cf. Timplerus, 85.

[38] Smiglecius, II 10–14.

[39] Pardo, cxlix^{vo}. Cf. Raulin.

[40] Coimbra, II 48.

[41] Fonseca, I 40.

[42] Pardo, cxlix^{vo}.

[43] Cf. Celaya, *Dial. Introd.* For two later references see Villalpandeus, 39^{vo}f.; John of St. Thomas, *Formal Logic*, 33.

[44] Fonseca, I 40–42.

[45] Tartaretus, *Expositio*, 50vo.

[46] See also Coronel, *Prima Pars Rosarii*.

[47] E.g. Gebwiler; Bartholomaeus de Usingen; Eckius, *El. Dial*; Coronel, *Termini*.

[48] Clichtoveus. 12^{vo}f.

[49] Pardo, clx.

[50] Gebwiler; Margalho, 106–108; Bartholomaeus de Usingen. The latter wrote: "homo est homo: chymera est chymera: quia sinonimum predicatur essentialiter de suo sinonimo. Pater est paternitas: homo est humanitas: risibile est risibilitas: quia sinonimum predicatur de sinonimo: nec differunt illi termini nisi in modo significandi grammaticali: que est significare concretive vel abstractive: ille autem non mutat sinonimitatem in logica. In via enim moderna relatio non distinguitur a suo fundamento: nec natura a supposito: nec proprio passio a suo subiecto in significatis."

[51] Tartaretus, *Expositio*, 50vo; Dolz, *Termini*, xxii^{vo}f.

[52] Keckermann, *Systema*, 317: "Syncategorematicum signum est, quod in propositione non significat rem aliquam certam, sed rei tantum modum." Cf. Du Trieu, 6; Jungius, 54. In the early sixteenth century Hieronymus of St. Mark said: "Terminus syncathegorematicus est qui nec per se nec cum alio significat aliquid vel aliqua sed solum aliqualiter ut omnis nullus et similes." The word 'consignification' was often given as an alternative way of expressing the same idea. E.g. Clichtoveus, 8; and the later writers Alsted, *Systema*, 41; Campanella, 15; J. Sanderson, 7. This usage goes back to Priscian: see discussion in Nuchelmans, *op. cit.*, 124.

[53] E.g. Paul of Pergula, *Logica*, 7, in the fifteenth century: Clichtoveus, 8, in the sixteenth century: and Carvisius, 103; Alsted, *Systema*, 41; and Campanella, 15, in the seventeenth century.

[54] E.g. Clichtoveus, 8vo. For later references see Hunnaeus, *Prodidagmata*, 72; Kecker-

mann, *Systema*, 14.

[55] Clichtoveus, 13ff.; Angelus, lxxxvii. For later references, see Carbo, 255–256; John of St. Thomas, *Formal Logic*, 36.

[56] Crab: "Sed terminus secunde intentionis est terminus significans res ea ratione qua sunt signa propositionalia: vel ea ratione qua significantur per alios terminos. Ponitur prima particula propter istos terminos nomen / propositio / oratio / sillogismus. Et ponitur secunda particula propter istos terminos univocum univocatum / equivocum equivocatum / diffinitum."

[57] For Ockham, no precise parallel could be established between the two groups. For instance, terms of second imposition referred only to properties of the spoken language and had no mental counterparts; whilst the terms of both first and second intention could, in their spoken or written form, be treated as terms of first imposition. See P. Boehner, 'Ockham's Theory of Signification', *Franciscan Studies* **6**(1946) 163–167.

[58] Blanchellus Faventinus, 6vo, 7vo; Paul of Pergula, *Logica*, 9; Hieronymus of St. Mark; Javellus, 16vo. For later sources, see Villalpandeus, 46f.; Carvisius, 103, 104.

[59] Clichtoveus, 13. For later sources, see Campanella, 17; Fonseca, I 88–90; Hunnaeus, *Prodidagmata*, 77; J. Sanderson, 8; Pedro de Oña, 15.

[60] N. Kretzmann, 'Medieval Logicians on the meaning of the *Propositio*', *Journal of Philosophy* **67** (1970) 767.

[61] Raulin. For text, see appendix.

[62] E.g. Pardo, ii^{vo}: "Et ideo iste terminus chymera significat omnia entia. Et licet iste terminus chymera significet sortem non potest supponere pro sorte quia non potest verificari de sorte propter repugnantiam partium..." Cf. Lax, *Termini*.

[63] Domingo de Soto, xxviii^{vo}.

[64] Coronel, *Prima Pars Rosarii*, "Esse incomplexe significabile est significatum per terminum incomplexum. Sortes secundum esse cognitum est incomplexe significabilis. Secunda est stat Sortem non habere esse et habere esse cognitum." Cf. Pardo, if.

[65] John of Glogovia, xvii. For some later references to this commonplace doctrine, see Fonseca, II 690, 692; Hunnaeus, *Prodidagmata*, 68; Ormazius, 27; Alcalá, 10. John of Glogovia wrote: "Notandum primo quod terminus communis habet duplex significatum. Quoddam est significatum eius principale et primarium et directum. quod scilicet significat ex impositione eius primaria et principali. ut iste terminus homo significatione principali et primaria significat naturam humanam et universale universaliter sumptum.... Secundo terminus communis habet significatum secundarium minus principale et indirectum, et isto modo terminus communis significat supposita: ut homo significat Iohannem Petrum et alios homines particulares qui participant naturam humanam...."

[66] Sbarroya, *Dial. Introd.*, xxiii.

[67] Cenali, *Termini*, said: "Terminus cognotativus est qui ultra materiale significatum aliquid importat et illud vocatur formale significatum." Celaya, *Dial. Introd.*, said: "Terminus cognotativus est terminus qui ultra hoc quod significat denotat rem aliqualiter se habere." Cf. Clichtoveus, 10^{vo}f.; Eckius, *El. Dial.* For a later source, see Fonseca, I 68.

[68] E.g. Clichtoveus, 5vo: "Propositio est oratio indicativa verum vel falsum significans." Cf. Paul of Pergula, *Logica*, 10; Melanchthon, *Erotemata*, 577; and many other sources. For later references see Fonseca, I 136; Villalpandeus, 9vo. Another version read: "Propositio est oratio verum vel falsum significans indicando": Enzinas, *Primus Tractatus*, iv^{vo}. For the history of this definition, see Nuchelmans, *op. cit.*, 166ff.

[69] E.g. Celaya, *Expositio*; Enzinas, *Primus Tractatus*, iiii^{vo}; Dolz, *Termini*, ii; Caubraith, lxviii^{vo}.

[70] Tartaretus, *Insolubilia*, 200vo; Pardo, vii.

[71] Major, *Termini*; Celaya, *Expositio*.

[72] Tartaretus, *Expositio*, 4^{vo}f., Domingo de Soto, xxxix^{vo}, adopted the view provisionally.

[73] Pardo, xiv^{vo}. See also xvi^{vo}.

[74] He noted that some people maintained that Heytesbury believed that a proposition such as "*Homo est homo*" corresponded to only one *notitia*.

[75] Sbarroya, *Expositio Primi*, x.

[76] Pardo, ii. Synonymous mental propositions would presumably occur in two or more minds, or in one mind at different times. Pardo wrote (lxiiii) "Sed ille equivalent in inferendo et significando simul que eandem rem penitus significant. ita quod si sint vocales vel scripte eidem mentali subordinantur si autem sint mentales idem omnino significant. ita quod si ponerentur complexe significabilia complexe significabile unius esset complexe significabile alterius." For the last point, cf. Coronel, *Prima Pars Rosarii*.

[77] See Dorp; Hieronymus of St. Mark. In his discussion of conversion, Dorp gives an interesting example of two synonymous propositions, namely "*Ego sum Johannes*" and "*Johannes est tu*" when said by Johannes and another man. He commented: "Ex quo patet quod pronomen demonstrativum prime persone et pronomen demonstrativum secunde persone si eandem rem demonstrent sunt synonima et hoc probatur ratione. Nam si ego proferam istam vocalem: ego sum Johannes petro audiente mentalis quam formabit petrus de illa vocali: et mentalis quam ego formabo erunt synonime."

[78] Hieronymus of St. Mark; Pardo, xxf.

[79] Dorp. Cf. Hieronymus of St. Mark; Pardo, ii; Celaya, *Expositio*.

[80] E.g. Eckius, *Summulae*, ci^{vo}; Enzinas, *Primus Tractatus*, xx; Celaya, *Suppositiones*; Caubraith, lxviii^{vo}.

[81] Pardo, x; Almain.

[82] E.g. Peter of Ailly.

[83] Eckius, *Summulae*, cviii^{vo}.

[84] Caubraith, lxviii^{vo}; Eckius, *Summulae*, cviii^{vo}; Pardo, viii^{vo}. The latter accepted the rule if an extra condition was added, as in: "hec est vera homo est asinus et significat hominem esse asinum ergo ita est quod homo est asinus."

[85] Clichtoveus: Le Fèvre, 136.

[86] Pardo, xix^{vo}–xx^{vo}. See also Enzinas, *Primus Tractatus*, v.

[87] For a discussion of Gregory of Rimini and other medieval sources, see the following: M. dal Pra, 'La teoria del "significato totale" della proposizione nel pensiero di Gregorio da Rimini', *Rivista critica di storia della filosofia* 11 (1956) 287–311; H. Elie, *Le complexe significabile*, Paris 1936; N. Kretzmann, *op. cit.*, 767–787; E. A. Moody, 'A Quodlibetal Question of Robert Holkot, O. P., on the Problem of the Objects of Knowledge and Belief', *Speculum* 39 (1964) 53–74; Pagallo; M. A. Reina, *Il problema del linguaggio in Buridano*, Vicenza 1959; T. K. Scott, 'John Buridan on the Objects of Demonstrative Science', *Speculum* 40 (1965) 654–673. Some of the points made were raised by Abelard. For a very full discussion of the whole debate up to and including Paul of Venice, see Nuchelmans, *op. cit.*

[88] Enzinas, *Primus Tractatus*, iiii^{vo}. Cf. Cenali, *Termini*.

[89] Pardo, i–v. The other sources are Peter of Ailly; Hieronymus of St. Mark; Bricot, *Insolubilia*. Briefer references can be found in Stephanus de Monte; Major, *Insolubilia*; Major, *Opera*, i–ii; Domingo de Soto, xxxix^{vo}; Trutvetter, *Summule*; Enzinas, *Primus Tractatus*, iiii^{vo}; Dolz, *Termini*, v–vi^{vo}; Raulin. See also A. Coronel, *Prima Pars Rosarii*.

[90] Coronel, *Prima Pars Rosarii*, said that in the third sense *aliquid* was taken "pro significabili incomplexe quod potest existere in rerum natura."

[91] Coronel (*Prima Pars Rosarii*) described what Andreas de Novo Castro was trying to do

in a slightly different way. According to Coronel, he was trying to prove that a complex signifiable must be *aliquid* in the third sense, since it must contain God as an entity. The alternative that one can understand God-to-be without understanding God was dismissed as absurd. For Andreas de Novo Castro's own discussion, see *Primum Scriptum Sententiarum*, Parrhisiis [1514], iii^vof.

[92] Hieronymus of St. Mark gave this view. He said that according to it, a proposition was false if the First Truth did not assent to it. Cf. A. Coronel, *Prima Pars Rosarii*.

[93] Raulin gave a similar argument.

[94] Coronel, *Prima Pars Rosarii*, in his exposition of the doctrines of Gregory of Rimini said that such predicates as 'eternal' and 'temporal' applied properly only to things in the third and strictest sense, so that it was improper to ask whether complex signifiables were eternal.

[95] Bricot; Major, *Insolubilia*; Pardo, ii^vo.

[96] Dolz, *Termini*, vf.; Duns Scotus, 284f. For a discussion of the significate of negative and false propositions, cf. Pagallo, 187f. Domingo de Soto, xxxix^vo, said: "Quod quidem significatum (pro nunc) non distinguitur realiter a significatis per extrema, quod capreolus 4. q. prologi ex dictis S. tho. corroborat, et fere doctores amplectuntur, sed est res ipsa significata per subiectum, cui convenit aut disconvenit res significata per predicatum, ut significatum huius propositionis / homo est animal / est homo qui existit animal."

[97] Coronel, *Prima Pars Rosarii*, said that the negative proposition "An animal is not a man" signified an animal which was not a man. He agreed that "A man is not an animal" signified nothing.

[98] He wrote: "significat significatum subiecti aliqualiter se habere in ordine ad predicatum."

[99] Coronel, *Prima Pars Rosarii*, rejected this kind of identity in his exposition of Buridan's view.

[100] Eckius, *Summulae*, xci^vo; Gebwiler; Major, *Logicalia*.

[101] Pardo, iiii–v.

[102] Elie, *op. cit.*, 186.

[103] Enzinas, *Primus Tractatus*, iiii^vo, also discusses God as a proposition, and makes much the same points as Bricot. Cf. Celaya, *Expositio*; Dolz, *Disceptationes*; Domingo de Soto, xxxviiif. Sbarroya, *Expositio primi*, xi^vof., said that although nominalists believed God to be a proposition, Thomists denied this.

[104] Enzinas, *Primus Tractatus*, iiii^vo. Cf. his discussion in *Prop. Ment.*, xxxv–xxxvi.

[105] Domingo de Soto, xxxviii^vo.

[106] Celaya, *Expositio*.

[107] Mainz; Dorp; *Commentum*.

[108] Eckius, *Summulae*, viii.

[109] Celaya, *Expositio*. Cf. Dolz, *Disceptationes*.

[110] Breitkopf, *Compendium*; Celaya, *Expositio*. Cf. Mainz.

[111] Domingo de Soto, xxxvii^vo; Tartaretus, *Expositio*, 5vo; Dolz, *Disceptationes*.

[112] Celaya, *Expositio*. For a lengthy discussion of the whole question, see A. Coronel, *Prima Pars Rosarii*.

[113] Versor, 13vo, wrote "Veritas propositionis est adaequatio eius ad suum significatum et falsitas est inadaequatio." In the seventeenth century Smiglecius said (II, 45): Logica veritas consistit in conformitate iudicii cum re iudicata." Derodon's formula (549f.) was similar to that of Versor.

[114] The common tag was "Veritas est adequatio intellectus et rei", though *conformitas* could be used instead of *adequatio*, as in Breitkopf, *Compendium*. For typical sources, see e.g. Hundt, xxix; Mainz; Trutvetter, *Summule*. For a history of the tag, see P. Boehner,

'Ockham's Theory of Truth' *Franciscan Studies* **11** (1951) 203–230. '*Intellectus*' can refer to an individual act of the understanding, or it can refer to the intellect as a whole. The latter meaning seems more prevalent in the late fifteenth and sixteenth centuries. For instance, in his explanation of the phrase Hundt drew a diagram comparing the *intellectus humana* with a mirror. The *intellectus humana* is related through the *res intellecta* to the *res ad extra*, just as the *speculum* is related through the *imago* to the *res ad extra*. Another example of this use of '*intellectus*' is found in a 1496 edition of the *Logica* of Thomas Aquinas, where we read: "Unde in hoc consistit veritas: quod res sic apprehenditur ab intellectu sicut est in rerum natura et per oppositum falsitas est in difformitate rei ut apprehensa est ab intellectu ad se ipsam: ut est in natura sua...."

[115] Stephanus de Monte. Cf. Celaya, *Expositio*; Dolz, *Disceptationes*; Sbarroya, *Expositio primi*, xii^vo.

[116] Domingo de Soto, xxxix^vo.

[117] John of St. Thomas, *Cursus*, 145f.

[118] Cf. Derodon, 507f. He distinguishes between *enuntiatio apprehensiva* and *enuntiatio iudicativa*.

[119] Cf. Smiglecius, II 38.

[120] Derodon, 552. Cf. Pardo's discussion of the *propositio plures* (see above). For Derodon's text, see appendix.

[121] Hieronymus of St. Mark; Hundt, xxviii^vo; Domingo de Soto, xxxvii^vo; Dolz, *Disceptationes*; Clichtoveus, 22; Pardo, vi. For later sources, cf. Villalpandeus, 9vo; Burgersdijck, 176; Dietericus, 227; Isendoorn, 518.

[122] E.g. Pardo, vii^vo: "Propositio eo dicitur vera quia qualitercunque per ipsam significatur sententia totali et propositionali esse vel non esse: fuisse vel non fuisse: fore vel non fore aut possibiliter vel impossibiliter: necessario vel contingenter: ita est vel non est fuit vel non fuit: erit vel non erit."

[123] E.g. Bartholomaeus de Usingen; Major, *Abbreviationes*; Trutvetter, *Summule*; Pardo, viiif.; Manderston: Gebwiler; Hieronymus of St. Mark.

[124] See Hieronymus of St. Mark; Pardo, viii; Major, *Logicalia*; Manderston.

[125] Gebwiler; Pardo, viii; Cf. Peter of Spain, *Summulae*, de Rijk, 218.

[126] Acerbus, 87vo.

[127] See also John of St. Thomas, *Cursus*, 192.

[128] Major, *Consequentie*; Pardo, xxiiii, Celaya, *Suppositiones*. Cf. Albert of Saxony, 25.

[129] E.g. Pardo, vi: "Propositio vera est que significat taliter qualiter est esse..." Pardo, vi^vo: "Propositio necessaria est que significat taliter qualiter necesse est esse." Cf. Hieronymus of St. Mark; Celaya, *Expositio*; Dolz, *Disceptationes*; Domingo de Soto, xxxviii.

[130] Peter of Spain, *Summulae*; Bocheński, 1.15, 6; de Rijk, 7. See commentaries, e.g. Enzinas, *Primus Tractatus*, vii^vof.; Domingo de Soto, xliiii–xlv^vo.

[131] Tartaretus, *Insolubilia*, 201f.

[132] Tartaretus, *Insolubilia*, 202. Cf. Pardo, ix.

[133] Trutvetter, *Breviarium*. Cf. Domingo de Soto, xix^vo. He quoted '7+3=10' as an example of a proposition which the *iuniores* took to be absolutely necessary. "If a man exists, a man is an animal" was the example of a conditionally necessary proposition.

[134] Major, *Insolubilia*.

[135] E.g. Clichtoveus: Le Fèvre, 23.

[136] Domingo de Soto, xix^vo: "Non enim volumus asserere veritates huiusmodi propositionum, eo quod subiecta supponant simpliciter pro essentiis rerum que sunt perpetue, sed eo potius quod supponant personaliter, pro individuis ipsis quamvis non existant."

[137] Enzinas, *Primus Tractatus*, iii.

[138] Cologne, cvii^{vo}. For text, see appendix.
[139] Cologne, c^{vo}. For text, see appendix.
[140] Cologne, cvii^{vo}f.
[141] Smiglecius, II 52.
[142] Isendoorn, 527.

SUPPOSITION THEORY

So far meaning has been discussed in fairly general terms, but an important part of logical theory throughout the period was concerned with the establishment of the precise meaning of particular propositions in the light of the supposition of terms, together with such allied properties as restriction, ampliation and appellation.[1] No simple account or neat definition of supposition can be offered in modern terms, for a whole range of topics, both syntactical and semantical were dealt with under this one heading. The syntactical part of supposition theory, which deals with the relationship between quantified propositions and unquantified propositions containing singular terms, will be discussed in chapter four. So far as semantics is concerned, a starting point is to be found in the realization that even if one can give a definition and specify a total denotation for a word such as 'man', one is still not fully equipped to discuss the meaning and reference of propositions in which the word 'man' occurs. Much depends on the presence of such syncategorematic words as 'all', 'some', and 'not', on the presence of other nouns and adjectives, on the mood and type of the verb; and a great deal of supposition theory concerned the establishment of the varying partial denotations of terms in the light of these considerations. As Domingo de Soto put it, a supposing term is related to the thing for which it supposes, to the concept through which it supposes, to the copula, and to the determining signs in the proposition; and it is in accordance with the nature of these various relationships that the precise import of a term, and hence of a proposition, is determined.[2] These attempts to establish both the type of reference of terms, whether to names, concepts or things, and the range of reference of terms, were naturally linked with a further type of inquiry, that into the truth conditions of propositions and the means for their verification. Indeed, Boehner seems sometimes to have felt that this was the most important part of supposition theory;[3] and

his view is supported both by the use made of supposition theory when
conditions for the truth of propositions were listed and by the emphasis
various authors placed on the need for the correct analysis of propositions by means of supposition theory. For instance, Gebwiler said that
we can only properly assess "Every man has a head" as true when we
know that it is a range of separate heads that is referred to rather than
one single head. He also made it clear that establishing the correct supposition of terms plays a vital role in syllogistic. It is supposition theory
that tells us whether terms are properly distributed and whether they
have the same range of reference in both premises and conclusion.

1. SUPPOSITION, ACCEPTANCE AND VERIFICATION

Supposition was usually defined either as "the acceptance of a term
for itself or for its significate";[4] or as "the acceptance of a term as standing for something of which it may be verified."[5] Various questions were
raised about these definitions. In the first place, what was being defined?
Is supposition a relational property of a term which can be seen as distinct from that term, or is it an inseparable aspect of a term, so that one
can say with the nominalists, "Supposition is a term"?[6] Celaya compared this to the debate on the truth of true propositions; and Domingo
de Soto said that it was another of the metaphysical problems which he
did not intend to discuss.[7] In the second place, does the acceptance of the
term have to be actual, or merely potential? At the end of the fifteenth
century Johannes Magister outlined three possibilities. First is the belief
of Dorp and some of the nominalists that a term in a closed book can
have supposition if somebody would take it to refer it they were to take
notice of it. Tartaretus and Eckius both echoed this view.[8] Second is the
belief of Marsilius and most of the nominalists that a term can only suppose in relation to a mental term, so that if "God exists" is written in a
closed book, it is not a proposition, and the word 'God' does not have
supposition. This view was adopted by Hieronymus of St. Mark, who
argued that a term had to be accepted by somebody as standing for
something before it could be said to have supposition. The last view is
that of the realists, who drew a distinction between potential and actual
supposition, and thus were able to combine the two other views.

In the third place, does the term have to appear in a proposition or not? Peter of Spain had denied that it did, saying that a term such as 'man' when taken by itself supposes naturally for all men past, present, or future;[9] and he was followed by a few men such as Breitkopf and Gutkius.[10] However, the majority held that it must appear in a proposition, either because a supposing term has to be verified, which can take place only through the copula of the proposition in which it appears,[11] or because the whole point of supposition theory is to determine the truth and falsity of propositions.[12]

The next group of questions was concerned with which kinds of term could be said to have supposition. It was normally assumed that they had to be meaningful, but an exception was made for such terms as 'bu' and 'baf' when they were mentioned rather than used. That is, they were admitted when they had material supposition and only under those conditions. Fonseca said that all terms which were mentioned rather than used, and hence were taken non-significatively, could be excluded from the account of supposition on the grounds that they appeared not so much as parts of a sentence but as the things pointed to by such phrases as "This term".[13] He missed the point however, for one can say that all mentioned terms are meaningful, no matter what their status is when used. "Baf" is meaningless, but "'baf'" means the concatenation of 'b', 'a' and 'f'. It was also normally assumed that the terms having supposition were substantive terms, and this was sometimes built into the definition.[14] Adjectives were sometimes said to have *copulatio*,[15] but usually they were discussed only later, under "Appellation". It was recognized that in some contexts, as in "A white (thing) runs", an adjective could have supposition, since it took the place of a substantive term;[16] and the same was said of verbs, as in "To read is to do", and of some adverbs such as "today".[17] Such verbs as 'runs' in "A man runs" could also be said to have supposition in so far as they were equivalent to a phrase with a participle such as "A man is running" or "A man is a running thing".[18] Tartaretus said that pronouns could suppose, as in "I run", for 'I' can be verified through the phrase "This is I", but that in some contexts, such as "I, Peter, run" they were purely syncategorematic.[19]

In the early sixteenth century, various questions were raised about the nature of acceptance, and about its relationship to signification on the one hand and to supposition on the other. It has already been noted that the signification of a term was taken to be its total denotation, past,

present, and future. A term when taken as merely significant thus has
the largest possible range of reference. However, this range of reference
can be narrowed in various ways, both through the imposition of con-
text-related restrictions and through the imposition of an existence-
requirement. To see what the acceptance of a term is, or, in other words,
what it is taken to refer to on a particular occasion, one must consider
the proposition in which it appears. In some cases, the range of reference
of an accepted term is the same as the range of reference of that term
when viewed as merely significant. For instance, in "A man is an animal", 'man' is accepted for or taken to refer to all men who were, are and
will be. By contrast, 'animal' in "The animal which is a man is running"
is taken to refer only to men, since the term is restricted by a qualifying
clause.[20] Acceptance is dependent on signification, and it frequently involves a narrower range of reference. In turn, supposition is dependent
on acceptance, and frequently involves an even narrower range of reference. Domingo de Soto took as an example the proposition "Some man
disputes."[21] Here, he said, 'man' signifies all humans of either sex who
are or can be imagined; it is accepted for all males, including those who
can be imagined; and it supposes for those males who actually exist.
Logicians agreed that such terms as 'chimera' and 'Antichrist' could have
acceptance even though they could have no supposition.[22] Thus acceptance obviously offers a device whereby failures to refer can be dealt with
when supposition itself is said to be a property only of referring terms, as
the verificationists demanded. One must be able to discuss both the
meaning of and the truth conditions for a sentence in the absence of
information as to whether the terms have referents or not. In the sentence
"There are some unicorns in the zoo" 'unicorn' can be taken as referring
to a certain kind of creature, and the range of reference (i.e. to some
presently existent unicorns rather than to all past unicorns) can be
specified before one knows whether there are any unicorns in the world.
Indeed, it is only because the term can be taken as having reference
that one can find out that in fact there are no unicorns. One must know
what one is looking for.

   The distinction between acceptance and signification was also used to
explain how it is that the same sentence can have different truth values.
Tartaretus, Bricot and Pardo all drew a distinction between two kinds
of *significatio* which could belong to a proposition.[23] The first belongs to

it by virtue of the meaning of the terms, and it does not change except when the linguistic conventions themselves change. To be concerned with this kind of signification is not to be concerned about truth and falsity, but rather with simple understanding of the words, independently of their assertive power in a given context. Tartaretus tried to explain this by saying that if this kind of meaning had anything to do with truth and falsity then the indefinite sentence "Man is white" (normally taken as equivalent to "Some man is white") would be false, since 'man' signifies every man, and the sentence would have to be regarded as equivalent to "Every man is white." The second kind of meaning belongs to a sentence by virtue of the *acceptio* of the terms, or what they are taken to refer to in a specific context. The *acceptio* or acceptance can and does change, and it is this which determines truth values. The cases in which a sentence can be said to be true by virtue of its signification alone were taken as special cases of acceptance [see section on natural supposition].

It was common in the late fifteenth and early sixteenth centuries to insist that a term should be verified before it could be said to have supposition.[24] In order to verify a term one took an elementary proposition of the form "This is *A*" (or "This was *A*", "This will be *A*", depending on the tense of the verb in the original proposition) and checked its truth value. Of course, the terms in a proposition could be verified in this sense without the proposition as a whole being verified. In "A man is a stone", both terms are verifiable.[25] Moreover, as Clichtoveus emphasized, the number of referents required for verification was very different from the number of possible referents a term with supposition was said to have; and the verifying proposition was frequently different in type from the proposition containing the term to be verified.[26] The subject of the negative proposition "No horse is a stone" is verified through the affirmative proposition "This is a horse"; the subject term of a universal proposition is verified by a singular proposition; the subject term of a modal proposition such as "Every man is impossibly a stone" [*Omnis homo impossibiliter est lapis*] is verified by pointing to Socrates and saying "This is possibly a man" [*subjectum sic verificatur demonstrato Sorte hoc possibiliter est homo*]. Nor was there any requirement of empirical verification, for as we have seen, all terms appearing in past, future, and modal propositions were taken to be verifiable. As John of St. Thomas said, "it suffices to demonstrate the thing to the intellect, since past and future

things cannot be pointed out to the sense." [27] Such terms as 'Adam' and
'chimera' were allowed to have supposition in such contexts as "Adam
was" and "A chimera is imagined" but otherwise they were denied it. [28]
This aroused the indignation of Fonseca, who argued that the reason
such propositions as "Adam exists" are false is that the predicates do not
belong to the things for which the subjects suppose. [29]

There were two problems connected with verification. One concerned
spoken terms which could not be repeated [*qui secundum se repeti non
possunt, quia volat irrevocabile verbum inquit poeta*]. [30] These, said Eckius,
have to be verified through synonymous terms, that is, through another
token of the same type. The other problem concerned such predicates as
"is not indicated". If one takes the sentence "A thing which is not indicated [or pointed to] is in the corner" [*Non demonstratum est in angulo*]
and tries to verify the subject term by formulating the proposition "This
is a thing which is not indicated", a paradox results. [31] The usual way of
dealing with this paradox was to say that verification was either through
a demonstrative pronoun or through some such noun as 'stone' which
was not demonstrative in nature. It is not paradoxical to say "A stone is
a thing which is not indicated" [*Lapis est ens quod non demonstratur*]. [32]
Domingo de Soto offered another argument, to the effect that verification could be taken in two ways. [33] In the first sense it involves predication in a true proposition, but in the second sense it only involves the use
of a proposition which signifies things to be as they are. "This is not
indicated" can be used to verify in the second sense but not in the first.
He seems to be distinguishing between a demonstrative and a non-
demonstrative use of the word 'this'.

2. PROPER, IMPROPER, RELATIVE AND ABSOLUTE SUPPOSITION

A great many types of supposition were discussed, and there were almost
as many organizational schemes as there were writers. I shall not attempt
to analyze the variations, since they were usually of little importance. [34]
The distinctions between proper and improper, absolute and relative
supposition may be dealt with first of all. Improper supposition is a feature of words used in an extended or metaphorical sense. [35] 'Wolf' in
"A wolf is in a story" is used improperly, as are 'man' used of a dead or
painted man, 'The Lion of Judah' used of Christ, or 'The Philosopher'

used of Aristotle. Proper supposition is a feature of words used in their normal sense. Relative supposition concerns the function of such relative words and phrases as 'who', 'that' or 'the same as', and discussion covered such matters as identity and diversity of reference, or the difference between "Peter is learned and he argues" and "Peter argues and another talks".[36]

Absolute supposition belongs to non-relative terms and phrases. Both improper and relative supposition are parasitic upon supposition proper, in so far as they deal with the clarification of ambiguous or misleading expressions in the light of the canons already laid down, and in the early seventeenth century Villalpandeus remarked that he felt that the topic of relative supposition really belonged to the grammarians.[37] However, at the beginning of the sixteenth century, a separate chapter or section was usually devoted to relative supposition, and a number of rules were given.[38]

3. MATERIAL SUPPOSITION

The category of material supposition embraced all those terms which are mentioned rather than used, but the discussion was often more lengthy than it need have been because of the absence of the useful device of quotation marks. Logicians were compelled to list the devices which might be used instead of quotation, and Celaya said that there were three things to look for.[39] First, the presence of such words as *'ly'* and 'this term'; second, the presence of such terms of second intention as 'noun'; and third, the presence of predicates which could not belong to the proper significate of the word, such as 'utterance' in "Man is an utterance". These signs were not infallible, for there are such contexts as "A sound is an utterance" in which the subject term is used and not mentioned, despite the presence of the term 'utterance'.[40] Generally there were said to be three kinds of material supposition.[41] In the first, the word stands for itself alone [*pro se*], that is, for a specific token as in "'Dog' is written in red ink here". In the second it stands for all tokens of the same type [*pro sibi simili vel in voce vel in scripto vel mente*] as in "'Dog' is a noun". In the third it stands for the same word used in another grammatical case. What characterized all these kinds was that a term was taken to refer to its non-ultimate rather than to its ultimate

significate; or to operate through the non-ultimate rather than the ultimate concept corresponding to it. Paul of Pergula and Javellus claimed
that some words such as 'being' and 'something' were incapable of
material supposition, since they had only one significate, the ultimate or
formal.[42] They are verifiable of themselves both with and without '*ly*',
said Paul of Pergula. In this he and Javellus both followed Paul of Venice,
who had argued that just as a being is a being, so too 'being' is a being,
and just as a noun is a noun, so too 'noun' is a noun (or 'name' a name).[43]
Eckius criticized this view, citing such sentences as "'Being' is a participle" and "'Something' is of neutral gender" to show that even these
words could be mentioned as well as used.[44]

Some problems concerning mental terms were discussed by Pardo.[45]
He described the view (attributed to Manfred of Cremona) that terms
have three kinds of signification. First, they signify whatever they were
imposed to signify; second, they signify themselves objectively, as all
things do; third, they signify themselves and all things like themselves.
This third type of signification corresponds to material supposition.
Leaving aside the second type of signification, written and spoken terms
can enjoy one or both of the first and third types. 'Man' has both, but
'every' has only the third type, and so does 'but'. However, mental terms
can only have the first kind of signification, since they cannot lose their
primary signification. Pardo rejected both the claim that there is a third
kind of signification and the claim that mental terms cannot have
material supposition. He said that vocal or written terms have material
supposition through being subordinated to a non-ultimate mental concept (i.e. the concept of the sound or written sequence in question) and
that there is a sense in which they may lose their primary signification in
the process, if the mind attends just to the sound or to the sequence of
letters. Similarly, mental terms can have material supposition through a
non-ultimate concept which is the reflexive concept of that first concept.
It is true that they cannot lose their primary significance, but this in no
way prevents them from enjoying material supposition.

4. SIMPLE SUPPOSITION

The category of simple supposition was one which gave rise to a good
deal of controversy, because of its link with the theory of universals and

with the claim that terms had both a primary and a secondary meaning. Eckius gave a useful survey of the possible interpretations.[46] First, simple supposition can be used to refer to the opposite of mixed supposition, or the supposition of phrases such as "the term 'man'" where part is taken personally, as referring to members of the class of terms, and part is taken materially.[47] Simple supposition in this sense embraces both material and personal supposition, and is not of any great importance. Second, simple supposition is said by some to be distinct from material supposition and to be the property of a term which supposes for a mental intention [*intentio animae*], but which is not taken significatively, such as 'stone' in "A stone is in my mind" [*lapis est in anima*].[48] According to Ockhamists, said Eckius, 'man' in "Man is a species" has this type of supposition because it stands for the appropriate mental intention without being a natural or conventional sign for that mental intention.[49] Eckius rejected this position on the grounds that 'man' in such a context does not stand for a mental intention any more than it stands for a spoken or written word. The third view, which was prevalent especially among realists, was that in "Man is a species" 'man' stands for the universal or common nature which is the primary meaning of that term. Eckius also rejected this view, because he felt that there were no common natures; but many people held it, some in a modified form.[50] Domingo de Soto said that human nature is not really distinguished from men, but that the word 'man' in "Man is a species" stands for man in so far as he is known through the concept to which the term is subordinated.[51] Javellus added that it was more consonant with the peripatetic road to consider universals as natures rather than terms, even if one denied their existence apart from singular things, as did Aristotle.[52] The view which Eckius himself held was that in "Man is a species" 'man' does not have any form of simple supposition.[53] Instead, it has material supposition because it "supposes for the concept of man which it signifies conventionally".

A few of those who adopted the third interpretation of simple supposition followed Peter of Spain in allowing terms to stand for their primary significates in a wide range of contexts. Normally terms were said to have simple supposition, if they had it at all, just when they appeared in a sentence whose predicate was a term of second intention such as 'genus' and 'species'; but the commentators of Cologne, for instance, said that a term also had simple supposition when it was the predicate of a universal affirmative proposition such as "All men are animals"; when it appeared after a verb of desiring, as in "I want wine"; and when it appeared after a superlative, as in "Man is the worthiest of creatures" [*homo est dignissima creaturarum*].[54] Other examples were 'horse' in "A horse is necessary for riding"; 'pepper' in "Pepper is sold here and in Rome"; and 'man' in "Only man is a laughing thing" [*tantum homo est risibilis*]. Domingo de Soto commented that there was a danger of so multiplying simple supposition that all confused terms would be said to have it.[55] The main drawback of the extended usage of simple supposition was the effect it would have on quantificational inference, especially in the case of "All men are animals", which is a standard *A*-proposition. Domingo de Soto expressed the common assumption when he said that "one cannot descend or syllogize when terms are taken with simple supposition,"[56] yet *A*-propositions are precisely those which are used to syllogize, which figure in rules of conversion, and from which descent is said to take place. The Cologne commentators did not mention these difficulties; and the majority of authors adopted a firmly extensionalist interpretation of propositions such as "All men are animals" without bothering to note that an alternative position was possible. In the seventeenth century John of St. Thomas made it quite clear that simple supposition could only be a property of terms in sentences where the predicate was a term of second intention.[57] All real predicates can belong to individuals, he said, and it is not enough for simple supposition that the predicate can belong to a nature. It must belong *only* to a nature. In other words, even if "All men are animals" can be interpreted intensionally as involving a relation between natures (or essences or concepts), this does not entitle one to attribute anything other than personal supposition to the terms in that proposition.

Not only common nouns but also singular terms were allowed to have simple supposition in certain contexts such as "Socrates is individual".[58] Just as one could not descend from a common term with simple supposition, so one could not ascend from a singular term with simple supposition. That is, just as one cannot go from "Man is a species" to "Socrates is a species", so one cannot go from "Socrates is an individual" to "Man is an individual", for individuality belongs to Socrates in a way that it does not belong to man.[59] The precise status of a singular term such as

"Socrates" was a matter of dispute, but since meaning was largely viewed in terms of denotation, its status was taken to be not entirely dissimilar from that of a common noun. Hieronymus of St. Mark said that unlike a common noun, 'Socrates' had only a primary significate, that thing which is Socrates. Domingo de Soto agreed that it had only one kind of formal significate, but said that in a way a primary significate is referred to in "Peter is an individual" and a secondary in "Peter disputes." [60] On the other hand, John of St. Thomas argued that 'Peter' has just the same kind of double meaning that common nouns do, only in reverse. [61] The immediate significate of a common noun is a nature [*natura*] and the mediate significate is the person to whom the nature belongs; but with a singular term, the immediate significate is the person or individual [*persona seu individuum*] and the mediate significate is the nature of that person, whereby he is defined as a person, i.e. an individual substance of a rational nature [*rationalis naturae individua substantia*].

Simple supposition was usually contrasted with personal supposition, by which a term was taken to be used in its secondary meaning as standing for all its instances, but some authors suggested that these two kinds of supposition had a meeting place in what earlier authors called simple supposition *secundum quid*, [62] but which later authors called absolute supposition (not to be confused with absolute as opposed to relative supposition). [63] Greve, for instance, said that in "Man is a rational animal", 'man' has simple supposition but nevertheless the referents are included; [64] and John of Glogovia said that whereas in "Man is a species" 'man' is accepted only for a universal and common nature, in "Man is the worthiest of creatures" 'man' is accepted primarily for the universal and common nature, but with "an inclination and relationship to the referents." [65] Later in the sixteenth century, Fonseca had a longer discussion. [66] He contrasted "Man is an animal" with "Man is a species" and "Every animal dies". In "Man is a species", 'man' must have simple supposition, since no individual is a species; 'animal' in "Every animal dies" must have personal supposition, since a universal cannot die; but in "Man is an animal", 'man' can be taken to have absolute supposition, for man is said to be animal by reason of the nature which belongs to individual men. He denied that any term which had purely simple supposition could be taken absolutely; but he claimed that all terms taken absolutely could also be taken personally, and that they were analogous to terms having simple supposition because they involved the immediate significate of the term, though not precisely. What they all seem to have been groping towards is that some propositions can be given both an intensional and an extensional interpretation. "Man is an animal" can be looked on as involving a relation between concepts or abstract entities of some kind, or as involving a relationship of identity between the members of two classes.

5. NATURAL PERSONAL SUPPOSITION

The usual divisions of personal supposition are more appropriately discussed in chapter four, so here I will confine myself to the distinction which was sometimes drawn between natural personal supposition and accidental personal supposition. There were three possible but closely linked interpretations of natural supposition. The first attributed natural supposition to a term which, taken by itself outside a proposition, stood for its total denotation.[67] 'Man' for instance, supposes for all men, past, present, and future. The second attributed natural supposition only to terms within a proposition, but retained the clause about total denotation. In "Every man is an animal", 'man' stands for all men that were, are, and will be.[68] The third interpretation also frequently retained the clause about total denotation, but introduced the additional notion of an essential relationship between subject and predicate. In "A man is an animal", the copula 'is' was said to be abstracted from time, and to signify a union between subject and predicate, rather than any temporal modality. [69] Accidental supposition was the property of terms which appeared in sentences whose copula had temporal reference and which were not taken as standing for their total denotation.

The most popular interpretation of natural supposition was the third one; but this itself was open to various interpretations, not all of which are equally plausible. Probably the most consistent view was that of Trutvetter and the Mainz commentators who tied natural supposition firmly to existence.[70] Propositions whose terms had natural supposition were necessarily true, but only *ex hypothesi*. A man is an animal given that the course of nature instituted by God does not change, and the copula is absolved from time only in the sense that all times are denoted indifferently. Eckius and Clichtoveus held a view which was closer to that of the realists, for they agreed that such propositions as "The rose is a beautiful flower" and "A man is an animal" were true even if there were neither roses nor men.[71] Clichtoveus said that "A man is an animal" is equivalent to "A man is by nature an animal" [*homo natus est esse animal*], and that the proposition is true and the terms suppose even if there are no men, no animals, and no time. They did not explain what the theoretical basis for their view was, though Eckius said that natural supposition appears when genus is predicated of species, difference of species, property of species, or a definition of a thing defined.[72] The view of the realists was explained by Javellus who said that unlike the nominalists they allowed the essential predicates of a subject to be verified of that subject even when it did not exist in nature;[73] or, as Tartaretus put it, "the terms do not have to suppose for something existent, it is sufficient that they suppose for something known."[74] Javellus added that for cases of natural supposition the realists rejected the rule that from a proposition, "*S* is *P*", in which 'is' is used predicatively, one can infer a proposition, "*S* is", in which 'is' is used existentially [*Ab est tertii adiecti ad est secundi adiecti valet consequentia*].[75] Some authors even allowed propositions with singular subjects such as "Adam is an animal" to have natural supposition, and to be true in the absence of a referent;[76] but Eckius rejected these on the grounds that science does not deal with singulars, and propositions with natural supposition are the propositions of science.[77] The realist view does not seem very satisfactory, for it is odd to assert that "A man is an animal" is about individual men and animals whilst also asserting that it is unconditionally true, and that its truth is independent of the existence of either man or animals. To introduce thought-objects which are not identified with either concepts or essences does not seem to solve the problem. Greve dealt with the problem of necessary truth much more convincingly when he said that one can save the perpetual truth of "A man is an animal" by taking both 'man' and 'animal' to have simple rather than personal supposition.

6. AMPLIATION

Propositions whose terms had personal accidental supposition were time-dependent, and the theory of ampliation was introduced in order to codify the temporal range of terms in different contexts. A term was said to have ampliation when it signified things existing not only at the time designated by the verb of the proposition in which it appeared, but also at other times.[78] There were normally said to be five kinds of ampliation, to things past, present, future, possible and imagined,[79] though some people rejected the idea of imagined things. Fonseca, for instance, thought that if a term is taken to refer to things, it can be taken to refer to possible things, but never to fictitious things, which destroys the point of the fifth kind of ampliation.[80] It was assumed that terms could only be ampliated when they were not restricted, and they had supposition.[81] 'Adam' in "Adam was" cannot be ampliated to refer to the present time, since 'Adam' has no supposition when placed in the context of a verb of present time [*in ordine ad copulam de presenti*]. Hieronymus of St. Mark added that since 'chimera' has no supposition it does not strictly speaking have ampliation, but is accepted as ampliated in some contexts [*dicitur teneri vel accipi ample*]. A standard set of rules for ampliation was given by Domingo de Soto:[82]

(1) A verb of present time makes the terms preceding and following it stand for what now exists.

(2) A verb of past time, or a past participle, ampliates the terms preceding it so that they stand for what is or was.

This rule was used to justify sophisms such as "A virgin was a mother", on the grounds that this is equivalent to "She who is or was a virgin was a mother". Presumably, this is true if she was a virgin at t_1 and a mother at t_2.

(3) A verb of future time or a future participle ampliates the terms preceding so that they stand for what is or will be.

This rule was used to justify sophisms such as "An old man will be a boy" on the grounds that this is equivalent to "He who is or will be an old man will be a boy". Presumably this is true if he will be an old man at t_2 and a boy at t_1.

(4) A term signifying some corruption ampliates the term in which such a corruption is said to take place to what is or was. For instance, in "Peter destroys a house" 'house' is ampliated to what is or was a house.

(5) A term signifying some action through which something begins to be, ampliates the term affected by the action to what is or will be. In "Peter makes a tunic", 'tunic' is ampliated to stand for what is or will be a tunic; and in "Peter begins to be a man", both 'Peter' and 'man' are ampliated,

so that this sentence is equivalent to "What is or will be Peter is or will be a man."

(6) A term signifying priority or posteriority ampliates the term which has priority to what is or was, and the term which has posteriority to what is or will be. In "Adam is prior to Antichrist", 'Adam' is ampliated to what is or was Adam and 'Antichrist' to what is or will be Antichrist.

(7) The verb 'can be' and the modes 'possibly', 'impossibly', 'necessarily', and 'contingently', when taken adverbially, ampliate both preceding and succeeding terms to what is, was, will be, and can be.

(8) Verbal nouns ending in 'ibile' and the like ampliate the preceding terms to what can be, as long as these terms denote the thing and not just the nature of the thing. He cited the examples of 'generabile' and 'corruptibile', which he compared with 'risibile'. John of St. Thomas explained that generability and corruptibility require only that their subject be able to exist, whereas other modifications require that their subject be able to act, and hence the existence of that subject must be presupposed.[83]

(9) 'Imaginary' ampliates both preceding and succeeding terms to what is, was, will be, can be, or is imagined to be.

(10) A term denoting an interior act of mind such as 'understand' and 'will', or connoting [importans] some relationship to the mind, such as 'signifies', ampliates the terms it governs to what can be imagined to be. In "Peter understands a chimera" and "'Chimera' signifies a chimera", 'chimera' stands for what is or is imagined to be.

Some people saw this rule as raising problems, since it licensed the truth of some propositions containing non-referring terms. Hieronymus of St. Mark said that "I know a rose" only implies the passive form, "A rose is known", when constantia is added. That is, there has to be an extra premiss, "A rose exists", for otherwise more will be signified by the consequent than is signified by the antecedent. Breitkopf, on the other hand, said that it did not matter whether one used the active or the passive formulation;[84] and Paul of Pergula pointed out that no existential inferences could be made from a proposition with ampliative terms.[85] An extra clause was added by Eckius, who said that when the terms had natural supposition, both subject and predicate were ampliated to what is, was, will be, can be or is imagined to be.[86] Domingo de Soto mentioned this as a possible means of explicating necessary propositions.[87]

Ampliation was usually discussed in connection with *status* and restriction.[88] *Status* covered those cases such as "He who is dead, lived", where there was no ampliation and the temporal range of reference was the same as the mood of the verb, that is, either past, present or future alone. In restriction the range of reference was restricted in some way, though not only temporally. For instance, in "Just men fear God", the range of reference of 'men' is restricted by the addition of the qualifying adjective. Restriction was linked with alienation, in which a term is used improperly in an extended or metaphorical sense; remotion, where the reference of one term is destroyed by another, as in 'irrational man'; and diminution, where only a part of each object denoted by the subject-term is in fact referred to, as in "An Ethiopian is white with respect to his teeth."

7. APPELLATION

The last topic associated with supposition was that of appellation. Originally a term was said to have appellation when it denoted some actually existing object, and this was the usage of Peter of Spain who said that 'Antichrist' had supposition but no appellation and that a general term such as 'man' picks out [*appellat*] only individual existent men.[89] In our period only Breitkopf seems to have followed Peter of Spain;[90] and the usual view was that appellation concerned the meaning and reference of connotative terms when they appeared in propositions.[91] In order to understand the discussion, the distinction between the formal and material significates of terms must be made clear. The formal significate was the primary significate, the universal or common nature; whereas the material significates were the secondary significates, or the things to which that common nature belonged. In the case of an absolute term such as 'man', the formal significate uniquely determines the group of material significates. All things sharing human nature are men, and they are distinct from all other individual substances. However, a connotative term such as 'white' does not uniquely determine any group of individuals, for men, flowers and swans may all share in the common nature of whiteness. Nominalists did not, of course, make these references to common natures, but they too distinguished between whiteness and those things which are white. Since connotative terms may be combined both with other connotative terms and with substantive terms in complex sentences, it was thought to be necessary to find some way of deciding whether the formal significate of one term was related to the material or to the formal significate of another. For instance, if I take a logician called Peter and say that he is good, I may be claiming that he is a skilled logician even though he is a morally disreputable man, or I may be claiming that he is a virtuous man, even though he is a poor logician. In the first case the formal significate of 'good' is predicated of the formal significate of 'logician', but in the second case it is predicated of the material significate of 'logician', i.e. of that thing which happens to be a logician, though it is not uniquely determined by this characterization. A closely related problem was brought about by the presence in sentences of words like 'know' and 'see'. If John is said to know a logician, does he know him under the description of a logician, i.e. through the formal significate, or does he merely know a person who happens to be a logician, i.e. a material significate of the word 'logician'? In the second case, he may well know a logician without knowing that he is a logician.

There was no completely standard account of appellation, and Sbarroya gave a good survey of the three main alternatives.[92] He said that the Scotists defined appellation as the acceptance of a connotative term for its formal significate in so far as this belongs to some other thing, and that their first rule was that when a connotative term appears alone, its formal significate belongs to the thing or things for which that term supposes. Otherwise their rules were the same as those of the Thomists. The nominalists' view was very similar, except that they defined appellation as a connotative term in a proposition, rather than as some relationship of such a term. They made the Thomist distinction between formal and rational appellation, and their rules, though fewer in number, do not seem to be essentially different from those of the Thomists. The Thomist view, which Sbarroya himself adopted,[93] was set out very clearly and in great detail by Domingo de Soto, and I shall now turn to his account of the matter.[94]

Domingo de Soto defined appellation as "the application of the formal significate of one term to the significate of another" [*Appellatio est applicatio formalis significati alicuius termini ad significatum alterius*]; and he began by distinguishing between connotation and appellation. A term can have connotation outside a proposition, but it can only have appellation within a proposition. Moreover, a connotative term signifies

that its formal significate belongs to its own material significate (or significates) whereas an appellative term involves the significate (or significates) of some other term. He then went on to make the usual
division between appellation of the real (sometimes called 'formal appellation') and appellation of reason. The latter was so called because it
involved operations of the intellect, both by virtue of the presence of
verbs such as 'know' and 'understand', and by virtue of the presence of
terms of second intention such as 'species' and 'genus' which can only be
predicated of things as conceptualized, or terms of first intention.[95]
Real appellation does not involve operations of the intellect, and it
concerns connotative terms which are taken adjectivally rather than sub-
stantively. He gave four rules for real appellation, and two for appellation
of reason.

Domingo de Soto's first rule was that in a proposition whose predicate
is an adjective and whose subject is a substantive term, the predicate "applies its formal significate to the material significate of the substantive"
[*appellat suum formale ad materiale substantivi*].[96] For instance, "This
logician is great [*magnus*]" means that the person who is a logician is
great in size rather than that he has any outstanding logical skills. He
said that modern logicians did not use this rule, since they claimed that
propositions with an adjectival predicate were subordinated to propositions in which the substantive term appeared in the predicate, as in "This
logician is a great logician", [*Hic logicus est logicus magnus*] and that
the appellative term applied to the substantive term on the part of the
predicate, and not on the part of the subject. He also noted that some
logicians extended the rule to absolute terms such as 'man' in "An animal
is a man", where the predicate is said to apply humanity to individual
animals;[97] but he argued that since 'man' has supposition for its own
peculiar significates, it could not properly be said to have appellation.

Domingo de Soto's second rule was that when two connotative terms,
one of which is substantive and one adjectival, appear together in subject
or predicate position, if the adjectival term precedes the other, it applies
its formal significate to the material significate of the substantive term
by reason of that substantive term's formal properties, so long as such
an interpretation is not clearly impossible. For instance, in "Peter is a
great logician" [*Petrus est magnus logicus*] 'greatness' is predicated of
Peter (the material significate) by virtue of his logical skill. Eckius used

the example of "Young Eckard is an old teacher", where 'old' applies to the length of his tenure, and he contrasted it with "Botzhemus is a tall teacher", where 'tall' has nothing to do with being a teacher. Celaya used the example "*Sortes est bonus logicus*", and said that the alternative sentence, "*Sortes est logicus bonus*", is false if Socrates is a bad man, since '*bonus*' does not precede '*logicus*' and hence is taken to apply directly to the material significate. The rule led to some debate about such examples as "Peter is a white monk", since whiteness could belong either to a man's habit, and hence indicate his monastic order, or to his skin.[98] De Soto, Celaya and Manderston all noted that some people wanted to give "*Petrus est albus monachus*" and "*Petrus est monachus albus*" different interpretations, but they did not find this convincing because of the analogy with such examples as "Peter is a white musician", in which whiteness must be taken as belonging to the material significate. Celaya said that '*monachus*' is not a connotative term, and that the habit does not make a monk, as can be shown by pointing to a totally nude religious [*demonstrato uno religioso totaliter nudo*]. Hieronymus of St. Mark took a different appoach. He argued that the order of words made no difference, and that in both "*Sortes est albus monachus*" and "*Sortes est monachus albus*" whiteness is predicated of Socrates's habit rather than of Socrates himself. Both these sentences are true when the habit is white, even if Socrates himself is black, he said.

The third rule was that a verb and an object denote their formal significates to belong to their material significates at the same time, so long as one or both are connotative and so long as the verb precedes the object. For instance, in "Peter saw the Pope", he must have seen the Pope at the time when he was Pope for the sentence to be true; and in "Brownie was the black horse of a white man", Brownie must have belonged to that man at a time when he was black and the man white. On the other hand, in "*Petrus papam vidit*" where the object precedes the verb, Peter could have seen the man who became Pope at a time when he did not hold that position. Thus, said Manderston, using familiar examples, it is possible for both these sentences to be true: "Something raw I ate" [*crudum comedi*] and "I did not eat something raw" [*non comedi crudum*].

The fourth rule, in Celaya's formulation , is that such modes as 'possibly', 'impossibly', 'necessarily', and 'contingently' appellate or denote these modes to belong to the formal significates of the terms following, so long as these are connotative. If the terms are absolute, or if they precede the modal terms, then the words are applied to the material significate. "God necessarily is creating" [*Deus necessario est creans*] is false, because necessity is said to belong to his creative activity, and God could have refrained from creation. Unlike Celaya, Domingo de Soto explicitly excluded the two modes *possibiliter* and *impossibiliter* from this rule.

Celaya added another rule, to the effect that words such as 'make', 'do', 'produce', 'begin', and 'destroy' bring it about that their formal significate belongs to the formal significate of the following term, so long as that is connotative. Thus one can say truly both that Christ begins to be Christ and that Christ does not begin to be. It was only at the incarnation that he took on the formal characteristic of being Christ, but he had existed materially from eternity.

The two rules for appellation of reason given by Domingo de Soto were first that a term of second intention such as 'species' applies this property to the formal significate of the subject term, and not to its material significates; and second that a term importing an interior act of mind, such as 'knows', indicates that the proper concept of the term immediately following belongs to its significate. The first rule is just a spelling-out of what had already been said in the discussion of simple supposition, namely that only universals and not individuals could be said to be species or genus; but the second rule is new. Its purpose is to distinguish between the case in which an object is known by virtue of a certain description, and the case in which it is not. For instance, to use Manderston's example, to say "I know a man" [*cognosco hominem*] is to claim that I have an adequate concept of man, and that I know a man by means of that concept, whereas to say "A man I know" [*hominem cognosco*] is merely to claim that I have an acquaintance with some being or other who happens to be a man. Domingo de Soto said that in a context such as "'Man' signifies man" 'signifies' applies to the primary (or formal) significate of 'man' and he contrasted it with "'Man' Peter signifies" [*ly homo petrum significat*] in which the material significate of Peter rather than the formal is involved. That is, 'man' is said to signify an actual person rather than humanity. These remarks could have been expanded into a discussion of the distinction between connotation and denotation (in the modern sense), but certainly Domingo de Soto did not pursue the point, and I am unaware of others who did. The second rule was more frequently used to analyze such claims as "No one desires evil" (that is, under that description) and "A poisoned drink is what I desire" (though not under that description).[99] Later logicians, such as Caramuel and Hunnaeus, often dismissed the whole topic of appellation as being useless and trivial, though they still discussed the other parts of supposition theory; and it was this last rule which particularly aroused their scorn.[100]

NOTES

[1] I have found discussions of supposition in at least fifty authors, including such seventeenth century figures as Pedro de Oña, John of St. Thomas, and Gabriel of St. Vincent.

[2] Domingo de Soto, xvii.

[3] P. Boehner, 'Ockham's Theory of Supposition and the Notion of Truth', *Franciscan Studies* 6 (1946) 261, 291f.

[4] "... acceptio termini pro se vel pro suo significato": Alcalá, 10. Cf. Domingo de Soto, xvi, and many others.

[5] "... acceptio termini pro aliquo de quo verificatur mediante copula suae propositionis": Eckius, *El. Dial.* Cf. Clichtoveus: Le Fèvre, 21, and many others. For a later source, see John of St. Thomas, *Formal Logic*, 60.

[6] "Suppositio est terminus existens in propositione qui accipitur pro aliquo suo significato": Celaya, *Suppositiones.* Cf. Gebwiler. For a general discussion, see Sbarroya, *Dial. Introd.*, xlii^{vo}f.

[7] Domingo de Soto, xvi.

[8] Tartaretus, *Expositio*, 51; Eckius, *Summulae*, lxxxiiii^{vo}.

[9] Peter of Spain, *Summulae*: Bocheński, 6.04, 58; de Rijk, 81.

[10] Breitkopf, *Compendium*; *Parv. Log.*; Gutkius, 282. Cf. Versor, 209vo; Fonseca, II 698.

[11] Hieronymus of St. Mark; Greve, vi^{vo}.

[12] Hieronymus of St. Mark; Gebwiler; Tartaretus, *Expositio*, 51.

[13] Fonseca, II 682–686.

[14] E.g. Breitkopf, *Parv. Log.* Cf. Celaya, *Suppositiones*; Domingo de Soto, xvi^{vo}; Campanella, 352; Ormazius, 26vo.

[15] Breitkopf, *Parv. Log.*; Greve, v; Versor, 209vo. Cf. Peter of Spain, *Summulae*: Bocheński, 6.03, 58; de Rijk, 80.

[16] Breitkopf, *Parv. Log.*; Javellus, 165vo.

[17] E.g. Tartaretus, *Expositio*, 51.

[18] Eckius, *Summulae*, lxxxiiii^{vo}.

[19] Tartaretus, *Expositio*, 51.

[20] Celaya, *Suppositiones.* Cf. Naveros, xxvi; Enzinas, *Termini.* The latter said (*Prop. Ment.*, xxix): "Accipi... non est nisi significare in propositione."

[21] Domingo de Soto, xvi^{vo}.

[22] E.g. Manderston.

[23] Pardo, viii^{vo}; Tartaretus, *Insolubilia*, 204f. The latter wrote: "Adverte tamen circa hoc, quod ipsius propositionis duplex est significatio. Quaedam est, quae sibi convenit ratione significationis terminorum suorum: et ista significatione propositio significat quicquid termini eius significant: et istam significationem propositio non potest mutare, sine nova

impositione terminorum. Et ex parte illius non attenditur veritas vel falsitas propositionis: quia tunc ista esset falsa, homo est albus: quia homo significat omnem hominem: et tunc significaret omnem hominem esse album. Alia est significatio propositionis, quae sibi convenit ratione acceptionis terminorum. Et illa significatione propositio solum significat illud, pro quo subiectum et praedicatum accipiuntur, saltem si supponat."

[24] E.g. Manderston; Major, *Logicalia*; Celaya, *Suppositiones*; Bartholomaeus de Usingen; Hieronymus of St. Mark; and others.

[25] John of St. Thomas, *Formal Logic*, 62.

[26] Clichtoveus: Le Fèvre, 21vo. Cf. Javellus, 166; Tartaretus, *Expositio*, 51.

[27] John of St. Thomas, *Formal Logic*, 62.

[28] Villalpandeus, 57.

[29] Fonseca, II 682.

[30] Eckius, *Summulae*, lxxxiiii[vo].

[31] Major, *Logicalia*. Cf. Manderston; Bartholomaeus de Usingen; Hieronymus of St. Mark; Tartaretus, *Expositio*, 51; Mainz.

[32] Eckius, *Summulae*, lxxxiiii[vo].

[33] Domingo de Soto, xvi[vo]f.

[34] For details see Ashworth[1].

[35] See e.g. Eckius, *El. Dial.*; Celaya, *Suppositiones*; Hieronymus of St. Mark. For two later sources see Fonseca, II 688 and Carvisius, 106[vo].

[36] John of St. Thomas, *Formal Logic*, 70; Campanella, 356.

[37] Villalpandeus, 71[vo].

[38] E.g. Domingo de Soto, xxi–xxiii[vo]; and most commentaries on the *Parva Logicalia* of Peter of Spain.

[39] Celaya, *Suppositiones*. Cf. Domingo de Soto, xviii.

[40] Celaya, *Suppositiones*; Domingo de Soto, xviii. For a later source, see Fonseca, II 684.

[41] E.g. Trutvetter, *Summule*; Breitkopf, *Parv. Log.* For a later source see Hunnaeus, *Prodidagmata*, 14.

[42] Javellus, 169[vo]; Paul of Pergula, *Logica*, 24f.

[43] Paul of Venice, *Logica Parva*, 14[vo]. He wrote: "nam sicut illa est vera ens est ens. Ita ista ly ens est ens. Et sicut illa est vera nomen est nomen, ita ista ly nomen est nomen."

[44] Eckius, *Summulae*, lxxxvi[vo].

[45] Pardo, cxlvii[vo]ff.

[46] Eckius, *Summulae*, lxxxvii.

[47] Cf. Hieronymus of St. Mark; Tartaretus, *Expositio*, 51[vo].

[48] Bartholomaeus de Usingen; Gebwiler; Enzinas, *Termini*.

[49] Trutvetter, *Summule*; Otto, xviif. Bartholomaeus de Usingen said that 'man' in "Man is a species" could have simple or material supposition; Gebwiler said that it had material supposition.

[50] E.g. Breitkopf, *Parv. Log.*; Greve, xi[vo]; Hundeshagen, 39; Hundt, clxx[vo]; Hieronymus of St. Mark; for later sources, see Du Trieu, 111; R. Sanderson, 76.

[51] Domingo de Soto, xvii[vo]. "... ly homo in his propositionibus / homo est species / homo disputat, pro eodem supponere, esto adhuc natura realiter distinguatur a supposito, nam supponit ly homo in prima pro concreto nature humane, quod non distinguitur realiter a suppositis, pro quibus supponit ly homo. Differt tamen, quod in prima supponit pro homine inquantum est cognitus per eius proprium conceptum. scilicet homo, in secunda tamen supponit pro eo absolute. i. non inquantum sic aut sic cognitus."

[52] Javellus, 168[vo].

[53] Gebwiler; Major, *Logicalia*.

[54] Cologne, xviii^{vo}. Cf. Breitkopf, *Parv. Log.*; Greve, xi; John of Glogovia, xviii; Hundt, clxxi; Versor, 212. Sbarroya (*Dial. Introd.*, vii) claimed that the *antiqui* tended to give a term simple supposition where the *moderni* would give it merely confused supposition because they were not acquainted with the latter type of supposition. They only recognized two types of descent, he said.

[55] Domingo de Soto, xviii^{vo}.

[56] Domingo de Soto, xvii^{vo}.

[57] John of St. Thomas, *Cursus*, 177: "Hoc autem solum contingit in praedicatis secundae intentionis.... Non ergo sufficit ad suppositionem simplicem dari aliquod praedicatum, quod conveniat immediato significato nominis, sed requiritur quod conveniat cum aliqua praecisione ita uni significato, quod non alteri."

[58] Tartaretus, *Expositio*, 52; *Dialectica*.

[59] Hieronymus of St. Mark. For two later sources, see R. Sanderson, 76f.; Marsh, 81.

[60] Domingo de Soto, xvii^{vo}. He wrote: "Unde esto ly petrus non habeat nisi unicum proprium significatum, nihilominus in hac / petrus est individuum, supponit pro suo primario significato / et in hac petrus disputat, pro secundario." Hieronymus of St. Mark wrote: "Termini discreti habent significatum primarium et non secundarium ut ly sortes qui de significato primario significat illam rem que est sortes. Ex quo sequitur falsitas aliquorum qui imaginantur quod solum terminus communis habet significatum primarium."

[61] John of St. Thomas, *Cursus*, 178.

[62] Breitkopf, *Parv. Log.*; Greve, xi; Hundt, clxx^{vo}; Cologne, xx; John of Glogovia, xviii.

[63] Gabriel of St. Vincent, 12; Carbo, 35–36.

[64] Greve, xi^{vo}. He said "homo supponit simpliciter et tamen supposita includitur."

[65] John of Glogovia, xviii. He wrote: "Alia autem est suppositio simplex. non tamen simpliciter sed secundum quid et improprie simplex. quando scilicet terminus communis supponit pro natura communi: cum inclinatione tamen et habitudine ad supposita licet minus principaliter. et sic propositio in qua terminus supponit simpliciter verificatur pro natura universali in ordine ad supposita et inclinatione ad supposita. ut homo est dignissima creaturarum. esse enim dignissimam creaturarum: et esse creaturam convenit nature humane in ordine ad supposita in quibus est illa natura humana."

[66] Fonseca, II 694–696.

[67] Breitkopf, *Parv. Log.* For a later source, see Gutkius, 282.

[68] For a number of later sources, see Carbo, 36; Ormazius, 27vo; Fonseca, II 698; Pedro de Oña, 40f.

[69] Clichtoveus: Le Fèvre, 23. Cf. Eckius, *Summulae*, lxxxvi; Trutvetter, *Summule*. For later sources, see John of St. Thomas, *Formal Logic*, 65; Alcalá, 10. Alcalá said: "Suppositio naturalis est positio termini pro omnibus suis significatis tam existentibus quàm non existentibus... illa copula *est* non importat tempus praesens, sed unionem quandam perpetuam inter praedicatum & subjectum."

[70] Trutvetter, *Breviarium*. Cf. Trutvetter *Summule*.

[71] Eckius, *El. Dial.*; Clichtoveus: Le Fèvre, 23.

[72] Cf. Trutvetter, *Brevarium*.

[73] Javellus, 170vo.

[74] Tartaretus, *Expositio*, 52vo.

[75] Javellus, 171^{vo}f. Cf. Carvisius, 107vo. For the rule see below.

[76] Tartaretus, *Expositio*, 52vo; Domingo de Soto, xix^{vo}; Cologne, c^{vo}.

[77] Eckius, *Summulae*, lxxxv. Cf. Clichtoveus: Le Fèvre, 24.

[78] Carbo, 40; Campanella, 357; John of St. Thomas, *Formal Logic*, 72. For an earlier source, see Breitkopf, *Parv. Log.*

[79] For five kinds see e.g. Breitkopf, *Parv. Log.*; Eckius, *Summulae*, xciiii[vo]; Gebwiler; Hieronymus of St. Mark; Mainz. For a later source, see Carvisius, 112. Carbo (40) said that some added a fifth kind, but that it was unnecessary.

[80] Fonseca, II 728.

[81] E.g. Celaya, *Suppositiones.* Cf. Eckius, *El. Dial.*

[82] Domingo de Soto, xxvi[vo]f. Cf. Celaya, *Suppositiones*; Eckius, *El. Dial.*; Otto, xviii[vo]f. For later sources, see Carvisius, 111[vo]–113; Campanella, 357–359; John of St. Thomas, *Formal Logic*, 73f.; and others.

[83] John of St. Thomas, *Formal Logic*, 74.

[84] Breitkopf, *Parv. Log.*

[85] Paul of Pergula, *Logica*, 41.

[86] Eckius, *Summulae*, xcvi.

[87] Domingo de Soto, xix[vo].

[88] For later sources, see Carbo, 39–41; Fonseca, II 738–744; John of St. Thomas, *Formal Logic*, 74f.; Villalpandeus, 75f. For earlier sources, see Eckius, *El. Dial.*; Celaya, *Suppositiones*; Domingo de Soto, xxix[vo]f. and others.

[89] Peter of Spain, *Summulae*: Bocheński, 10.01, 10.02, 10.03, 102–103; de Rijk, 197f.

[90] Breitkopf, *Compendium*: "Appellatio est acceptio termini pro re existente."

[91] E.g. Manderston; Eckius, *El. Dial.*; Clichtoveus: Le Fèvre, 30[vo], discusses the double signification of appellative terms. He wrote: "Terminus appellativus duplex habet significatum. Unum pro quo supponit et illud non appellat: ipsumque vulgari nomine significatum materiale nuncupatur. Aliud pro quo non supponit sed quod preter id pro quo supponit importat. Et id vocant significatum formale / appellatum / sive connotatum termini / ratione cuius terminus est connotativus et designatur per abstractum termini connotativi: ut album supponit pro quolibet albo: denotando albedinem pro qua non supponit sed quam appellat."

[92] Sbarroya, *Dial. Introd.*, xxiiif.

[93] Sbarroya, *Dial. Introd.*, xviii[vo]ff.

[94] Domingo de Soto, xxx–xxxii[vo].

[95] Cf. Eckius, *El. Dial.*; Celaya, *Suppositiones.*

[96] Cf. Carbo, 42; Fonseca, II 746; John of St. Thomas, *Formal Logic*, 76. For an earlier source, see Manderston.

[97] Cf. W. Burleigh, *De Puritate Artis Logicae Tractatus Longior*, (ed. by P. Boehner), St. Bonaventure, N.Y., Louvain, Paderborn, 1955, 1, 47ff. See also Albert of Saxony, 16.

[98] Cf. Carbo, 42.

[99] Eckius gives the first example (*El. Dial.*); Paul of Pergula, the second (*Logica*, 44). Cf. Campanella, 359.

[100] Caramuel, *Philosophia*, 9; Caramuel, *Praecursor*, 15; Hunnaeus, *Prodidagmata*, 52.

SEMANTIC PARADOXES

1. PROBLEMS ARISING FROM SELF-REFERENCE

Semantic paradoxes were discussed under the heading of *insolubilia*, although it was realized that the title was misleading, since insolubles were not incapable of solution, and since they involved only one kind of difficulty.[1] The root of the problem was their characteristic of self-reference, although not all kinds of self-reference were involved. For instance, as Bricot said, any proposition containing a transcendental term such as 'being' can refer to itself, since all propositions are beings, but this very general kind of self-reference does not lead to semantic difficulties. The important kind, at least from the point of view of generating paradoxes, arose from the presence of terms such as 'true', 'false', 'singular', 'negative', 'believed', and 'doubted', which range over propositions. Of course, it was realized that the presence of such terms is not sufficient to guarantee self-reference. "This sentence is this sentence" is not self-referential when it points to another sentence;[2] and "Socrates says what is false" is only self-referential when this is all that Socrates says. Precisely what kind of self-reference was involved in an insoluble was a matter of dispute, but it was agreed that any sentence which asserted its own falsity whether directly or as a consequence was an insoluble, for it turns out to be false if and only if it is true. Favourite examples were: "Socrates says what is false", "This is true" said of "This is not true", and "Socrates says 'Plato says what is false' while Plato says 'Socrates says what is false'." Many elaborations were possible, including "This is this false proposition" said of "This is this false proposition" said of "This is this false proposition" said of the first sentence.[3]

It was realized that distinctions could be drawn within this group of self-falsifying propositions, and various classifications were offered. The standard division, found in a great many authors, was between those propositions which falsified themselves immediately and those which did so mediately, through some further proposition or propositions.[4] The author of the *Libellus Sophistarum*, echoing Paul of Venice, added that in the case of immediate falsification, some propositions falsify themselves alone, and some, such as "Every proposition is false", have a more general reference. The most elaborate classification is found in Peter of Ailly. His first distinction was between propositions which signify themselves to be false, and those, such as "This is true" which do not signify themselves to be false. His second distinction was between those propositions which are self-falsifying in any circumstances, such as "This (very) proposition is false", and those which are self-falsifying in a particular situation, such as "Socrates says what is false". The third distinction was between propositions which falsify themselves directly, because they contain the term 'false' and those such as "This is not true", which do so indirectly or as a consequence. Tartaretus rejected this distinction, preferring "Socrates says 'Plato says what is false' and Plato says 'Socrates says what is false'" as an example of indirect falsification.[5] Peter's fourth distinction was between those propositions which falsify themselves immediately, even though the word 'false' does not appear, such as "This is not true", and those which do so mediately through some other proposition or propositions such as "This is true" when said of its contradictory. The fifth distinction was between those propositions which falsify themselves mediately through a proposition which they signify, such as "This is true" which signifies "This is not true", and those, such as "Every spoken proposition is false" which do so only through propositions they do not signify, such as "This is a spoken proposition." Finally, a proposition can be mediately falsified through another of which it is not a part, or through another of which it is a part, as with the second conjunct in "God exists and this conjunction is false."

There was some controversy as to whether other groups of self-referential propositions such as "No proposition is negative" and "I am silent" were insolubles or not. The author of the tract attributed to Peter of Spain seemed to feel that "No proposition is negative" was an insoluble; and the Cologne commentators and John of Glogovia accepted "I am silent."[6] They agreed that it contained no word referring to a property of a proposition, but said that nevertheless it contained an implicit reference to truth and falsity. However, most authors who discussed the matter felt that such propositions could not be accepted as genuine insolubles.

Major said that a genuine insoluble must "signify that things are as they are" which is not the case here. Tartaretus and Bricot objected that from the assumption that things were as signified, the falsity of the proposition in question did not follow;[7] whereas Clichtoveus said that if one assumed their falsity, their truth did not follow, so that there were no paradoxical consequences.[8] Clichtoveus, followed by Eckius, gave an account of the difference between being true at a time and being true for a time.[9] For instance, "John sits" can be true both at and for the time of utterance; whereas "John sat" can be true at the time of utterance, but only for some previous time. The peculiar characteristic of "No proposition is negative" or "I am silent" is that these propositions can be true at the time of utterance but never for the time of utterance. They are paradoxical, because their statement with reference to the present time is incompatible with their truth at the time; but they are not insolubles, because they are not false if and only if they are true.

Another favourite kind of paradox about whose classification people were uncertain, concerned a bridge whose keeper, often called Socrates, said that he would throw anyone who spoke falsely into the water. The man who wanted to cross, often called Plato, said "You will throw me in the water." Did he speak truly or falsely?[10] A similar puzzle concerned a country where all the healthy people, and none of the sick people, spoke the truth. One of their number said "I am ill", thus generating the paradox.[11] Paul of Pergula, the anonymous author of *Libellus Sophistarum*, and David Derodon were all happy to accept such paradoxes as insolubles;[12] but Peter of Ailly, Eckius, Major and Clichtoveus did not agree.[13] Peter of Ailly, whose arguments were echoed by the later writers, pointed out that "You will throw me from the bridge" contains no word referring to a proposition, and it does not signify its own falsity. It is indeed impossible for Socrates both to make Plato's statement come true and to fulfil the conditions he laid down, for the two are incompatible; but the problem is more one of an ill-formed promise than anything else.

Finally, some reference must be made to those paradoxes which involve knowing, believing and doubting. I have in mind such examples as "Socrates believes that he is deceived", "Socrates knows that he errs", when these are his sole beliefs; and "Socrates doubts the proposition written on the wall", when this is the only proposition written on the wall. Buridan had discussed such problems at length; but, apart from

Domingo de Soto, the people in our period did not, although they appear in the lists of insolubles given by Paul of Pergula, Stephanus de Monte, Major and the author of *Libellus Sophistarum*.[14] Again, there was doubt about their status. Peter of Ailly said they were not properly insolubles since they did not signify themselves to be false. Major said that although they were reflexive they were not insolubles; whereas Paul of Pergula argued that an insoluble is not restricted to the true and the false. It is enough to be able to establish that the case is as adequately signified by the proposition in question if and only if it is not as adequately signified.[15]

2. SOLUTION ONE: SELF-REFERENCE IS ILLEGITIMATE

A number of different approaches were made to the solution of those propositions such as "Socrates says what is false" which everyone agreed to have the status of a genuine insoluble. One popular solution, which was discussed by George of Brussels, Tartaretus, Bricot, Trutvetter and Eckius, found its standard formulation in the work of Ockham.[16] He argued that the part of a proposition cannot suppose for the whole, or in other words, that the proposition in which a term such as 'true' appears cannot be included within that term's range of reference. His view, which effectively debarred all kinds of self-reference, was based on the claim that words such as 'true' and 'false' as well as words such as 'negative' and 'particular' were words of second intention, and hence applicable only to first intentions. Ockham could be credited with a theory of language hierarchies; but his theory can also be interpreted in terms of pre-suppositions. When I say "This proposition is false" it is presupposed that I am referring to some other proposition and the truth or falsity of the presupposition has a bearing upon the truth or falsity of my proposition. For Ockham, unlike Strawson, if the presupposition was false, the proposition too was false. Thus he translates "Socrates speaks falsely", when this is all that Socrates says, into "Socrates says something false other than this, 'Socrates says what is false'", and assesses it as being false. On the other hand "Socrates does not speak truly" is translated into "Socrates does not say something true other than 'Socrates does not speak truly'", which is true even when Socrates has uttered only the one proposition. This latter interpretation in terms of presuppositions is far closer to the views of the fifteenth and early sixteenth century writers

I have mentioned than is the first interpretation, for they tended to speak, not of the distinction between terms of first and second intention, but of common usage and the assumption that some proposition other than the one being uttered was being referred to. Bricot, for instance, argued that we normally assume that propositions do not refer to themselves, for when we ask a silent man what he is saying, and he replies "I am saying nothing" we accept this as true. Although Ockham's solution was much discussed, it was not widely accepted. Tartaretus said that although it was useful it was not very subtle;[17] but others had more concrete objections. Bricot objected to the equivocal use of 'false' in "Socrates says 'Socrates says what is false' and Plato says 'Socrates says what is false'", where the second occurrence of 'false' has a referent which the first lacks. He also said that Ockham's view would not only exclude such harmlessly self-referential propositions as "Every being exists" (for a proposition is a being) but would make it possible to argue that "No proposition exists" is true, when this is the only proposition that exists. Eckius objected that a term must suppose for everything of which it is verified, so that self-reference cannot be escaped by Ockham's means.[18] If I say "Every proposition is false", 'proposition' must range over all propositions, since of any proposition including the one I now utter I can say "This is a proposition". Domingo de Soto grouped Ockham's view with that of Peter of Ailly, and objected to them both on the grounds that the arguments offered in support of them were weak, especially the appeal to experience. We cannot use the example of "I say nothing" to show that "This is false" cannot be self-referential by virtue of its meaning; nor can arguments against the self-referential use of such demonstratives as 'this' be applied to such generally phrased insolubles as "Every proposition is false." Moreover, if we reject the legitimacy of "Some proposition is false" on the grounds that a part supposes for the whole, we will also have to reject "Some proposition is a sentence" which is clearly acceptable even when this is the only proposition that exists.[19] Ockham was not often explicitly attacked on the grounds that he excluded even harmless self-reference; but clearly other people agreed that the latter could be accepted, and Clichtoveus cited such cases as "Some proposition is affirmative."[20] The latter both signifies itself and is verified of itself, said Clichtoveus, showing that there are reflexive propositions which are neither insoluble nor self-falsifying.

3. Solution Two: All Propositions Imply Their Own Truth

The most common types of solution were offered by those logicians who were unwilling to dispose of insolubles by ruling that all self-reference was illegitimate. I shall begin by examining a solution which rested on the claim that a proposition implies its own truth, whether logically, or virtually as Buridan preferred to assert.[21] The solutions of Buridan and Paul of Venice have already been discussed by Moody, Prior and Bocheński,[22] so I shall concentrate upon that outlined by Lefèvre d'Etaples and explained by Clichtoveus in the accompanying commentary.[23] First, a number of rules were laid down: (1) Insolubles are to be assessed by means of propositions which are equivalent to them; (2) every proposition implies itself; (3) every proposition implies its own truth; (4) if a proposition implies several others, it also implies their conjunction; (5) every proposition is equivalent to a conjunction of the proposition and an assertion of its truth; (6) equivalent propositions have the same truth-value and imply one another. Clichtoveus pointed out that (5) was derived from (2), (3) and (4) with the aid of a further rule that a conjunction implies one of its conjuncts. That is, we start with '$P \supset P$' and '$P \supset T^\circ P$'', get '$P \supset (P . T^\circ P')$' by (4) and with the aid of '$(P . T^\circ P') \supset P$', finish with (5), '$P \equiv (P . T^\circ P')$'. If we take the insoluble, "I say something false", and call this 'a', we can see at once how an insoluble is to be solved through an equivalent proposition, for this insoluble is, by (5), equivalent to "I say something false and a is true." If one assumes the truth of the first conjunct, the second conjunct is obviously false, for if a is true and a is what I say, I cannot be saying something false. Since this conjunct is false, the whole conjunction is, and hence so is the proposition equivalent to it, namely the original insoluble. One can also argue the other way, by assuming the truth of the second conjunct and thus showing the first conjunct to be false, for whatever interpretation one adopts, the two parts are incompatible. Equally, the negation of the insoluble is true, for the disjunction equivalent to the negated conjunction, "I do not say something false or a is not true", is true. Clichtoveus did not explicitly examine the crucial question of whether the assumption that the insoluble proposition is false would lead to an assertion that it is true. Since he agreed that the assertion of its truth implied its falsity, this is the test of the validity of his solution, for it is only a genuine solution if it is impossible to obtain the biconditional "*a* is true if and only if *a* is false." That he succeeded by following a line of argument very similar to that of Paul of Venice and which involves no distinction between use and mention or different language levels, could be shown informally as follows. Suppose we assume that '*a*', where '*a*' is '*a* is false', is false. If '*a*' is false, then its equivalent "*a* and *a* is true" will also be false and we obtain "It is false that (*a* and *a* is true)". By De Morgan we get "Either it is false that *a* or it is false that *a* is true." But we can replace '*a*' in the first disjunct by '*a* is false' and argue that if it is false that *a* is false, then *a* must be true. Hence we get '*a*', when false, is equivalent to "Either *a* is true or it is false that *a* is true." Since "*a* is either true or not true" is a tautology, the original assumption has not led to any contradictory consequences and a paradoxical conclusion has been avoided. It may be added that the claim that the disjunction is a tautology accords well with Clichtoveus's explicit statement that the original conjunction is made from repugnant parts, and hence is a logical contradiction

The solution offered by Clichtoveus was not novel in its substance,[24] but the formulation, especially the use of propositional rules, was particularly neat. This did not, however, lead to its acceptance. Eckius outlined the argument with care, but rejected the claim that every proposition implies its own truth on various grounds.[25] Firstly he said that if one argues "God exists, therefore 'God exists' is true", one is putting forward a consequence whose antecedent is necessary and whose consequent is contingent, because the proposition "God exists", viewed as an occurrent entity, may not exist. Secondly, if one argues "No proposition is negative, therefore 'No proposition is negative' is true" one is putting forward a consequence whose antecedent is possible, but whose consequent is impossible, since this particular proposition can only be true if it is stated, but the moment it is stated it becomes false. Thirdly, if one argues "God exists, therefore 'God exists' is true", one is overlooking the possibility that the quoted words may be reinterpreted to mean something other than "God exists". Finally, the view means that all propositions will become reflexive, which Eckius found to be as unacceptable a conclusion as had Peter of Ailly before him. Peter had added that it was possible to represent the proposition "A man is an ass" without conceiving or understanding it to be true; and that "A man is an ass" did not mean precisely the same as "'A man is an ass' is true."

4. SOLUTION THREE: INSOLUBLES ASSERT THEIR OWN FALSITY

A more common approach was that whereby an insoluble was seen as asserting its own falsity. One important version of this view was given by Peter of Ailly, whose work was taken into account by most of his successors,[26] despite its dependence on a doctrine of mental propositions which not many people were willing to accept. As has already been stated, he drew a distinction between written, spoken and mental propositions improperly so-called, all of which had conventional meaning, or some element of conventional meaning because of their object, and mental propositions properly so-called which had natural meaning, and to which all conventionally meaningful propositions were subordinated. To some extent Peter adopted the Ockhamist solution to insolubles, for he argued that in the case of mental propositions no self-reference was possible, although it was possible in other cases. To do this, he made certain claims about objective and formal signification. The image of a king signifies the king objectively, he said, for to signify objectively is simply to be the object of a formal cognition. All created things can signify themselves objectively, for they can be the object of some cognition. However, only the concept of a king will signify the king formally, for to signify formally is to be a formal cognition of the object, or an apprehension of its essential properties. No created thing can signify itself formally, for no created thing can have a proper and distinct cognition of itself. That is, no concept can at one and the same time involve apprehension both of the properties which belong to it as a concept and of the properties which belong to its object. A confused apprehension of self is possible in certain cases, as with the cognition of 'being' or 'quality'; but the cognition of a mental proposition which, in Peter's view, is a simple entity like a concept, can never involve the cognition that the mental proposition is true or false, universal or particular, or has any of the other properties which belong to a proposition. A separate cognition is necessary. He supported his case with remarks about the consequence of accepting self-reference. For instance, one would have to accept that two mental propositions, with the same meaning and reference, "This is false", said of itself, and "This is false", said of the first, would have different truth-values; and that the same mental proposition, "This is false", would be both false, because it falsifies itself, and true, because it signifies that things are as they are. To the objection that self-referential mental propositions such as "All mental propositions are false" or "This mental proposition is true" could be formed, he replied that these were not genuinely self-referential. We are misled into thinking that mental propositions have parts because spoken propositions do. If we did form the mental proposition, "This mental proposition is false", and we were possessed of no other mental proposition for it to refer to, then it would be false, not because it was an insoluble, but because the subject term would have no supposition. Self-reference is possible in spoken and written propositions because these have conventional meaning, and we can make them mean what we wish, but we have no such power over mental propositions.

Peter of Ailly solved the problem of self-reference among spoken and written propositions by claiming that an insoluble was a *propositio plures*. Normally this phrase was used of such sentences as "The bank is on fire" which can be given at least two separate interpretations, depending on what kind of bank one has in mind, but here he meant that an insoluble such as "This is false" corresponds at the same time to two separate mental propositions, one of which is true, and one of which is false, so that the insoluble itself can be said to be both true and false. He offered a scheme like this:

This is false   spoken proposition
          referent of spoken proposition

 ↑

This is false   ←   This is false
[true mental]   [false mental]

referent   This is not true   ←   This is true   [spoken proposition]

      ↑

This is true   ←   This is false
[true mental]   [false mental]

He agreed that there were certain awkward results. For instance, one can have similar propositions of which one is a *propositio plures* and one is not; or one can have apparent contradictories which are not in fact contradictory. If Socrates says, "Socrates says what is false", he is uttering a *propositio plures*, but if Plato says "Socrates does not say what is false", he is uttering a simple proposition. Peter was willing to accept these anomalies for the sake of the general solution.

Some authors such as Bricot, criticized Peter's view because they could not accept his claim that mental propositions were incapable of self-reference; but Eckius presented more detailed criticisms.[27] Every proposition, he said, must be either true or false, so one cannot say that an insoluble is both. If an insoluble is to be a proposition, it cannot be a *propositio plures*, for these are not genuine propositions. Finally there is no good reason to say that of two contradictories, one corresponds to two categorical mental propositions and the other does not.

5. SOLUTION FOUR: TWO KINDS OF MEANING

A view very similar to that of Peter of Ailly, but which did not involve his claims about mental propositions, found its starting point in the claim that all propositions have two kinds of meaning. This view was presented by Paul of Pergula, who argued that if an insoluble is taken in its precise signification, then a contradiction is generated and the insoluble is impossible, but if it is taken imprecisely, then it is admissible, for it can be shown to be false.[28] This theory was presented in a sharper form by George of Brussels and other later exponents, such as Trutvetter.[29] John of Glogovia said "An insoluble proposition is a proposition which is difficult to assess as true or false because of the relationship of its secondary reflexive meaning to its direct meaning."[30] George of Brussels argued that the primary or direct meaning, sometimes called the formal meaning of a proposition, is that whereby the terms are taken in their normal sense as referring to a state of affairs, or as he put it, denoting that the subject and predicate, at least in an affirmative proposition, suppose for the same objects. The secondary, indirect or reflexive meaning, sometimes called material, arises when a term supposes for the whole proposition by reason of its meaning, and falsifies the proposition, alone or with some added premiss. Eckius, in his account of the solution, attributed it to both Paul of Venice and George of Brussels, but said that whereas Paul of Venice took the secondary meaning to be "This is true" George of Brussels took it to be "This is false", which Eckius saw as *expeditior et melior*.[31] It was agreed that if an insoluble had added to it "and according to its primary and adequate signification" it could not be accepted.

All admissible insolubles turn out to be false on this view, since they are equivalent to a conjunction at least one of whose parts is false. As Eckius put it, it is not sufficient for the truth of a proposition that things should be as it signifies, for things should also be in whatever way it signifies. Things are as they are stated to be, but the clause "in whatever way it signifies" brings reflexive meaning into play, and here we get falsehood arising. Eckius added that one will not get valid inferences with an non-insoluble antecedent and an insoluble consequent, such as "This consequent is false, therefore this consequent is false" because they are not synonymous. The antecedent is categorical and the consequent is hypothetical. Nor do contradictories have a common form, for one is conjunctive and one disjunctive. This aspect is brought out very clearly by Trutvetter who in his account of the theory said "Henry says what is false" is equivalent to "Henry is a thing saying what is false and that proposition which signifies precisely that Henry says what is false is false." The first part of the conjunction is true, but the second false, so the whole conjunction is false. The contradictory of the original insoluble is equivalent to "Either the thing which is Henry is not the thing which is saying what is false or this proposition is not false", where 'this' refers to the first part of the conjunction; and this disjunction is true.[32]

This solution like others raised the question of how the insoluble was to be regarded. Was it a simple categorical proposition, or some kind of disguised hypothetical, or did it, as Peter of Ailly held, correspond to more than one proposition? Ockham and those who followed him, held that insolubles were categorical propositions, and so did the author of the tract attributed to Peter of Spain.[33] He argued that "the secondary signification is as it were adventitious and accidental," and "there is not a multiple proposition but rather one, because both significations are involved in judging about truth or falsity." The same view as presented by George of Brussels and Trutvetter involved the equivalence of an insoluble to a conjunction whose first conjunct signified that things were as described and whose second conjunct signified the first to be false, in accordance with the insoluble's secondary signification. But this view was not always found satisfactory. As both Peter of Ailly and Tartaretus remarked, there seemed to be no good reason to suppose that an insoluble is equivalent in meaning to a hypothetical proposition, and if it is so equivalent, why choose a conjunction rather than the other types?[34]

6. SOLUTION FIVE:

TWO TRUTH-CONDITIONS

One way of saving the categorical nature of an insoluble was to see it, not as having a double signification, but as having to meet more than one truth-condition while itself remaining simple. There were two versions of this doctrine. The first version was that of John Major, Gaspar Lax, Celaya, the *Libellus Sophistarum* and the anonymous author of the *Insolubilia*. According to them, a true proposition is one which satisfies two conditions, it signifies that things are as they are, and it does not falsify itself. A false proposition fails to meet either one or both of these two conditions.[35] As a result, "This is false" is false because it falsifies itself, but its contradictory, "This is not false", when said of the first proposition, is also false because it denies that things are as they are. Thus the problem of insolubles was solved at the expense of various awkward results. The solution applies only to self-falsifying propositions without impinging upon less harmful forms of self-reference, and it does show that insolubles are false. Nevertheless, as well as the result that two contradictories may both be false, it is also the case that there can be valid inferences whose antecedent is true and whose consequent is false, as in "This consequent is false, therefore this consequent is false." Moreover, one can have an invalid inference where it is impossible for the antecedent to be true when the consequent is false, for example, "Every consequence is invalid, this is a consequence, therefore this consequence is invalid." Domingo de Soto who also accepted these results, accused those such as Bricot who sought a formulation which would rule them out, of *petitio principii*.[36]

These paradoxical results were not generally found acceptable, and the alternative solution presented by Tartaretus, Trutvetter and Bricot, which the latter two thought the most probable of all that they surveyed, distinguished between affirmative and negative propositions.[37] Two conditions must be satisfied before an affirmative proposition can be said to be true. That is, it must signify things to be as they are and it must not falsify itself. A negative proposition, on the other hand, is true just in case either it signifies that things are not as they are not, or it has a self-falsifying contradictory. This distinction between affirmative and negative propositions had two important results. In the first place, rather paradoxically, it means that "This is false" and "This is not true" have different truth-values when they are both self-referential; and indeed it turns out that all propositions which formally signify themselves to be false are false; and all propositions which formally signify themselves not to be true are true. This is because the first group are affirmative and have to satisfy two conditions for truth, whereas the second are negative and have to satisfy only one condition. In the second place, it means that of any two contradictory propositions, one will be true and one false. "This is false" is false because it falsifies itself, and "This is not false" is true because its contradictory falsifies itself. One consequence of both this solution and the previous one is that the formula "$T'P' \equiv P$" can no longer be appealed to, even with the additional premisses that P exists and that 'P' signifies P, for P may be the case when 'P' is false, as when P is "This is false". That is, it is now possible for a false proposition to signify that things are as they are.

The Aristotelian solution, whereby insolubles were classed as examples of the fallacy *secundum quid et simpliciter*, was sometimes mentioned in relation to these solutions via the notion of truth conditions. The author of the *Libellus Sophistarum* wrote that those who objected to his solution on the grounds that Aristotle had said something different, should be aware that to argue "This proposition signifies precisely as things are, therefore it is true" commits just that fallacy. The proposition in question is indeed true in a certain respect, but not simply, because there is a second condition it has to satisfy. This fallacy was sometimes mentioned in other contexts.[38] Trutvetter, for instance, appealed to it in his account of Ockham's solution; but Aristotle was obviously not regarded as having done more than provide a support for other people's solutions.

A variant solution was provided by Eckius, who said that every insoluble falsifies itself "*per modum sequelae et consecutive*", and that "Socrates says what is false" is false not because it signifies things to be other than they are, but because its falsity follows from the assumption of its truth; which ought, he said, to be added to the definition.[39] He claimed that Trutvetter, to whose "beautiful way of solving insolubles" he had earlier referred, would not have abhorred this solution. What Eckius seems to have been getting at was the definition "A proposition is true if and only if it signifies that things are as they are and it has no false consequences;" which is closely related to the usual rules that from a true proposition only true propositions may follow.

7. LATER WRITING ON INSOLUBLES

After the beginning of the sixteenth century, when men such as Eckius and Trutvetter were writing, there was a sudden and abrupt change in the approach to insolubles. Even their name was changed, for the Ciceronian *inexplicabilia* came to be used instead of *insolubilia*. For once it is obvious that the change was due to humanism, and in particular to the revival of interest in classical texts. A great many paradoxes, though not many of logical interest, had been current in the ancient world, and information about them was obtainable in the sixteenth century from such sources as Diogenes Laertius, Cicero (especially *Academica Priora* II 95 and 96) and Aulus Gellius, whose *Noctes Atticae* was very popular and received a number of editions. Adrian Turnebus, who commented on Cicero's *Academica*, referred to Diogenes Laertius by name,[40] but usually it was only Cicero and Aulus Gellius who were cited. Of the scholastics, only Eckius and Major showed any awareness of these sources,[41] but their successors were almost united in ignoring the scholastic sources and quoting the classical.[42] The favourite examples were the standard liar, or "I am lying"; the claim of Epimenides the Cretan that all Cretans were liars; and the crocodile. In this classical story, which appeared in Politian's *Miscellanea*, first published in 1489, the crocodile seizes a child and after saying that it will be returned if the mother speaks the truth, asks the mother whether the child will be returned or not. Of the later authors only Villalpandeus and Aldrich wrote at any length, and only Aldrich and Thomas Oliver made much reference to scholastic sources, though Cardano has a brief reference to Heytesbury.[43] Aldrich cited Ockham, and Oliver cited Buridan, Clichtoveus, Heytesbury and Marsilius of Inghen. He surveyed the literature, but seems to have added nothing of his own, except an apparently unique example of the written liar:[44]

> omne enuntiatum
> intra hoc quadratum
> scriptum est falsum.

Most of these authors did not offer any solutions to the paradoxes they mentioned, but some of them solved the problem of Epimenides's statement by refusing to recognize its paradoxical nature. They said that it was fallacious to take a general or indefinite statement like "Cretans are liars" and to conclude that one particular man, Epimenides, was therefore a liar.[45] Carbo offered as an explanation that anyone who calls men liars is excluding himself; and Melanchthon said that "Cretans are liars" is a particular statement, and nothing follows from two particulars. They did not consider what would be the case if Epimenides said "All Cretans without any exception are liars," and if nothing else was said by a Cretan.

But it would be a mistake to think that none of those who were influenced by classical writers had anything of interest to say, for Aldrich and Valentia joined the more traditional authors, Savonarola, Ormazius, and Derodon in offering a solution which does not seem to have been taken into account by the scholastics I have discussed, although it would be found acceptable today.[46] This solution is based on the claim that insoluble sentences are not propositions, and hence cannot be assessed as true or false. Savonarola alone did not offer an argument to support his claim, but said that an insoluble was to a genuine proposition as a dead man was to a live one. Derodon argued that an insoluble cannot be a proposition since it leads to an impossible situation, and hence, being itself impossible, says nothing. He explained the impossibility in two ways. Firstly the insoluble demands both assent and dissent; and secondly the predicate is incompatible with the tacit assertion of truth which is contained in every proposition. His view bears considerable similarity to that known as *cassatio*, which is found in more than one medieval manuscript.[47] Such views were also mentioned by Paul of Venice.[48] Valentia agreed with Derodon about the status of insolubles, but his reasons, like those of Ormazius and Aldrich, rested on a doctrine of presuppositions rather than the notion of impossibility. Who, asked Valentia, says "I lie", wishing to refer to that very proposition? If he is referring to some previous proposition he does indeed make a statement [*sermonem facit*]; otherwise, since he says nothing it is neither true nor false. Aldrich argued that Socrates's claim, "Socrates speaks falsely", signifies nothing unless there is some previous utterance, for "whoever makes a judgement necessarily presupposes something about which he judges." Ormazius gave an even more elaborate justification, though the arguments he used were standard, even if their conclusion was novel. He first outlined some of the untoward consequences of taking an insoluble to be true or false, such as the acceptance of two contradictories both of which are false, or of a valid inference with a true antecedent and a false consequent; and he then said that in fact insolubles were not propositions but *orationes imperfectae*, for one cannot accept a situation in which part of a proposition refers to (or stands for) the very proposition of which it is part. He added that experience substantiates this, for if someone remarks "This proposition is false", his audience will not judge the remark to be true or false, but will listen avidly for some other proposition.

NOTES

[1] Peter of Ailly, and many others.

[2] Celaya, *Insolubles*, 259, 289.

[3] Celaya, *Insolubles*, 263, 292. He wrote: "Hec est hec falsa."

[4] See Paul of Venice, *Logica Magna*, 194f.; Cologne, xcvii; John of Glogovia, ciiii^{vo}; *Insolubilia*; Major, *Insolubilia*.

[5] Tartaretus, *Insolubilia*, 203.

[6] Peter of Spain, *Syncategoremata*, 137; Cologne, xcvii; John of Glogovia, ciiii^{vo}.

[7] Tartaretus, *Insolubilia*, 205vo.

[8] Clichtoveus: Le Fèvre, 135vo.

[9] Eckius, *Summulae*, cviii; Clichtoveus: Le Fèvre, 134^{vo}f.

[10] E.g. J. Buridan, *Sophisms*, 219; Paul of Venice, *Logica Magna*, 197^{vo}f.; Major, *Insolubilia*; Eckius, *Summulae*, cx^{vo}; Peter of Ailly; Clichtoveus: Le Fèvre, 139f.

[11] E.g. Stephanus de Monte; *Lib. Soph.*; Clichtoveus: Le Fèvre, 139f.

[12] Paul of Pergula, *Logica*, 145f. For a later source, see Derodon, 554.

[13] Cf. Clichtoveus: Le Fèvre, 139f. Eckius (*Summulae*, cx^{vo}f.) quoted Clichtoveus.

[14] Buridan, *Sophisms*, 207ff.; Paul of Pergula, *Logica*, 145. Domingo de Soto devoted chapters 4 and 5 of his work on insolubles to problems of knowledge and doubt.

[15] Paul of Pergula, *Logica*, 145.

[16] Ockham, 487–489. Cf. George of Brussels, *Expositio*, cclxx^{vo}; Eckius, *Summulae*, cviii^{vo}. See Prantl, n. 159, 41; and de Rijk, 'Some Notes on the Mediaeval Tract *De Insolubilibus*', *Vivarium* **4** (1966) 88, 96, for references to earlier sources where the view is called '*restrictio*'.

[17] Tartaretus, *Insolubilia*, 205vo.

[18] Eckius, *Summulae*, cviii^{vo}.

[19] Domingo de Soto, cxliiii^{vo}.

[20] Clichtoveus: Le Fèvre, 135vo. Cf. Eckius, *Summulae*, cviiif.

[21] Buridan, *Sophisms*, 195.

[22] See Bocheński[1]; E. A. Moody, *Truth and Consequence in Medieval Logic*, Amsterdam 1953; A. N. Prior, 'Some Problems of Self-Reference in John Buridan', *Proceedings of the British Academy* **48** (1962) 281–296.

[23] Clichtoveus: Le Fèvre 135vo–136vo.

[24] Paul of Pergula, *Logica*, 143.

[25] Eckius, *Summulae*, cviii^{vo}.

[26] Tartaretus, *Insolubilia*, 203^{vo}ff.; Trutvetter, *Summule*; Eckius, *Summulae*, cviii^{vo}.

[27] Eckius, *Summulae*, cviii^{vo}f.

[28] Paul of Pergula, *Logica*, 135ff. Cf. Paul of Venice, *Logica Magna*, 192^{vo}f.

[29] George of Brussels, *Expositio*, cclxxi; Tartaretus, *Insolubilia*, 204[vo]; Stephanus de Monte; Eckius, *Summulae*, cix; Peter of Spain, *Syncategoremata*, 135f.; Silvester de Priero. The latter wrote: "Omnis propositio mundi habet significatum hypoteticum. Significat tamen suum primarium significatum et ultra hoc significat se esse verum." He added that both parts of the conjunction which corresponded to a non-insoluble had the same truth-value, but that in the case of an insoluble the parts would have different truth-values.

[30] John of Glogovia, cii[vo]: "Propositio insolubilis est propositio habens difficultatem an vera dici debeat aut falsa: propter secundam significationem reflexam supra significationem directam."

[31] Eckius, *Summulae*, cix. He wrote: "Non sufficit ad veritatem propositionis quod ita sit sicut significat: sed requiritur quod ita sit qualitercunque significat / quod non faciunt insolubilia: ut Socrates dicit falsum: valet illam: Sortes est dicens falsum: et haec est vera demonstrando eam ipsam propositionem: licet igitur ita sit sicut propositio illa significat: quia significat sortem dicere falsum et ita est: non tamen ita est qualitercunque significat / cum secunda pars sit falsa."

[32] Trutvetter, *Summule*: "Hec propositio: Henricus dicit falsum in casu quo Henricus solum dicat illam aequivalet huic copulative. Henricus est res dicens falsum et illa propositio que significat precise. Henricum dicere falsum est falsa. ...At contradictoria dicte propositionis. Non Henricus dicit falsum aequivalet huic disiunctive. Illa res que est Henricus non est illa res que est dicens propositionem falsam vel hec propositio non est falsa: per ly hec demonstrando priorem partem copulative."

[33] Peter of Spain, *Syncategoremata*, 137.

[34] Tartaretus, *Insolubilia*, 205: "... sed non est hypothetica: quia non aequivalet sibi in significando, licet bene in inferendo: quia non videtur quod in ipsis ponatur aliquod syncategorema, quod includat coniunctionem ideo non videtur quod debeant dici hypotheticae."

[35] Celaya, *Insolubles*, 263f., 293; Major, *Insolubilia*.

[36] Domingo de Soto, cxlv[vo].

[37] Tartaretus, *Insolubilia*, 205[vo]. See also David Cranston.

[38] Cf. Eckius, *Summulae*, cix, in relation to Paul of Venice; and George of Brussels, *Expositio*, cclxxi, in relation to an example of an insoluble.

[39] Eckius, *Summulae*, cix[vo].

[40] *M. Tulli Ciceronis Academica. Recensuit ... et Hadr. Turnebi Petrique Fabri. Commentarius adjunxit Joannes Davisius*, Cantabrigiae, 1725, no. 7, 161.

[41] Eckius, *Summulae*, cviii, cx[vo].

[42] For detailed references, see Ashworth [3].

[43] Cardano, *Dialectica*, 301.

[44] Oliver, 9.

[45] Carbo, 233f.; Gorscius, 991; J. Sanderson, 105; Valerius, 174; Villalpandeus, 180f. For two earlier sources, see Willichius, 258f.; Melanchthon, *Erotemata*, 749.

[46] Aldrich, 74f.; Derodon, 554; Ormazius, 54[vo]–56; Valentia, 63. Cf. Isendoorn, 521f.

[47] Prantl, n. 159, 41; de Rijk, *op. cit.*, 92, 88.

[48] Paul of Venice, *Logica Magna*, 192[vo].

CHAPTER III

FORMAL LOGIC
PART ONE: UNANALYZED PROPOSITIONS

It is sometimes asserted that traditional logic was devoted exclusively to the study of analyzed propositions of the subject-predicate form, and to their relationships, but this is not the case. Practically every logician had something to say about both hypothetical propositions and hypothetical syllogisms, and use was made of propositional rules, particularly in the reduction of the syllogism. There was a tendency to claim that hypothetical syllogisms could be reduced to categorical syllogisms, but this should not be allowed to obscure the fact that a large number of un-reduced propositional rules can be gleaned from the literature. Moreover, the theory of consequence (or inference) continued to be discussed throughout the period, even though it must be admitted that a decline in both quantity and quality of treatment is apparent. At the end of the fifteenth and beginning of the sixteenth century authors such as Almain, Martinus de Magistris, Major, and Coronel were still writing complete treatises on the theory of consequence, while others gave a detailed account of the subject in their more general works. At least forty good sources from this period can be found. However, after the middle of the sixteenth century only about twenty of the many authors discussed consequence, and often very briefly. Scholastics such as Fonseca, Carbo and Gabriel of St. Vincent had the most to say, but even they do not stand up well to close comparison with the earlier authors. As a result, most of what I have to say in the section on valid inference will be drawn from these earlier authors, although by way of contrast many of the rules for specific propositional connectives will come from later authors.

No light will be shed on the relationship which was thought to obtain between the logic of unanalyzed propositions and the logic of analyzed propositions. It was not unusual for a syllogism to be called a consequence, and it was not unusual for hypothetical propositions to be rewritten in subject-predicate form with quantifiers, but this evidence is not sufficient to sustain any general theory in the absence of an explicit discussion of the matter. As I have said before, it seems that only when one has the notion of a formal system can one sensibly discuss the relationship between different kinds of formal systems; and this notion was lacking.

THE THEORY OF CONSEQUENCE

1. THE DEFINITION OF CONSEQUENCE

The most usual definition of consequence was "a consequence is a discourse [*oratio*] with an antecedent, a consequent, and a sign of illation such as '*si*', '*quia*', '*ergo*', '*ideo*' or '*igitur*'".[1] The presence of '*si*' and the use of words such as 'antecedent' and 'consequent' rather than 'premiss' and 'conclusion' suggests that the distinction between a consequence and a conditional proposition was blurred; but although conditionals frequently appeared as instances of consequences it was made quite clear in practice that a consequence was not a proposition but a sequence of propositions which purported to be an instance of a rule justifying that sequence. John of St. Thomas said explicitly that consequences were not propositions; and that they were therefore assessed not as true or false but as valid or invalid.[2] To be more precise, consequences were assessed in two ways, as instances of rules, or as instances of valid rules. They could fail because they were not in fact instances of the rule appealed to, as was often said to happen in the case of consequences involving self-referential propositions; or they could fail because the rule itself failed. While consequences were clearly seen to be distinct from conditional propositions, the relationship between the two was rightly regarded as close, especially as conditionals were interpreted in terms of strict rather than material implication [see below]. Clichtoveus said that every valid consequence was a true conditional and vice versa;[3] and the Cologne commentators said with regard to syllogistic consequences that if the antecedent, which could be taken as a conjunction of propositions, were taken together with the consequent, it would make a conditional proposition.[4]

One question which was frequently raised was whether a consequence could legitimately be called invalid or not. When a consequence was defined just as an *oratio* there was no problem, but when, as sometimes happened, the condition that the consequent should be derived from or follow from the antecedent was added, it seemed contradictory to turn around and deny that such a relationship held. Eckius dealt with the problem by saying that one can take 'consequence' in a broad sense, as a sequence of propositions in which the consequent is said to follow from the antecedent; or in a strict sense, as a sequence in which the consequent does follow from the antecedent.[5] The broad sense of 'consequence', unlike the narrow sense, is neutral with respect to validity. Other writers relied upon analogy and presented the curious argument that an invalid consequence stands to a valid consequence as a painted man stands to a living man.[6] Celaya alone realized that a third division could be made when he said that one could have not only invalid consequences, but formally invalid, or contravalid, ones as well. He cited '$P \vee -P \to Q . -Q$' as an instance of what he had in mind.[7]

2. THE DEFINITION OF VALID CONSEQUENCE

The topic to which the earlier authors devoted most of their time and ingenuity was that of the definition of a valid consequence; but before I examine their arguments, it is necessary to make some preliminary remarks about their attitude to propositions, and about the place semantical issues played in the general discussion. As has already been established, a proposition was not viewed as some kind of timeless entity, an intermediary between a sentence and a state of affairs; but rather as an actual occurrent, that is, as a declarative sentence which was either written, spoken or thought. That this was so, complicated matters in two ways. In the first place, it was possible to conceive of a consequence which failed because of the non-existence of one of its parts. In the second place, some propositions were such that their very existence produced a paradoxical situation. "No proposition is negative" was a favourite example of this. Nor could the authors ignore such awkward examples on the ground that the paradox was not a formal one, for the distinction between formal and material consequences, or between syntactical and semantical issues, was a subordinate one. Any definition of validity produced was supposed to cover both inferences such as '$P . Q \to P$' and inferences such as "'Smith is a bachelor' implies 'Smith is male'." They did not seek to escape from problems of self-reference or problems produced by the reinterpretation of constituent parts (suppose 'bachelor' came to mean 'has red hair') by retreating into a formal system containing either uninterpreted theorems, or theorems interpreted in the austerest possible manner, by the assignment of letters, numbers, or members of a domain to the constituent parts.

The starting point for the discussion of validity was an examination of the most obvious definition, "A consequence is valid if and only if it is impossible for the antecedent to be true and the consequent false." A few people accepted it as adequate,[8] but many felt that it expressed neither the necessary nor the sufficient conditions for validity. There were two reasons for rejecting it as a necessary condition. In the first place, it was sometimes claimed that where self-reference was involved, one could have a valid consequence with a true antecedent and a false consequent, or at least, one which was not true. Pardo, for instance, accepted "Every proposition is affirmative, therefore no proposition is negative" as valid, even though the consequent could not be true. To be true it must exist, and the moment it comes into existence it falsifies itself.[9] In the second place, such a definition overlooks the requirement of existence. Almain felt that "Socrates runs, therefore a man runs" could have a true antecedent and a consequent which was not true because it did not exist. As a result, his first step towards an adequate definition was to say "It is impossible for the antecedent to be true when an existing consequent is false."

One might object at this point that it makes no sense to speak of a consequence which has an antecedent but no consequent, but Almain's claim may easily be explicated in terms of the type-token distinction. If a consequence is defined as a set of sentence-types such that whenever the tokens of the antecedent sentences are true, then the token of the consequent sentence is true, one can indeed argue that there may be situations in which some but not all of the tokens exist, and hence that the definition is inadequate. However, as Pardo's example suggests, there were situations in which the actual existence of a proposition (as a sentence-token) was most inconvenient, and such authors as Caubraith modified their final definition in such a way that existence was not viewed as a necessary condition.

The fullest and most elaborate discussion of the question whether the definition provides a necessary condition for validity was offered by

Niphus, though he obviously owed much of his argument to Pseudo-Scotus.[10] Using the same example as Pardo, he said that the definition does not cover the obviously valid consequence, "Every proposition is affirmative, therefore no proposition is negative." Here the antecedent can be true, because all negative propositions could be annihilated, yet in such a situation the consequent would be false, because it would not exist. If it did exist, then one could immediately demonstrate the truth of its contradictory, "Some proposition is negative." One could try to modify the definition by introducing the requirement that the antecedent and consequent should be formed together, but this will not work, for if all negative propositions are annihilated, the consequent cannot be formed at all. Hence the definition must be modified by the addition of the words "if they were formed together," so that a counter-factual conditional is produced. This is all right, he said, because if it is the case that all propositions are affirmative, it certainly follows that no proposition is negative, even though "No proposition is negative" is itself impossible, because it cannot exist.

The chief quarrel with the definition in terms of truth was that it failed to give a sufficient condition for validity, allowing as it did a number of obviously unacceptable consequences.[11] The two fullest discussions are to be found in the works of Celaya and Almain, so I shall concentrate upon their arguments.[12] Celaya took as his chief example "No proposition is negative, therefore a man is an ass." One can argue, he said, that it is impossible to have a true antecedent and a false consequent here because if the antecedent is assumed to be true, then it is, as an existent proposition, false, and if the consequent is false, then the falsity of the antecedent follows by an acceptable rule. Yet the consequence is clearly invalid, because it violates the rule that an impossible proposition cannot follow from a possible proposition. Those who attempt to solve the problem by saying that the antecedent refers to a future time and hence can be true now, while the consequent is false, are easily refuted by the formulation of a new antecedent, "No proposition is or will be or was negative." Almain's example was virtually the same, namely "No proposition is negative, therefore God does not exist," which is, he said, invalid because it violates the rule that in a valid consequence the contradictory opposite of the consequent implies the contradictory opposite of the antecedent. He went on to discuss the whole matter of truth and possibility. It does not follow, he said, that because a proposition cannot be true it is impossible, or that because it cannot be false, it is necessary. One can have two propositions which are compossible, such as "No proposition is negative" and "God exists", even though they cannot be true together; and one can have two propositions which are synonymous, though only one is true, as where "There is no spoken proposition" is both spoken and written. Finally, a proposition such as "Some proposition is negative" can be false even though its contradictory, "No proposition is negative", cannot be true. In other words, a proposition is possible when the state of affairs it refers to is possible, but it is possibly true when its existence as a sentence-token does not conflict with the state of affairs described. Almain, like Celaya and a number of others, turned therefore towards a definition of validity in which the notion of possibility was clearly applied to states of affairs rather than to the truth of propositions.

The new definition offered by Celaya took the form, not so much of a new set of words, as of a new gloss upon the old set of words. He still held that a consequence was valid if and only if it was impossible for the antecedent to be true and the consequent false, but he drew a distinction between two senses of 'true' and the two corresponding senses of 'false'. The antecedent could be true in the sense that it signified things to be as they in fact were, or it could be true in the sense that it signified things to be as they in fact were by means of a true proposition. Only the first sense is applicable here. Almain, however, made his meaning immediately explicit when he dropped all reference to truth and said that in a valid consequence it was impossible for whatever the antecedent signified to obtain without what the consequent signified also obtaining.[13] This definition was not, of course, original to Almain, for it goes back to Buridan and Albert of Saxony;[14] and some of Almain's contemporaries gave very elaborate versions of it in order to guard against the pitfalls which are contained even in this new formulation.[15]

In the first place, existence was still seen to be a problem. Caubraith took as his example "God exists, therefore some proposition is indefinite." He did not wish to accept such a consequence as valid; yet if one admits that things are as signified by the antecedent, one is committed to the claim that the antecedent proposition exists, which in turn renders the conclusion true, so that it is impossible for things to be as signified by the antecedent without their being as signified by the consequent.[16]

His way of escape, which was also used by men such as Major, Pardo, Enzinas, and Domingo de Soto, was to add the clause "or as can be signified."[17] One can agree that things are as can be signified by the sentence-type "God exists" without committing oneself to the existence of any particular sentence-token. Other awkward cases, such as "No proposition is negative, therefore some proposition is negative" or "Every proposition is particular, therefore some proposition is universal" can equally well be ruled out by the use of this clause, whereas legitimate cases such as "Every proposition is affirmative, therefore no proposition is negative" are not affected.[18]

The problems arising from syntactical self-reference were easily dealt with, but those arising from semantical self-reference were more intractable. Enzinas, Caubraith and Celaya all produced the same two examples of this second kind of self-reference: "This consequent does not signify things to be as they are, therefore this consequent does not signify things to be as they are" and "This consequence is valid, therefore a man is an ass."[19] The first case seemed to be an instance of the valid rule leading from synonym to synonym, yet when the consequent referred to is its own, the antecedent signifies (or can signify) things to be as they are, but the consequent does not. In his discussion of insolubles, Trutvetter commented that such consequences as "This is false, therefore this is false" may not be genuine cases of the inference from synonym to synonym, since the antecedent and consequent differ in their secondary or reflexive signification [see above].[20] The second case seems to be invalid, for the impossible is derived from the possible, yet it is not possible for the antecedent to signify things to be as they are without the consequent also so signifying, for it is not possible for the antecedent to signify things to be as they are at all. Both Enzinas and Caubraith added two clauses to their definition: that the consequent should not have "does not signify things to be as they are" appended to it; and that the entire consequence should not invalidate itself.[21] Celaya said that his definition did not apply to insolubles, where it is quite possible for an invalid consequence to be subordinated to a valid one, as in the first case above. He added that in the case of insolubles one could have a true conditional which was an invalid consequence, as in "If this is a valid consequence then man is a lion", or a valid consequence which was a false conditional, as in "If this conditional is true, a man is an ass."

This is valid, because the antecedent is impossible, but a false conditional because it falsifies itself. He seems to be denying the equivalence between '$P \rightarrow Q$' and "'$P \dashv Q$' is valid" which was normally assumed to hold. For further details he, like Enzinas, referred the reader to his treatise on insolubles.

Since propositions were regarded as sentence-tokens another type of problem arose from the arbitrariness of the connection between a set of words and a state of affairs, or between a set of words and the group of things to which the words refer, depending on which view of meaning was adopted. That is, a sentence such as "An ass runs" can be reinterpreted to mean "God exists", or it can be taken to refer to just one aspect of the state of affairs that it signifies, namely that an animal is running. These possibilities could wreak havoc with an otherwise valid consequence, or at least with a consequence whose validity was dependent upon the semantical rather than the syntactical properties of its constituents; and various clauses were added to ensure that propositions retained their original and total significance.[22] Caubraith was more lengthy in his discussion than most.[23] He required that the propositions appearing in a consequence should maintain their virtual, adequate and total signification to exclude the following three cases (among others): (1) "A man runs, therefore an ass runs" when read as meaning only "Socrates runs, therefore an animal runs;" (2) "Socrates runs, therefore every man runs" where the consequent can be taken in its partial signification as meaning "Socrates runs"; and (3)"Socrates runs, therefore a man runs", where "Socrates runs" is taken to be convertible in meaning with "God exists". He went on to rule out the inference from "'P' is true" to "P", since the quoted sentence could receive a new meaning whilst the total and propositional signification of the antecedent was unvaried [non variantem significationem totalem et propositionalem antecedentis]. It could thus be the case that things were as signified by "This is true 'A man is an ass'" but not as signified by "A man is an ass".

It should be noted that one other definition was sometimes appealed to, namely that a consequence is valid if and only if the contradictory opposite of the consequent is incompatible with the antecedent. Both Paul of Venice and Paul of Pergula had offered this as a definition, and they were followed by Blanchellus Faventinus,[24] while others such as Celaya and Domingo de Soto mentioned it as a possibility.[25] More frequently, it was appealed to as a criterion for a valid consequence, together with the rule that the contradictory opposite of the consequent entails the contradictory opposite of the antecedent.[26] Two problems are associated with the criterion of incompatibility, the definition of incompatibility, and the status of certain consequences in relation to it. Most usually, propositions were said to be incompatible if they could not be true (or false) together,[27] but Hieronymus of St. Mark pointed out that this is inadequate, for it will make "No proposition is negative" incompatible with any other proposition. He preferred the alternative interpretations, that two propositions are incompatible if it is impossible for things to be as signified by them together,[28] and that they are incompatible if they form an impossible conjunction.[29] It was often added that both impossible and false propositions were incompatible with any other, whereas necessary and true propositions were not.[30] It was this fact which was appealed to in order to solve the problem of the status of consequences such as "Only a father exists, therefore not only a father exists" (because there must be a child) or "A man is an ass therefore a man is not an ass."[31] In each of these cases the contradictory opposite of the consequent is identical with the antecedent, and it seems odd to say that identical propositions can be incompatible. However, it was decided that an impossible proposition is incompatible even with itself, and that no conjunction containing such a proposition can ever be consistent. As Hieronymus of St. Mark pointed out, it is a sufficient condition for the impossibility of a conjunction that just one part be impossible. Not every one was convinced, for Domingo de Soto said that although 'the moderns' accepted "If God does not exist, then God exists" on the grounds that the impossible leads to anything, he could not bring himself to accept an inference of this form [*Hoc autem (fateor) non possum mihi suadere*].[32]

Later logicians did not indulge in these elaborate discussions of what it was for a consequence to be valid, and they contented themselves with the claim that it was impossible in a valid consequence for the antecedent to be true and the consequent false.[33] Some also added the criterion of incompatibility.[34] The only alternative approach to be found is that of Melanchthon, who defined a valid consequence as one which did not violate the precepts of dialectic.[35] He was followed in this by Vincentius who, like Melanchthon, failed to realize that such a definition was

valueless, given that the point of defining validity was to produce a
standard for the assessment of the precepts of dialectic themselves.[36]

3. FORMAL AND MATERIAL
CONSEQUENCE

Having established the general conditions of validity, logicians went on
to distinguish between two kinds of valid consequence, formal and
material.[37] This division corresponds to that between inferences valid
on syntactical grounds and those valid on semantical grounds, for a
formal consequence was said to be one whose validity depended on the
form of the propositions alone, whereas a material consequence was one
whose validity depended on the presence of certain terms, or on a
certain kind of antecedent or consequent. One could find examples of
material consequences having the same form, only one of which was
valid. For instance, "A man runs, therefore God exists" and "A man runs
therefore an ass exists" have the same form, but only the first is materially
valid, since it has a materially necessary consequent.[38] Some time was
devoted to the discussion of what it was for two propositions to be
identical in form, and it was agreed that they must have the same copula
or connective, the same quantity, quality and relation of terms, and
the same acceptance or supposition of terms.[39] That is, "'Man' is a
word", "Man is a species", and "Man is an animal" were not taken to
be similar in form. The relationship between the two types of inference
was not so frequently discussed. Strode and Cajetan of Thiene had
remarked that all valid formal consequences were also valid material consequences, for, Cajetan explained, if a consequence is valid because of
its mode of arguing, it follows that the terms are also linked;[40] but it
should be noted that they had a special theory about formality, and
that they did not accept the paradoxes of strict implication as formal
consequences. As will be seen below, both Eckius and Niphus realized
that a materially valid consequence could be turned into a formally valid
consequence by the addition of an extra premiss, but other authors did
not consider this possibility.

The special view of formality which Strode and Cajetan held was not
without influence on the period with which I am concerned. Strode had
said that a formally valid consequence was one in which the consequent

was understood in the antecedent; and Cajetan in his commentary on Strode discussed the matter at some length.[41] He first made the usual distinction between formal consequences which held because of the mode of arguing, and material consequences (including the paradoxes of strict implication) which held because of the terms [*gratia terminorum et non gratia modi arguendi*]. He then divided formally valid consequences into two kinds, those valid *simpliciter*, where the contradictory opposite of the consequent could not be imagined together with the antecedent without a contradiction, and those valid *secundum quid*, where the opposite of the consequent could not be imagined together with the antecedent without incompatibility. Some called the latter sort material consequence, he said. He cited "You know you are a stone, therefore you do not know you are a stone", and commented that it was not clear what attitude Strode would have adopted to this consequence. Moreover, he said, Strode's requirement that the consequent be understood in [*de formali intellectu*] the antecedent was difficult to apply to a consequence which was formally valid *simpliciter*. He offered three interpretations of Strode's requirement. It might mean that antecedent and consequent were linked in being [*in essendo*], just as one cannot be a man without being an animal. It might mean that antecedent and consequent were linked in inferring [*in consequendo*], as in "You are an ass therefore man is ass" where the consequent is understood in the antecedent but is neither included in it nor presupposed by it; or it might mean that antecedent and consequent were linked both in being and in inferring, as in "A man runs, therefore an animal runs". He added that the existence of the things in question was not required. Instead, it was sufficient for one to be so included in or presupposed by the other that it was not possible to imagine one to be present and the other not. For instance, one cannot imagine something to be a man and not to be an animal, or something not to be an animal and not also not to be a man. His final remark was that Strode's requirement should be added to the definition of a formally valid consequence.

Not surprisingly, such a view was severely criticized by subsequent logicians. Enzinas said that it was worthless, for one can easily understand that a man is running without understanding that an animal is running;[42] and Dolz rejected it with scorn.[43] What, he asked, does "imaginable with" mean: "apprehended with"; "assented to together with" or what?

In many cases of obviously formal consequences like syllogisms, one can certainly both apprehend and assent to the conjunction of the negated consequent and the antecedent, so how can this be used as a criterion? In the seventeenth century Kesler rejected Javellus's version of the position because, he said, the distinction between form and matter has nothing to do with the obviousness of the inference. He clearly felt that psychological criteria were inappropriate.[44]

Nevertheless, a few people did follow Strode and Cajetan. The Cologne commentators, Greve, and John of Glogovia all seem to have accepted the claim that the consequent should be understood in the antecedent without comment; while Major added that a relationship of pertinence between the terms was required; and the author of the *Libellus Sophistarum* said that the antecedent formally contains the consequent just when verifying the antecedent verifies the consequent.[45] A more elaborate discussion is to be found in Paul of Pergula, who followed his predecessor Paul of Venice very closely.[46] He made a two-fold division of valid consequences into formal and material and then again into formal *de forma* and formal *de materia*, the last two divisions being those normally called formal and material. In his interpretation a formally valid consequence was one in which the contradictory opposite of the consequent could not be imagined together with the antecedent without contradiction, and a materially valid consequence was one in which such a conjunction could be imagined, though it was in fact impossible. The example given was "God does not exist and some man does exist", which can be imagined to hold by atheists. Not all formally valid consequences were also valid *de forma* and such inferences as "Only a father exists, therefore not only a father exists" and "You know that you are a stone, therefore you do not know that you are a stone" were cited as exceptions. Both Blanchellus Faventinus and Javellus reproduced these arguments exactly, though Javellus said that realists, unlike terminists, denied the father and stone examples to be even formally valid, since no valid consequence can lead to a contradiction.[47]

4. 'UT NUNC' CONSEQUENCE

A number of authors divided consequences into those valid *simpliciter*, those valid *per accidens*, and those valid *ut nunc* (as of now).[48] Celaya,

Pardo and Domingo de Soto gave very similar accounts of the matter.[49]
A consequence is valid *simpliciter* when at no time is it possible for the
antecedent to be true (or for things to be as signified by the antecedent)
without the consequent also being true (or things being as signified by
the consequent); it is valid *per accidens* when the antecedent cannot now
or in the future be true without the consequent, although this would
once have been possible; and it is valid *ut nunc* when the antecedent
cannot be true without the consequent, things being as they are now.
Initially these distinctions seem rather curious, but they can be elucidated
with the aid of other distinctions, in particular that between sentence-
types and sentence-tokens. Some sentence-types are such that all their
tokens are true. For instance, any sentence-type of the form '$P \vee -P$' will
have only true tokens. Similarly, a consequence-type can be such that
all its tokens are valid (where a consequence-type is a sequence of
sentence-types together with some word like 'therefore'), and this consequence-type will be valid *simpliciter*. Some sentence-types are such that
all their tokens are now true because they contain reference to a particular
thing located at a particular time and place. "Adam was" is a sentence-
type of this sort, given that 'Adam' was always taken to have unique
reference to the first man. Tokens of this type cannot now be false,
although any which existed before the creation of Adam would have been
false at that time. The use of such sentences gives us consequence-types
such as "Adam did not exist, therefore God does not exist", all of whose
tokens are now valid, because the antecedent is impossible *per accidens*
(or *secundum quid*). This consequence-type is said to be valid *per accidens*.
Finally, there are sentence-types such as "John sits" which can be uttered
in various contexts with various referents. Some of the tokens of this type
are true, others are false. The use of such sentences gives us consequence-types which are valid at certain times, in the sense that given the
circumstances obtaining at those times it is impossible for the antecedent
to be true and the consequent false. These consequences are called valid
ut nunc. I shall not give any examples at this point, because there was
some dispute as to whether antecedent and consequent should be linked
in meaning or not.

The other distinction which is relevant to an understanding of these
three kinds of consequence is that between formal and material validity.
Following Pseudo-Scotus, Niphus explicitly identified consequences

which were valid *simpliciter* with formally valid consequences, and he said
that what he called consequences valid *per accidens simpliciter* and consequences valid *per accidens ut nunc* were both materially valid consequences. His example of a consequence valid *per accidens simpliciter* was
"A man runs, therefore an animal runs", and he said that it becomes
formally valid with the addition of the necessarily true premiss, "Every
man is an animal." His example of a consequence valid *per accidens ut
nunc* was "Socrates runs, therefore something white runs" and he said
that it becomes formally valid with the addition of the true premiss,
"Socrates is white." In this way, all valid material consequences can be
reduced to valid formal consequences.[50] Since material consequences
involve a relationship of terms, it is clear that he took *ut nunc* consequences to involve such a relationship, and that 'white' was somehow
linked with 'Socrates'. Eckius seems to have had in mind an account
similar to that of Niphus, since he said that an *ut nunc* consequence such
as "Every man is a thinker, therefore you are a thinker" was not really
valid unless one added the premiss "You are a man."[51] Otherwise, there
was a conspicuous absence of attempts to explain the relationships
between the three types of consequence in terms of previous distinctions,
or in any terms at all. Celaya remarked that every consequence which is
simply valid is also valid *ut nunc*, but that is the only reference I have.

The exact nature of the consequences said to be valid *ut nunc* was a
matter of some discussion. Some people either rejected them or only
accepted them in a form which identified them with the consequences
otherwise known as *per accidens*. Almain, for instance, said that "Adam
did not exist, therefore God does not exist" was a valid *ut nunc* consequence but that "Socrates runs, therefore Plato runs" was not, even if
both were running. Pardo, who also seemed to accept *ut nunc* consequences when these were equated with consequences *per accidens*, said
that although "John sits, therefore William runs" was valid *ut nunc* given
the definition in terms of the antecedent not being true without the consequent under present conditions, it should be rejected. The vulgar sometimes used it, but it was not a kind of consequence employed by
logicians.[52]

Others, such as Niphus, accepted *ut nunc* consequences given the
assumption that some link of meaning between antecedent and consequent was involved, and there was a tendency to associate this view with

an existence requirement. The author of the treatise on consequences attributed to Peter of Spain reported that some people tied a consequence *ut nunc* to the existence of the subject of the consequent, as in "A man is an animal, therefore this man is an animal"; but he added that this was invalid because the antecedent is necessary, whereas the consequent is a possible proposition and will be false after the man is dead. Apart from consequences which were valid *simpliciter*, he would accept as valid only those such as "John exists, therefore Aristotle did exist", which can never become invalid, since they have a consequent which is necessary *per accidens*.[53] The Cologne commentators, however, said that "A man is an animal, therefore Socrates is an animal" can be accepted as valid because, despite the modern contention that "Socrates is an animal" means "Socrates exists as an animal", all that is really entailed is a link between subject and predicate. Socrates is a man and an animal whether he exists or not.[54] Like Hundt áfter them, they said that a simply valid consequence involved a perpetual connection of terms, and a consequence valid *ut nunc* a contingent connection of terms.[55]

At least two people did accept *ut nunc* consequences in their most uncomplicated form. John of Glogovia said that "A man is sitting, therefore a stick is in the corner" was valid, provided that things were as described;[56] and John Major accepted "John is a priest, therefore John is an ass." (I take it that John was not a priest, so that both antecedent and consequent were false). Since they obviously assumed no connection between antecedent and consequent other than one of truth-value, one might be tempted to credit these authors with a recognition of the modern distinction between strict and material implication, but the temptation should be resisted. No mention was made of cases in which antecedent and consequent differed in truth-value; no attempt was made to link *ut nunc* consequences with conditional propositions; and no attempt was made to explain in what sense *ut nunc* consequences were inferential. These omissions suggest a degree of imprecision in the thinking of John of Glogovia and Major which makes it hardly plausible to claim that they had an important logical distinction in mind.

5. The Paradoxes of Strict Implication

How logicians distinguished between formal and material consequence

often had a close bearing upon their classification of the so-called
paradoxes of strict implication, that is, that from an impossible proposition anything follows, and that a necessary proposition follows from anything. Some people listed them without comment;[57] while others mentioned that they followed because of the criterion of incompatibility, the
impossible being incompatible with anything.[58] Clichtoveus offered one
of the most succinct arguments when he said that if one takes an antecedent A and a consequent B, the only reason for denying the inference
of B from A is that A is true and B false.[59] If A is true by
hypothesis, then it can be true. But in the case of the first paradox,
A is assumed to be impossible and it is contrary to the definition
of 'impossible' to say that it is possible for an impossible proposition
to be true. Hence the impossible implies anything. By a parallel
argument, if B does not follow from A this is because A is true
and B false. Yet it is contradictory to say that it is possible for a
necessary proposition to be false. Other authors took the distinction between formal and material consequence, and showed that one could have
two corresponding types of paradox.[60] From the formally impossible,
which either is or implies a formal contradiction, anything follows by a
formally valid consequence; but from the materially impossible, such
as "God does not exist", anything follows by a materially valid consequence. Niphus alone added that from a false proposition anything
follows by a consequence valid *ut nunc*, for either an arbitrary proposition follows immediately; or if it does not, one can produce a proof by
assuming the true proposition which is the contradictory opposite of the
original false proposition.[61] In the second case, that of the materially
impossible, he noted similarly that one must assume the materially
necessary proposition '$-P$' to cover the cases where Q does not otherwise follow from P. For all three cases he offered the standard proof:[62]

$$P . - P \rightarrow P$$
$$P \rightarrow P \vee Q$$
$$P . - P \rightarrow - P$$
$$P \vee Q, \ - P \rightarrow Q$$

Therefore: $P . - P \rightarrow Q$

This proof yields a proof for the case of a necessary consequent by
appeal to the principle that the contradictory opposite of the consequent

implies the contradictory opposite of the antecedent. It also follows, he said, that a true proposition will follow from any other.

Those logicians who believed that the consequent had to be understood in the antecedent for a consequence to be formally valid, tended to list the paradoxes as being only materially valid.[63] The author of the *Libellus Sophistarum* gave a typical account which was very close to that which had been offered by Ferebrich. There are, he said, three kinds of materially valid consequence, that whose validity depends on the terms employed, that where the antecedent is both impossible and irrelevant to the consequent, as in "A man is an ass, therefore the stick is in the corner", and that where the consequent is both necessary and irrelevant to the antecedent, as in "You run, therefore God exists." It was, of course, acknowledged that there were some formally valid consequences whose antecedents were impossible, such as "A man is an ass, therefore a man is an animal", but these held by virtue of some other rule. Javellus said that realists would not even allow the paradoxes to be materially valid, because they exhibited no inferential link [*sequela*], no dependence, and no incompatibility between the antecedent and the negated consequent.[64] In the fifteenth century Maiolus had also rejected the paradoxes, for, he said, he could not see how the impossible was imaginable together with anything, and he certainly did not wish to call them formally valid.

In at least three cases the paradoxes were denied to be formally valid even though the standard formal proof for the first was carefully set out. Sermonete, in his remarks on Strode, said that a consequence of Strode's view was that something could follow formally from the consequent of a valid consequence without so following from the antecedent, since in the case of the paradox "c is understood in b, b in a, but c is not understood in a."[65] The Cologne commentators said that even though every step in the derivation of Q from '$P. - P$' is formal, one cannot accept the last step.[66] This is because '$P. - P$' can be taken in two ways, absolutely, as a virtual contradiction, or for the sake of the argument. In this proof, it is accepted for the sake of the argument, and since both P and $-P$ have thus been conceded, one cannot use part of the formal contradiction to deny the other part. That is, '$P \vee Q, -P \to Q$' has to be rejected! De Soto agreed that '$P. - P \to Q$' could be proved only if the contradiction were taken absolutely; and he also appealed to common usage to support his doubts about the paradoxes: who would say that if you are a stone, it follows both that you are and that you are not?[67]

In the later period a completely new interpretation was given to the rules that from an impossible proposition anything follows and that anything implies a necessary proposition. It was carefully explained that by 'anything' was meant a necessary, contingent, or impossible proposition;[68] and Fonseca's examples show that a close link between antecedent and consequent was assumed. For instance, he gave "Every stone subsists by itself, man is a stone, therefore man subsists by himself" as an example of how the necessary is derived from anything. Only Regius referred to the original interpretation, whereby 'anything' meant some arbitrary proposition.[69] He reported that Javellus and the doctors of Cologne had rejected this view on the grounds that in a case such as "Man is an ass, therefore the stick is in the corner", there is no relation of dependence between the propositions, and the negation of the consequent is not incompatible with the antecedent. The earliest parallel to Fonseca's view of the paradoxes in the period I am concerned with is found in the Cologne commentary on Peter of Spain, which said that the impossible could lead to anything with respect to the genus of propositions, but not with respect to their species or number.[70]

6. RULES OF VALID CONSEQUENCE

The corollary of the interest in semantic problems which is displayed throughout the discussion of the nature of valid consequence was a failure to develop any syntactically adequate system. The authors made no attempt to draw up a list of axioms and rules from which theorems could be derived; nor did they employ any symbolism apart from the occasional use of A, B and C to indicate either propositions or terms. Nevertheless, a large number of rules are to be found in their works, and I shall list them in as orderly a manner as I can. The rules which deal with particular connectives will appear below, in the sections devoted to those connectives.

Some explanation of my symbolism is now in order. When one is formalizing a logical rule such as *modus ponens*, one can present it in at least four different guises:

(1) As a theorem: '$(((p \dashv3 q).p) \dashv3 q)$'. This uses the object language; and p and q are proposition letters.

(2) As a meta-theorem: '$(((P \dashv3 Q).P) \dashv3 Q)$'. This uses the meta-

language; and P and Q are metalinguistic variables which range over propositions.

(3) As a rule: '$P \dashv Q, P \to Q$.' This also uses the metalanguage.

(4) As a meta-rule: '$P \to Q, P \vdash Q$'. This uses a meta-metalanguage.

As is well-know, methods (3) and (4) are the most appropriate for the texts I am concerned with. Accordingly I shall use '$\to$' as a metalinguistic sign for "formally implies", '$\Rightarrow$' as a metalinguistic sign for "materially implies" (in the medieval sense); and '$\vdash$' as a meta-metalinguistic sign to indicate that from one valid consequence another can be formed. I shall also use '$=$' to indicate mutual implication; and '$P \bigcirc Q$' to indicate that P and Q are compossible. Similarly '$-(P \bigcirc Q)$' will indicate that P and Q are incompatible or that they are not compossible. My other symbols need no explanation. If any reader fears that I am talking of letters rather than propositions, he may insert Quine's corners to his taste.

1. *Truth*

(1.111) $P \to Q, T'P' \vdash T'Q'$

(1.112) $P \to Q, F'P' \vdash T'Q' \lor F'Q'$

(1.121) $P \to Q, T'Q' \vdash T'P' \lor F'P'$

(1.122) $P \to Q, F'Q' \vdash F'P'$

"From the true only the true follows; but the true follows from both the true and the false." [71]

"From the false follows both the false and the true; but the false only follows from the false." [72]

These rules were standard; but one or two later writers did cast some doubt upon them. Dietericus, for instance, said that the true can only follow from the false *per accidens* or by reason of matter rather than of form [73]; and Timplerus argued that the rule applied only to inferences when considered formally. [74] When they were considered materially, it could be seen that the true gives rise only to the true and the false to the false.

(1.211) $P = Q, T'P' \vdash T'Q'$

(1.212) $P = Q, T'Q' \vdash T'P'$

(1.221) $P = Q, F'P' \vdash F'Q'$

(1.222) $P = Q, F'Q' \vdash F'P'$

"From the truth of one equipollent proposition follows the truth of the other, and from the falsity of one follows the falsity of the other." [75]

(1.311) $T^{\iota}P' \to F^{\iota} - P'$
(1.312) $T^{\iota} - P' \to F^{\iota}P'$
(1.321) $F^{\iota}P' \to T^{\iota} - P'$
(1.322) $F^{\iota} - P' \to T^{\iota}P'$

"From the truth of one contradictory follows the falsity of the other; and from the falsity of one follows the truth of the other." [76]

2. *Modal Consequences*

(2.11) $P \to Q, - \diamond - P \vdash - \diamond - Q$

"If the antecedent of a valid consequence is necessary, the consequent similarly is necessary." [77]

This rule is a standard one and none of the earlier authors I have read explicitly considered the case of a necessary antecedent and a possible consequent, even though an analogous rule appears in the inference from an illative conditional to a promissory conditional. However, Pardo could be interpreted as allowing a possible consequent, for the rule he gives is simply that from a necessary antecedent a contingent consequent does not follow.[78] Later in the century Mercado explicitly allowed a possible consequent:

(2.12) $P \to Q, - \diamond - P \vdash - \diamond - Q \lor \diamond Q$

"The contingent cannot follow from the necessary, but the possible can." [79]

He saw no need to point out that an impossible conclusion was debarred.

Carvisius also offered the following rules:

(2.131) $- \diamond - P \to P$
(2.132) $- \diamond - - P \to - P$

"From a necessary proposition whether assertoric [*de inesse*] or negatoric [*de non inesse*] to a simply assertoric proposition there is a formal consequence. For instance, from it is necessary that every swan is white it follows that every swan is white." [80]

He did not explain how this rule was compatible with two others which he gave:

(2.141) $P \rightarrow \lozenge - P . \lozenge P$
(2.142) $-P \rightarrow \lozenge P . \lozenge - P$

"From a simply assertoric proposition to a contingent negatoric proposition and from a simply negatoric proposition to a contingent assertoric proposition there is a formal consequence."[81]

(2.151) $-\lozenge - Q \vdash P \rightarrow Q$

"The necessary follows from anything. That is, any consequence whose consequent is necessary is valid."[82]

This version of the rule appears only in the earlier period. After the mid-sixteenth century it was always replaced with the following version which appeared as early as 1529, in Domingo de Soto:

(2.152) $P \rightarrow Q, \ -\lozenge - Q \vdash -\lozenge - P \vee (\lozenge P . \lozenge - P) \vee -\lozenge P.$

"The necessary follows from anything, that is, the necessary, the contingent, or the impossible."[83]

(2.16) $P . - \lozenge - Q \rightarrow R \vdash P \rightarrow R$

"If from some proposition together with a necessary proposition (or propositions) follows some consequent, that consequent follows from the same proposition without the addition of the necessary proposition (or propositions). This rule is proved because either that proposition to which the necessary is joined is contingent or it is impossible. If it is impossible the whole antecedent is impossible and since anything follows from the impossible, the consequence is valid. If it is contingent, then I ask whether the consequent is impossible. It is clear that it is not, for then from the possible would follow the impossible. Either the consequent is necessary, and then from that contingent proposition that necessary proposition would follow, because the necessary follows from anything; or the consequent is contingent, and then it is clear that the consequent does not follow from the antecedent by reason of the necessary proposition, but by reason of the contingent proposition. Therefore from that contingent proposition without the addition of the necessary the contingent consequent follows no less than it does with the addition of the necessary proposition."[84]

(2.2) $P \to Q, \, \Diamond P \vdash \Diamond Q$

"If the antecedent of a valid consequence is possible, the consequent must be possible." [85]

(2.31) $P \to Q, (\Diamond P . \Diamond - P) \vdash - \Diamond - Q \vee (\Diamond Q . \Diamond - Q)$
(2.32) $P \to Q, (\Diamond Q . \Diamond - Q) \vdash - \Diamond P \vee (\Diamond P . \Diamond - P)$

"From the contingent never follows the impossible, but either the necessary or the contingent; the contingent never follows from the necessary, but from the contingent or the impossible." [86]

(2.41) $P \to Q, \, - \Diamond Q \vdash - \Diamond P$

"The impossible only follows from the impossible." [87]

(2.42) $- \Diamond P \vdash P \to Q$

"From the impossible follows anything; every consequence whose antecedent is impossible is valid." [88]

After the mid-sixteenth century this version of the rule was replaced by the following:

(2.422) $P \to Q, \, - \Diamond P \vdash (- \Diamond - Q \vee (\Diamond Q . \Diamond - Q) \vee - \Diamond Q)$

"From the impossible follows anything, that is, the necessary, the contingent and the impossible." [89]

(2.51) $P \to Q \vdash -(P \bigcirc - Q)$

"In every valid formal consequence the contradictory opposite of the consequent is incompatible with the antecedent of that same consequence." [90]

(2.52) $P \to Q, \, -(Q \bigcirc R) \vdash -(P \bigcirc R)$

"Whatever is incompatible with the consequent is incompatible with the antecedent." [91]

(2.6) $P \to Q, (\dot{P} \bigcirc R) \vdash (Q \bigcirc R)$

"Whatever is consistent with the antecedent is consistent with the consequent.[92]

(2.71) $P \to Q, R \to S, \vdash -(Q \bigcirc S) \to -(P \bigcirc R)$

"Whenever from some antecedents follow some consequents if the consequents are incompatible, the antecedents are also incompatible."[93]

This rule was proved by appeal to rule (3.92), '$P \rightarrow Q, R \rightarrow S, \vdash (P.R) \rightarrow \rightarrow (Q.S)$'. It was argued that if Q and S were repugnant, then the consequent was impossible, and that if P and R were consistent, then their conjunction was possible. This would violate the rule that the possible does not imply the impossible. Hence, if Q and S are incompatible, P and R must also be incompatible, and thus we get rule (2.71).

3. *Other Consequences*

(3.1) $P \rightarrow P$

"From synonym to synonym there is a formal consequence."[94]

(3.21) $P = --P$

"Two negations are equivalent to an affirmative."[95] This rule is usually given in the context of the discussion of term-negation but it clearly applied to the propositions in which the terms appeared as well. Some people also noted that:[96]

(3.22) $-P = ---P$
(3.31) $P, P = Q \vdash Q$
(3.32) $Q, P = Q \vdash P$

"The first type of consequence is when a proposition is inferred from itself or from its equipollent."[97]

(3.4) $P \rightarrow Q, P \vdash Q$

"In every valid consequence, given the antecedent, the consequent is given."[98]

(3.5) $P \rightarrow Q \vdash -Q \rightarrow -P$

"If a consequence is valid, from the contradictory opposite of the consequent follows the contradictory opposite of the antecedent."[99]

(3.61) $P \rightarrow Q, R \rightarrow P \vdash R \rightarrow Q$

"Whatever precedes the antecedent of a valid consequence precedes the consequent."[100]

(3.62) $P \to Q, Q \to R \vdash P \to R$

"Whatever follows the consequent of a valid consequence follows the antecedent."[101]

From this we get the general principle "from first to last" [*de primo ad ultimum*], or the rule that in any sequence of consequences the antecedent of the first entails the consequent of the last, so long as all the intermediary consequences are valid.[102]

(3.71) $(P \cdot Q) \to R \vdash (-R \cdot P) \to -Q$
(3.72) $(P \cdot Q) \to R \vdash (-R \cdot Q) \to -P$

"If a consequence is valid and the antecedent is a conjunction, from the opposite of the consequent together with one part of that conjunction there follows the opposite of the other part."[103]

(3.81) $P \to Q, P = R \vdash R \to Q$
(3.82) $(P \cdot Q) \to R, (P \cdot Q) = (Q \cdot P) \vdash (Q \cdot P) \to R$

"Whatever follows from one proposition follows from another equivalent to it."[104]

This principle is applied to the syllogism, since the transposed premisses are equivalent to the original premisses.

(3.91) $P \to Q, P \to R \vdash P \to (Q \cdot R)$

"If a proposition implies several others, it implies their conjunction."[105]

(3.92) $P \to Q, R \to S \vdash (P \cdot R) \to (Q \cdot S)$

"If from some antecedents follow some consequents, then from the conjunction composed of the antecedents follows the conjunction composed of those consequents."[106]

NOTES

[1] Major, *Consequentie*. Cf. Gebwiler; Greve, lii^{vo}; Eckius, *Summulae*, c; Trutvetter, *Summule*; Caesarius. For two later sources, see Regius, *Libri IV*, 647; Timplerus, 612.
[2] John of St. Thomas, *Formal Logic*, 103. Cf. Pedro de Oña, 111.
[3] Clichtoveus: Le Fèvre, 69.

[4] Cologne, xcixf.

[5] Eckius, *Summulae*, cf. Cf. Major, *Consequentie*; Cologne, xcix; John of Glogovia, lxxviii[vo]. For a later source, see John of St. Thomas, *Formal Logic*, 103.

[6] Marsilius of Inghen, *Parv. Log.*, 201; Hieronymus of St. Mark. For a later source, see Oddus, 55.

[7] Celaya, *Suppositiones*. "Quelibet consequentia in qua consequens formaliter est impossibile: et antecedens formaliter est necessarium est formaliter mala... ...arguendo a disiunctiva composita ex partibus contradicentibus inter se ad copulativam compositam ex partibus contradicentibus inter se consequentia est formaliter mala."

[8] E.g. Gebwiler; Clichtoveus: Le Fèvre, 6[vo].

[9] Pardo, x.

[10] Niphus, *Libros Priorum*, 11[vo]. Cf. Duns Scotus, 287.

[11] See Eckius, *Summulae*, xviii and c[vo]f; Enzinas, *Primus Tractatus*, xx; John of Glogovia, lxxixf; Pardo, x. For an earlier source, see Albert of Saxony, 23[vo].

[12] Celaya, *Suppositiones*.

[13] John of Glogovia, lxxix[vo].

[14] Albert of Saxony, 24. Cf. Cajetan in Strode, 34; Marsilius of Inghen, *Parv. Log.*, 201[vo].

[15] Caubraith, lxviiif; Enzinas, *Primus Tractatus*, xx. Caubraith wrote "Dicitur quod ad consequentiam esse bonam requiritur et sufficit quod secundum aliquam significationem antecedentis formalis virtualis vel propositionis illi correspondentis impossibile sit ita esse sicut per ipsum vel ipsam significatur vel significari potest de significatione totali et adequata quin ita sit sicut per consequens formale virtuale vel propositionem correspondentem significatur vel significari potest manente significatione totali et propositionali antecedentis et consequentis adequate eadem: et hoc dummodo consequens non habeat non significare sicut est annexum: nec tota consequentia se maleficet...."

[16] Caubraith, lxviii[vo].

[17] Pardo, ix[vo]; Enzinas, *Primus Tractatus*, xx; Domingo de Soto, lxxiii.

[18] Enzinas, *Primus Tractatus*, xx. Cf. Eckius, *Summulae*, xviii; Major, *Consequentie*.

[19] Enzinas, *Primus Tractatus*, xx; Celaya, *Suppositiones*; Caubraith, lxviii.

[20] Trutvetter, *Summule*.

[21] Cf. Niphus, *Libros Priorum*, 11[vo].

[22] Almain; Enzinas, *Primus Tractatus*, xx; Domingo de Soto, lxxiii. Pardo, ix[vo].

[23] Caubraith, lxviiif.

[24] Blanchellus Faventinus, 90.

[25] Paul of Venice, *Logica parva*, 27[vo]; Paul of Pergula, *Logica*, 87; Celaya, *Suppositiones*; Domingo de Soto, lxxiii[vo].

[26] Cf. Eckius, *Summulae*, ci; *Lib. Soph.* Niphus, *Libros Priorum*, 12[vo], said that the first was the regulative principle of all consequences, though he also mentioned the second as a candidate (11).

[27] E.g. Greve, liiii[vo]; Gebwiler. The author of *Lib. Soph.* said that two propositions are incompatible if the verification of one falsifies the other.

[28] Cf. Almain; Pardo, xxii[vo].

[29] Cf. Eckius, *Summulae*, ci; Major, *Consequentie*; Pardo, xxii[vo].

[30] E.g. Mainz; Trutvetter, *Summule*; Bartholomaeus de Usingen; Gebwiler.

[31] E.g. Eckius, *Summulae*, ci.

[32] Domingo de Soto, lxxiiiif.

[33] Kesler, 8; Caesarius; Carvisius, 117; Santolaria, 156; Regius *Libri IV*, 648; Scharfius, *Institutiones*, 490; Timplerus, 613.

[34] Campanella, 372; Carbo, 122; Carvisius, 117; Gabriel of St. Vincent, 35; Regius, *Libri IV*, 649; Scharfius, *Institutiones*, 491; Timplerus, 613; Kesler, 9; Fonseca, I 332.

³⁵ Melanchthon, *Erotemata*, 595. Melanchthon was quoted by Regius, *Libri IV*, 648.
³⁶ Vincentius, 49.
³⁷ E.g. Almain; Breitkopf, *Parv. Log.*; Celaya, *Suppositiones*; Domingo de Soto, lxxiiii; Dolz, *Syllogismi*; Eckius, *Summulae*, ci; Enzinas, *Primus Tractatus*, xx; John of Glogovia, lxxviii^{vo}; Gebwiler; Greve, lii^{vo}; Hundt, cli^{vo}; Clichtoveus: Le Fèvre, 65; Niphus, *Libros Priorum*, 11vo; Pardo, xi.
³⁸ Celaya, *Suppositiones*.
³⁹ Celaya, *Suppositiones*; Cologne, ci^{vo}; Dolz, *Syllogismi*; Eckius, *Summulae*, ci^{vo}; Clichtoveus: Le Fèvre, 65; Pardo, xi; Hundt, clii; Mainz. For later sources, see Kesler, 14–16; Carbo, 123; Gabriel of St. Vincent, 35; Fonseca, I 334–336.
⁴⁰ Cajetan in Strode, 35; Strode, 2vo.
⁴¹ Cajetan in Strode, 35f.
⁴² Enzinas, *Oppositiones*, l. ['50'].
⁴³ Dolz, *Syllogismi*. He wrote: "…sed ista diffinitio improbatur quia vel per esse imaginabile cum antecedente intelligitur quod quis posset simul illa apprehendere vel simul illis assentire vel aliquid aliud non ultimum quia non videtur posse dari aliud nec aliquod illorum quia tunc multe essent consequentie sillogistice non formales quia in aliqua tali possumus simul apprehendere antecedens et oppositum consequentis et etiam illis assentire ideo aliter oportet diffinire."
⁴⁴ Kesler, 13.
⁴⁵ Cologne, ciiii; Greve, lii^{vo}; John of Glogovia, lxxix^{vo}; *Lib. Soph.* The author of the latter wrote: "Consequentia illa est bona et formalis cuius consequens formaliter intelligitur in antecedente ut homo currit ergo animal currit. Et dico consequens formaliter intelligi in antecedente quando ex verificationis antecedentis verificatur consequens."
⁴⁶ Paul of Pergula, *Logica*, 87. Cf. Paul of Venice, *Logica parva*, 27vo.
⁴⁷ Javellus, 195–196; Blanchellus Faventinus, 60vo–61; Paul of Venice, *Logica Magna*, 140^{vo}ff.
⁴⁸ Almain; Eckius, *Summulae*, c^{vo}; John of Glogovia, lxxix^{vo}; Greve, liii; Hieronymus of St. Mark; Hundt, cli^{vo}; Major, *Consequentie*.
⁴⁹ Celaya, *Suppositiones*; Domingo de Soto, lxxiiii^{vo}; Pardo, xf.
⁵⁰ Niphus, *Libros Priorum*, 11vo. Niphus draws his material from Duns Scotus, 287f.
⁵¹ Eckius, *Summulae* c^{vo}.
⁵² Pardo, x^{vo}. Cf. Hieronymus of St. Mark.
⁵³ Peter of Spain, *Syncategoremata*, 142f.
⁵⁴ Cologne, c^{vo}.
⁵⁵ Hundt, cli^{vo}.
⁵⁶ John of Glogovia, lxxix^{vo}.
⁵⁷ Enzinas, *Primus Tractatus*, xx^{vo}.
⁵⁸ E.g. Gebwiler; Trutvetter, *Breviarium*.
⁵⁹ Clichtoveus: Le Fèvre, 71.
⁶⁰ Hieronymus of St. Mark; Pardo, xxii.
⁶¹ Niphus, *Libros Priorum*, 12. Cf. Duns Scotus, 288.
⁶² Cf. Pardo, xxii.
⁶³ E.g. John of Glogovia, lxxxi. Cf. Cajetan in Strode, 35; Ferebrich in Strode, 93vo.
⁶⁴ Javellus, 194vo.
⁶⁵ Sermonete in Strode, 3vo.
⁶⁶ Cologne, ciiii.
⁶⁷ Domingo de Soto, lxxiiiif.
⁶⁸ Kesler, 26f. Cf. Carvisius, 118; Mercado, *Commentarii*, 67vo; Toletus, *Introductio*, 179; Fonseca, I 342–344.

[69] Regius, *Libri IV*, 654.

[70] Cologne, ciiii.

[71] Kesler, 22.

[72] Kesler, 24.

[73] Dietericus, 266.

[74] Timplerus, 620.

[75] Alsted, *Systema*, 386.

[76] Alsted, *Systema*, 386. Cf. Kesler, 38.

[77] Almain. Cf. Domingo de Soto, lxxiii[vo]; Enzinas, *Primus Tractatus*, xx[vo]; Celaya, *Suppositiones*; Savonarola. For later sources see Kesler, 25; Carvisius, 118; John of St. Thomas, *Formal Logic*, 126; Mercado, *Commentarii*, 67[vo]; Timplerus, 590; Toletus, *Introductio*, 177.

[78] Pardo, xxii[vo].

[79] Mercado, *Commentarii*, 67f.

[80] Carvisius, 119[vo].

[81] Carvisius, 119[vo].

[82] Celaya, *Suppositiones*. Cf. Hieronymus of St. Mark; Enzinas, *Primus Tractatus*, xx[vo]; Caubraith, cvii[vo].

[83] Kesler, 25. Domingo de Soto, lxxiii[vo]. Cf. note 68.

[84] Hieronymus of St. Mark. Cf. Pardo, xxiiii.

[85] Almain. Cf. Domingo de Soto, lxxiii[vo]. John of Glogovia, lxxx[vo]; Savonarola; Celaya, *Suppositiones*; Cologne, cii[vo].

[86] Kesler, 25–26. Cf. Santolaria, 157; Timplerus, 590; Toletus, *Introductio*, 177; Dietericus, 266. For 2.32 cf. Almain; Domingo de Soto, lxxiiii[vo]; Celaya, *Suppositiones*; Major, *Consequentie*.

[87] Domingo de Soto, lxxiii[vo]. Cf. John of St. Thomas, *Formal Logic*, 126; Mercado, *Commentarii* 67[vo]; Kesler, 26f.

[88] Celaya, *Suppositiones*. Cf. Enzinas, *Primus Tractatus*, xx[vo]; Caubraith, cvii[vo].

[89] Kesler, 26f. Cf. Carvisius, 118; Mercado, *Commentarii*, 67[vo]; Santolaria, 157; Toletus, *Introductio*, 179.

[90] Breitkopf, *Parv. Log.* See earlier discussion.

[91] Hieronymus of St. Mark. Cf. Domingo de Soto, lxxiii[vo]; Eckius, *Summulae*, ci; Major, *Consequentie*; Pardo, xxiii[vo]; Savonarola; Trutvetter, *Summule*. For later sources, see Kesler, 28; Alsted, *Systema*, 385; John of St. Thomas, *Formal Logic*, 126; Mercado, *Commentarii*, 68; Oddus, 58; Timplerus, 590; Pedro de Oña, 112; Fonseca, I 346.

[92] Hieronymus of St. Mark. Cf. Enzinas, *Primus Tractatus*, xx[vo]; Eckius, *Summulae*, ci; Pardo, xxiii[vo]; Fonseca, I 344; Kesler, 27; Alsted, *Systema*, 385; Timplerus, 590.

[93] Hieronymus of St. Mark. Cf. Pardo, lvi[vo].

[94] Eckius, *Summulae*, ci[vo]. Cf. Enzinas, *Primus Tractatus*, xx; Celaya, *Suppositiones*;

[95] Dietericus, 248. Cf. Jungius, 175; Alsted, *Systema*, 356; Titelmanus, 212. For an earlier source, see Eckius, *Summulae*, xi[vo].

[96] Eckius, *Summulae*, xi[vo]; Titelmanus, 212.

[97] Fonseca, I 328. Cf. Carbo, 121–122; Gabriel of St. Vincent, 35. For an earlier source, see Breitkopf, *Parv. log.*

[98] Kesler, 23. Cf. Oddus, 58; Carvisius, 118.

[99] Almain.

[100] Celaya, *Suppositiones*. Most authors give this rule.

[101] Celaya, *Suppositiones*. Most authors give this rule.

[102] Cf. Eckius, *Summulae*, ci; Greve, lvi; Major, *Consequentie*; Pardo, xxiii; Bartholomaeus de Usingen; Javellus, 197f.; Gebwiler; John of Glogovia, lxxxviii[vo].

[103] Celaya, *Suppositiones.* Cf. John of Glogovia, lxxxix[vo]; Major, *Consequentie*; Savonarola.

[104] Enzinas, *Sillogismi*, ii. He said: "…solum quarta figura et prima differunt penes transpositionem premissarum. ergo premisse quarte figure et premisse prime equivalebunt. at quicquid sequetur ex una propositione: sequitur ex alia sibi equivalenti: ergo quicquid sequetur ex premissis prime figure: sequitur ex premissis quarte sibi equivalentibus…."

[105] Clichtoveus: Le Fèvre, 135vo.

[106] Hieronymus of St. Mark.

PROPOSITIONAL CONNECTIVES

1. COMPOUND PROPOSITIONS IN GENERAL

Compound (or hypothetical) propositions were normally said to have a set of properties which distinguished them from categorical propositions.[1] Their parts were not terms but propositions, so that they had no subject and predicate *per se*, although subjects and predicates did of course appear in their constituent parts. Their copula was a connective, not a verb. Their quality depended solely upon the affirmation or negation of the main connective, so that "It is not the case that if the sun shines it is day" was negative, whereas "If the sun does not shine it is not day" was affirmative. Properly speaking they had no quantity, so that a hypothetical proposition could have a contradictory but no contrary. However, they could be said to have something analogous to quantity by virtue of their truth-values and, as I will show, tables of opposition between different kinds of hypothetical propositions were frequently drawn up.

A number of different connectives were discussed. The three most usual were the conditional, the conjunction and the disjunction, but to these were frequently added the rational and the causal. The temporal and the local were also mentioned, and they were normally assimilated to conjunctions, though Fonseca mentioned them in his chapter on conditionals.[2] Examples are "Where the sun shines it is day" and "When the sun shines it is day." Rational propositions according to the Roman grammarian Priscian, are those compound propositions which exhibit such connectives as 'ergo', 'igitur' and 'itaque',[3] and they seem to be in a different category from other compound propositions. The connectives are of the sort which join a sequence of separate propositions to produce an argument, rather than a new proposition. A rational proposition was said to be true just in case all its parts were true and the corresponding conditional was true, which, given the non-truth-functional view of the conditional which prevailed, would justify one in identifying a true rational proposition with a sound argument. That is, it is a valid sequence with true premises and a true conclusion. A causal proposition had to meet the same conditions as a rational proposition, together with the extra condition that there really was a causal connection between antecedent and consequent. A few logicians such as Martinus de Magistris, mentioned that one could validly infer a conditional and a conjunction from both causal and rational propositions,[4] but otherwise no use was made of them, and they were normally assimilated to conditional propositions.[5]

Rational and causal propositions did, however, feature in tables of opposition. Some of these were very elaborate,[6] but the two following examples will give an idea of what was included:

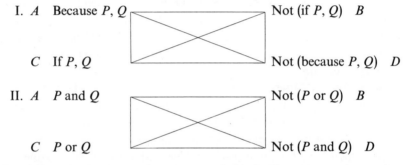

I. *A* Because *P*, *Q*   Not (if *P*, *Q*)   *B*

    C If *P*, *Q*   Not (because *P*, *Q*)   *D*

II. *A* *P* and *Q*   Not (*P* or *Q*)   *B*

    C *P* or *Q*   Not (*P* and *Q*)   *D*

A and *B* were seen as analogous to universal affirmative and negative and *C* and *D* to particular affirmative and negative propositions, because of the relationships which obtained between them. *A* and *B* were contraries, for they could both be false but could not both be true. *C* and *D* were subcontraries because they could both be true, but could not both be false. *A* and *D*, *B* and *C* were contradictories; and *C* and *D* were subalternate to *A* and *B* respectively because they could be inferred from *A* and *B*, although the reverse did not hold. *B* and *D* in the second table were sometimes written as "Not *P* and not *Q*" and "Either not *P* or not *Q*"[7] and Eckius remarked that '*P*.*Q*' and '$-P \vee -Q$' were contradictories even though both were affirmative.[8] Like Caubraith, he claimed that conditional propositions had neither contraries nor subalternates. Neither '*P* $\vee$ *Q*' nor '*P*.*Q*' follow from '*P* $\dashv$ *Q*'; and '$-(P \vee Q)$' and '$-(P.Q)$' are both compatible with '*P* $\dashv$ *Q*'.[9]

2. CONDITIONAL PROPOSITIONS

Conditional propositions were normally said to be true under exactly the same conditions that consequences were said to be formally valid;[10] and even those later logicians who did not mention valid consequences in this context made it clear that there must be more than a merely truth-functional link between antecedent and consequent. It was emphasized that the truth of a conditional did not depend on the truth of the parts, but on the connection between them.[11] "If an ass flies, an ass has wings" was true even though both parts were false because when the antecedent was given, the consequent was also given.[12] The connection was seen as an inferential one, but those logicians who did not discuss valid consequence in general did not offer an alternative discussion of what this inferential connection depended on. Certainly their examples suggest that it depended on the meaning of the terms involved, so that a true conditional would be more closely related to a materially valid consequence than to a formally valid consequence, but in the absence of further textual evidence one can only speculate about what the authors had in mind. It is perfectly possible that the average writer of text-books merely repeated what others had said about the conditional without bothering to consider why they had said it.

Those who linked true conditionals with valid consequences also made the traditional claim that all true conditionals were necessary and all false ones impossible;[13] but the basis for this statement was never examined closely and it seems to rest on a confusion. Pardo said, quite correctly, that if one contradictory is necessary then the other is impossible;[14] and if one takes a series of formulae all of which are valid or necessary, then certainly their negations will be contravalid or impossible. One can even set up a system in which given any formula and its negation at least one is valid, so that every formula is either necessary or impossible. However, ordinary language and many formal systems are not like this, in so far as they allow for contingent formulas which are invalid without being contravalid, so that neither they nor their negations are valid. Our authors seem to have overlooked the possibility that a conditional was false not because it was impossible but because it was contingent, so that the negation of such a conditional would also be false. The confusion may have arisen because of the assimilation of truth to validity. Conditional propositions, being propositions, were said to be true or false, which suggests only two possibilities; but their truth depended on their necessity, and this introduces three possibilities, necessity, impossibility and contingency. They paired truth with necessity, and falsity with impossibility, forgetting about contingency.

Not all fell into the trap equally deeply. Pardo examined "If Adam does not exist, then God does not exist" which seems, he said, to be contingent.[15] He referred back to his discussion of consequences which were valid *secundum quid* and said that although this conditional was false *simpliciter*, it was true *secundum quid*. However, he seems to have been reluctant to draw the desirable conclusions from such examples. Some later authors did explicitly set aside the traditional claim that all true conditionals were necessary and all false ones impossible.[16] For instance Fonseca claimed that many conditionals dealing with future contingents and some dealing with the present such as "If she is a mother, she loves her son" were only probably true and hence were contingent. However, this position is not wholly satisfactory, for if one wishes to say that some conditionals are contingently true, then one cannot define the truth of a conditional in terms of validity. A distinction analogous to that between strict and material implication would have been very useful at this point.

So far nothing has been said to support the claim that some logicians of the fifteenth, sixteenth and seventeenth centuries were implicitly aware of material as opposed to strict implication. Usually historical figures are credited with this implicit awareness on two grounds. The first is their use of consequences valid *ut nunc*, on which I have already commented. The second is their (equally implicit) awareness of two biconditionals, which do not hold when '⊃' is replaced by '⥽', namely:

$$(P \supset Q) \equiv (-P \lor Q)$$
$$(P \supset Q) \equiv -(P.-Q)$$

As we shall see, people did accept the inference from a conditional proposition to the disjunction composed of the negated antecedent and the affirmed consequent, and they also accepted both the rule '$-P \lor Q$, $--P \to Q$' and the principle of double negation. However, in order to obtain the first biconditional one has to discard the explicit condition that the disjunction obtained from a conditional should be a necessary one; and one also has to credit them with the principle of conditionalization in order to obtain '$(-P \lor Q) \supset (P \supset Q)$' from '$-P \lor Q, P \rightarrow Q$'. This last move begs the question, for it can only be made by those who already accept material implication. The same stricture applies to attempts to read the second biconditional into various historical texts. Fonseca, for instance, allowed that from "If P then Q" one could obtain '$-(P.-Q)$',[17] and he also recognized the rule '$-(P.-Q), P \rightarrow Q$' but without conditionalization one cannot get '$-(P.-Q) \supset (P \supset Q)$'. Nor should one wish to, since he explicitly denied the inference from "It is not the case that Socrates is both a stone and not an animal" to "If Socrates is a stone, then he is an animal" on the grounds that the antecedent was true and the consequent false in the light of his earlier definitions.[18]

Some seventeenth century writers do complicate the issue by explicitly allowing relevant equivalences to hold. Jungius said that the negated conjunction, '$-(P.Q)$' was equivalent to two conditionals, 'If P then $-Q$' and 'If Q then $-P$';[19] and Wallis said that a disjunction gives rise to the two conditionals 'If $-P$ then Q' and 'If $-Q$ then P'.[20] Marsh listed the following ways of resolving a disjunction:[21]

> $P \lor Q$ is resolved into: If $-P$ then Q.
> $-(P \lor Q)$ is resolved into: $-($if $-P$ then $Q)$
> $-P \lor -Q$ is resolved into: If P then $-Q$.
> $-(-P \lor -Q)$ is resolved into: $-($if P then $-Q)$.

In their discussion of the conditional proposition they gave no hint that they were aware of more than one interpretation, so whether they should be credited with inconsistency or with an implicit awareness of material implication is a nice point. Marsh is a particularly curious case, for he gave all of De Morgan's laws while firmly defining the disjunction in terms of strong rather than weak disjunction. Perhaps the fairest comment is that their work would have gained much from the introduction of distinctions which they did not themselves see the need for.

The most fruitful way of ascertaining whether logicians were aware of various kinds of conditional is to look at what they had to say about the conditional itself. The vast majority have nothing to add to what has already been discussed; but those who taught or studied in Paris at the beginning of the sixteenth century were more acute. They were aware that '*si*' could have various uses. It might have illative force, but it might also be used in questions, vows, promises, or statements about the conditions necessary for performing some activity as in "If I had books, I would study". [22] The promissory use was that which was singled out for special attention, the most common example being "If you come to me, I will give you a horse". Not all the discussion was relevant to logic, some later authors insisting that the truth of a promissory conditional depended on the presence of an intention, and that even if I gave you a horse, the above conditional would be false if I had not so intended at the time of uttering the sentence. [23]

Caubraith, whose account was the fullest and clearest, began by stating that for the truth of "If Socrates comes to me, I will give him a horse", it is not required either that the antecedent be true or that the consequent be true, nor is it required that it be impossible for the antecedent to be true without the consequent also being true. [24] The necessary and sufficient condition for truth is simply that if the antecedent is true, then the consequent is also true. For the truth of a negated promissory conditional the falsity of the corresponding affirmative is necessary and sufficient, that is, the antecedent should be true and the consequent false. Both Enzinas and Domingo de Soto added a temporal element. [25] They agreed that it was not required that the negation of the consequent should be incompatible with the antecedent, or form an impossible conjunction, but they thought that the conjunction so formed should never be true. Pardo said that it was sufficient tor the truth of a promissory conditional that the conjunction of the antecedent and the negation of the consequent should be false, whether it was possible or impossible, and it was sufficient for the falsity of a promissory conditional that such a conjunction should be true. [26] So far this sounds very much like material implication, but he went on to discuss whether 'If P then Q' was convertible with '$-P \vee Q$'. He decided that it was not because of the case when both P and Q were false. Unless P is true, no one except God knows whether the promissory conditional itself is true because they do not know whether the promise would have been kept or not. He thought that it was a necessary condition for the truth of promissory conditionals that the promise should be fulfilled. [27] Hieronymus of St. Mark agreed with him; but Enzinas made it obvious in his discussion of impossible consequents that he took a promissory conditional to be true when its antecedent was false. Hieronymus of Hangest went further. He said explicitly that it was not required that the promise should be fulfilled, and that since what was involved was the concomitance of the antecedent and consequent, such conditionals were more rightly called '*concomitativa*' than '*promissiva*'.[28]

Caubraith went on to say that promissory conditionals can be either impossible, necessary or contingent. If the antecedent is contingent and the consequent impossible, the conditional is impossible, but it must be noted that here Caubraith is for once in error, as is Major who made the same claim. Enzinas pointed out that "If you come to me, I will turn you into an ass" is not impossible, "as some assert", but true provided that you never come to me. Celaya's example of an impossible promissory conditional, "If God exists then I will give you a horse and I will not give you a horse" is correct, given that the antecedent was regarded as necessary.[29] Caubraith said that if the antecedent is impossible or the consequent necessary, then the conditional is necessary. Otherwise it is contingent. If a promissory conditional turns out to be equivalent to a valid inference when '*si*' is taken illatively, it is necessarily true, but not all those which are equivalent to an invalid inference can be labelled as false or impossible. All illative conditionals imply a promissory conditional with the same terms, but the reverse does not hold. No further rules were given, except by Hieronymus of Hangest [see below], but this one is sufficient to generate a large number.

The distinction between illative and promissory conditionals is closely analogous to that between strict and material implication. That the correspondence is not entirely exact is due to the fact that such men as Pardo were thinking not about truth-functions, but about ordinary language and the nature of the promising activity itself.

In the seventeenth century there is one author who gives the impression that he did distinguish between strict and material implication. This is Dietericus, who began by defining a true conditional in what look like truth-functional terms. "A conditional is judged to be true if when the antecedent is given, so is the consequent," he said.[30] On the next page he said that some conditionals were necessary, "if their parts are linked by a necessary connection," and others were contingent, when it was possible for the antecedent to hold even when the consequent did not.[31] However, I would not wish to place too much emphasis on those few remarks in the absence of a more detailed discussion in the text.

3A. RULES FOR ILLATIVE CONDITIONALS

(1) $P \dashv Q, P \to Q$

"Arguing from a conditional together with its antecedent to the consequent is a formal consequence."[32]

It was noted that in certain cases the consequent can be affirmed. For instance, one can argue '$P \dashv (Q. - Q)$, $(Q. - Q) \to P$.' However, this consequence only holds by virtue of another rule, that governing impossible propositions.[33]

(2) $(P \dashv Q), -Q \to -P$

"Arguing from a conditional together with the negation of the consequent to the negation of the antecedent is a valid consequence."[34]

(3) $(P \dashv Q) = (-Q \dashv -P)$

"From one conditional to a conditional which is composed of the negation of the first consequent as antecedent and the negation of the first antecedent as consequent there is a mutual consequence."[35]

(4.1) $(P \dashv Q) \to (-P \lor Q)$
(4.2) $(-P \lor P) \to (P \dashv P)$

"From an affirmative conditional to a disjunction composed of the negation of the antecedent and the consequent there is a valid formal consequence; but the contrary consequence does not hold unless the parts of that disjunction are formally contradictory or participate in the law of contradictories."[36]

It was noted that the disjunction in (4.1) must be necessary because of the rule that a necessary proposition cannot imply a contingent proposition.[37]

(5) $(P \dashv Q) \to -(P. - Q)$

"... there are conjunctions which are inferred from conditionals as when you infer from this conditional if Socrates is a man he is an animal, this negative conjunction: it is not the case that Socrates is a man and he is not an animal."[38]

(6.1) $(P.Q) \dashv R), (-R.P) \to -Q$
(6.2) $(P.Q) \dashv R), (-R.Q) \to -P$

"Arguing from a conditional whose antecedent is a conjunction together with the negation of the consequent and one part of the conjunction to the negation of the other part is a valid consequence."[39]

(7.1) $(P \dashv (Q \vee R), (P. - Q) \to R$

(7.2) $(P \dashv (Q \vee R), (P. - R) \to Q$

"Arguing from a conditional whose consequent is a disjunction together with the antecedent and the negation of one part of the disjunction to the other part is a valid consequence."[40]

(8.1) $(P.Q) \dashv (R.S), - R.P \to - Q$

(8.2) $(P.Q) \dashv (R.S), - R.Q \to - P$

(8.3) $(P.Q) \dashv (R.S), - S.P \to - Q$

(8.4) $(P.Q) \dashv (R.S), - S.Q \to - P$

"Arguing from a conditional whose antecedent and consequent are conjunctions together with the negation of one part of the second conjunction and the affirmation of one part of the first conjunction to the negation of the other part of the first conjunction is a valid consequence."[41]

(9.1) $P \dashv Q, R \dashv P \to R \dashv Q$

"From every conditional follows another conditional with the same consequent, whose antecedent is antecedent to that of the first conditional."[42]

(9.2) $P \dashv Q, R \dashv P, Q \dashv S \to R \dashv S$

"Arguing from an affirmative conditional to another affirmative conditional which is such that the antecedent of the conditional which is the consequent implies the antecedent of the conditional which is the antecedent, and the consequent of the conditional which is antecedent implies the consequent of the conditional which is consequent, is a valid consequence."[43]

(10) $P \dashv Q \to - \Diamond - (\text{if } P \text{ then } Q)$

"Arguing from a conditional to a categorical with 'necessarily' applying to that whole conditional is a valid consequence."[44]

3B. RULES FOR PROMISSORY CONDITIONALS

(1.1) $P \dashv Q \rightarrow P \supset Q$

"From an illative conditional to a promissory conditional with the same terms is a valid argument, but not the reverse."[45]

(1.2) $P . Q \rightarrow P \supset Q$

"Any affirmative conjunction implies a promissory conditional."[46]

(1.3) $P . -Q \rightarrow -(P \supset Q)$

"Every conjunction which is composed of the antecedent and the opposite of the consequent of an affirmative promissory conditional implies the negative promissory conditional which is the contradictory of the affirmative."[47]

Hieronymus of Hangest also gave *modus ponens* and *modus tollens* for promissory conditionals. He is the only author I know of who provided such a comprehensive listing of inferences involving promissory conditionals.

4. BICONDITIONALS

The higher-order relationship of logical equivalence was frequently discussed, but only Crellius gave a clear account of the biconditional as a propositional connective.[48] He did not introduce any new vocabulary. Instead he contrasted the proposition "If the sun is risen it is day" with the proposition "If a man exists, an animal exists". The second is a case of *consecutio imperfecta*, for it can be used as a premiss only in two valid inferences, *modus ponens* and *modus tollens*, but the first is a case of *consecutio perfecta*, giving rise not only to *modus ponens* and *modus tollens*, but to the inference from consequent to antecedent and from negated antecedent to negated consequent

(1) $P \equiv Q, P \rightarrow Q$
(2) $P \equiv Q, Q \rightarrow P$
(3) $P \equiv Q, -P \rightarrow -Q$
(4) $P \equiv Q, -Q \rightarrow -P$

5. CONJUNCTIONS

There is not much to be said about the conjunction, which was viewed as a purely truth-functional connective. Everyone agreed that a conjunction was true if and only if all its parts were true. More interesting is the attitude of later logicians to the use of the conjunction in inference. Scholastics were usually perfectly at home with the inference from a conjunction to one of its parts, but others regarded it with doubt. Caesarius denied its utility; and Horstius said that nothing could be done with '$P.Q$' as a premiss, since one had already conceded all one might conclude.[49] The one standard inference found in non-scholastic sources was that from a negated conjunction and the assertion of one of its parts to the negation of the other. Oddly enough, it is not to be found in the scholastic sources of the earlier period. This may have something to do with the growing influence of classical authors, for of the five Stoic indemonstrables only the first two were used in the late fifteenth and early sixteenth centuries, unless by such humanists as George of Trebizond, whereas later they were to appear in almost every text-book. The five inferences in question are:

$$P \dashv Q, P \to Q$$
$$P \dashv Q, -Q \to -P$$
$$P \not\equiv Q, P \to -Q$$
$$P \not\equiv Q, -P \to Q$$
$$-(P.Q), P \to -Q$$

(1.1) $T'(P.Q)' \to T'P'$
(1.2) $T'(P.Q)' \to T'Q'$

"From the truth of a conjunction to the truth of either part there is a valid consequence." [50]

(2.1) $-\diamondsuit-(P.Q)=(-\diamondsuit-P.-\diamondsuit-Q)$

"From the necessity of an affirmative conjunction to the necessity of each principal part and the reverse, is a valid consequence. For the necessity of a conjunction it is necessary and sufficient that each part be necessary." [51]

(2.2) $\diamondsuit(P.Q)=(\diamondsuit P.\diamondsuit Q).(P \bigcirc Q)$

"From the possibility of a conjunction to the possibility of each part and their compossibility, and the reverse, is a valid consequence. ...for the possibility of a conjunction it is necessary and sufficient that each part should be possible and the parts should be compossible." [52]

$$(2.3) \qquad -\Diamond(P.Q) = -\Diamond P \vee -\Diamond Q \vee -(P \bigcirc Q)$$

"For the impossibility of a conjunction it is necessary and sufficient that one part should be impossible or that the parts should be incompatible." [53]

$$(2.4) \qquad (\Diamond(P.Q).\Diamond -(P.Q)) =$$
$$= ((\Diamond P.\Diamond -P).(P \bigcirc Q)) \vee ((\Diamond Q.\Diamond -Q).(P \bigcirc Q))$$

"If one part of an affirmative conjunction is contingent and is not incompatible with the other part then the conjunction is contingent, and the reverse. This is enough for if one part is not incompatible with the other it is clear that it is not impossible, for the impossible is incompatible with anything..." [54]

$$(3) \qquad (P.Q) = (Q.P)$$

"Nevertheless in conjunctions and disjunctions there can be simple conversion or transposition of the extremes: for it follows validly "A man is an animal and God exists, therefore God exists and a man is an animal"." [55] The author suggests that the reverse also follows.

$$(4.11) \qquad P.Q \rightarrow P$$
$$(4.12) \qquad P.Q \rightarrow Q$$

"From a conjunction to each of its parts is a formal consequence." [56]

$$(4.21) \qquad -P \rightarrow -(P.Q)$$
$$(4.22) \qquad -Q \rightarrow -(P.Q)$$

"From the destruction of part of a conjunction to the destruction of the whole conjunction is a formal consequence." [57]

$$(5.1) \qquad P.Q \rightarrow P \vee Q$$

"From a conjunction to a disjunction constituted out of the same parts is a formal consequence." [58]

This is so because a conjunction implies each of its parts and these in turn imply a disjunction. [59] In the later period, Mercado gave this rule, but Campanella explicitly rejected it, even though he recognized weak disjunction.[60]

From (5.1) Enzinas derived:[61]

(5.2) $-(P \vee Q) \rightarrow -(P.Q)$
(6) $(P.Q) \rightarrow -(-P.-Q)$

"Arguing from an affirmative conjunction to a negative conjunction whose first principal part contradicts the first part of the affirmative conjunction and whose second contradicts the second is a formal consequence."[62]

(8) $(P.Q) \rightarrow -(P \dashv -Q)$

"From a conjunction to a negative conditional constituted from the first part and the contradictory of the second part of that conjunction is a valid consequence."[63]

(9.1) $P.Q, P \rightarrow R, Q \rightarrow S \vdash R.S$

"Arguing from a conjunction to another conjunction of which one part is inferred from one part of the first conjunction and the other from the other is valid."[64]

(9.211) $P \rightarrow R \vdash P.Q \rightarrow R$
(9.212) $Q \rightarrow R \vdash P.Q \rightarrow R$
(9.221) $P \Rightarrow R \vdash P.Q \Rightarrow R$
(9.222) $Q \Rightarrow R \vdash P.Q \Rightarrow R$

"Whatever follows formally from one part of a conjunction follows from the whole, and whatever follows materially similarly follows materially."[65]

(9.311) $P \rightarrow P, P \rightarrow Q \vdash P \rightarrow P.Q$
(9.312) $Q \rightarrow Q, Q \rightarrow P \vdash Q \rightarrow P.Q$
(9.321) $P \rightarrow P, P \Rightarrow Q \vdash P \Rightarrow P.Q$
(9.322) $Q \rightarrow Q, Q \Rightarrow P \vdash Q \Rightarrow P.Q$

"... arguing from a principal part of an affirmative conjunction to the whole conjunction is not necessarily valid: however, it sometimes holds: but this only materially in a very few instances, as when arguing "Socrates runs therefore Socrates runs and God exists" ... Sometimes it holds formally when one part formally implies each part as in "Socrates runs therefore Socrates runs and Socrates runs or Socrates does not run." As a corollary it follows that when one part of a conjunction implies each part materially or one materially and the other formally that part materially implies the whole conjunction: and if one part of a conjunction implies each part formally that part formally implies the whole conjunction..."[66]

Sometimes these rules appeared in the following guise:[67]

(9.411) $P \to Q \vdash P \to P.Q$
(9.412) $Q \to P \vdash Q \to P.Q$
(9.421) $P \Rightarrow Q \vdash P \Rightarrow P.Q$
(9.422) $Q \Rightarrow P \vdash Q \Rightarrow P.Q$
(9.51) $\Diamond P . \Diamond - P, - \Diamond - Q \vdash P \to P.Q$
(9.52) $\Diamond Q . \Diamond - Q, - \Diamond - P \vdash Q \to P.Q$

"...when a conjunction has one contingent part and one necessary part then arguing from the contingent part to the whole conjunction is valid."[68]

(9.61) $\Diamond P, - \Diamond Q \vdash Q \to P.Q$
(9.62) $\Diamond Q, - \Diamond P \vdash P \to P.Q$

"...when a conjunction is composed of a possible proposition and an impossible proposition, then arguing from the part of the conjunction which is impossible to the whole conjunction is a valid consequence."[69]

(9.71) $- T'Q' \to - T'P' \vdash P \to P.Q$
(9.72) $- T'P' \to - T'Q' \vdash Q \to P.Q$

"...when a conjunction is made out of two parts of which one cannot be true without the other: then arguing from that part of the conjunction which cannot be true without the other to the whole conjunction is a valid consequence as with "You are sitting therefore you are sitting and you are a man."[70]

The last set of rules is that which does not appear in the earlier scholastic sources:

(10.1) $- (P.Q), P \to - Q$
(10.2) $- (P.Q), Q \to - P$

"From the affirmation of one part of a conjunction to the negation of the other is a valid consequence when the major is negative...."[71]

Some authors also listed the possible valid variations on the above. For instance, in the end-papers of one edition of George of Trebizond we find the following:[72]

(10.3)	$-(-P.-Q), -P$	$\rightarrow Q$
(10.4)	$-(-P.-Q), -Q$	$\rightarrow P$
(10.5)	$-(P.-Q), P$	$\rightarrow Q$
(10.6)	$-(P.-Q), -Q$	$\rightarrow -P$
(10.7)	$-(-P.Q), -P$	$\rightarrow -Q$
(10.8)	$-(-P.Q), Q$	$\rightarrow P$

As has already been noted, some problems about the definition of the conditional were raised by the inclusion of the two following equivalences:[73]

(11.1)	$-(P.Q)=(\text{If } P \text{ then } -Q)$
(11.2)	$-(P.Q)=(\text{If } Q \text{ then } -P)$

These are valid if '⊃' is used instead of '⊰', but the texts do not explicitly license such a step.

6. DISJUNCTIONS

There are two kinds of disjunction, the weak disjunction which is true when either one or both of its parts are true, and the strong disjunction which is true when just one part is true. In the earlier part of the period with which I am concerned those logicians who were working in the scholastic tradition took it for granted that the disjunction was to be interpreted in the weak sense. However, those who were influenced by classical sources and most logicians of the later period took it for granted that it was to be interpreted in the strong sense. It was argued that the parts of a disjunction must be opposed to one another;[74] and C. Martinus added that a true disjunction must list all possibilities. It is no use saying that "Either Peter is white or Peter is black," because he may also be red, blue or green.[75] A few logicians recognized that two kinds of disjunction could be given,[76] and Fonseca, Jungius and Pedro de Oña listed inference forms for both weak and strong disjunctions.[77] Of the later scholastics,

John of St. Thomas recognized only the weak disjunction.[78]

(1.1) $T'P' \vee T'Q' = T'(P \vee Q)'$
(1.2) $F'P' . F'Q' = F'(P \vee Q)'$

"For the truth of an affirmative disjunction it is necessary and sufficient that one or the other principal part be true and for falsity that each should be false." [79]

(2.11) $-\diamondsuit-(P \vee Q)=(-\diamondsuit-P \vee -\diamondsuit-Q \vee -(P \bigcirc Q))$

"For the necessity of a disjunction it is necessary and sufficient for either part to be necessary or for the parts to be incompatible." [80]

Later writers offered an alternative to the effect that if one part were necessary the other had to be impossible. [81] Otherwise, it would have been possible for both parts of the disjunction to be true.

(2.12) $-\diamondsuit-(P \not\equiv Q)=$
                         $=((-\diamondsuit-P.-\diamondsuit Q) \vee (-\diamondsuit-Q.-\diamondsuit P) \vee -(P \bigcirc Q))$
(2.2) $\diamondsuit(P \vee Q)=(\diamondsuit P \vee \diamondsuit Q)$

"For the possibility of a disjunction it is necessary and sufficient for one principal part to be possible." [82]

(2.31) $-\diamondsuit(P \vee Q) \rightarrow -\diamondsuit P. -\diamondsuit Q$

"For impossibility it is required that each principal part be impossible." [83]

An alternative rule was offered by later writers on the grounds that when both parts are necessary they are always true, and hence that the disjunction will always be false. [84]

(2.32) $-\diamondsuit(P \not\equiv Q) \rightarrow (-\diamondsuit P. -\diamondsuit Q) \vee (-\diamondsuit-P.-\diamondsuit-Q)$
(2.41) $(\diamondsuit(P \vee Q). \diamondsuit-(P \vee Q))=$
                         $=(((\diamondsuit P. \diamondsuit-P).-\diamondsuit Q) \vee ((\diamondsuit Q. \diamondsuit-Q).-\diamondsuit P) \vee$
                         $\vee (((\diamondsuit P. \diamondsuit-P).(\diamondsuit Q. \diamondsuit-Q)).(P \bigcirc Q)))$

"For contingency it is necessary and sufficient that one part should be contingent and the other impossible or for both to be contingent so long as the parts are not incompatible." [85]

Later writers added an extra clause to the effect that one part may be necessary. If one part is necessary and the other contingent, the disjunction is contingent because if the contingent part is true, the whole disjunction will be false.[86]

(2.42) $(\Diamond(P \vee Q). \Diamond -(P \vee Q)) = (((\Diamond P. \Diamond -P). -\Diamond Q) \vee$
$\vee ((\Diamond Q. \Diamond -Q). -\Diamond P) \vee (((\Diamond P. \Diamond -P). (\Diamond Q. \Diamond -Q)).$
$. (P \bigcirc Q)) \vee ((\Diamond P. \Diamond -P). -\Diamond -Q) \vee$
$\vee ((\Diamond Q. \Diamond -Q). -\Diamond -P))$

A number of people noted that whereas a conjunction followed its weakest part, a disjunction followed its strongest part. That is, if part of a conjunction is false or impossible or contingent the whole conjunction is false, impossible or contingent, whereas if part of a (weak) disjunction is true, necessary or possible, the whole disjunction is true, necessary, or possible.[87]

(3) $P \vee Q = Q \vee P$

"Nevertheless in conjunctions or disjunctions there can be simple conversion or transposition of the extremes..."[88]

(4.11) $P \to P \vee Q$
(4.12) $Q \to P \vee Q$

"Arguing from the principal part of a disjunction to the whole disjunction is a formal consequence."[89]
Pedro de Oña noted that this rule holds only for weak disjunctions.[90]

(4.21) $-(P \vee Q) \to -P$
(4.22) $-(P \vee Q) \to -Q$

"From the destruction of a whole disjunction to the destruction of one of its parts is a formal consequence."[91]

(5.11) $P \vee Q, -P \to Q$
(5.12) $P \vee Q, -Q \to P$

"From a whole disjunction with the destruction of one principal part to the other principal part there is a valid consequence."[92]

(5.211) $P \not\equiv Q, P \to -Q$
(5.212) $P \not\equiv Q, Q \to -P$
(5.221) $P \not\equiv Q, -P \to Q$
(5.222) $P \not\equiv Q, -Q \to P$

"In affirmative disjunctions... there are two figures, if the disjunction is made of incompatible parts.... In the former one part is asserted so that the other is denied; in the latter one part is denied so that the other is asserted." [93]

A complete list of the sixteen possible combinations of negative and affirmative propositions in these rules can be found in George of Trebizond, in the end-papers of the edition cited.

(6.11) $-\Diamond P, (\Diamond Q . \Diamond - Q) \vdash P \vee Q \rightarrow Q$

(6.12) $-\Diamond Q, (\Diamond P . \Diamond - P) \vdash P \vee Q \rightarrow P$

(6.21) $-\Diamond_m P, (\Diamond Q . \Diamond - Q) \vdash P \vee Q \Rightarrow Q$

(6.22) $-\Diamond_m Q, (\Diamond P . \Diamond - P) \vdash P \vee Q \Rightarrow P$

"If there is an affirmative disjunction of which one part is impossible and the other contingent, from that disjunction to the contingent part is a valid consequence. And if the impossible part is materially impossible the consequence will be material and if it is formally impossible the consequence will be formal." [94]

(7.11) $-\Diamond - P, (\Diamond Q . \Diamond - Q) \vdash P \vee Q \rightarrow P$

(7.12) $-\Diamond - Q, (\Diamond P . \Diamond - P) \vdash P \vee Q \rightarrow Q$

(7.21) $-\Diamond_m - P, (\Diamond Q . \Diamond - Q) \vdash P \vee Q \Rightarrow P$

(7.22) $-\Diamond_m - Q, (\Diamond P . \Diamond - P) \vdash P \vee Q \Rightarrow Q$

"If there is a disjunction of which one part is contingent and the other necessary, to the necessary part there is a valid formal consequence if that part is formally necessary, and material if it is materially necessary." [95]

(8.11) $P \rightarrow P, Q \rightarrow P \vdash P \vee Q \rightarrow P$

(8.12) $Q \rightarrow Q, P \rightarrow Q \vdash P \vee Q \rightarrow Q$

(8.21) $P \rightarrow P, Q \Rightarrow P \vdash P \vee Q \Rightarrow P$

(8.22) $Q \rightarrow Q, P \Rightarrow Q \vdash P \vee Q \Rightarrow Q$

"When one part of a disjunction is inferred from each part by a valid consequence, from the disjunction to that part is a valid consequence and not otherwise. And if that part is inferred from one part of the disjunction materially and from the other formally the consequence is material. And if it is inferred formally from each the consequence is formal. It formally follows: Socrates runs and Socrates does not run or Plato disputes, therefore Plato disputes." [96]

The sources cited above also license the following versions of the rules:

(8.31) $Q \to P \vdash P \lor Q \to P$
(8.32) $P \to Q \vdash P \lor Q \to Q$
(8.41) $Q \Rightarrow P \vdash P \lor Q \Rightarrow P$
(8.42) $P \Rightarrow Q \vdash P \lor Q \Rightarrow Q$
(9.1) $-T'P' \to -T'Q' \vdash P \lor Q \to P$
(9.2) $-T'Q' \to -T'P' \vdash P \lor Q \to Q$

"When a disjunction is made from two parts of which one cannot be true unless the other is true, then arguing from the whole disjunction to that part without which the other cannot be true is a valid consequence as in: you are moving or you are running, therefore you are moving."[97]

As has already been noted, some problems about the definition of the conditional were raised by the inclusion of the following inferences:

(10.11) $P \not\equiv Q = P \dashv -Q$
(10.12) $P \not\equiv Q = Q \dashv -P$
(10.21) $P \not\equiv Q = -P \dashv Q$
(10.22) $P \not\equiv Q = -Q \dashv P$[98]
(11.11) $P \lor Q = -P \dashv Q$
(11.12) $P \lor Q = -Q \dashv P$[99]

Marsh added:[100]

(11.21) $-(P \lor Q) = -(-P \dashv Q)$
(11.22) $-(P \lor -Q) = P \dashv -Q$
(11.23) $-(-P \lor -Q) = -(P \dashv -Q)$

The above are valid if '$\dashv$' is replaced by '$\supset$', but the texts do not explicitly license such an interpretation of the conditional.

Jungius gave a number of more elaborate equivalences.[101] For instance:

(12.11) $(P \not\equiv Q) \not\equiv R = P \dashv Q \downarrow R$
(12.12) $(P \not\equiv Q) \not\equiv R = Q \dashv P \downarrow R$
(12.13) $(P \not\equiv Q) \not\equiv R = R \dashv P \downarrow Q$
(12.21) $(P \not\equiv Q) \not\equiv R = -P \dashv Q \not\equiv R$
(12.22) $(P \not\equiv Q) \not\equiv R = -Q \dashv P \not\equiv R$
(12.23) $(P \not\equiv Q) \not\equiv R = -R \dashv P \not\equiv Q$

7. DE MORGAN'S LAWS

These laws are dependent for their validity on the use of the weak disjunction, and it is not surprising that they are usually found only in the earlier sources. There were, however, one or two later logicians who made the mistake of citing these laws when they professed to be dealing only with the strict disjunction.[102]

(1) $P \vee Q = -(-P. -Q)$

"Arguing from an affirmative disjunction to a negative conjunction composed out of contradictory parts is a mutual consequence."[103]

(2) $P.Q = -(-P \vee -Q)$

"From a whole conjunction to a negative disjunction composed of parts contradicting the parts of that conjunction is a formal and mutual consequence."[104]

(3) $-(P \vee Q) = -P. -Q$

"From a negative disjunction to an affirmative conjunction composed of the [contradictory] parts of that disjunction is a mutual consequence."[105]

(4) $-(P.Q) = -P \vee -Q$

"From a negative conjunction to an affirmative disjunction composed of parts contradicting the parts of that conjunction is a mutual consequence."[106]

8. OTHER PROPOSITIONAL CONNECTIVES

Two other propositional connectives were used by Joachim Jungius.[107] He called the first of these *posterior subdisjunctiva* and he described it as a disjunction whose parts cannot both be true but yet can both be false. This is clearly equivalent to non-conjunction or '$P \mid Q =_{\text{def}} -(P.Q)$'. Like other writers, he can also be credited with a knowledge of non-disjunction or '$P \downarrow Q =_{\text{def}} -(P \vee Q)$' by virtue of his use of 'neither-nor'.[108]

Jungius listed a large number of inferences, including those of the following forms:

(1) $P \mid Q, P \to -Q$

(2.11) $(P \lor Q) \lor R, P \downarrow Q \to R$

(2.12) $(P \lor Q) \lor R, -P \to Q \lor R$

(2.21) $(P \not\equiv Q) \not\equiv R, P \not\equiv Q \to R$

(2.22) $(P \not\equiv Q) \not\equiv R, -P \to Q \not\equiv R$

(3.11) $(P \not\equiv Q) \not\equiv R, P \to Q \downarrow R$

(3.12) $(P \not\equiv Q) \not\equiv R, P \not\equiv Q \to -R$

(3.21) $((P \mid Q) \mid (P \mid Q)) \mid R, P \to Q \downarrow R$

(3.22) $((P \mid Q) \mid (P \mid Q)) \mid R, P \mid Q \to -R$

(3.22) is invalid whether one has '$P \mid Q$', '$P \not\equiv Q$' or '$P \lor Q$' as the second premiss.

NOTES

[1] E.g. Eckius, *Summulae*, xvi^{vo}–xviii. For later sources see Pedro de Oña, 109f.; Fonseca, I 194–196, 208–210.

[2] E.g. Eckius, *Summulae*, xvii. For later sources, see Titelmanus, 232; Fonseca, II 200.

[3] Priscian, *Institutionum Grammaticarum libri XVIII* in *Grammatici Latini*, (ed. by H. Keil) Leipzig 1855, III, 100.

[4] Cf. Hieronymus of St. Mark; Domingo de Soto, lxxiiii.

[5] For rational and causal propositions, see e.g. Eckius, *Summulae*, xviif. For later sources, see Campanella, 333; Villalpandeus, 148f; Titelmanus, 231; Pedro de Oña, 111f.; Oddus, 52.

[6] E.g. Caubraith, cxxi. Table I is based on Caubraith; Eckius, *Summulae*, xviii^{vo}; Hieronymus of St. Mark. Table II is based on these; together with Gebwiler; Mainz; Stephanus de Monte; Trutvetter, *Summulae*.

[7] E.g. Mainz.

[8] Eckius, *Summulae*, xviii^{vo}.

[9] Eckius, *Summulae*, xviii^{vo}; Caubraith, cxxf.

[10] E.g. Pedro de Oña, 112; John of St. Thomas, *Formal Logic*, 96; and all commentaries on Peter of Spain's first tract.

[11] E.g. Burgersdijck, 165; Wasius, 101, and many others.

[12] E.g. Alsted, *Systema*, 322; Jungius, 99.

[13] E.g. Caesarius; Campanella, 333; John of St. Thomas, *Formal Logic*, 97; and all commentaries on Peter of Spain's first tract.

[14] Pardo, xxxvii^{vo}.

[15] Pardo, xl^{vo}.

[16] Fonseca, I 198. Cf. Dietericus, 243; Alsted, *Systema*, 322; Polanus, 333. Carbo, 103, echoes Fonseca.

[17] Fonseca, I 194.

[18] Fonseca, I 224.

[19] Jungius, 101, 157. Cf. Kesler, 142.

[20] Wallis, 214. Cf. Fonseca, I 194.

[21] Marsh, 96.

[22] Caubraith, lxviii; Celaya, *Expositio*; Dolz, *Disceptationes*; Enzinas, *Primus Tractatus*,

xx; Eckius, *Summulae*, xvii; Domingo de Soto, lxxvi; Major, *Consequentie*; Pardo, xl^{vo}; Hieronymus of St. Mark.

[23] Alcalá, 17; Oddus, 53.

[24] Caubraith, lxxi^{vo}f. Major, *Consequentie*. Later references to promissory conditionals are found in Mercado, *Commentarii*, 64vo; and Pedro de Oña, 111.

[25] Domingo de Soto, lxxvi; Enzinas, *Primus Tractatus*, xxi.

[26] Pardo, xl^{vo}f. He wrote (xli) "...ad veritatem promissive sufficit quod ex contradictorio consequentis et antecedente fiat copulativa falsa sive sit possibilis sive impossibilis. et ad falsitatem talis promissive sufficit quod ex contradictorio consequentis et antecedente fiat copulativa vera."

[27] Pardo, xl^{vo}. "...ad veritatem propositionis ubi ly si tenetur promissive requiritur adimpletio promissionis... Ex quo sequitur quod non cognoscitur veritas propositionis in qua ly si tenetur promissive donec promissio sit adimpleta."

[28] Hieronymus of Hangest, *Exponibilia*. For text, see appendix.

[29] Celaya, *Expositio*.

[30] Dietericus, 242.

[31] Dietericus, 243.

[32] Celaya, *Expositio*. Most authors give this rule.

[33] Celaya, *Expositio*. Cf. Hieronymus of St. Mark.

[34] Celaya, *Expositio*. Most authors give this rule.

[35] Enzinas, *Primus Tractatus*, xx. Cf. Domingo de Soto, lxxiiii; Clichtoveus: Le Fèvre, 71.

[36] Caubraith, lxx. Cf. Celaya, *Expositio*; Dolz, *Disceptationes*; Pardo, xli; Domingo de Soto, lxxiiii; Enzinas, *Primus Tractatus*, xx^{vo}; Major, *Consequentie*. For an earlier source, see Paul of Venice, *Logica Magna*, 136vo.

[37] Enzinas, *Oppositiones*, lii^{vo}.

[38] Fonseca, I 194.

[39] Dolz, *Disceptationes*. Cf. Hieronymus of St. Mark; Pardo, lvif.

[40] Dolz, *Disceptationes*.

[41] Dolz, *Disceptationes*.

[42] Hieronymus of St. Mark. Cf. Pardo, xlv; Clichtoveus: Le Fèvre, 71.

[43] Caubraith, lxx. Cf. Dolz, *Disceptationes*; Enzinas, *Primus Tractatus*, xx^{vo}.

[44] Caubraith, lxx^{vo}. Cf. Celaya, *Expositio*; Dolz, *Disceptationes*; Enzinas, *Oppositiones*, lii^{vo}. For an earlier source, see Paul of Venice, *Logica Magna*, 138vo.

[45] Caubraith, lxii. Cf. Major, *Consequentie*; Hieronymus of Hangest, *Exponibilia*.

[46] Hieronymus of Hangest, *Exponibilia*.

[47] Hieronymus of Hangest, *Exponibilia*.

[48] Crellius, 240f.

[49] Horstius, 318. Cf. Fonseca, I 434; Isendoorn, 627f.

[50] Hieronymus of St. Mark.

[51] Pardo, lvi^{vo}. Cf. Enzinas, *Primus Tractatus*, xxi^{vo}; Caubraith, lxxx^{vo}; Versor, 34vo; Trutvetter, *Summule*; Trutvetter, *Breviarium*; Eckius, *Summulae*, xvii^{vo}; Dolz, *Disceptationes*; Domingo de Soto, lxxviii; Gebwiler; Hieronymus of St. Mark. For later sources, see Titelmanus, 232; Pedro de Oña, 114; John of St. Thomas, *Formal Logic*, 97; Carbo, 103; Mercado, *Commentarii*, 69.

[52] Pardo, lvi^{vo}f. Cf. references in note 51.

[53] Caubraith, lxxx^{vo}. Cf. references in note 51.

[54] Pardo, lvii^{vo}. Cf. references in note 51.

[55] Gebwiler. Cf. Jungius, 102: "Eadem enim manet ejus sive veritas sive falsitas, quocunque ordine membra proponantur."

[56] Celaya, *Expositio*. Most scholastic authors give these rules. Cf. Kesler, 86; Regius, *Libri IV*, 658; Pedro de Oña, 115.

[57] Clichtoveus: Le Fèvre, 72.

[58] Clichtoveus: Le Fèvre, 73. Cf. Caubraith, lxxxii; Dolz, *Disceptationes*; Domingo de Soto, lxxxiii; Enzinas, *Primus Tractatus*, xxi^vo; Sbarroya, *Expositio primi*, xlii^vo.

[59] Martinus de Magistris.

[60] Mercado, *Commentarii*, 69; Campanella, 380.

[61] Enzinas, *Primus Tractatus*, xxi^vo.

[62] Caubraith, lxxxii.

[63] Martinus de Magistris.

[64] Dolz, *Disceptationes*.

[65] Dolz, *Disceptationes*. Cf. Caubraith, lxxxii.

[66] Caubraith, lxxxii. Cf. Enzinas, *Primus Tractatus*, xxi^vo; Gebwiler; *Lib. Soph. Oxon.* [It does not appear in all versions of the *Lib. Soph.*]

[67] See note 66.

[68] *Lib. Soph. Oxon.*

[69] *Lib. Soph. Oxon.*

[70] *Lib. Soph. Oxon.*

[71] Kesler, 141. Cf. Caesarius; Horstius, 318; and various others.

[72] Cf. Fonseca, I 434–436.

[73] Jungius, 101, 157; Kesler, 142.

[74] Marsh, 72; Burgersdijck, 166. See also Polanus, 151; Dietericus, 246; Caesarius; Crellius, 242; Wallis, 138.

[75] Martinus, *Commentarii*, 263.

[76] Caesarius; Titelmanus, 232; Villalpandeus, 160–161; Toletus, 65; Hunnaeus, *Dialectica*, 176; Carbo, 102; Oddus, 53f. In most cases they correctly attributed the strict disjunction to the *veteres* or *antiqui* such as Cicero and Boethius, and the weak to the *recentiores*. In the fifteenth century Menghus Blanchellus Faventinus (*Logica*, 26f.) had also recognized two kinds of disjunction. He referred to Thomas Aquinas and Algazel as sources for strong disjunction.

[77] Jungius, 105; 159–161. Fonseca I 436–438; Pedro de Oña, 118. Jungius echoed Priscian (*op. cit.*, 97f.) when he called the strong disjunction *disjunctiva* and the weak *subdisjunctiva*.

[78] John of St. Thomas, *Formal Logic*, 96–98.

[79] Enzinas, *Primus Tractatus*, xxi^vo.

[80] Celaya, *Dial. Introd.* Cf. Trutvetter, *Summule* and *Breviarium*; Caubraith, cvi; Enzinas, *Primus Tractatus*, xxi^vo; Pardo, lxii^vo; Hieronymus of St. Mark; Dolz, *Disceptationes*; Domingo de Soto, lxxxiii; Carbo, 103; Tartaretus, *Expositio*, 11; Eckius, *Summulae*, xviii.

[81] Toletus, 68.

[82] Caubraith, cvi. For other references, see note 80.

[83] Caubraith, cvi. For other references, see note 80.

[84] Pedro de Oña, 118.

[85] Enzinas, *Primus Tractatus*, xxi^vo. For other references see note 80.

[86] Pedro de Oña, 118.

[87] E.g. John of St. Thomas, *Formal Logic*, 98; Mercado, *Commentarii*, 69; Domingo de Soto, lxxxiii.

[88] See note 55.

[89] Celaya, *Expositio*. Most earlier authors give these rules. Cf. Kesler, 86; Campanella, 380; Mercado, *Commentarii*, 71; John of St. Thomas, *Formal Logic*, 98.

[90] Pedro de Oña, 118.

[91] Clichtoveus: Le Fèvre, 72vo.
[92] Celaya, *Expositio*. These rules were standard, no matter what interpretation of the disjunction was adopted.
[93] Fonseca, I 436. These rules were standard in later authors.
[94] Caubraith, cviii. Cf. Clichtoveus: Le Fèvre, 74; *Lib. Soph. Oxon.*; Gebwiler.
[95] Caubraith, cviii. Cf. *Lib. Soph. Oxon.*; Gebwiler.
[96] Caubraith, cvii^{vo}. Cf. Enzinas, *Primus Tractatus*, xxii; Gebwiler; *Lib. Soph. Oxon.*
[97] *Lib. Soph. Oxon.*
[98] Jungius, 104.
[99] Jungius, 105. Cf. Wallis, 214; Fonseca, I 194.
[100] Marsh, 96.
[101] Jungius, 104. Cf. Wallis, 140.
[102] Marsh, 97; Carbo, 105.
[103] Enzinas, *Primus Tractatus*, xxii. Cf. Sbarroya, *Expositio primi*, xlii^{vo}; Caubraith, cviii; Domingo de Soto, lxxxiii; Enzinas, *Oppositiones*, lxi. For later sources, see Fonseca, I 224–226; Carbo, 105.
[104] Celaya, *Expositio*. Cf. Caubraith, cviii; Dolz, *Disceptationes*; Domingo de Soto, lxxxiii. For later sources, see Fonseca, I 224; Kesler, 86.
[105] Enzinas, *Oppositiones*, lx^{vo}; Hieronymus of St. Mark; Javellus, 208vo; Clichtoveus: Le Fèvre, 74; Pardo, lxiii^{vo}; Enzinas, *Primus Tractatus*, xxi^{vo}. For a later source, see Fonseca, I 224.
[106] Enzinas, *Oppositiones*, lx^{vo}; Dolz, *Disceptationes*; Hieronymus of St. Mark; Javellus, 208vo; Pardo, lxiii^{vo}; Clichtoveus: Le Fèvre, 73; Enzinas, *Primus Tractatus*, xxi^{vo}. For later sources, see Fonseca, I 226; Mercado, *Commentarii*, 69.
[107] Jungius, 105; 160f.
[108] Jungius, 104, 160f; Cf. Burgersdijck, 302; Wallis, 140. Erastus, 53, gives (3.11).

AN ANALYSIS OF THE RULES FOUND IN
SOME INDIVIDUAL AUTHORS

In the previous two parts I have offered a summary of the rules which someone who had read a number of sixteenth and early seventeenth century logic texts would be acquainted with. However, the reader might well wonder how these rules would be presented by a single author, and I have therefore done two things. In the first place, I have summarized the valid consequences and some, if not all, of the rules for propositional connectives which are to be found in a number of authors, with especial emphasis on those writing in early sixteenth century Paris. In the second place, I have transcribed the texts which serve as the basis for my summaries, and these will be found in the appendix. The reader who wishes to know how the transition was made from one rule to the next, and what explanation was given of each rule, should read the appendix, although I must confess that some of this material has had to be omitted, owing to limitations of space. In one or two cases where a rule is clearly invalid, or clearly belongs to the logic of analyzed propositions, I have omitted it from my summaries.

1. PARIS IN THE EARLY SIXTEENTH CENTURY

A. *Caubraith*[1]

I. Illative Conditionals

(1)	$P \dashv Q, P \to Q$	[II, 3a, 1]
(2)	$P \dashv Q, -Q \to -P$	[II, 3a, 2]
(3a)	$P \dashv Q \to (-P \lor Q)$	[II, 3a, 4.1]
(3b)	$(-P \lor Q) \to P \dashv Q,$ when $-P$ and Q are contradictories.
	E.g. $(-P \lor P) \to P \dashv P$	[II, 3a, 4.2]
(4)	$P \dashv Q, R \dashv P, Q \dashv S \to R \dashv S$	[II, 3a, 9.2]

(5a) $P \dashv Q \rightarrow - \diamondsuit - (\text{if } P \text{ then } Q)$ [II, 3a, 10]
(5b) $-(P \dashv Q) \rightarrow - \diamondsuit - - (\text{if } P \text{ then } Q)$

II. Conjunctions

(1a) $P.Q \rightarrow P$ [II, 5, 4.11]
(1b) $P.Q \rightarrow Q$ [II, 5, 4.12]
(2) $P.Q \rightarrow P \vee Q$ [II, 5, 5.1]

Corollaries

(i) $P.Q \rightarrow -(-P.-Q)$ [II, 5, 6]
(ii) $-(P \vee Q) \rightarrow -P.-Q$ [II, 7, 3]
(iiia) $P \Rightarrow R \vdash P.Q \Rightarrow R$ [II, 5, 9.221]
(iiib) $Q \Rightarrow R \vdash P.Q \Rightarrow R$ [II, 5, 9.222]
(iiic) $P \rightarrow R \vdash P.Q \rightarrow R$ [II, 5, 9.211]
(iiid) $Q \rightarrow R \vdash P.Q \rightarrow R$ [II, 5, 9.212]

(3a) $P \rightarrow P, P \Rightarrow Q \vdash P \Rightarrow P.Q$ [II, 5, 9.321]
(3b) $Q \rightarrow Q, Q \Rightarrow P \vdash Q \Rightarrow P.Q$ [II, 5, 9.322]
(3c) $P \rightarrow P, P \rightarrow Q \vdash P \rightarrow P.Q$ [II, 5, 9.311]
(3d) $Q \rightarrow Q, Q \rightarrow P \vdash Q \rightarrow P.Q$ [II, 5, 9.312]
           E.g. $\vdash P \rightarrow (P.(P \vee -P))$

III. Disjunctions

(1a) $P \rightarrow P \vee Q$ [II, 6, 4.11]
(1b) $Q \rightarrow P \vee Q$ [II, 6, 4.12]
(2a) $P \vee Q, -P \rightarrow Q$ [II, 6, 5.11]
(2b) $P \vee Q, -Q \rightarrow P$ [II, 6, 5.12]
(3a) $P \rightarrow P, Q \Rightarrow P \vdash P \vee Q \Rightarrow P$ [II, 6, 8.21]
(3b) $Q \rightarrow Q, P \Rightarrow Q \vdash P \vee Q \Rightarrow Q$ [II, 6, 8.22]
(3c) $P \rightarrow P, Q \rightarrow P \vdash P \vee Q \rightarrow P$ [II, 6, 8.11]
(3d) $Q \rightarrow Q, P \rightarrow Q \vdash P \vee Q \rightarrow Q$ [II, 6, 8.12]
           E.g. $\vdash ((P.-P) \vee Q) \rightarrow Q$

Corollaries

(ia) $-\diamondsuit_m P, \quad \diamondsuit Q.\diamondsuit -Q \vdash P \vee Q \Rightarrow Q$ [II, 6, 6.21]
(ib) $-\diamondsuit_m Q, \quad \diamondsuit P.\diamondsuit -P \vdash P \vee Q \Rightarrow P$ [II, 6, 6.22]
(ic) $-\diamondsuit P, \quad \diamondsuit Q.\diamondsuit -Q \vdash P \vee Q \rightarrow Q$ [II, 6, 6.11]

(id) $-\Diamond Q, \quad \Diamond P. \Diamond -P \vdash P \vee Q \to P$ [II, 6, 6.12]
(iia) $-\Diamond_m -P, \ \Diamond Q. \Diamond -Q \vdash P \vee Q \Rightarrow P$ [II, 6, 7.21]
(iib) $-\Diamond_m -Q, \ \Diamond P. \Diamond -P \vdash P \vee Q \Rightarrow Q$ [II, 6, 7.22]
(iic) $-\Diamond -P, \quad \Diamond Q. \Diamond -Q \vdash P \vee Q \to P$ [II, 6, 7.11]
(iid) $-\Diamond -Q, \ \Diamond P. \Diamond -P \vdash P \vee Q \to Q$ [II, 6, 7.12]

(4a) $P \vee Q \to -(-P. -Q)$ [II, 7, 1]
(4b) $P \vee Q \to -(-P \vee -Q)$ [II, 7, 2]

B. *Celaya*[2]

I. Consequences

(1) $P \to Q, T`P' \vdash T`Q'$ [I, 1.111]
(2) $P \to Q, F`Q' \vdash F`P'$ [I, 1.122]
(3) $P \to Q, \Diamond P \vdash \Diamond Q$ [I, 2.2]
(4) $P \to Q, -\Diamond Q \vdash -\Diamond P$ [I, 2.41]
(5) $P \to Q, -\Diamond -P \vdash -\Diamond -Q$ [I, 2.11]
(6) $P \to Q, \Diamond Q. \Diamond -Q \vdash -(-\Diamond -P)$ [Cf. I, 2.42]
(7) $-\Diamond P \vdash P \to Q$ [I, 2.42]
(8) $-\Diamond -Q \vdash P \to Q$ [I, 2.151]
(11) $P \to Q \vdash -Q \to -P$ [I, 3.5]

Corollaries

(i) $P.Q \to R \vdash -R.P \to -Q$ [I, 3.71]
(ii) $P.Q \to R \vdash -R.'Q \to -P$ [I, 3.72]
(iii) $P \to Q, -(Q \bigcirc R) \vdash -(P \bigcirc R)$ [I, 2.52]

(13a) $P \to Q, R \to P \vdash R \to Q$ [I, 3.61]
(13b) $P \to Q, Q \to R \vdash P \to R$ [I, 3.62]

II. Conditionals[3]

(1) $P \dashv Q. P \to Q$ [II, 3a, 1]
(2) $P \dashv Q. -Q \to -P$ [II, 3a, 2]
(3) $P \dashv Q \to -P \vee Q$ [II, 3a, 4.1]
(4) $P \dashv Q \to -\Diamond -(\text{if } \text{ then } Q)$ [II, 3a, 10]
(5)   There are two cases in which one can argue

$$P \dashv Q, Q \to P$$

(5a) $P \dashv (Q. -Q), Q. -Q \to P$

(5b) $P \dashv P, P \vdash P$

(6)   There are also certain cases in which one can argue:

$$P \dashv Q, -P \to -Q$$

For an explanation, see 5 above.

III. Conjunctions

(1a) $P.Q \to P$ [II, 5, 4.11]

(1b) $P.Q \to Q$ [II, 5, 4.12]

(3) $P.Q = -(-P \vee -Q)$ [II, 7, 2]

IV. Disjunctions

(1a) $P \to P \vee Q$ [II, 6, 4.11]

(1b) $Q \to P \vee Q$ [II, 6, 4.12]

(2a) $P \vee Q, -P \to Q$ [II, 6, 5.11]

(2b) $P \vee Q, -Q \to P$ [II, 6, 5.12]

(3a) $-\Diamond P \vdash P \vee Q \Rightarrow Q$ [Cf. II, 6, 6.21]

(3b) $-\Diamond Q \vdash P \vee Q \Rightarrow P$ [Cf. II, 6.22]

C. *Clichtoveus: Le Fèvre*[4]

(4) $P \to Q \vdash -Q \to -P$ [I, 3.5]

(5) $-Q \to -P \vdash P \to Q$

(6) $P \to Q, Q \to R \vdash P \to R$ [I, 3.62]

(7a) $-\Diamond P \vdash P \to Q$ [I, 2.42]

(7b) $-\Diamond -Q \vdash P \to Q$ [I, 2.151]

(8) $P \dashv Q . P \to Q$ [II, 3a, 1]

(9) $P \dashv Q . -Q \to -P$ [II, 3a, 2]

(10) $P \dashv Q, R \dashv P \vdash R \dashv Q$ [II, 3a, 9.1]

(11) $P \dashv Q \to -Q \dashv -P$ [Cf. II, 3a, 3]

(14a) $P.Q \to R \vdash -R.P \to -Q$ [I, 6.1]

(14b) $P.Q \to R \vdash -R.Q \to -P$ [I, 6.2]

(15a) $P.Q \to P$ II, 5, 411]

(15b) $P.Q \to Q$ [II, 5, 4.12]

(16a) $-P \to -(P.Q)$ [II, 5, 4.21]

(16b) $-Q \to -(P.Q)$ [II, 5, 4.22]

(19a) $P \to P \lor Q$ [II, 6, 4.11]
(19b) $Q \to P \lor Q$ [II, 6, 4.12]
(20a) $-(P \lor Q) \to -P$ [II, 6, 4.21]
(20b) $-(P \lor Q \to -Q$ [II, 6, 4.22]
(21a) $P \lor Q, -P \to Q$ [II, 6, 5.11]
(21b) $P \lor Q, -Q \to P$ [II, 6, 5.12]
(22a) $-Q \to -((P \lor Q) . -P)$
(22b) $-P \to -((P \lor Q) . -Q)$
(23) $P . Q \to P \lor Q$ [II, 5, 5.1]
(24a) $-(P . Q) \to -P \lor -Q$ [II, 7, 4]
(24b) $-(P . Q) = -P \lor -Q$ [II, 7, 4]
(25) $-(P \lor Q) \to -P . -Q$ [II, 7, 3]
(26) $P \lor Q \to -(-P . -Q)$ [II, 7, 1]
(27) $-(P \lor Q) = -P . -Q$ [II, 7, 3]
(28a) $-\Diamond P, \Diamond Q \vdash P \lor Q \to Q$ [Cf. II, 6, 7.11]
(28b) $-\Diamond Q, \Diamond P \vdash P \lor Q \to P$ [Cf. II, 6, 7.12]

D. *Dolz*[5]

I. Conditionals

(1) $-\Diamond P \to T'P \dashv Q'$
(2) $-\Diamond -Q \to T'P \dashv Q'$
(3) $P \dashv Q, P \to Q$ [II, 3a, 1]
(4) $P \dashv Q, -Q \to -P$ [II, 3a, 2]
(5a) $P . Q \dashv R, -R . P \to -Q$ [II, 3a, 6.1]
(5b) $P . Q \dashv R, -R . Q \to -P$ [II, 3a, 6.2]
(6a) $P \dashv Q \lor R, P . -Q \to R$ [II, 3a, 7.1]
(6b) $P \dashv Q \lor R, P . -R \to Q$ [II, 3a, 7.2]
(7a) $P . Q \dashv R . S, -S . P \to -Q$ [II, 3a, 8.1]
(7b) $P . Q \dashv R . S, -S . Q \to -P$ [II, 3a, 8.2]
(7c) $P . Q \dashv R . S, -R . P \to -Q$ [II, 3a, 8.3]
(7d) $P . Q \dashv R . S, -R . Q \to -P$ [II, 3a, 8.4]
(8a) $P \dashv Q \to -P \lor Q$ [II, 3a, 4.1]
(8b) $-\Diamond -(-P \lor Q) \to P \dashv Q$ [II, 3a, cf. 4.2]
(9) $P \dashv Q, R \dashv Q \to R \dashv Q$ [II, 3a, 9.1]
(10) $P \dashv Q \to -\Diamond -(\text{if } P \text{ then } Q)$ [II, 3a, 10]

II. Conjunctions

(a) Truth and Modality

(1)	$T'P.Q' \rightarrow T'P'.T'Q'$	[Cf. II, 5, 1.1]
(2a)	$F'P' \rightarrow F'P.Q'$	
(2b)	$F'Q' \rightarrow F'P.Q'$	
(3)	$\Diamond(P.Q) \rightarrow \Diamond P.\Diamond Q.P \bigcirc Q$	[Cf. II, 5, 2.2]
(4a)	$-\Diamond P \rightarrow -\Diamond(P.Q)$	[Cf. II, 5, 2.3]
(4b)	$-\Diamond Q \rightarrow -\Diamond(P.Q)$	[Cf. II, 5, 2.3]
(4c)	$-(P \bigcirc Q) \rightarrow -\Diamond(P.Q)$	[Cf. II, 5, 2.3]
(5a)	$\Diamond P.\Diamond -P.P \bigcirc Q \rightarrow \Diamond(P.Q).\Diamond-(P.Q)$	[Cf. II, 5, 2.4]
(5b)	$\Diamond Q.\Diamond -Q.P \bigcirc Q \rightarrow \Diamond(P.Q).\Diamond-(P.Q)$	[Cf. II, 5, 2.4]
(6)	$-\Diamond-(P.Q) \rightarrow -\Diamond-P.-\Diamond-Q$	[Cf. II, 5, 2.1]

(b) Rules

(1a)	$P.Q \rightarrow P$	[II, 5, 4.11]
(1b)	$P.Q \rightarrow Q$	[II, 5, 4.12]
(2)	$P.Q \rightarrow -(-P \vee -Q)$	[II, 7, 2]
(3)	$-(P.Q) \rightarrow -P \vee -Q$	[II, 7, 4]
(4)	$P.Q, P \rightarrow R, Q \rightarrow S \vdash R.S$	[II, 5, 9.1]
(5)	$P.Q \rightarrow P \vee Q$	[II, 5, 5.1]
(6a)	$P \rightarrow R \vdash P.Q \rightarrow R$	[II, 5, 9.211]
(6b)	$Q \rightarrow R \vdash P.Q \rightarrow R$	[II, 5, 9.212]
(6c)	$P \Rightarrow R \vdash P.Q \Rightarrow R$	[II, 5, 9.221]
(6d)	$Q \Rightarrow R \vdash P.Q \Rightarrow R$	[II, 5, 9.222]
(7a)	$-\Diamond-(P.Q) \rightarrow -\Diamond-P$	[Cf. II, 5, 2.1]
(7b)	$-\Diamond-(P.Q) \rightarrow -\Diamond-Q$	[Cf. II, 5, 2.1]
(8a)	$P.Q \rightarrow R \vdash -R.P \rightarrow -Q$	[I, 3.71]
(8b)	$P.Q \rightarrow R \vdash -R.Q \rightarrow -P$	[I, 3.72]

III. Disjunctions

(a) Truth and Modality

(1)	$T'P \vee Q' = T'P' \vee T'Q'$	[II, 6, 1.1]
(2)	$F'P \vee Q' = F'P'.F'Q'$	[II, 6, 1.2]
(3)	$\Diamond(P \vee Q) = \Diamond P \vee \Diamond Q$	[II, 6, 2.2]
(4)	$-\Diamond(P \vee Q) = -\Diamond P.-\Diamond Q$	[II, 6, 2.31]

(5) $-\Diamond-(P\vee Q)=-\Diamond-P\vee-\Diamond-Q\vee-(P\bigcirc Q)$
       [II, 6, 2.11]
(6) $\Diamond(P\vee Q).\Diamond-(P\vee Q)=((\Diamond P.\Diamond-P).(\Diamond Q.\Diamond-Q).$
       $.(P\bigcirc Q))\vee((\Diamond P.\Diamond-P).-\Diamond Q)\vee((\Diamond Q.\Diamond-Q).-\Diamond P)$
       [II, 6, 2.41]

(b) Rules

(1a) $P\to P\vee Q$ [II, 6, 4.21]
(1b) $Q\to P\vee Q$ [II, 6, 4.22]
(2a) $P\vee Q,-P\to Q$ [II, 6, 5.11]
(2b) $P\vee Q,-Q\to P$ [II, 6, 5.12]
(3a) $-\Diamond_m P\vdash P\vee Q\Rightarrow Q$ [Cf. II, 6, 6.21]
(3b) $-\Diamond_m Q\vdash P\vee Q\Rightarrow P$ [Cf. II, 6, 6.22]
(3c) $-\Diamond P\vdash P\vee Q\to Q$ [Cf. II, 6, 6.11]
(3d) $-\Diamond Q\vdash P\vee Q\to P$ [Cf. II, 6, 6.12]

E. *Enzinas*[6]

I. Conditionals

(1) $P\dashv Q, P\to Q$ [II, 3a, 1]
(2) $P\dashv Q,-Q\to-P$ [II, 3a, 2]
(3) $P\dashv Q=-Q\dashv-P$ [II, 3a, 3]
(4) $P\dashv Q=-P\vee Q$ [II, 3a, 4.1]
(5a) $P\dashv Q, R\dashv P\to R\dashv Q$ [II, 3a, 9.1]
(5b) $P\dashv Q, Q\dashv R\to P\dashv R$

II. Consequences

(1) $P\to Q,\Diamond P\vdash-(-\Diamond Q)$ [Cf. I, 2.2]
(2) $P\to Q,-\Diamond-P\vdash-\Diamond-Q$ [I, 2.11]
(3) $P\to Q, F`Q'\vdash F`P'$ [I, 1.122]
(4) $P\to Q, P\bigcirc R\vdash Q\bigcirc R$ [I, 2.6]
(5) $P\to Q,-(Q\bigcirc R)\vdash-(P\bigcirc R)$ [I, 2.52]
(6) $P\to Q, Q\to R\vdash P\to R$ [I, 3.62]
(7) $-\Diamond P\vdash P\to Q$ [I, 2.42]
(8) $-\Diamond-Q\vdash P\to Q$ [I, 2.151]

III. Conjunctions: Truth and Modality

(1)	$T^{\iota}P.Q^{\jmath}=T^{\iota}P^{\jmath}.T^{\iota}Q^{\jmath}$	[II, 5, 1.1, 1.2]
(2a)	$F^{\iota}P^{\jmath} \to F^{\iota}P.Q^{\jmath}$	
(2b)	$F^{\iota}Q^{\jmath} \to F^{\iota}P.Q^{\jmath}$	
(3)	$\Diamond(P.Q)=\Diamond P.\Diamond Q.(P\bigcirc Q)$	[II, 5, 2.2]
(4)	$-\Diamond(P.Q)=-\Diamond P \vee -\Diamond Q \vee -(P\bigcirc Q)$	[II, 5, 2.3]
(5)	$-\Diamond-(P.Q)=-\Diamond-P.-\Diamond-Q$	[II, 5, 2.1]
(6)	$\Diamond(P.Q).\Diamond-(P.Q)=$	

$$=(\Diamond P.\Diamond -P \vee \Diamond Q.\Diamond -Q).(P\bigcirc Q) \qquad \text{[II, 5, 2.4]}$$

IV. Disjunctions: Truth and Modality

(1)	$T^{\iota}P \vee Q^{\jmath}=T^{\iota}P^{\jmath} \vee T^{\iota}Q^{\jmath}$	[II, 6, 1.1]
(2)	$F^{\iota}P \vee Q^{\jmath}=F^{\iota}P^{\jmath}.F^{\iota}Q^{\jmath}$	[II, 6, 1.2]
(3)	$\Diamond(P \vee Q)=\Diamond P \vee \Diamond Q$	[II, 6, 2.2]
(4)	$-\Diamond-(P \vee Q)=-\Diamond -P \vee -\Diamond -Q \vee -(P\bigcirc Q)$	

[II, 6, 2.11]

(5)	$\Diamond(P \vee Q).\Diamond-(P \vee Q)=((\Diamond P.\Diamond -P).-\Diamond Q) \vee$

$\vee((\Diamond Q.\Diamond -Q).-\Diamond P)\vee((\Diamond P.\Diamond -P).(\Diamond Q.\Diamond -Q).$
$.(P\bigcirc Q))$ [II, 6, 2.41]

V. Rules for Conjunctions

(1a)	$P.Q \to P$	[II, 5, 4.11]
(1b)	$P.Q \to Q$	[II, 5, 4.12]
(2a)	$P \to P, P \Rightarrow Q \vdash P \Rightarrow P.Q$	[II, 5, 9.321]
(2b)	$Q \to Q, Q \Rightarrow P \vdash Q \Rightarrow P.Q$	[II, 5, 9.322]
(2c)	$P \to P, P \to Q \vdash P \to P.Q$	[II, 5, 9.311]
(2d)	$Q \to Q, Q \to P \vdash Q \to P.Q$	[II, 5, 9.312]
(3a)	$P.Q \to P \vee Q$	[II, 5, 5.1]
(3b)	$-(P \vee Q) \to -(P.Q)$	[II, 5, 5.2]
(4)	$-(P.Q)=-P \vee -Q$	[II, 7, 4]
(5)	$-(P \vee Q)=-P.-Q$	[II, 7, 3]

VI. Rules for Disjunctions

(1a)	$P \to P \vee Q$	[II, 6, 4.11]
(1b)	$Q \to P \vee Q$	[II, 6, 4.12]

(2a) $P \rightarrow P, Q \Rightarrow P \vdash P \vee Q \Rightarrow P$ [II, 6, 8.21]
(2b) $Q \rightarrow Q, P \Rightarrow Q \vdash P \vee Q \Rightarrow Q$ [II, 6, 8.22]
(2c) $P \rightarrow P, Q \rightarrow P \vdash P \vee Q \rightarrow P$ [II, 6, 8.11]
(2d) $Q \rightarrow Q, P \rightarrow Q \vdash P \vee Q \rightarrow Q$ [II, 6, 8.12]
(3a) $P \vee Q, -P \rightarrow Q$ [II, 6, 5.11]
(3b) $P \vee Q, -Q \rightarrow P$ [II, 6, 5.12]
(4) $P \vee Q = -(-P.-Q)$ [II, 7, 1]

F. *Major* [7]

Consequences

(1) $P \rightarrow Q, T'P' \vdash -F'Q'$ [I, 1.111]

Corollaries

(i) $P \rightarrow Q, -Q \vdash -P$ [I, 3.5]
(ii) $P \rightarrow Q, P \vdash Q$ [I, 3.4]
(iii) $-\Diamond P \vdash P \rightarrow Q$ [I, 2.42]
(iv) $-\Diamond -Q \vdash P \rightarrow Q$ [I, 2.151]
(v) $P \rightarrow Q, -\Diamond Q \vdash -\Diamond P$ [I, 2.41]
(vi) $P \rightarrow Q, \Diamond P \vdash -(-\Diamond Q)$ [Cf. I, 2.2]
(vii) $P \rightarrow Q, -\Diamond -P \vdash -\Diamond -Q$ [I, 2.11]
(viii) $P \rightarrow Q, \Diamond Q. \Diamond -Q \vdash (\Diamond P. \Diamond -P) \vee -\Diamond P$ [I, 2.32]

(3) $P \rightarrow Q \vdash -Q \rightarrow -P$ [I, 3.5]
(5a) $P.Q \rightarrow R \vdash -R.P \rightarrow -Q$ [I, 3.71]
(5b) $P.Q \rightarrow R \vdash -R.Q \rightarrow -P$ [I, 3.72]
(6) $P \rightarrow Q \vdash -(P \bigcirc -Q)$ [I, 2.51]
(7) $P \rightarrow Q, R \rightarrow P \vdash R \rightarrow Q$ [I, 3.61]
(8) $P \rightarrow Q, Q \rightarrow R \vdash P \rightarrow R$ [I, 3.62]
(9a) $P \rightarrow Q, -(R \bigcirc Q) \vdash -(R \bigcirc P)$ [I, 2.52]
(9b) $P \rightarrow Q, R \bigcirc P \vdash R \bigcirc Q$ [I, 2.6]

G. *Pardo*

I. Consequences [8]

(1) $P \rightarrow Q, T'P' \vdash -F'Q'$ [Cf. I, 1.111]
(2) $P \rightarrow Q, \Diamond P \vdash -(-\Diamond Q)$ [Cf. I, 2.2]

(3) $-\Diamond P \vdash P \rightarrow Q$ [I, 2.42]

(4) $P \rightarrow Q, -\Diamond -P \vdash -(\Diamond Q . \Diamond -Q)$ [Cf. I, 2.11]

(5) $-\Diamond -Q \vdash P \rightarrow Q$ [I, 2.151]

(6) $P \rightarrow Q \vdash -(P \bigcirc -Q)$ [I, 2.51]

(7a) $P \rightarrow Q, Q \rightarrow R \vdash P \rightarrow R$ [I, 3.62]

(7b) $P \rightarrow Q, R \rightarrow P \vdash R \rightarrow Q$ [I, 3.61]

(8) $P \rightarrow Q, -(Q \bigcirc R) \vdash -(P \bigcirc R)$ [I, 2.52]

(9) $P \rightarrow Q, (P \bigcirc R) \vdash (Q \bigcirc R)$ [I, 2.6]

(10a) $P \rightarrow Q \vdash -Q \rightarrow -P$ [I, 3.5]

(10b) $P.Q \rightarrow R \vdash -R.P \rightarrow -Q$ [I, 3.71]

(10c) $P.Q \rightarrow R \vdash -R.Q \rightarrow -P$ [I, 3.72]

(11a) $P.Q \rightarrow R, -\Diamond -P \vdash Q \rightarrow R$ [I, 2.16]

(11b) $P.Q \rightarrow R, -\Diamond -Q \vdash P \rightarrow R$ [I, 2.16]

II. Hypothetical Propositions [9]

(1) $P \prec Q, T`P' \rightarrow T`Q'$ [Cf. II, 3a, 1]

(2) $P \prec Q, P \rightarrow Q$ [II, 3a, 1]

(3a) $P \prec Q, -Q \rightarrow -P$ [II, 3a, 2]

(3b) $P \prec Q \rightarrow -Q \prec -P$ [Cf. II, 3a, 3]

(4) $P \prec Q, R \prec P \rightarrow R \prec Q$ [II, 3a, 9.1]

(5a) $T`P.Q' \rightarrow T`P'$ [II, 5, 1.1]

(5b) $T`P.Q' \rightarrow T`Q'$ [II, 5, 1.2]

(6a) $P.Q \prec R \rightarrow -R.P \prec -Q$ [Cf. I, 3.71]

(6b) $P.Q \prec R \rightarrow -R.Q \prec -P$ [Cf. I, 3.72]

(7a) $-\Diamond -(P.Q) \rightarrow -\Diamond -P$ [Cf. II, 5, 2.1]

(7b) $-\Diamond -(P.Q) \rightarrow -\Diamond -Q$ [Cf. II, 5, 2.1]

(7c) $-\Diamond -(P.Q) = -\Diamond -P . -\Diamond -Q$ [II, 5, 2.1]

(8a) $\Diamond(P.Q) \rightarrow \Diamond P$ [Cf. II, 5, 2.2]

(8b) $\Diamond(P.Q) \rightarrow \Diamond Q$ [Cf. II, 5, 2.2]

(8c) $\Diamond(P.Q) \rightarrow (P \bigcirc Q)$ [Cf. II, 5, 2.2]

(8d) $\Diamond(P.Q) = \Diamond P . \Diamond Q . (P \bigcirc Q)$ [II, 5, 2.2]

(8 Cor) $P \rightarrow Q, R \rightarrow S, -(Q \bigcirc S) \vdash -(P \bigcirc R)$ [I, 2.71]

(9a) $\Diamond P . \Diamond -P . (P \bigcirc Q) = \Diamond(P.Q) . \Diamond -(P.Q)$ [II, 5, 2.4]

(9b) $\Diamond Q . \Diamond -Q . (P \bigcirc Q) = \Diamond(P.Q) . \Diamond -(P.Q)$ [II, 5, 2.4]

(10a) $P \rightarrow P \vee Q$ [II, 6, 4.11]

(10b) $Q \rightarrow P \vee Q$ [II, 6, 4.12]

(11a) $P \lor Q, -P \to Q$ [II, 6, 5.11]

(11b) $P \lor Q, -Q \to P$ [II, 6, 5.12]

(12a) $-\Diamond -P \lor -\Diamond -Q \lor -(P \bigcirc Q) \to -\Diamond -(P \lor Q)$

        [Cf. II, 6, 2.11]

(12b) $(\Diamond P.\Diamond -P).(\Diamond Q.\Diamond -Q).(P \bigcirc Q \to$

        $\to \Diamond(P \lor Q).\Diamond -(P \lor Q)$ [Cf. II, 6, 2.41]

(13a) $\Diamond P \to \Diamond(P \lor Q)$ [Cf. II, 6, 2.2]

(13b) $\Diamond Q \to \Diamond(P \lor Q)$ [Cf. II, 6, 2.2]

(14a) $-(P.Q) = -P \lor -Q$ [II, 7, 4]

(14b) $-(P \lor Q) = -P. -Q$ [II, 7, 3]

2. OXFORD IN THE EARLY SIXTEENTH CENTURY

A. *Hieronymus of St. Mark*[10]

I. Consequences

(1) $P \to Q, T'P' \vdash -F'Q'$ [Cf. I, 1.11]

(2) $P \to Q, \Diamond P \vdash -(-\Diamond Q)$ [Cf. I, 2.2]

(3) $-\Diamond P \vdash P \to Q$ [I, 2.42]

(4) $P \to Q, -\Diamond -P \vdash -(\Diamond Q.\Diamond -Q)$ [Cf. I, 2.11]

(5) $-\Diamond -Q \vdash P \to Q$ [I, 2.151]

(6) $P \to Q \vdash -(P \bigcirc -Q)$ [I, 2.51]

(7a) $P \to Q, R \to S, -(Q \bigcirc S) \vdash -(P \bigcirc R)$ [I, 2.71]

(7b) $P \to Q, R \to S \vdash (P.R) \to (Q.S)$ [I, 3.92]

(8a) $P \to Q, Q \to R \vdash P \to R$ [I, 3.62]

(8b) $P \to Q, R \to P \vdash R \to Q$ [I, 3.61]

(9) $P \to Q, -(R \bigcirc Q) \vdash -(P \bigcirc R)$ [I, 2.52]

(10) $P \to Q, P \bigcirc R \vdash Q \bigcirc R$ [I, 2.6]

(11a) $P \to Q \vdash -Q \to -R$ [I, 3.5]

(11b) $P.Q \to R \vdash -R.P \to -Q$ [I, 3.71]

(11c) $P.Q \to R \vdash -R.Q \to -P$ [I, 3.72]

(12a) $P.Q \to R, -\Diamond -Q \vdash P \to R$ [I, 2.16]

(12b) $P.Q \to R, -\Diamond -P \vdash Q \to R$ [I, 2.16]

II. Rules for Hypothetical Propositions

(1) $P \dashv_3 Q, P \to Q$ [II, 3a, 1]

(3)	$P \dashv Q, -Q \to -P$	[II, 3a, 2]
(4)	$P \dashv Q, R \dashv P \to R \dashv Q$	[II, 3a, 9.1]
(5a)	$T'P.Q' \to T'P'$	[II, 5, 1.1]
(5b)	$T'P.Q' \to T'Q'$	[II, 5, 1.2]
(5c)	$P.Q \to P$	[II, 5, 4.11]
(5d)	$P.Q \to Q$	[II, 5, 4.12]
(6a)	$P.Q \to R \vdash -R.P \to -Q$	[Cf. I, 3.71]
(6b)	$P.Q \to R \vdash -R.Q \to -P$	[Cf. I, 3.71]
(7)	$-\diamond-(P.Q) = -\diamond-P.-\diamond-Q$	[II, 5, 2.1]
(8)	$\diamond(P.Q) = \diamond P.\diamond Q.(P \bigcirc Q)$	[II, 5, 5.22]
(11a)	$P \to P \vee Q$	[II, 6, 4.11]
(11b)	$Q \to P \vee Q$	[II, 6, 4.12]
(12a)	$P \vee Q, -P \to Q$	[II, 6, 5.11]
(12b)	$P \vee Q, -Q \to P$	[II, 6, 5.12]

B. *Libellus Sophistarum ad usum Oxoniensium*[11]

I. Conjunctions

(1a)	$F'P' \to F'P.Q'$	
(1b)	$F'Q' \to F'P.Q'$	
(1c)	$T'P'.T'Q' \to T'P.Q'$	
(2a)	$P.Q \to P$	[II, 5, 4.11]
(2b)	$P.Q \to Q$	[II, 5, 4.12]
(3ia)	$P \to Q \vdash P \to P.Q$	[II, 5, 9.411]
(3ib)	$Q \to P \vdash Q \to P.Q$	[II, 5, 9.412]
(3iia)	$\diamond P.\diamond-P, -\diamond-Q \vdash P \to P.Q$	[II, 5, 9.51]
(3iib)	$\diamond Q.\diamond-Q, -\diamond-P \vdash Q \to P.Q$	[II, 5, 9.52]
(3iiia)	$\diamond P.-\diamond Q \vdash Q \to P.Q$	[II, 5, 9.61]
(3iiib)	$\diamond Q.-\diamond P \vdash P \to P.Q$	[II, 5, 9.62]
(3iva)	$P = Q \vdash P \to P.Q$	
(3ivb)	$P = Q \vdash Q \to P.Q$	
(3va)	$-T'Q' \to -T'P' \vdash P \to P.Q$	[II, 5, 9.71]
(3vb)	$-T'P' \to -T'Q' \vdash Q \to P.Q$	[II, 5, 9.72]

II. Disjunctions

(1a)	$T'P' \to T'P \vee Q'$	[Cf. II, 6, 1.1]

(1b) $T'Q' \rightarrow T'P \vee Q'$ [Cf. II, 6, 1.1]

(1c) $F'P'.F'Q' \rightarrow F'P \vee Q'$ [Cf. II, 6, 1.2]

(2a) $P \rightarrow P \vee Q$ [II, 6, 4.11]

(2b) $Q \rightarrow P \vee Q$ [II, 6, 4.12]

(3ia) $P \rightarrow Q \vdash P \vee Q \rightarrow Q$ [II, 6, 8.32]

(3ib) $Q \rightarrow P \vdash P \vee Q \rightarrow P$ [II, 6, 8.31]

(3iia) $\Diamond P . \Diamond - P, \, - \Diamond - Q \vdash P \vee Q \rightarrow Q$ [II, 6, 7.12]

(3iib) $\Diamond Q . \Diamond - Q, \, - \Diamond - P \vdash P \vee Q \rightarrow P$ [II, 6, 7.11]

(3iiia) $- \Diamond P . \Diamond Q \vdash P \vee Q \rightarrow Q$ [II, 6, 6.11]

(3iiib) $\Diamond P . - \Diamond Q \vdash P \vee Q \rightarrow P$ [II, 6, 6.12]

(3iva) $P = Q \vdash P \vee Q \rightarrow P$

(3ivb) $P = Q \vdash P \vee Q \rightarrow Q$

(3va) $- T'Q' \rightarrow - T'P' \vdash P \vee Q \rightarrow Q$ [II, 6, 9.2]

(3vb) $- T'P' \rightarrow - T'Q' \vdash P \vee Q \rightarrow P$ [II, 6, 9.1]

(4a) $P \vee Q, \, - P \rightarrow Q$ [II, 6, 5.11]

(4b) $P \vee Q, \, - Q \rightarrow P$ [II, 6, 5.12]

3. GERMANY IN THE EARLY SIXTEENTH CENTURY

Eckius

I. Consequences[12]

A $P \rightarrow Q \vdash - (P \bigcirc - Q)$ [I, 2.51]

(1) $- \Diamond P \vdash P \rightarrow Q$ [I, 2.42]

Corollary: $P \rightarrow Q \vdash - Q \rightarrow - P$ [I, 3.5]

(2.) $- \Diamond - Q \vdash P \rightarrow Q$ [I, 2.151]

B (a) $P \rightarrow Q, \, - (Q \bigcirc R) \vdash - (P \bigcirc R)$ [I, 2.52]

(b) $P \rightarrow Q, \, P \bigcirc R \vdash Q \bigcirc R$ [I, 2.6]

Corollary: $P \rightarrow Q \vdash - Q \rightarrow - P$ [I, 3.5]

C (a) $P \rightarrow Q, \, R \rightarrow P \vdash R \rightarrow Q$ [I, 3.61]

(b) $P \rightarrow Q, \, Q \rightarrow R \vdash P \rightarrow R$ [I, 3.62]

Corollary: The rule of 'first to last'.

II. Rules for Hypothetical Propositions[13]

(1a) $P . Q \rightarrow P$ [II, 5, 4.11]

(1b) $P.Q \rightarrow Q$ [II, 5, 4.12]
(2a) $P \rightarrow P \vee Q$ [II, 6, 4.11]
(2b) $Q \rightarrow P \vee Q$ [II, 6, 4.12]
(3a) $P \vee Q, -P \rightarrow Q$ [II, 6, 5.11]
(3b) $P \vee Q, -Q \rightarrow P$ [II, 6, 5.12]
(4a) $P \dashv Q, P \rightarrow Q$ [II, 3a, 1]
(4b) $P \dashv Q, -Q \rightarrow -P$ [II, 3a, 2]

4. SPAIN IN THE THIRD DECADE OF THE SIXTEENTH CENTURY

Domingo de Soto

I. Consequences[14]

(1) $P \rightarrow Q, T'P' \vdash T'Q'$ [I, 1.111]
(2) $P \rightarrow Q, F'Q' \vdash F'P'$ [I, 1.122]
(3) $P \rightarrow Q, \diamond P \vdash \diamond Q$ [I, 2.2]
(4) $P \rightarrow Q, -\diamond Q \vdash -\diamond P$ [I, 2.41]
(5) $P \rightarrow Q, -\diamond -P \vdash -\diamond -Q$ [I, 2.11]
(6) $P \rightarrow Q, \diamond Q . \diamond -Q \vdash -(-\diamond -P)$ [Cf. 1, 2.32]
(7) $P \rightarrow Q, -\diamond P \vdash -\diamond Q \vee -\diamond -Q \vee (\diamond Q . \diamond -Q)$ [I, 2.422]
(8) $P \rightarrow Q, -\diamond -Q \vdash -\diamond P \vee -\diamond -P \vee (\diamond P . \diamond -P)$ [I, 2.152]
(9a) $P \rightarrow Q, Q \rightarrow R \vdash P \rightarrow R$ [I, 3.62]
(9b) $P \rightarrow Q, R \rightarrow P \vdash R \rightarrow Q$ [I, 3.61]
(10a) $P \rightarrow Q, -(R \bigcirc Q) \vdash -(R \bigcirc P)$ [I, 2.52]
(10b) $P \rightarrow Q, (R \bigcirc P) \vdash (R \bigcirc Q)$ [I, 2.6]

II. Rules for Conditionals[15]

(1) $P \dashv Q, P \rightarrow Q$ [II, 3a, 1]
(2) $P \dashv Q, -Q \rightarrow -P$ [II, 3a, 2]
(3) $P \dashv Q \rightarrow -P \vee Q$ [II, 3a, 4.1]
(4) $P \dashv Q \rightarrow -Q \dashv -P$ [Cf. II, 3a, 3]

5. SPAIN IN THE SECOND PART OF THE SIXTEENTH CENTURY

Fonseca

I. Consequences[16]

(1a) $P \rightarrow Q, T'P' \vdash T'Q'$ [I, 1.111]

(1b)	$P \to Q,\ T`Q' \vdash T`P' \vee F`P'$	[I, 1.121]
(2a)	$P \to Q,\ F`P' \vdash T`Q' \vee F`Q'$	[I, 1.112]
(2b)	$P \to Q,\ F`Q' \vdash F`P'$	[I, 1.122]
(3a)	$P \to Q,\ -\Diamond - P \vdash -\Diamond - Q$	[I, 2.11]
(3b)	$P \to Q,\ -\Diamond - Q \vdash -\Diamond - P \vee -\Diamond P \vee (\Diamond P . \Diamond - P)$	[I, 2.152]
(4a)	$P \to Q,\ \Diamond P . \Diamond - P \vdash -(-\Diamond Q)$	[Cf. I, 2.31]
(4b)	$P \to Q,\ \Diamond P . \Diamond - P \vdash -\Diamond - Q \vee (\Diamond Q . \Diamond - Q)$	[I, 2.31]
(4c)	$P \to Q,\ \Diamond Q . \Diamond - Q \vdash -(-\Diamond - P)$	[Cf. I, 2.32]
(4d)	$P \to Q,\ \Diamond Q . \Diamond - Q \vdash (\Diamond P . \Diamond - P) \vee -\Diamond P$	[I, 2.32]
(5a)	$P \to Q,\ -\Diamond P \vdash -\Diamond - Q \vee -\Diamond Q \vee (\Diamond Q . \Diamond - Q)$	[I, 2.422]
(5b)	$P \to Q,\ -\Diamond Q \vdash -\Diamond P$	[I, 2.41]
(6)	$P \to Q,\ P \bigcirc R \vdash Q \bigcirc R$	[I, 2.6]
(7)	$P \to Q,\ -(R \bigcirc Q) \vdash -(R \bigcirc P)$	[I, 2.52]
(8a)	$P \to Q,\ R \to P \vdash R \to Q$	[I, 3.61]
(8b)	$P \to Q,\ Q \to R \vdash P \to R$	[I, 3.62]

II. Hypothetical Syllogisms [17]

(1a)	$P \dashv Q,\ P \to Q$	[II, 3a, 1]
(1b)	$P \dashv Q,\ -Q \to -P$	[II, 3a, 2]
(2a)	$-(P.Q),\ P \to -Q$	[II, 5, 10.1]
(2b)	$-(P.Q),\ Q \to -P$	[II, 5, 10.2]
(3a)	$P \not\equiv Q,\ P \to -Q$	[II, 6, 5.211]
(3b)	$P \not\equiv Q,\ Q \to -P$	[II, 6, 5.212]
(3c)	$P \not\equiv Q,\ -P \to Q$	[II, 6, 5.221]
(3d)	$P \not\equiv Q,\ -Q \to P$	[II, 6, 5.222]
(4a)	$P \vee Q,\ -P \to Q$	[II, 6, 5.11]
(4b)	$P \vee Q,\ -Q \to P$	[II, 6, 5.12]

6. GERMANY IN THE EARLY SEVENTEENTH CENTURY

Kesler

I. Consequences [18]

Kesler's eight rules are taken from Fonseca.

II. Hypothetical Propositions [19]

(1a)	$P.Q \to P$	[II, 5, 4.11]
(1b)	$P.Q \to Q$	[II, 5, 4.12]

(2) $\qquad -(P.Q) = \quad P \vee -Q \qquad$ [II, 7, 4]

(3a) $\qquad P \to P \vee Q \qquad$ [II, 6, 4.21]

(3b) $\qquad Q \to P \vee Q \qquad$ [II, 6, 4.22]

NOTES

[1] Caubraith, lxx–lxx^{vo}, lxxxii, cvii^{vo}–cviii. For text, see appendix.

[2] Celaya, *Suppositiones*. For text, see appendix.

[3] Celaya, *Expositio*. For text, see appendix.

[4] Clichtoveus: Le Fèvre, 70vo–74vo. For text, see appendix.

[5] Dolz, *Disceptationes*. For text, see appendix.

[6] Enzinas, *Primus Tractatus*, xx–xxii. For text, see appendix.

[7] Major, *Consequentie*. For text, see appendix.

[8] Pardo, xi–xxiiii. For text, see appendix.

[9] Pardo, xl^{vo}–lxiii^{vo}. For text, see appendix.

[10] For text, see appendix.

[11] For text, see appendix.

[12] Eckius, *Summulae*, ci. For text, see appendix.

[13] Eckius, *Summulae*, cii. For text, see appendix.

[14] Domingo de Soto, lxxiii^{vo}. For text, see appendix.

[15] Domingo de Soto, lxxiiii. For text, see appendix.

[16] Fonseca, I 342–348. For text, see appendix.

[17] Fonseca, I 432–438. For text, see appendix.

[18] Kesler, 22–29. For text, see appendix.

[19] Kesler, 86. For text, see appendix.

CHAPTER IV

FORMAL LOGIC. PART TWO:
THE LOGIC OF ANALYZED PROPOSITIONS

It is tempting to dismiss the logic of analyzed propositions offered in the fifteenth, sixteenth and seventeenth centuries as the mere repetition of Aristotelian syllogistic, and it is true that very little attempt was made to expand the list of inferences offered. Such non-Aristotelian elements as appeared were usually derived from early medieval sources, and the majority of the textbook discussions were wholly pedestrian, derivative and interchangeable one with another. However, it would be a mistake to suppose that the study of syllogistic in this period had nothing to offer us, for it turns out upon examination that on those occasions when an explanation is offered the way the system was interpreted is of great interest and some originality.

The main features can be described very briefly. It was made clear that those sentences which entered into syllogistic inferences were to be interpreted extensionally. Both subject and predicate referred to an individual or group of individuals at a given time or times; and the function of the copula was accordingly two-fold. It indicated the temporal range of reference [see section on ampliation]; and it asserted an identity between the members of the subject class and some, if not all, members of the predicate class. Furthermore, it was made clear that valid inferences were valid whether the subject class had members or not. In those cases where validity seemed to depend upon the existence of a given group of individuals, a separate premiss to that effect was added, so that the existential presuppositions of the system were made explicit. It should not be supposed that this interpretation is precisely that of the modern first-order quantificational calculus, for universal propositions were taken to have existential import, and universal affirmative propositions were taken to be false if the subject class was empty. Moreover, the domain of individuals in terms of which a sentence was interpreted was carefully restricted. A modern logician would interpret a quantified proposition such as "All men are animals" in relation to a finite or infinite domain, some of whose members are also members of the classes of men and of animals (or of whom the relevant predicates are true), but a sixteenth century logician would consider only individuals that were men and individuals that were animals.

After an introductory survey of categorical propositions and the relations which were thought to obtain among them, I shall examine the details of this interpretation as they are to be found in the discussion of personal supposition and the related topic of suppositional ascent and descent. I shall then examine the syllogistic system in the light of this interpretation.

SECTION I

THE RELATIONSHIPS BETWEEN PROPOSITIONS

1. THE QUALITY AND QUANTITY OF PROPOSITIONS

Before the relationships between categorical propositions can be determined, something must be said of their properties. At its simplest, a categorical proposition consists of a subject, a predicate and a copula, though the copula and the predicate may be joined together as in "A man runs", where 'runs' is equivalent to 'is running'. Before such a proposition can function within a logical system it normally has to have a sign of quantity such as 'all' or 'some' added to it, to indicate whether it is a universal or a particular proposition. An indefinite proposition such as "A man runs" was taken to have the force of a particular proposition, though this depended to some extent upon content. "Man is an animal" was more likely to be interpreted as having the force of "All men are animals".[1] Propositions containing singular terms such as 'Socrates' or 'this man' as subject or predicate or both were also admitted to the system. If just the predicate was singular, then the proposition was taken to have a standard form; but if the subject was singular, the proposition was called a singular proposition, and was treated as non-standard. More will be said of the precise interpretations given to quantified and singular propositions in the section on suppositional descent.

A standard quantified categorical proposition was also said to have one of two qualities, affirmative and negative; and it was assumed that as a result all standard propositions fell into one of four groups, universal affirmative (A), universal negative (E), particular affirmative (I) and particular negative (O). However, the question of just when a proposition is properly called negative is not as easy to answer as might be supposed. One can argue on the basis of the texts that there are three kinds of negation, the negation of a term, the negation of a predicate, and the negation of a proposition; and that the presence of either of the first two kinds of negation does not necessarily cause the proposition as a whole to be negative. A proposition is negated, and hence is negative, when the negation sign is placed in front of the proposition in such a way as to deny the entire proposition, whether it is categorical or hypothetical; but in most examples of categorical propositions, the negation sign appears somewhere within the proposition. It may even be built into the subject or predicate term; and these cases must be examined in more detail.

Eckius discussed three kinds of term-negation.[2] In the first place there was *negatio negans*, by which a term was simply denied, and nothing was asserted in its place. In the second place, there was *negatio infinitans*, by which a term was not only denied, but everything else was signified. For instance, 'non-man' does not refer to men but does refer to everything which is not a man. He pointed out that the disjunction of a finite with an infinite term extended over everything in the universe, and that if the finite term were transcendent then the corresponding infinite term must be fictitious. This was so because a transcendent term such as 'being' or 'existent' was taken to refer to everything, or to the universal class, while a so-called fictitious term referred only to what was imaginary, or to the null-class. If the finite term were fictitious, as is 'chimera', then the corresponding infinite term, 'non-chimera', referred to the universal class. In the third place, there was *negatio privans*, when the negation is included in the meaning of the term. For instance, 'blind' is applied to animals which have been deprived of the vision they are by nature capable of. Neither privative nor infinite terms deny the copula, Eckius said, and as a result no proposition can be called negative on the sole grounds that it contains either privative or infinite terms. However, as will be seen below, certain close relations were taken to exist between propositions with infinite terms and explicitly negative propositions.

Of *negatio negans* Eckius simply remarks that if the negation sign comes after the copula, the copula is not denied and hence the proposition is affirmative. Latin usage was such that a distinction was drawn between "*S* is not *P*" [*S non est P*] and "*S* is not-*P*" [*S est non P*], though none was drawn between "*S* is not-*P*" [*negatio negans*] and "*S* is non-*P*" [*negatio infinitans*]. However, English usage is such that term-negation of the first type (i.e. 'not *P*') is clearly related to predicate-negation, or the case in which "the predicate is removed from the subject"[3]; and the two

seem to raise identical problems. If we consider propositions of the form
"All *S* is not *P*" and "Some *S* is not *P*" we see that they could be interpreted in two ways. We could take them as affirming not-*P* of *S*, or we
could take them as denying *P* of *S*. In the first case, the sentence could be
called affirmative; in the second case it could be called negative. Although
the ambiguity is not so apparent in Latin, it is nevertheless the case that
one can ask the question whether the negation is internal to an affirmative
proposition, or whether it applies to the proposition as a whole, thus
rendering it negative. Moreover, the recognition of *negatio negans* and
the manipulation of negation signs in the rules of equipollence make it
clear that some further analysis of negation is needed for Latin as well
as for English sentences. F. Sommers has suggested drawing a distinction
between the term copulas 'is' and 'isn't', and predicative affirmation
and denial, for which he used 'iss' and 'ain't'.[4] Thus "Some *S* is not *P*"
could be written as either "Some *S* iss what isn't *P*" (affirmative predication) or "Every *S* ain't what is *P*" (negative predication). However, there
is no need to retain the notion of predicate-negation at all, for the propositions in question can be rewritten so as to employ either proposition-
negation or the second kind of term-negation (i.e. 'non-*P*'). If one wishes
to emphasize the negative aspect of "All *S* is not *P*", then one can write
"It is not the case that some *S* is *P*"; if one wishes to emphasize the
affirmative aspect, one can write "All *S* is non-*P*". Unfortunately the
latter method does not necessarily preserve logical equivalence [see be-
low], so it is better to adopt the former. This will give us the following
set of standard categorical propositions:

A	All *S* is *P*
E	It is not the case that some *S* is *P*.
I	Some *S* is *P*
O	It is not the case that all *S* is *P*.

While I wish it to be borne in mind that standard categorical propositions
can be put into a standard form which exhibits their quality clearly and
unambiguously, I shall nevertheless revert to the traditional form for the
purposes of subsequent discussion. Moreover, I shall make no attempt
to translate propositions into the notation of the first-order quantificational calculus for reasons which become apparent in the discussions of

existential import and of suppositional descent. I shall use the following symbolism:

$$A \quad SaP$$
$$E \quad SeP$$
$$I \quad SiP$$
$$O \quad SoP$$

non-S, non-P $\quad \bar{S}, \bar{P}$

Not $\quad -$

Singular terms $\quad x, y$

members of the subject/predicate class exist: $\quad S! \quad P!$

affirmative copula of a singular proposition: $\quad =$

negative copula of a singular proposition: $\quad \neq$

Thus, '$(\bar{S}e\text{-}\bar{P}).\bar{S}!$' is read: "No non-$S$ is not non-P and there are non-Ss." '$x = P$' is read "A named individual is a member of a class P", eg. "Socrates is a man." 'Six', on the other hand, will be used to translate "Some man is Socrates."

2. OPPOSITION

Categorical propositions of standard form were thought to stand in three relations to one another, those of opposition, equipollence and conversion. Opposition related propositions with the same terms whose truth-values were or could be different; equipollence related propositions with the same terms whose truth-values were necessarily the same; and conversion concerned the transformation of one proposition into another proposition with the same terms but a different form. I shall begin with opposition.

The square of opposition which appeared in all non-Ramist textbooks is as follows:

SaP	contraries	SeP
subalterns	contradictories contradictories	subalterns
SiP	subcontraries	SoP

It was explained in terms of the following rules:

(1.11) $T`(SaP)` \rightarrow F`(SeP)`$
(1.12) $T`(SeP)` \rightarrow F`(SaP)`$
(1.13) $\Diamond(F`(SaP)` . F`(SeP)`)$

"The law of contraries is such that if one is true, the other is false, and not the reverse. However, they may both be false when the matter is contingent, e.g. "Every man is white", "No man is white"."[5]

To prove the first point, Clichtoveus argued that if 'All A is B' is true, then both A and B can be verified of the same singular term, C. If 'C is A' and 'C is B' are both true, then 'Some A is B' is true. If 'Some A is B' is true, then its contradictory 'No A is B' is false. Since this is the contrary of 'All A is B', it follows that two contraries cannot both be true.[6]

(1.21) $F`SiP` \rightarrow T`SoP`$
(1.22) $F`SoP` \rightarrow T`SiP`$
(1.23) $\Diamond(T`SiP` . T`SoP`)$

"The law of subcontraries is such that if one is false, the other is true, and not the reverse. However, they may both be true when the matter is contingent."[7]

To prove that they cannot both be false, Clichtoveus argued that if 'Some A is B' is false, then its contradictory 'No A is B' is true. If 'No A is B' is true, then its contrary 'All A is B' is false. If 'All A is B' is false, then its contradictory 'Some A is not B' is true. Hence it follows that two subcontraries cannot both be false.[8]

(1.31) $T`SaP` = F`SoP`$
(1.32) $T`SoP` = F`SaP`$
(1.33) $T`SeP` = F`SiP`$
(1.34) $T`SiP` = F`SeP`$

"The law of contradictories is such that if one is true, the other is false and vice versa, for there is no material such that both can be true or both be false."[9]

(1.41) $T`SaP` \rightarrow T`SiP`$
(1.42) $T`SeP` \rightarrow T`SoP`$
(1.43) $F`SiP` \rightarrow F`SaP`$
(1.44) $F`SoP` \rightarrow F`SeP`$

"The law of subalternates is such that if one universal is true the particular is true, and not the reverse, for the universal can be false when its particular is true. And if the particular is false, the universal is false, and not the reverse."[10]

Paul of Pergula also gave squares of opposition for the cases where either subject or predicate or both were infinite terms.[11]

It should be noted that, despite some modern criticism, all the above inferences are valid given the interpretation of quantified propositions which had been adopted. If one assumes that when the subject class is empty, all affirmative propositions are false and all negative propositions are true, it follows that no two contraries can be true, and that sub-alternation must hold. If 'SaP' is false, then 'SiP' will also be false; and the same can be said of 'SeP' and 'SoP'.

3. EQUIPOLLENCE

Three rules dealt with the equipollence of contradictories, contraries and subalternates.

(2.11) $-(SaP) = SoP$
(2.12) $-(SeP) = SiP$
(2.13) $-(SiP) = SeP$
(2.14) $-(SoP) = SaP$

"If to some sign, whether universal or particular, a negation is prefixed, [the proposition] is equivalent to its contradictory."[12]

(2.21) $Sa - P = SeP$
(2.22) $Se - P = SaP$

"If some universal sign is followed by a negation, [the proposition] is equivalent to its contrary."[13]

(2.23) $Si - P = SoP$
(2.24) $So - P = SiP$

Fonseca remarked that the rule for contraries also applied to sub-contraries, although unlike Paul of Pergula, he gave no examples.[14] In opposition, John of St. Thomas argued that subcontraries could not enter into the relation of equipollence at all.[15] If the particular sign were preceded by a negation, he said, the proposition would become universal; and if the subject were followed by a negation, we would have either a formally negative proposition such as "Some man is not white", or a useless repetion, as in "Some man is not not white". Most authors did not mention the matter. Of those who did, Fonseca is clearly right, as can be shown with the help of a symbolization in which "Some S is not P" can be written either as 'SoP' or as '$Si-P$'.

(2.31) $-(Sa-P)=SiP$
(2.32) $-(Se-P)=SoP$
(2.33) $-(Si-P)=SaP$
(2.34) $-(So-P)=SeP$

"If a universal or a particular sign is preceded and followed by a negation, [the proposition] is equivalent to its subaltern."[16]

We thus obtain the following square of opposition:

SaP	contraries	SeP
$-(Si-P)$		$-(SiP)$
$Se-P$		$Sa-P$
$-(SoP)$		$-(So-P)$
subalterns		subalterns
SiP		SoP
$-(SeP)$		$-(Se-P)$
$-(Sa-P)$		$-(SaP)$
$So-P$	contraries	$Si-P$

contra dictories
contra dictories

4. SIMPLE AND ACCIDENTAL CONVERSION

The first two kinds of conversion were expressed in the following rules:

(3.11) $SeP=PeS$
(3.12) $SiP=PiS$

"Simple conversion occurs when a predicate is formed from a subject, and vice versa, with the quality and quantity being kept the same. The universal negative and the particular affirmative are converted in this way."[17]

(3.21) $SaP \rightarrow PiS$
(3.22) $SeP \rightarrow PoS$

"Conversion *per accidens* occurs when a predicate is formed from a subject and vice versa, with the quality being kept the same but the quantity being changed. In this way a universal negative is converted into a particular negative and a universal negative into a particular affirmative." [18]

Javellus pointed out that conversion *per accidens* could be proved with the aid of simple conversion and subalternation, and he described the proofs as follows: [19]

$$SaP \rightarrow SiP \qquad (1.41)$$
$$\underline{SiP \rightarrow PiS \qquad (3.12)}$$
$$SaP \rightarrow Pis$$

$$SeP \rightarrow PeS \qquad (3.11)$$
$$\underline{PeS \rightarrow PoS \qquad (1.42)}$$
$$SeP \rightarrow PiS$$

Niphus raised the wider question of whether all the rules of conversion could be proved by appeal to other rules when he asked whether they were enthymemes or not. [20] He said that those who responded affirmatively to this question did so on the grounds that Aristotle had said all arguments could be reduced to syllogistic form. He offered the following examples of reduction:

(3.11) by *Cesare*: SeP
                                     $\underline{PaP}$
                                     PeS
(3.21) by *Darapti*: SaS
                                     $\underline{SaP}$
                                     PiS
(3.12) by *Datisi*: SaS
                                     $\underline{SiP}$
                                     PiS

Niphus rejected these proofs on two grounds: there were only two terms instead of the three which are necessary for a syllogism; and propositions of the form 'Every A is A' are ridiculous.

Further rules were offered for propositions containing singular terms:

(3.311) $x = y . = . y = x$
(3.322) $x \neq y . = . y \neq x$

"A singular proposition with a singular predicate is converted simply both when it is affirmative and when it is negative: e.g. Marcus is Tullius, therefore Tullius is Marcus; John is not Peter, therefore Peter is not John."[21]

(3.321) $x = P \rightarrow Pix$
(3.322) $x \neq P \rightarrow Pex$
(3.323) $x \neq P \rightarrow Pox$

"A singular proposition with a common predicate is converted *per accidens*, e.g. Socrates is a man therefore a man is Socrates. It is the same with negative propositions, e.g. Socrates is not a man, therefore no man is Socrates."[22]

Fonseca added that in the latter case one could also convert the singular proposition into a particular negative proposition. Thus "Socrates is not a stone" converts into both "Some stone is not Socrates" and "No stone is Socrates."[23]

(3.331) $Sax \rightarrow x = S$
(3.332) $Six \rightarrow x = S$
(3.333) $Sex \rightarrow x \neq S$

"If they consist of a common subject and a singular predicate, the affirmatives and the universal negatives are said to be converted *per accidens* into singulars in this way: Every or some philosopher is Socrates, therefore Socrates is a philosopher; No shoemaker is Socrates, therefore Socrates is not a shoemaker. However, particular negatives are not to be converted for true *conversae* and false *convertentes* can be given, as when you say Some philosopher is not Socrates, therefore Socrates is not a philosopher."[24]

A number of authors warned their readers that care must be taken to preserve the properties of those terms which were being converted.[25] It was particularly important to preserve ampliation, and a case typical

of those cited is "A man is dead". This should be converted to "He is
dead who is or was a man".[26] Similarly, "A man was an animal" should
be converted to "An animal which was, was a man who is or was". The
supposition and appellation of terms should also be preserved. One
cannot argue "A dog his master knows, therefore knowing his master is
a dog" [*canis dominum suum cognoscit, igitur cognoscens dominum suum
est canis*], since this violates the rules of appellation whereby the first
proposition merely implies that the dog recognizes the man who is his
master, whereas the second implies that he has a concept of his master.
The correct conversion is to "His master knowing is a dog" [*dominum
suum cognoscens est canis*]. It was also necessary for valid conversion to
supply whatever was implicit in the antecedent, as in "No one runs,
therefore nothing running is a man". Gebwiler concluded his list of
errors to be avoided by commenting that if it was noted that the terms in
antecedent and consequent should be synonymous, that it should be
appropriate to transpose the terms, that the consequence should be valid,
and that what is implicit in one proposition should be explicit in the other,
then all difficulties would be evaded.

One puzzle case about conversion was discussed by Robert Caubraith
at the beginning of the sixteenth century: that is, the proposition "No *a* is
a predicate".[27] Even assuming that this is true, i.e. that the term '*a*' is not
a predicate in any existent proposition, it will immediately become false
upon conversion. One suggested solution was that '*a*' should be replaced
by a synonym '*b*', but this can be circumvented by a new formulation,
"a never is nor ever will be a predicate either in itself or through a
synonym". Caubraith concluded that if one assumes the truth of such a
proposition, one cannot convert it, for that the proposition should be
converted is not compossible with the first assumption. Similarly, he
said, if one assumes that no proposition now existing has or will have a
convertens, it follows that "A man is an animal" cannot be converted.

Another difficulty raised by John of St. Thomas in the seventeenth
century concerned the existential import of converted propositions.[28]
Some people, he said, objected to the conversion of the universal
affirmative proposition on the grounds that "Every white man is a
man, therefore some man is a white man" can have an antecedent which
is true, because it is necessary and a consequent which is false, because
in fact no white man exists. In effect, he replied by referring back to the

distinction between natural and accidental supposition, and by claiming
that both antecedent and consequent must be interpreted in the same
way. If 'est' is taken accidentally, then the terms suppose for existent
men, and both antecedent and consequent are false when there are no
white men. On the other hand, if 'est' is abstracted from time and the
propositions are to be viewed as necessary, then 'white' must be verified
not according to actuality, but according to possibility [*non debet ibi
verificari secundum existentiam sed secundum possibilitatem*]. Under this
interpretation the inference in question can be rephrased as "Every
possibly-white man is a man, therefore some man is a man who is
possibly white". Both antecedent and consequent will be true, and
necessarily true, even when no men are white. Indeed, he could have
added, they will be true even when there are no men, for terms with
natural supposition extend over (or are ampliated to) possible as well as
actual beings. He could presumably have replied more briefly by remarking that the interpretation necessary to the claim that the inference is
invalid violates the rule that the type of supposition should be the same
in antecedent and consequent, since the terms 'man' and 'white man'
were taken to have natural supposition in the first proposition and to
have accidental supposition in the second proposition. He would not
have fared so well in solving his problem had he been committed to an
interpretation of necessary propositions in terms of concept-inclusion,
rather than in terms of reference to an expanded domain of objects. The
moment one can claim to be talking about possible men, one can also
claim to be talking about possibly-white possible men, and it becomes
plausible to assert that "Some men are white men" is a necessary truth;
whereas if a necessary truth is such that the subject-concept includes the
predicate-concept, then "Some men are white men" is surely contingent.

5. CONVERSION BY CONTRAPOSITION

Peter of Spain and many other logicians gave the following rules for
contraposition:

(4.1) $SaP = \bar{P}a\bar{S}$
(4.2) $SoP = \bar{P}o\bar{S}$

"Conversion by contraposition occurs when a predicate is formed from the subject and vice versa, and the same quality and quantity are retained, but finite terms are changed to infinite. In this way a universal affirmative is converted to a universal affirmative, and a particular negative is converted to a particular negative."[29] Other authors emphasized that the resulting inferences were mutual.[30]

Two further rules were sometimes added:

(4.11) $SaP \rightarrow \bar{P}i\bar{S}$
(4.21) $SeP \rightarrow \bar{P}o\bar{S}$

The following proofs were offered:[31]

$$SaP \rightarrow \bar{P}a\bar{S} \qquad (4.1)$$
$$\bar{P}a\bar{S} \rightarrow \bar{P}i\bar{S} \qquad (1.41)$$
$$\overline{SaP \rightarrow \bar{P}i\bar{S}}$$
$$SeP \rightarrow SoP \qquad (1.42)$$
$$SoP \rightarrow \bar{P}o\bar{S} \qquad (4.2)$$
$$\overline{SeP \rightarrow \bar{P}o\bar{S}}$$

Jungius distinguished between two kinds of contraposition. Posterior contraposition was the standard kind; but prior contraposition was such that the quality varied and the inferences were not (in his view) mutual.[32] What he offered were these laws of partial contraposition:

(4.31) $SaP \rightarrow \bar{P}eS$
(4.32) $Sa\bar{P} \rightarrow PeS$
(4.33) $\bar{S}aP \rightarrow \bar{P}e\bar{S}$
(4.4) $SoP \rightarrow \bar{P}iS$

Various rules of obversion also appeared in the context of the discussion of conversion by contraposition. The simplest versions were as follows:

(5.11) $SeP = Sa\bar{P}$
(5.12) $SoP = Si\bar{P}$

"A negative with a finite predicate is equivalent to an affirmative with an infinite predicate, if the same quantity is preserved."[33]

(5.21) $SaP \rightarrow Se\bar{P}$
(5.22) $SiP \rightarrow So\bar{P}$

"From an affirmative to a negative without the constancy of the subject, the predicate being varied with respect to finite and infinite, is a valid inference."[34]

A number of authors rejected the rules for conversion by contraposition as they were given by Peter of Spain. Some did so on the grounds that contraposition was not a true case of conversion, since infinite terms were not synonymous with finite terms;[35] but others did so on the grounds that the resulting inferences were invalid.[36] The problem was caused by two standard assumptions: that propositions with infinite terms are affirmative (unless they contain some other sign of negation), and that affirmative propositions whose subjects do not suppose are false, whereas the corresponding negative propositions are true. Four kinds of counter-example were produced.[37] First, there are those affirmative propositions whose predicate terms are transcendental. The inference from "All men are beings" to "All non-beings are non-men" is invalid because there are no non-beings, and hence the consequent is false. Second, there are those affirmative propositions whose terms normally suppose but which can be false in some circumstances. "All men are animals, therefore all non-animals are non-men" has a false consequent if only men exist.[38] Third, there are those negative propositions whose subject terms are fictitious. In "Some chimera is not an animal, therefore some non-animal is not a non-chimera" the antecedent is true, because it is negative, but the consequent is false because its contradictory, "All non-animals are non-chimeras", is true.[39] Fourth, there are those negative propositions whose terms normally suppose but which can be false in some circumstances. Before the creation of the world "Some man is not an animal" was true, but "Some non-animal is not a non-man" was false, since its contradictory "All non-animals are non-men" was true.[40] Similar counter-examples can be produced to invalidate those rules of obversion which have a negative antecedent and an affirmative consequent. For instance, "Some chimera is not an animal" is true, but "Some chimera is a non-animal" is false, given the standard assumptions mentioned above.

Menghus Blanchellus Faventinus dealt with the problem cases by examining two possibilities, "of which the first is easier and the second more subtle."[41] The first involved the simple denial that transcendent terms, or terms such as 'chimera' which lack a referent, could be made

---

infinite.[42] To add a negation to a word such as 'being' will destroy its nature, he said, and if there are no roses then one cannot speak of a non-rose. The second possibility involved the claim that two useful principles could be extracted from Boethius. One was the principle that infinite terms could be verified both of non-beings and of beings, so that "A chimera is a non-man" is just as true as "An ass is a non-man".[43] Given simple conversion, it followed that "A non-man is a chimera" was also true. He noted that this principle entailed the rejection of the inference from 'S is P' to 'S exists', at least in the case of infinite terms. The other principle was that by which "Some non-animal is not a non-man" was equivalent to "Some non-animal is a man", or '$\bar{P}o\bar{S} = \bar{P}iS$'. With these principles in hand he was able to argue that the supposed counter-examples were in fact valid. For instance, given that no rose exists, "Some rose is not a substance" is true and so is "Some non-substance is not a non-rose", since the latter is equivalent to "Some non-substance is a rose".

The most usual solution to the problem cases involved the use of *constantia*, or an extra premiss which asserted the existence of those objects without which the inference would be invalid.[44] Such a premiss could be false, but if it were, then the entire antecedent would be false, and it would no longer be possible to have a true antecedent and a false consequent. In the case of particular negative propositions, the extra premiss required for valid contraposition and obversion asserted the existence of members of the subject class of the original antecedent; in the case of universal affirmative propositions the extra premiss asserted the existence of members of the subject class of the consequent. Most people had an existential proposition of the form "Man is" as their extra premiss, [45] but Enzinas preferred one in which 'is' was used predicatively (*tertius adiectus* or *adiacens*) and he wrote "Man is a man".[46] Unless it was claimed that 'man' had natural supposition in such a context, the effect would be the same, for "Man is man" is false if there are no men. Hieronymus of St. Mark and Pardo both claimed that in the case of universal affirmative propositions two extra premisses were required, the second of which asserted the existence of members of the predicate class of the consequent;[47] but this move was unnecessary. If we assume that 'All As are B' is true and that some non-Bs exist, then it follows that there are non-As. As long as something exists, then that thing is either an A or a non-A. If there are no non-As, then everything, including non-Bs, is an A, but to claim that any non-B is an A contradicts the original assumption that all As are B. Hence, either the antecedent is false or there are non-As. In neither case do we need an extra premiss to ensure validity.

With the extra premiss in hand, we obtain the following rules:

(6.1) $SaP, \bar{P}! \to \bar{P}a\bar{S}$
(6.2) $SoP, S! \to \bar{P}o\bar{S}$

"Conversion by contraposition is a consequence in which from one proposition, given the constancy of the subject or of the opposite of the predicate, is inferred another proposition whose subject is the term contradictory to the predicate [of the first] and whose predicate is the term contradictory to the subject of the first, the same quality being preserved... and the same quantity...."[48]

(7.11) $SeP, S! \to Sa\bar{P}$
(7.12) $SoP, S! \to Si\bar{P}$

"Arguing from a negative to an affirmative, the predicate being varied with respect to finite and infinite, given the constancy of the subject of the negative, is a valid inference."[49]

We also have one part of the original equivalences in (5.11) and (5.12):

(7.21) $Sa\bar{P} \to SeP$
(7.22) $Si\bar{P} \to SoP$

"From an affirmative with an infinite predicate to a negative with a finite predicate, both having the same subject and quantity, is a formal consequence."[50]

(5.21) and (5.22) remain unaltered, but we can also add:

(7.31) $Se\bar{P}, S! \to SaP$
(7.32) $So\bar{P}, S! \to SiP$

"From a negative with an infinite predicate with the constancy of the subject to an affirmative with a finite predicate is a necessary consequence."[51]

Formal proofs were offered for both (6.1) and (6.2). The most detailed proofs are found in Caubraith,[52] but others followed a similar pattern.[53]

Caubraith's proofs are as follows:

A. (1) $SaP \rightarrow Se\bar{P}$ (5.21)
    (2) $\bar{P}! \rightarrow \bar{P}!$ Valid consequence (3.1)
    (3) $SaP, \bar{P}! \rightarrow Se\bar{P}, \bar{P}!$ (1), (2) Valid Consequence (3.92)
    (4) $Se\bar{P} \rightarrow \bar{P}eS$ (3.11)
    (5) $Se\bar{P}, \bar{P}! \rightarrow \bar{P}eS, \bar{P}!$ (2), (4) Valid Consequence (3.92)
    (6) $\bar{P}eS, \bar{P}! \rightarrow \bar{P}a\bar{S}$ (7.11)
    (7) $SaP, \bar{P}! \rightarrow \bar{P}a\bar{S}$ (3)–(6). First to last: see discussion of valid consequence (3.62)

B. (1) $SoP, S! \rightarrow Si\bar{P}$ (7.12)
    (2) $Si\bar{P} \rightarrow \bar{P}iS$ (3.12)
    (3) $\bar{P}iS \rightarrow \bar{P}o\bar{S}$ (5.22)
    (4) $SoP, S! \rightarrow \bar{P}o\bar{S}$ (1)–(3) First to last

If any equivalences analogous to (4.1) and (4.2) are to be proved, then an additional rule is required, which allows the inference of S! Three versions of such a rule are obtainable.

(8.11) $SaP \rightarrow S!$
(8.12) $SiP \rightarrow S!$
(8.13) $x = P \rightarrow x!$

"From an affirmative proposition in which 'is' is used predicatively, there follows an affirmative proposition in which 'is' is used existentially." [54]

Various exceptions were made to this rule. [55] It did not hold for ampliative terms such as 'dead' or 'future'; and some people denied that it held for essential predicates when these were thought to involve natural supposition. [56] The following corollaries were seen to hold.: [57]

(8.21) $-S! \rightarrow -(SaP)$
(8.22) $-S! \rightarrow -(SiP)$
(8.23) $-x! \rightarrow -(x = P)$

Again, ampliative terms were excluded. One cannot argue "Adam is not, therefore Adam is not dead." [58]

Given (8.11) we can now argue in the following manner:

(1) $SaP \rightarrow S!$ (8.11)

(2) $SaP \rightarrow Se\bar{P}$ (5.21)
(3) $SaP \rightarrow Se\bar{P}, S!$ (1), (3) Valid consequence (3.91)
(4) $Se\bar{P}, S! \rightarrow SaP$ (7.31)

$$SaP = Se\bar{P}, S!   (3), (4)$$

Similar proofs can be produced for other cases of obversion and contraposition. However, I shall leave the reader to supply his own, as they are not to be found in the texts I am discussing.

NOTES

[1] Eckius, *Summulae*, cii, supports this view when he says, "Ab indefinita ad universalem in materia naturali est bona consequentia... ut homo est risibilis ergo omnis homo est risibilis."

[2] Eckius, *Summulae*, xif. Cf. Hieronymus of St. Mark.

[3] Peter of Spain, *Summulae*: Bocheński, 1.10, 4; de Rijk, 5, defined a negative categorical proposition as one in which the predicate was removed from the subject. The definition was commonplace in our period.

[4] F. Sommers, 'The Calculus of Terms', *Mind* **79** (1970) 6.

[5] Peter of Spain, *Summulae*: Bocheński, 1.16, 6; de Rijk, 7. I am quoting Peter of Spain since most texts followed him.

[6] Clichtoveus: Le Fèvre, 61vo.

[7] Peter of Spain, *Summulae*: Bocheński, 1.17, 6; de Rijk, 7.

[8] Clichtoveus: Le Fèvre, 61vo.

[9] Peter of Spain, *Summulae*: Bocheński, 1.17, 6; de Rijk, 7.

[10] Peter of Spain, *Summulae*: Bocheński, 1.17, 6; de Rijk, 7.

[11] Paul of Pergula, *Logica*, 13.

[12] Peter of Spain, *Summulae*: Bocheński, 1.25, 8; de Rijk, 10. De Rijk omits "tam universali quam particulari", but this phrase is found in early printed editions. Cf. Versor, 36.

[13] Peter of Spain, *Summulae*: Bocheński, 1.25, 8f.; de Rijk, 10.

[14] Fonseca, I 150–152. Cf. Paul of Pergula, *Logica*, 15.

[15] John of St. Thomas, *Formal Logic*, 85.

[16] Peter of Spain, *Summulae*: Bocheński, 1.25, 9; de Rijk, 10.

[17] Peter of Spain, *Summulae*: Bocheński, 1.18, 6; de Rijk, 8.

[18] Peter of Spain, *Summulae*: Bocheński, 1.20, 7; de Rijk, 8.

[19] Javellus, 43vo.

[20] Niphus, *Libros Priorum*, 9. Cf. I. Thomas, 'Kilwardby on Conversion', *Dominican Studies* **6** (1953) note 22, 74f., for the medieval antecedents of this way of proving the rules of conversion.

[21] Gebwiler.

[22] Gebwiler.

[23] Fonseca, I 156.

[24] Fonseca, I 156.

[25] Most of the material in this paragraph comes from Gebwiler. Cf. Breitkopf, *Compendium*; Mainz.

[26] Breitkopf, *Compendium*.

[27] Caubraith, liii. Cf. Tartaretus, *Expositio*, 10.

[28] John of St. Thomas, *Cursus*, 195f.

[29] Peter of Spain, *Summulae*: Bocheński, 1.20, 7; de Rijk, 8.

[30] Jungius, 120; John of St. Thomas, *Formal Logic*, 86.

[31] Clichtoveus: Le Fèvre, 67^{vo}f.

[32] Jungius, 120.

[33] Jungius, 88. Cf. Blanchellus Faventinus *Logica* 135vo; Javellus, 45.

[34] Caubraith, lvii^{vo}; Enzinas, *Primus Tractatus*, xlii^{vo}; Clichtoveus: Le Fèvre, 67. For a later source, see John of St. Thomas, *Cursus*, 194.

[35] Gebwiler; Niphus, *Libros Priorum*, 9vo; Clichtoveus: Le Fèvre, 66vo. For later sources, see Isendoorn, 531; Newton, 68.

[36] Caubraith, lvii^{vo}; Celaya, *Expositio*; Clichtoveus: Le Fèvre, 68vo; Domingo de Soto, lxix^{vo}; Enzinas, *Primus Tractatus*, xlii^{vo}; Gebwiler; Hieronymus of St. Mark; Tartaretus, *Expositio*, 10; Trutvetter, *Summule*.

[37] Caubraith, lvii^{vo}. Cf. Domingo de Soto, lxxi^{vo}; Eckius, *Summulae*, xvi; Enzinas, *Primus Tractatus*, xlii^{vo}; Gebwiler; Hieronymus of St. Mark; Mainz; Pardo, xl^{vo}.

[38] Pardo, xl^{vo}, gives this example.

[39] Clichtoveus gives this explanation in Clichtoveus: Le Fèvre, 68vo.

[40] Caubraith, lvii^{vo}. Presumably he had in mind that before the creation no man existed, but God, who is a non-animal, did exist.

[41] Blanchellus Faventinus, 135vo.

[42] Cf. Clichtoveus-Le Fèvre, 68.

[43] Enzinas, *Primus Tractatus*, xlii^{vo}, speculated that Peter of Spain had this principle in mind when he gave his unqualified rules of contraposition. Enzinas himself rejected the principle.

[44] Caubraith, lvii^{vo}; Clichtoveus: Le Fèvre, 67^{vo}f.; Celaya, *Expositio*; Enzinas, *Primus Tractatus*, xlii^{vo}; Hieronymus of St. Mark; Pardo, xl^{vo}. For a later source, see John of St. Thomas, *Cursus*, 194.

[45] E.g. Caubraith, lvii^{vo}.

[46] Enzinas, *Primus Tractatus*, xlii^{vo}.

[47] Pardo, xl^{vo}.

[48] Caubraith, lvii^{vo}.

[49] Caubraith, lvii^{vo}. Cf. Clichtoveus: Le Fèvre, 67; Enzinas, *Primus Tractatus*, xlii^{vo}; Strode, 25vo; Almain. For a later source, see John of St. Thomas, *Cursus*, 194.

[50] Clichtoveus: Le Fèvre, 67. Cf. Strode, 25vo; Almain.

[51] Clichtoveus: Le Fèvre, 67.

[52] Caubraith, lvii^{vo}. For the text, see appendix.

[53] Clichtoveus: Le Fèvre, 67vo; Domingo de Soto, lxxi^{vo}; Enzinas, *Primus Tractatus*, xlii^{vo}. For a later source, see John of St. Thomas, *Cursus*, 194. For proofs not using *constantia*, see Javellus, 44^{vo}f.; Versor, 31f.

[54] Almain. Cf. *Lib. Soph.*; Marsilius of Inghen, *Parv. Log.*, 212vo; Melanchthon, *Erotemata*, 634; Eckius, *Summulae*, cii; Mainz; Bartholomaeus de Usingen. For later sources, see Kesler, 88; Carvisius, 119vo.

[55] Peter of Spain, *Syncategoremata*; 155; Paul of Pergula, *Logica*, 99; Breitkopf, *Parv. Log.*; Mainz; Eckius, *Summulae*, cii.

[56] Cologne, cxii. They explained that because the inference only held for accidental predicates, it was materially rather than formally valid. Cases of essential predicates were also excluded by Breitkopf, *Parv. Log.* Carvisius, 119vo, said that the rule did not hold "in materia necessaria."

[57] Eckius, *Summulae*, cii.

[58] Marsilius of Inghen, *Parv. Log.*, 212vo.

SUPPOSITION THEORY AND QUANTIFICATION

1. The divisions of personal supposition

Terms were said to have personal supposition when they referred (or were taken to refer) to individuals rather than to universals, and when they were used rather than mentioned. Natural personal supposition, which belonged to terms in necessary propositions, and did not presuppose the existence of the individuals in question, has already been discussed, and was of far less importance in determining the range of reference of propositions than was accidental personal supposition. Indeed, for the purposes of debate necessary propositions were sometimes treated as if their terms had accidental rather than natural supposition, and as if the existence of referents was presupposed.[1] There were several main divisions of accidental supposition. The first was between discrete and common supposition; though it should be noted that some authors did not see discrete supposition as a subdivision of personal supposition at all.[2] Common supposition was divided into determinate and confused; and confused supposition was in turn normally divided into three, distributive, merely confused, and collective, though again some variations in these categories can be found.

A term was said to have discrete supposition when it referred to just one object, not merely as a matter of fact, but by virtue of its properties. That is, such terms as 'sun' and 'world' were not discrete, because they could be used to refer to a number of suns and worlds, had more been created. Proper names had discrete supposition, except in certain contexts. 'Nero' could be used to refer to tyrants and 'Crassus' to refer to rich men, and in such cases these names had common supposition.[3] Nouns could also have discrete supposition when they were preceded by a demonstrative such as 'this' or when they were supplemented by a relative clause as in "A man who is called Jesus healed me."[4] Sentences containing terms with discrete supposition were not thought to raise any problems of analysis; and there was obviously no attempt to produce any sentence or set of sentences to which they were logically equivalent by virtue of containing a singular term, since such attempts usually involved the introduction of singular terms into contexts where they did not originally appear.

The other four kinds of personal supposition involved those cases where a common term referred (or was taken to refer) to the members of a class; and they were explained by means of a sentence or group of sentences containing singular terms to which the sentence containing the common term in question was logically equivalent. A term with determinate supposition had disjunctive reference, in the sense that the sentence in which it appeared was equivalent to a set of disjoined sentences, each with a singular term in the place of the original noun. For instance, "Peter is a man" is equivalent to "Peter is man$_1$ or Peter is man$_2$ or ... or Peter is man$_n$"; and the original sentence is true only if one of the disjuncts is true. A term with distributive supposition had conjunctive reference, in the sense that the sentence in which it appeared was equivalent to a set of conjoined sentences, each with a singular term in place of the original noun. For instance, "All men are mortal" is equivalent to "Man$_1$ is mortal and man$_2$ is mortal and ... and man$_n$ is mortal"; and the original sentence is true only if all the conjuncts are true. A term with merely confused supposition had disjoint reference, in the sense that the sentence in which it appeared was equivalent to another sentence whose predicate (or subject) was a disjunction. For instance, "All men are animals" is equivalent to "All men are animal$_1$ or animal$_2$ or ... or animal$_n$"; and the original sentence is true only if each man is identical to just one animal. A term with collective supposition had conjoint reference in the sense that the sentence in which it appeared was equivalent to another sentence whose subject (or predicate) was a conjunction. For instance, "All the apostles are twelve" is equivalent to "Apostle$_1$ and apostle$_2$ and ... and apostle$_n$ are twelve"; and the original sentence is true only if the number of referents taken together is twelve.

There were, of course, a number of restrictions imposed upon the interpretation which I have just outlined. In some cases, extra existential premisses were needed before genuine logical equivalence could be achieved. For instance, a universal affirmative proposition is only equiv-

alent to a set of conjoined singular propositions when members of the
subject class exist, and when the singular terms employed successfully
name members of that class. The details of these requirements will be
examined below, in the section on ascent and descent. It was pointed out
that the subject of a universal affirmative proposition could be distributed
even when it did not have distributive supposition. For instance, 'chimera'
has no kind of supposition, because it does not refer, and no descent can
be made from it to a set of singular propositions; nevertheless it can be
taken as if it does range over members of a class.[5] Even when the subject
class is non-empty, it may not have enough members for descent to a set
of singular propositions to be possible. For instance, there is only one
world, so "Some world is created" cannot be rewritten as a disjunction
of singular propositions. Eckius dealt with this case by pointing to the
distinction between the acceptance of a term, which concerns its logical
properties, and descent from a term, which concerns its actual reference.
'World' is accepted determinately, even though descent from it is not
possible. It is sufficient, he said, for a term to have determinate supposition that descent can be made from another term similarly accepted.[6] In
yet other cases, descent from a distributive or merely confused term was
said to be impossible, even though it had more than one referent. Not all
made this claim; but those who did so spoke in terms of the distinction
between mobile and immobile supposition.[7] If a term is mobile, the
equivalent to the sentence in which it appears can be spelled out; but if
it is immobile, this is not possible. For instance, one cannot rewrite "Necessarily all men are animals" as a series of singular propositions; nor
can one replace 'penny' in "I promise you a penny" by a disjunction of
singular terms [see below]. Finally, there were cases in which normal descent was not possible because of the presence of a reciprocal relation.[8]
In "Every man is himself", the subject term is distributed, but the predicate term does not have merely confused supposition as do other sentences of this form, and any descent must involve both terms at once. One
must write "Man_1 is man_1 and man_2 is man_2 and ... and man_n is man_n,"
in order to capture the sense of the original sentence.

A number of standard rules were offered in order to determine how
syncategorematic signs affected the type of supposition a term was said
to have.[9] If a sentence was unquantified, or if it was a particular
affirmative sentence, then both subject and predicate were said to have

determinate supposition. The same was true of a predicate in a singular affirmative proposition. If a sentence was a particular negative, then just the subject had determinate supposition, for the predicate was governed by the negation sign. Since signs could impede each other, it turns out that in any particular sentence which is preceded by a negation sign the terms which would otherwise have had determinate supposition will have confused supposition, either distributive as in '$-(SiP)$' which is equivalent to 'SeP', or a mixture of distributive and merely confused as in '$-(SoP)$', which is equivalent to 'SaP'. Some people introduced a special sign, 'b', which was supposed to produce determinate supposition in the term following it, in cases where this would not otherwise be possible. For instance, in "Every man is some animal", 'animal' was said to have confused supposition because of the presence of 'every', but in "Every man is b animal" 'animal' has determinate supposition, because terms governed by 'b' are not affected by previous signs.[10] Another special sign which was sometimes used was 'a', which produced merely confused supposition in the term immediately following it. One use of 'a' was to ensure that a term was shown to have the correct type of supposition when it appeared in non-standard propositions. For instance, if "Every man is an animal" is converted to "a. animal is every man", the presence of 'a' will prevent the reader from taking the second proposition as equivalent to "Some animal is every man".[11] The use of these special signs seems to be peculiar to the early sixteenth century.

The two most common causes of distributive supposition were negation and universal affirmation. An affirmative universal sign such as 'every' or 'all' which preceded the entire sentence distributed the term immediately following it, that is, the subject term. Eckius noted that if such a sign appeared within a sentence and preceded the predicate term, then the result could in one case be a true proposition, that is, when the predicate class contained only one member.[12] He cited "This sun is every sun" as an example. *Negatio negans* distributed all the terms which followed it, subject to the usual restrictions about impeding signs. Negative universal signs such as 'no' and 'none' distributed the subject and predicate, but when 'not' appeared within a sentence as in "Some man is not an animal", it distributed just the predicate term. If 'not' preceded a sentence which already had syncategorematic signs as in "It is not the case that every man is an animal", then it was impeded by those signs. In

this case, the predicate does have distributive supposition, but the subject had determinate supposition.[13] *Negatio infinitans* distributed the
term preceded by 'non-', such as 'man' in 'non-man', but the resulting
phrase had determinate supposition, because it was equivalent to "Something which is a non-man".[14] One could rewrite this more clearly as
"There is a thing which is not identical with any man."

Among the other distributive signs were comparatives, superlatives,
signs of difference, and signs of similarity, all of which distributed the
term immediately following. For instance, 'man' is distributed in "A
lion is stronger than man" and "A lion differs from a man." Sometimes
a gloss was necessary. In "Peter is the most just of men", it was understood that 'men' referred to men other than Peter.[15] Exceptive signs distributed the terms immediately and mediately following them. For instance,
in "Every animal except man is irrational" both 'man' and 'irrational'
are distributed.[16] Exclusive signs such as 'only' distributed the term
which they governed mediately. For instance, in "Only an animal is a
man", 'man' is distributed.

Merely confused supposition is a property of those terms which are
governed mediately by a universal affirmative term, that is, the predicate
in such sentences as "Every man is an animal". Similarly, it is a property
of terms governed immediately by an exclusive sign such as 'only', and
as a result we can see that a sentence such as "Only an animal is a man"
is equivalent to "Every man is an animal".[17] Enumerative terms such
as 'twice', certain types of conjunction such as 'here and at Rome', acts
of mind such as 'desire' and 'understand', and verbs of obligation such
as 'promise' and 'owe' were also said to produce merely confused supposition in the terms they governed. Various restrictions had to be born
in mind. One had to be sure that the term did not have simple supposition, as it could in such a context as "I know a rose" [*scio ro'sam*].[18]
Moreover, said Javellus, one had to ask whether the acts enumerated
could be repeated with respect to the same object or not.[19] In "I saw a
man twice", 'man' has mobile supposition, for the sentence is equivalent
to "I saw this man or that man or the other man twice", but in "I sang
mass twice" or "I ate bread twice", 'mass' and 'bread' have immobile
supposition, for no descent can be made to a sentence with singular
terms, without losing the sense of the original. Similarly, he said, 'pepper'
in "Pepper is sold here and at Rome" and 'penny' in "I promise you a

penny" have merely confused immobile supposition. In the latter case it is
false that any specific penny has been promised to you, and the penny
which will be used to pay the debt may not even have been minted yet.

Of collective supposition there is little to be said. A term had
collective supposition when it was preceded by a collective sign such as
'all' and had a numerical predicate, or when it was preceded by 'only' and
had a numerical subject, as in "There are only five universals".[20] A term
could also have collective supposition in such contexts as "These are all
men", i.e. all the men there are.

In the light of these rules, the standard quantified and singular
categorical propositions were said to exhibit the following types of
personal supposition:[21]

A The subject has distributive supposition and the predicate has
merely confused supposition.

SaP $(S_1 = P_1 \vee P_2 \vee \dots \vee P_n) . (S_2 = P_1 \vee P_2 \vee \dots \vee P_n) \dots$
$$\dots . (S_n = P_1 \vee P_2 \vee \dots \vee P_n)$$

E The subject and predicate both have distributive supposition.

SeP $(S_1 \neq P_1 . S_1 \neq P_2 \dots S_n \neq P_n) . (S_2 \neq P_1 . S_2 \neq P_2 \dots S_2 \neq P_n) .$
$$\dots . (S_n \neq P_1 . S_n \neq P_2 \dots S_n \neq P_n)$$

I The subject and predicate have determinate supposition.

SiP $(S_1 = P_1 \vee S_1 = P_2 \vee \dots \vee S_1 = P_n) \vee (S_2 = P_1 \vee S_2 = P_2 \vee \dots$
$\vee S_2 = P_n) \vee \dots \vee (S_n = P_1 \vee S_n = P_2 \vee \dots \vee S_n = P_n)$

O The subject has determinate supposition and the predicate has distributive supposition.

SoP $(S_1 \neq P_1 . S_1 \neq P_2 \dots S_1 \neq P_n) \vee (S_2 \neq P_1 . S_2 \neq P_2 \dots$
$S_2 \neq P_n) \vee \dots \vee (S_n \neq P_1 . S_n \neq P_2 \dots S_n \neq P_n)$

Singular affirmative: the subject has discrete supposition and the predicate has determinate supposition.

$x = P$ $x = P_1 \vee x = P_2 \vee \dots \vee x = P_n$

Singular negative: The subject has discrete supposition and the predicate has distributive supposition.

$$x \neq P \qquad x \neq P_1 . x \neq P_2 ..... x \neq P_n$$

In carrying out a translation, it should be noted that one first translates from the term with determinate supposition, then from the term with distributive supposition, and finally from the term with merely confused supposition.[22] If both terms in a proposition have the same type of supposition, it does not matter where one starts with the translation as the results will be logically equivalent, owing to the commutability of '.' and ' $\vee$ '. These translations are, of course, subject to a number of restrictions, especially those concerning existential assumptions. They are offered only as a guide to the way in which sentences were interpreted. The restrictions will be discussed in the section on ascent and descent.

2. DESCENT AND ASCENT

The interpretation of propositions which has just been examined was more fully worked out in the discussion of suppositional ascent and descent. Descent was the inference of a set of singular propositions from a quantified proposition, and ascent was the inference of a quantified proposition from a set of singular propositions. There were four kinds of ascent and descent, which corresponded to the four types of personal common supposition which have already been discussed. That is, there were disjunctive, conjunctive, disjoint, and conjoint ascent and descent. It was normally held both that the inferences should be formally valid,[23] and that they should be mutual.[24] Descent (or ascent) could only be valid if the corresponding ascent (or descent) was also valid. The relationship of these inferences to the truth and falsity of sentences was thought to be a very intimate one. Partly this was a theoretical matter. If the truth of a proposition depends on the supposition of its terms in the ways that have been suggested, then ascent and descent must be valid, for they provide a means of explaining how it is that terms are taken to refer, and when it is that the subject and predicate do or do not refer to the same individuals.[25] If a universal affirmative proposition asserts an identity between every member of the subject class and members of another class, then we must agree that the production of an individual of whom the identity does not hold will falsify the original proposition. To reject this is both to reject the conditions laid down for the truth of affirmative propositions, and to reject the validity of descent. Pragmatic considerations were also involved, for descent and ascent were seen as clarifying and simplifying the conditions under which quantified sentences were known to be true or false.[26] For instance, if one considers "Every man is every man", one may not know how to assess it. However, if one takes three men, Socrates, Plato, and Cicero, and carries out a descent, it will become obvious that the sentence is false, for one will obtain: "(Socrates is Socrates and Socrates is Plato and Socrates is Cicero) and (Plato is Socrates and Plato is Plato and Plato is Cicero) and (Cicero is Socrates and Cicero is Plato and Cicero is Cicero)."[27] John of St. Thomas remarked that in the cases of conjoint and disjoint supposition, enumeration did not "serve to clarify and resolve the proposition's truth" as it did in the case of disjunctive and conjunctive supposition.[28]

As will be seen below, careful conditions were laid down to ensure that ascent and descent remained formally valid inferences whether the terms succeeded in referring or not. Nevertheless, there was a strong tendency to require that ascent and descent should be not only valid but sound. People spoke of descents which were good for today but not good for tomorrow, because of the death of one or more of the individuals referred to by the singular terms in the consequent.[29] It was frequently stated that only common terms with supposition could be employed;[30] and that these common terms should refer to more than one individual.[31] No descent could be made from terms like 'sun' and 'world', even though they enjoyed the logical status of a common term. Only Hieronymus of St. Mark questioned this attitude. He pointed out that one could define 'descent' as "arguing from a term accepted as common either to its singulars by virtue of acceptance, or to its singulars by virtue of supposition." 'This chimera' would be accepted as a singular term, even though it lacked discrete supposition. His approach is the most fruitful one, since the discussion of ascent and descent involved the question of possible rather than actual interpretations, and nothing seems to be gained by restricting the name 'descent' to those inferences which meet some material conditions as well as the required formal conditions. On the other hand, it is true that formal validity is not enough for an acceptable descent, given the requirement that the corresponding ascent should also hold. That is, cases in which the antecedent was false and the consequent true could not be accepted. Either both had to be true, or both false.

The requirement of soundness is reflected in the discussion of what kind of singular terms should be admitted. There were said to be three kinds of singular term: those which were singular *in significando*, such as 'Adam', those which were singular *in supponendo*, such as 'this man', and those which were singular *in significando et in supponendo*, such as 'Maximilian' (Emperor at the time when Eckius wrote).[32] It was agreed that it was not enough for a term to be singular by virtue of its meaning, for it might well lack a referent. Nor was it enough for a term to be singular by virtue of both meaning and supposition, for the bearer of that name might die. Hence only terms which were singular by virtue of supposition should be employed. No one commented that the phrase 'this man' was also singular by virtue of its meaning, for it was clearly the use of proper names that they were seeking to debar. Gebwiler produced further reasons for doing this.[33] He pointed out that unless one used a noun phrase, one could not be sure that the number of terms had not varied, and that only materially valid inferences would be possible. There is no formal distinction between arguing from 'man' to 'Socrates' and 'Plato' on the one hand, and from 'man' to 'Favellus' and 'Grisellus' on the other hand, yet the latter names are used only of animals. Proper names, one could say, have a special kind of connotation, which must be taken into account informally, but which cannot be taken into account formally. However, Pardo in his discussion of the phrase '*et sic de aliis*' produced reasons for claiming that a descent could be valid even if inappropriate proper names were used [see below].

The further requirements for the soundness of ascent and descent were worked out in response to the examination of a number of apparent counter-examples. These were all stated as if they involved just a difference in modality between antecedent and consequent, but some of these differences can be seen to rest on an assumption about the relationship between demonstrative words such as 'this' and the thing referred to. If 'this' has the function of pointing to a man, then "This is an ass" becomes an impossible proposition, because it is taken as equivalent to "This man is an ass."[34] Thus, "Every running thing is an ass, therefore this running thing is an ass" was said to exemplify the apparent inference of an impossible singular proposition from a possible universal proposition, given that men were running.[35] The other examples were more straightforward.[36] One could apparently have a necessary antecedent, such as "All men are animals", with a consequent, "This man is an animal", which was contingent because the existence of any particular man is contingent. Similarly one could have a contingent antecedent, "This man does not exist", with a consequent, "No man exists", which was impossible, at least according to Aristotle.[37] One could also have a contingent antecedent, "Every being is God", and a consequent, "This being is God", which was necessary, given that only God existed.[38] One could even have a universally quantified antecedent, "No being is pointed to", with a consequent "This being is not pointed to", which could not be true given that the utterance of 'this' is a method of pointing to an object.[39] However, one could never have a true universal proposition whose singulars were actually false, unless insolubles were involved. Hieronymus of St. Mark gave as an example the false self-referential singulars "This singular proposition is false and this singular proposition is false and this singular proposition is false", and the true universal proposition (given that there were only three singular propositions), "Every singular proposition is false."

The apparent counter-examples were all neutralized by the addition of an extra premiss, "These are all the *A*'s there are", without which the consequent could not be inferred from the antecedent.[40] In the first example, "These are all the running things there are" is not compossible with "Every running thing is an ass", given a situation in which men are running and are indicated by 'these'. Similarly, "These are all the men there are" is not compossible with "This man does not exist, and this man does not exist, and so on." Hence, in each case the antecedent is impossible, just like the consequent. In the second case cited, "These are all the men there are" is a contingent premiss, and when added to "All men are animals", renders the whole antecedent contingent. "These are all beings" is not compossible with "No beings are pointed to", since 'These' is an indicator word, with the result that the antecedent is not possibly true, any more than the consequent is possibly true. The only case which seems not to fit in is that of the contingent antecedent and the necessary consequent. Presumably the solution lies with the fact that *constantia* will have to be added to what is the consequent when it becomes the antecedent of an ascent, so that one can derive a biconditional: "Every being is God if and only if this being is God and these are all beings", in which both parts are contingent.

Even with the provision of an extra premiss, some counter-examples could still be generated. These all seemed to involve the activity of verbal pointing, and the problem arising from the relationship between the phrases used and the thing or things pointed to. The following cases were given. First, "Every man is a laughing thing and these are all the men, therefore this man is a laughing thing", given that 'this man' refers to Antichrist.[41] Second, "All non-white men are running and these are all the non-white men, therefore this non-white man is running", given that only Ethiopians are men, that all are running, and that one of them becomes white.[42] Third, "Every being is created, these beings are all the beings, therefore this being is a created being and this being is a created being", given that Peter and Paul, who were referred to by the consequent, die, but their matter and form, which were referred to by the second premiss, still remain.[43] Another version of this problem involved the argument "All men are running and these are all the men, therefore this man is running and this man is running", given that the consequent originally refers to Socrates and Plato, out of whose matter and form a non-running Cicero is later constructed.[44]

So that it could deal with these new counter-examples as well as the ones already discussed, *constantia* was given a dual function. In the first place, it had to ensure that the modalities and the truth-values of the antecedent and consequent did not differ, in order to preserve the relationship of mutual implication between ascent and descent; and in the second place it had to guarantee that those things referred to by the antecedent were just those things referred to by the consequent. In other words, *constantia* was introduced both to ensure the consistency of the interpretation, and to ensure that, given a consistent interpretation, the conditions for validity were met. In order to ensure the consistency of the interpretation it was insisted that those things referred to by 'these' in the antecedent should be those things referred to by 'this', 'this', and so on in the consequent.[45] These terms together with the common noun had to be related by synonymy, so that the same things were referred to,[46] and they had to be so related that the same number of things was referred to.[47] If matter and form were to be referred to as well as men, then these had to be pointed to in both antecedent and consequent. Celaya laid down two further conditions for *constantia*.[48] First, "it must denote that the term beneath which descent is made belongs to all its referents." For instance, all the referents of 'non-white men' must be non-white, else they cannot count as referents. Second, "it must denote that the term beneath which descent is made belongs only to its referents." I take this to mean that 'man' can be used only of men, and not of Antichrist, and that 'ass' can be used only of asses, and not of men. Celaya's requirements are more restrictive than the others since they do not allow "This is a man" or "These are all the men there are" to be said of non-men, but they have the same effect. In one case, one cannot refer to non-men by means of these phrases; in the other case one can, but one must do so consistently in both antecedent and consequent.

Precisely how the needed extra premiss was to be phrased and interpreted was a matter of discussion. There were two main alternatives, true *constantia* and the *antiquum medium*, which was frequently used as equivalent to true *constantia*. The chief characteristic of the latter was that 'is' was used existentially, and in the context of ascent and descent it turned out to be a conjunction of singular propositions, such as "This man is and this man is and so for all the others."[49] 'Was' or 'will be' could of course be substituted for 'is' where the context required this.[50] The terms in *constantia* were taken to have accidental supposition, and it was therefore always a contingent proposition.[51] Although some people apparently argued that it should be true, Celaya rightly rejected this,[52] for such a requirement would have preserved the invalidity of such descents as that from "All men are animals and these are all men" to "Socrates is an animal", where the consequent is false.

In the so-called *medium antiquum* 'is' was used predicatively. The subject of the proposition was a demonstrative pronoun, which referred to the significates of the predicate. The predicate itself was the term from which descent (or to which ascent) was to be made, and it was preceded by a collective sign.[53] Thus we obtain "These are all the men", or "These men are all the men there are." The demonstrative pronoun could be interpreted in two ways, as standing for a series of singular terms, or as indicating a group of individuals collectively taken.[54] The latter interpretation was thought to give rise to some difficulties. "These are all the things not pointed to" was found unacceptable because 'these' is a term which has the function of pointing; whereas "Socrates and Plato and so on are all the things not pointed to" was taken to be unproblematic.[55] As a result, people preferred the other interpretation, whereby "These *A*s are all the *A*s there are" was thought to be shorthand for "A_1 and A_2 and... and A_n are all the *A*s there are."[56] More elaborate versions were possible, such as "This man is and this man is and so for the others and every man is this man or this man or this man and so for the others,"[57] but they did not substantially alter the principle involved. It is clear that given the latter interpretation, *medium antiquum* will be true only if *constantia* in its proper form is true, so that using it instead of *constantia* posed no problems.

Some logicians had tried to do the work of *constantia* with an addition to the consequent, but only John of Glogovia seems to have accepted this in our period.[58] The addition took the form of 'if he exists', as in "This man, if he exists, is an animal"; and it was said to preserve the necessity of the consequent so that a contingent proposition could not be inferred from a necessary proposition. However, as the commentators of Mainz pointed out, this applied only to natural matter, and not to such contingent sentences as "This man is white." "This man, if he exists, is white" can be false, yet it could be derived from a true universal proposition. Gebwiler said that two interpretations of this addition were possible, neither of which was acceptable. It could be seen as producing a conditional sentence, in which case the descent was improper, since conditional sentences have no quantity, and hence cannot be singular. Alternatively, it could be seen as producing the equivalent to "This existing man is an animal", which would be contingent, and could be false.

Constantia was not the only addition necessary for adequate ascent and descent, for the formula '*et sic de aliis*' or '*et sic de singulis*' had also to be added, in order to ensure that formal reference was made to all members of a class, even if these were not, or could not be, explicitly enumerated and named. There was some discussion about the interpretation of this clause. Some people saw it as meaning "There is no *A* other than those demonstrated but that it is *B*";[59] and Pardo argued that this had the advantage of retaining the formal validity of a descent or ascent even if the wrong singular terms were used. "Brunellus runs,

Favellus runs, and there is no man other than these who does not run, therefore every man runs" was to him quite acceptable. However, this interpretation was frequently rejected on the grounds that it would produce an infinite series of descents, since every set of singular propositions produced would include a proposition with common terms, from which a further descent would have to be made.[60] It would thus make the truth or falsity of the original proposition more obscure, rather than more manifest.[61] Moreover, the phrase could not be interpreted in the same way in all contexts, for in disjunctive descent "Some man is a man who runs" would appear instead of "No man is a man but that he runs".[62] The most popular interpretation was that '*et sic de aliis*' stood for those propositions or terms which had not been enumerated, and asserted that whatever was true of those enumerated was also true of those which had not been enumerated.[63] Whether the phrase stood for a conjunction or disjunction depended on the context; though Domingo de Soto seemed to think that '*et sic de aliis*' should be used for a disjunctive context, and '*et sic de singulis*' for a conjunctive context, since only by means of the latter phrase was the common term distributed.[64] If everything had been enumerated, then '*et non sunt plura*' was substituted for '*et sic de aliis*'. The problem of infinitely large classes was also mentioned. Domingo de Soto discussed the argument that one could not descend from a term with infinitely many referents, since one could not conceive of so many singulars;[65] and Manderston believed that no finite capacity could do this. Celaya seemed to think that descent was still possible, and that one could still judge the truth of the original proposition, although one might be mistaken. He cited the case of "All mules are sterile", which, he said, had been falsified in his time.[66]

How often *constantia* and the phrase '*et sic de aliis*' were needed was a matter of debate. Some people held that they were necessary for every type of affirmative ascent or descent;[67] but Domingo de Soto omitted *constantia* from his examples of disjoint and conjoint ascent and descent.[68] He also said that '*et sic de aliis*' could be omitted from affirmative copulative descent, and affirmative disjunctive descent.[69] This argument makes sense, for if "All men are animals" is true, then "This man is an animal" is true, and the truth of the consequent will not vary with the number of singulars enumerated. Similarly, if "This man is running" is true, "Some man is running" is also true. On the other hand, even if "This man is running" is false, "Some man is running" may be true, and by omitting 'et sic de aliis' one will have produced a situation in which antecedent and consequent have different truth-values, which is inconsistent with the requirement of mutual implication. Hence, 'et sic de aliis' will have to be included if it is intended to demonstrate the relationship between ascent and descent. So far as negative ascent and descent were concerned, 'et sic de aliis' was still required,[70] but *constantia* was only required in the case of negative disjunctive ascent.[71] "This being does not exist or this being does not exist or similarly for the others, therefore some being does not exist" is only valid if one adds "And these are all the beings" to the antecedent, thus making it as impossible as the consequent.[72] Without this addition, the antecedent is true, for if reference is made to just one non-existent being, a true proposition is automatically produced, by virtue of the fact that any negative proposition whose subject does not suppose is true. On the other hand, "These are all the beings" will be false in the same situation, since it is an affirmative sentence which refers to at least one non-existent being.

It should be noted in conclusion that although ascent and descent were discussed throughout the period I am concerned with,[73] the requirement of *constantia* and the problem of the interpretation of 'et sic de aliis' virtually dropped from sight after the first part of the sixteenth century. Carvisius did include the premiss "And these are all the *A*s", but he did not discuss the reasons for its presence.[74] Thus we see yet another example of a medieval doctrine which failed to survive.

NOTES

[1] Domingo de Soto, xx.

[2] For details, see Ashworth[1], 273.

[3] Eckius, *El. Dial.*

[4] Eckius, *El. Dial.*

[5] Eckius, *Summulae*, xc.

[6] Eckius, *Summulae*, lxxxix^{vo}. "sufficit enim quod sub alio consimiliter tento valet descensus disiunctivus."

[7] Paul of Pergula, *Logica*, 30ff. Cf. Javellus, 175.

[8] Eckius, *Summulae*, xc^{vo}f., xcii^{vo}. He said (xc^{vo}) that the subject has *distributio sigillata* when it can only be distributed in relation to another distributed term. Cf. Breitkopf, *Parv. log.*

[9] E.g. Clichtoveus: Le Fèvre, 24ff.; Eckius, *Summulae*, lxxxix^{vo}ff.; Domingo de Soto, xxf.;

Celaya, *Suppositiones*; Hieronymus of St. Mark; Cologne, xxviii[vo]f.; Javellus, 175[vo]ff.; Paul of Pergula, *Logica*, 27ff.

[10] Domingo de Soto, xx.

[11] Domingo de Soto, lxix[vo]; xx.

[12] Eckius, *Summulae*, xci.

[13] See John of St. Thomas, *Formal Logic*, 69, for an explanation.

[14] Hieronymus of St. Mark; Clichtoveus: Le Fèvre, 25[vo]f.; Major, *Abbreviationes*; Mainz; Celaya, *Suppositiones*; Eckius, *Summulae*, xci[vo].

[15] Domingo de Soto, xx[vo].

[16] Domingo de Soto, xx[vo].

[17] Eckius, *Summulae*, xcii[vo].

[18] Javellus, 177vo.

[19] Javellus, 177ff.

[20] Eckius, *Summulae*, xciiif.

[21] E.g. Clichtoveus: Le Fèvre, 24.

[22] Domingo de Soto, xxv[vo].

[23] Eckius, *Summulae*, lxxxix; Major, *Abbreviationes*; Domingo de Soto, xxiii[vo].

[24] Eckius, *Summulae*, lxxxix; Pardo, cxlv. Cf. Domingo de Soto, xxiiii.

[25] Pardo, cxlv; Hieronymus of St. Mark.

[26] Domingo de Soto, xxiiii; Hieronymus of St. Mark.

[27] Pardo, cli.

[28] John of St. Thomas, *Formal Logic*, 67.

[29] Celaya, *Suppositiones*.

[30] Celaya, *Suppositiones*; Manderston; Pardo, cxlv[vo].

[31] Hieronymus of St. Mark; Tartaretus, *Expositio*, 79.

[32] Eckius, *Summulae*, lxxxix; Mainz; Hieronymus of St. Mark; John of Glogovia (lxxvii) said he preferred the third kind of singular.

[33] Cf. Eckius, *Summulae*, xc[vo].

[34] Enzinas, *Termini*, gives a clear account of this process. He considered the example of saying "This man is an animal" while pointing to a horse, and he wrote: "...omnis actus sincathegoreumaticus demonstrativus causatur mediante notitia rei quam demonstrat communi vel singulari. In proposito dico quod si ille actus demonstrat equum oportet quod subintelligatur notitia equi: ita quod erit sensus: iste equus homo est animal..."

[35] Eckius, *Summulae*, lxxxix[vo]; Celaya, *Suppositiones*; Hieronymus of St. Mark.

[36] Major, *Insolubilia*; Major, *Logicalia*; Eckius, *Summulae*, lxxxix[vo]; Gebwiler; Hieronymus of St. Mark; Pardo, cxl[vo].

[37] Hieronymus of St. Mark. Cf. Domingo de Soto, xxv.

[38] Hieronymus of St. Mark.

[39] Hieronymus of St. Mark.

[40] Major, *Insolubilia*; Gebwiler; Celaya, *Suppositiones*; Hieronymus of St. Mark; Major, *Logicalia*.

[41] Domingo de Soto, xxiiii.

[42] Celaya, *Suppositiones*; Manderston.

[43] Domingo de Soto, xxiiii.

[44] Celaya, *Suppositiones*; Manderston; Enzinas, *Primus Tractatus*, xiiii[vo]. Sbarroya, *Dial. Introd.*, xii[vo], commented that this kind of example arose from the nominalist view that the whole is nothing but the parts.

[45] Eckius, *Summulae*, lxxxix.

[46] Major, *Logicalia*; Domingo de Soto, xxiiii. The latter wrote: "Habet enim esse inter

subiectum constantie et subiecta singularium talis connexio, ut si constantia ponatur per singularia determinata singula eorum et non alia sint subiecta in singularibus, quod si ponatur per pronomen demonstrativum collective sumptum, nihil habet demonstrari in singularibus quod non demonstretur in constantia, et illa synonimitas inter subiecta illa singularium et constantie est ita intrinseca ut si in alia non servetur non erit similis forme."

[47] Domingo de Soto, xxiiii[vo].

[48] Celaya, *Suppositiones*.

[49] Eckius, *Summulae*, lxxxix; Hieronymus of St. Mark; Mainz; Pardo, cxlv[vo]; Gebwiler.

[50] Hieronymus of St. Mark; Mainz; Pardo, cxlv[vo].

[51] Mainz.

[52] Celaya, *Suppositiones*. Manderston said that *constantia* must be true.

[53] Eckius, *Summulae*, lxxxix; Domingo de Soto, xxiiii; Hieronymus of St. Mark; Manderston; Margalho, 234; Enzinas, *Primus Tractatus*, xiiii; Pardo, cxlv[vo].

[54] Domingo de Soto, xxiiii[vo]; Celaya, *Suppositiones*.

[55] Mainz; Celaya, *Suppositiones*.

[56] Celaya, *Suppositiones*; Enzinas, *Primus Tractatus*, xxiii; Pardo, clvi.

[57] Manderston; Enzinas, *Primus Tractatus*, xiiii[vo].

[58] John of Glogovia, lxxvii[vo].

[59] Domingo de Soto, xxiiii; Celaya, *Suppositiones*; Pardo, cxlvi[vo].

[60] Domingo de Soto, xxiiii; Celaya, *Suppositiones*.

[61] Celaya, *Suppositiones*.

[62] Enzinas, *Primus Tractatus*, xiiii[vo]. Cf. Pardo (cxlvii) who had "Some man who is not one of these men, runs" in the disjunctive context. 'These men' were those already enumerated.

[63] Celaya, *Suppositiones*; Manderston.

[64] Domingo de Soto, xxiiii[vo]; Cf. Manderston.

[65] Domingo de Soto, xxiiii.

[66] Celaya, *Suppositiones*.

[67] Celaya, *Suppositiones*.

[68] Domingo de Soto, xxv; cf. Gebwiler.

[69] Domingo de Soto, xxiiii[vo]. Cf. Margalho, 242, 244.

[70] Hieronymus of St. Mark.

[71] Domingo de Soto, xxiiii[vo]; Pardo, cxlvii.

[72] Pardo, cxlvi.

[73] E.g. Caramuel, *Philosophia*, 30–31; Pedro de Oña, 62–66; Fonseca, II 698–702; John of St. Thomas, *Formal Logic*, 104–107.

[74] Carvisius, 109.

CATEGORICAL SYLLOGISMS

1. FIGURES AND MODES

"A categorical syllogism is a formal consequence whose conclusion is inferred from the premisses by means of a middle term", said John Major.[1] It contains three terms, major (*P*), minor (*S*), and middle (*M*), arranged in three categorical propositions, the major premiss, the minor premiss, and the conclusion. The middle term appears in both premisses, but not in the conclusion. When regarded as a unit, the syllogism is a hypothetical proposition whose antecedent is the conjunction of the two premisses. It is divided into a number of figures, according to the position of the middle term; and each figure is divided into a number of modes, according to the possible combinations of *A*, *E*, *I* and *O* propositions. So far there is nothing controversial about this characterization, but when one attempts to specify either the total number of figures and modes or the number of valid modes, controversy does arise. This is largely because there were various possible definitions of the major and minor term, and which modes could consistently be accepted depended on the definition which was adopted.

Three separate definitions of the major and minor term were current during the fifteenth, sixteenth and seventeenth centuries, but they were not always carefully distinguished, and it is not uncommon to find authors paying lip service to one while using another. At the end of the fifteenth century the most common definition was that of Peter of Spain, who had said that the major term was the one appearing in the first or major premiss, and that the minor term was the one appearing in the second or minor premiss.[2] By the seventeenth century it was more usual to follow Philoponus, who had defined the major and minor terms as the predicate and subject of the conclusion.[3] The third definition, which was used more frequently than it was stated, was the Aristotelian one in terms of comprehension. In the first figure, the major term was said to have the most outstanding place [*praestantiorem locum*],[4] because it was predicate to the middle term, and as such greater, more universal, more common.[5] Where there was parity, as in the second and third figures, then the major term was defined as that which appeared first. Some of the difficulties arising from this approach will be stated below.

For the moment I will assume that there are four figures, and consider just the problem of indirect modes. An indirect mode was said to be one in whose conclusion the major term was subject and the minor term was predicate. Such a situation is impossible given the second definition of these terms, as Arnauld realized,[6] but it was usual for logicians to list the five indirect modes of the first figure, no matter which definition of major and minor terms they had adopted. Of course, given the first definition, there is no problem, and it turns out that there is an indirect mode corresponding to every direct mode. Clichtoveus explained that this was so because of the propositional law governing the transposition of premisses, '$(P.Q) \rightarrow R \vdash (Q.P) \rightarrow R$'.[7] From any syllogism another syllogism with transposed premisses can be inferred, and the mere transposition of premisses is enough to produce an indirect mode. Normally one would say that P and S must be interchanged throughout, but this is an unnecessary elaboration if P and S are defined according to their order of appearance. The situation can be shown diagrammatically by first employing A, B and C as ordinary term variables, and then substituting P, S and M to indicate where the major, minor, and middle terms appear:

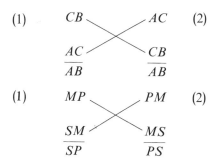

One of the interesting features of this process is that owing to the change in the position of the middle term all the indirect modes derived from the

first figure belong to the fourth, and all the indirect modes derived from
the fourth figure belong to the first, a relationship of which Wallis was
explicitly aware.[8] The number of modes listed varied considerably.
Clichtoveus gave mnemonic names for nineteen, including the indirect
modes of the five indirect modes of the first figure;[9] and Marsh listed five
indirect modes for each of the second and third figures;[10] but others
mentioned only two, *Faresmo* and *Firesmo* for the second figure, *Fapemo*
and *Fipemo* for the third figure.[11]

   The problem of indirect modes is closely associated with the problem
of the fourth figure, and in approaching this second question, it should
first of all be pointed out that there are two ways of determining the
number of figures. If one considers the position of the middle term in two
undifferentiated premisses there are only three possibilities, but if one
differentiates between the major and minor premisses then there are four
possibilities. At the beginning of the sixteenth century it was remarked
that in the broad sense of figure the fourth figure was included in the first
figure, since the middle term was subject in one premiss and predicate
in the other.[12] Thus the following scheme was accepted:

Figure 1: A	Figure 1: B	(Figure 4)
$M-$	$-M$	
$-M$	$M-$	
$--$	$--$	
Figure 2	Figure 3	
$-M$	$M-$	
$-M$	$M-$	
$--$	$--$	

If one adopts the first definition of major and minor terms, then filling
in the blanks in Figure 1 will produce the following four possibilities:

A.1	A.2	B.1	B.2
MP	MP	PM	PM
SM	SM	MS	MS
SP	PS	PS	SP

It was then claimed that there were nine modes belonging to the fourth figure, four indirect modes called *Bambara, Camerent, Dimari*, and *Fimero*, and five direct modes called *Bamalipton, Camentes, Dimatis, Fesmapo* and *Fremsisomorum*.[13] The inclusion of the latter amounts to a recognition of a separate fourth figure, but this may have been an accident arising from the unexamined desire of some logicians to include the counterparts of the five indirect modes of the first figure. Otto, who had no such desire for completeness, listed just *Bamana, Camene, Dimari* and *Fimeno* as the modes of the fourth figure, saying that they all concluded indirectly and were to be reduced by transposition of the premisses.[14] Similarly in the seventeenth century Campanella said that these four were the direct modes of the fourth figure, although they were indirect in relation to the first figure.[15] He listed the other five, but called them indirect. Thus, in so far as logicians regarded *Bamana* etc. as of primary importance, one cannot credit them with a precise and explicit knowledge of a separate fourth figure, even though they possessed all the necessary elements of such a knowledge.

It was possible for those who used the first definition of the major and minor terms both to accept the fourth figure, and to say that it involved merely a transposition of premisses, a claim which seemed to make the fourth figure both unimportant and innocuous. However, the situation is more complicated when the major and minor terms are defined either with reference to the conclusion or with reference to their comprehension. Some people defined the terms with reference to the conclusion, and then said that the fourth figure was merely the first with transposed premisses,[16] i.e.:

$$(1) \quad \begin{array}{cc} MP & SM \quad (4) \\ SM & MP \\ \hline SP & SP \end{array}$$

This, of course, does not work. If one defines the terms with reference to the conclusion, and figure with reference to the position of the middle term in differentiated premisses, then there must be four distinct figures.[17] Moreover, the transposition of premisses cannot possibly produce any change in figure, for it is the disposition of terms that is the crucial factor, and this is unaltered.[18] Thus, those who wished to reject the fourth figure had to make some further moves, most of which were derived from the influential discussion of Averroes.[19]

One move involved the extra-logical distinction between natural and
unnatural argumentation. It was claimed that people did not argue like
that;[20] that the premisses, owing to the inept and unnatural disposition
of terms, did not arouse the mind to arrive at a conclusion without the
addition of some intermediary;[21] and that the figure lacked necessity and
was obscure, contrary to nature, and useless in disputation.[22] Zabarella
in particular developed this theme at some length;[23] but it is not worth
dwelling on, except in so far as it reveals a blatant unwillingness to accept
the implications of a formal system, on the part of those who were devel-
oping just such a system. Certainly the discussion of the first three figures
of the syllogism was not linked to any empirical examination of how
people do in fact argue, or what psychological laws are involved.

The most nearly acceptable of a series of unacceptable moves depended
on the third definition of the major and minor terms as being more and
less comprehensive. Two principles were involved: that the predicate
contains the subject, and hence is greater than it; and that if A is predicated of B and B of C then A is predicated of C. In the fourth figure, it was
argued, M is predicated of P and is subject to S. Hence, by the first
principle, it is greater than the major term and less than the minor term.[24]
By the second principle, since M is predicated of P and S of M, it follows
that M is predicated of M. Thus, it is both greater than itself and contained
within itself, which is absurd.[25] Versor, the fifteenth century Thomist,
argued in a very similar manner.[26] If M is predicated of P, it is a whole
with respect to P; if it is subject to S, then it is a part with respect to S.
Yet if M is a whole with respect to P, and P is a whole with respect to S,
then M is a whole with respect to S. Thus M is both whole and part with
respect to S, which is impossible. Burgersdijck rules out these possibilities in advance by requiring that any term predicated of the middle
term should be a predicate in the conclusion and that any term which was
subject to the middle term should be subject in the conclusion.[27] This
rule did not apply to the second and third figures, in which order of
appearance in the premisses was the determining factor in distinguishing
between the major and minor terms.

The arguments which I have just reported would indeed provide good
reason for rejecting the fourth figure if the premiss that a predicate
contains and is greater than its subject were a plausible one. It was already
clear that it cannot be accepted with respect to the second and third

figures, and the modification that the predicate could be equal to the subject was a standard one, but even this is not enough. If one considers the following syllogism "All men are mortal and some physical objects are men, therefore some physical objects are mortal", it is obvious both that this is a valid syllogism of the first figure, and that as a matter of fact the class of physical objects is larger than the class of mortal things even though the latter is the predicate class and the former the subject class. Moreover, if one considers the extensionalist interpretation of categorical propositions which was offered by all those who considered the matter at all, it becomes apparent that there are no grounds for drawing any conclusions about the relative size of the classes involved. To say that a particular affirmative proposition is true is to say that some members of the subject class, A, are identical with some members of the predicate class, B, and this is compatible with class A including class B, class B including class A, class A and class B intersecting, and class A and class B being coextensive. Even when class B is in fact larger, this can justify no conclusions about the predicate, for when the original sentence is converted, A will become the predicate class.

Once it had been decided how many figures there were, the next step was to compute the number of possible syllogisms. The most usual procedure was to work out the number of ways in which the four types of categorical proposition could be combined in two premises, thus arriving at sixteen possibilities, to reject those which could lead to no conclusion, and to consider the remaining nine possibilities with reference to each figure.[28] A few logicians also took the conclusion into account, thus arriving at sixty four possible modes for each figure.[29] Some deviations from this procedure were possible, though the practical results were the same. For instance, some people derived thirty six possible modes for each figure by combining the two qualities of the premisses (i.e. affirmative and negative) with three of the quantities, universal, particular, and indefinite.[30] Hospinianus derived 512 modes by combining the two qualities with four quantities, including singular, for the conclusion as well as the premisses. However, since both indefinite and singular propositions were treated as either universal or particular in the context of the syllogism, no new kinds of mode were in fact added to those already known, nor was any advantage derived from treating quantity and quality separately.

2. How to Test the Validity of a Syllogism

Given the finite number of possible syllogisms, there are two ways of isolating those which are valid. Either one can test each possibility for validity, or one can attempt to prove each possibility by means of a set of axioms and rules. Traditionally, a combination of both methods was used. First, the invalid modes were rejected in the light of some general rules for testing validity, and then the modes of the first figure were adopted as axioms and used to prove the modes of the other figures. In this section I shall consider the first method.

It was usual, at least in the earlier period, to offer a number of guidelines which should be applied even before the final tests for validity came into play. Equivocation had to be avoided, for instance; and care had to be taken to see that the properties of the terms did not vary. A number of examples were given by both Gebwiler and Bartholomaeus de Usingen, whose work is curiously similar. "No living thing is dead and every man is living, therefore no man is dead" was rejected because of a variation in ampliation; "No man is a woman and the mother of John is a man [i.e. human], therefore the mother of John is not a woman" was rejected because of a variation in restriction; "Every man is a species and John is a man, therefore John is a species" was rejected because of a variation in the type of supposition. It was also usual to add some cautionary remarks about divine terms, or such words as 'father' and 'son' when said of God, since the doctrine of the Trinity raised certain problems concerning the reference of these terms.[31]

A good deal of the theoretical basis for the set of rules used to check the validity of particular syllogisms was provided by supposition theory, for it is here that we find the crucial notion of distribution. A term has distribution, or is distributed, when it is a common noun which either has personal distributive supposition, or would have personal distributive supposition if it succeeded in referring. A sentence containing such a term is logically equivalent to a set of conjoined singular sentences in which the common noun is replaced by a series of singular terms each of which names (or is taken to name) just one member of the class referred to by the common noun, and which together name (or are taken to name) all members of that class. The original sentence is true only if every singular sentence is true. A common noun which is undistributed is also taken to refer to a class, and any sentence containing such a name is equivalent either to a complex sentence, or to a set of singular sentences, in which the members of that class are exhaustively named; but there is one crucial difference. In a complex sentence, the names are disjoined; in a set of singular sentences, the sentences are disjoined. This has an obvious effect upon the truth-conditions for sentences containing undistributed terms. In "All men are animals", 'animals' is undistributed, and the original sentence is equivalent to a complex sentence with a disjoined predicate, "$animal_1$ or $animal_2$ or... or $animal_n$", so that the original sentence is true if each man is identical to just one animal, and there is no requirement that these identities should be exhaustive of the class of animals. There may be many animals to which no man is identical. In "Some animals are horses", 'animals' is undistributed, and the original sentence is equivalent to the series of disjoined sentences "$Animal_1$ is a horse or $animal_2$ is a horse or... or $animal_n$ is a horse", so that the original sentence is true if just one disjunct is true, irrespective of the truth or falsity of the others. It turns out that the subjects of A and E propositions and the predicates of E and O propositions are distributed, and that all other terms appearing in A, E, I and O propositions are undistributed. A full account of how these sentences were interpreted as a whole can be found in Section 2 of this chapter.

In the light of what has been said about distribution, two logical principles can be formulated, one of which applies to inferences in general, and one of which applies to the syllogism. The first principle is that from a proposition in which a given term is undistributed one cannot validly derive a proposition in which this term is distributed. For instance, from "Some men are animals" one cannot derive "All men are animals", because the first may be true even if only one man is an animal, whereas the second can only be true if every man is an animal. In the early sixteenth century, Sbarroya explained the matter very clearly.[32] One of his examples of the kind of invalid inference which arose when the principle was violated was: "Every man is an animal, no horse is a man, therefore no horse is an animal" in which 'animal' is distributed in the conclusion, but not in either premiss. Suppose, he said, that there are just ten animals in the world, five of which are men and five of which are horses. 'Animal' in the major premiss will be verified of just five things through the middle term, and the division in the minor premiss will apply only to those five things, i.e. to the five men, yet the truth of the conclusion depends on 'animal' being verified of ten referents.

The second principle, which applies to the syllogism alone, is that in a syllogism the middle term must be distributed in at least one premiss, since it is only through the middle term that the other two terms can be related to one another. If we know that every member of class A is identical (or non-identical) to some member of class B, whether class B is exhausted or not, we can infer that any member of class C which is identical to a member of class A is also identical (or non-identical) to a member of class B. However, if we only know that some members of A are identical (or non-identical) to some members of B, and that some members of A are identical to some members of C, we cannot relate B and C, for we have no guarantee that the same members of A will be named in the two sets of identity statements. It is true that some members of the class of human beings are identical to some members of the class of men, and it is true that some members of the class of human beings are identical to some members of the class of women, but no conclusion can be syllogistically derived from these premisses. We know that the first premiss can only be true of those members of the class of human beings of which the second premiss will be false, and vice versa, but we also know that it is possible for both premisses to be interpreted as true when the class of human beings is taken disjunctively. Hence, the premisses can be true when any possible affirmative conclusion ("Some men are women", "Some women are men", "All men are women", "All women are men") is false.

Dici (or *dictum*) *de omni* and *dici de nullo* were the two so-called regulative principles to which every author appealed in his account of the syllogism. There was surprisingly little discussion of these principles, but some of the earlier authors, particularly Gebwiler and Bartholomaeus de Usingen, stated them in such a way as to make clear what their significance was taken to be.[33] These principles, they said, can be captured by the following rules:

(1.1)   Whatever is affirmed of a distributed subject is also affirmed of whatever is subsumed under that subject.

(2.2)   Whatever is denied of a distributed subject is also denied of whatever is subsumed under that subject.

A corollary of these rules was said to be the rule that the middle term must be distributed in at least one premiss. Three conditions were specified under which the principles were said to govern a syllogism directly. First, the subsumption should be under the distributed subject of the major premiss. Second, the subject of the minor premiss should itself be subsumed under that distributed term. Third, the predicate of the major premiss should be predicated of the subject of the minor premiss in the conclusion. These three conditions excluded all indirect modes, and all modes of the second, third and fourth figures. These imperfect modes were said to be governed by *dici de omni* and *dici de nullo* only indirectly, by virtue of the fact that they could be proved through the four perfect modes of the first figure.

In a passage of outstanding clarity and interest Clichtoveus used the two regulative principles in order to prove each direct mode of the first figure. [34] For example, he argued that if anyone doubted the validity of *Barbara* they should grant the two premisses and doubt the conclusion. The two premisses "Every *b* is *a*" and "Every *c* is *b*" form a conjunction, and if a conjunction is true, then each conjunct is true. Hence the first premiss, "Every *b* is *a*", is true. Since it is a universal affirmative proposition, the principle of *dici de omni* applies to it, and nothing can be subsumed under the subject *b* of which the predicate *a* is not affirmed. Since by the second premiss *c* has been universally subsumed under *b*, it follows by *dici de omni* that "Every *c* is *a*" is true, which was the desired conclusion. Hence if the antecedent is true, it is necessary that the consequent is also true, and *Barbara* is a formally valid consequence. Alternatively, he said, one can prove *Barbara per impossibile*. If "Every *b* is *a* and every *c* is *b*, therefore every *c* is *a*" does not hold, it must be because the antecedent is true and the consequent is false. Let the antecedent be true and the consequent false. If the consequent is false, its contradictory, "Some *c* is not *a*", is true. By the previous argument it turns out that "Every *c* is *a*" is true. Thus, two contradictories are both true, which is impossible. He went on to give proofs for the indirect modes and for the modes of other figures which will be examined in the next section.

Once *dici de omni* and *dici de nullo* had been stated, it was usual to offer a set of five general rules together with two specific rules for each figure to which direct appeal could be made in the process of checking possible modes for validity.[35] One of these rules, that the middle term should not appear in the conclusion, can be ignored, since it concerns the structure of the syllogism rather than a test for validity.

(2.1)   Nothing follows from two particular premisses.

Either the middle term is not distributed, or a term distributed in the conclusion is not distributed in the premisses. If both premisses are affirmative, the middle term is undistributed. If one premiss is negative, the conclusion must also be negative. The predicate of both these propositions will be distributed, but if the term distributed in the conclusion is distributed in the premiss, then the middle term is not distributed. If the middle term is distributed in the premiss, then the term distributed in the conclusion is not distributed in the premiss.[36]

The earlier sources, such as Gebwiler, noted some exceptions to this rule. It did not apply to syllogisms with singular terms; nor did it apply to first and second figure syllogisms in which the middle term was restricted by the relation of identity. For instance, "Some white thing is an animal and some man is the same animal, therefore some man is white" is a legitimate argument. Another exception was provided by cases in which the middle term was preceded by a universal affirmative sign, as in "Some animal is a stone and some man is every animal, therefore some man is a stone."

(2.2)   Nothing follows from two negative premisses.

It is not the case that if two terms are denied of a third term, they are also denied of each other. Moreover, it is otherwise possible to have true premisses and a false conclusion, as in "No man is an ass and no laughing thing is an ass, therefore no laughing thing is a man." Distribution is not an issue here, in so far as all the terms in a sequence of three E propositions would be distributed, and all the predicates in a sequence of three O propositions would be distributed. In the latter case, however, the middle might still be undistributed, and the predicate of the conclusion might not have been distributed in either premiss, so that some syllogisms with negative premisses would violate more than one rule.

(2.3)   If one premiss is particular, the conclusion is also particular.

If the conclusion is universal, then at least one of the terms is distributed and either a term distributed in the conclusion is not distributed in the premisses or the middle term is undistributed. If the particular premiss is negative, then its predicate is distributed. However, the other premiss must be a universal affirmative proposition with only one distributed term (by (2.1) and (2.2)) and the conclusion must be a universal negative proposition with two distributed terms. Either the middle term is not distributed, or one of the terms in the conclusion was not distributed in a premiss. If the particular premiss is affirmative, it has no distributed term. If the other premiss is a universal affirmative proposition it has one distributed term. Either this term is the one distributed in the universal affirmative conclusion and the middle term is not distributed, or it is the middle term and there is a term distributed in the conclusion which was not distributed in a premiss. If the other premiss is a universal negative proposition, it will contain two distributed terms, one of which is the middle term. However, the conclusion will now be a universal negative proposition containing two distributed terms, one of which has not been distributed in the premisses.

(2.4)   If one premiss is negative, the conclusion must be negative.

If two terms have been separated through the middle term, they must also be separated in the conclusion. Moreover, it is otherwise possible to have true premisses and a false conclusion, as in "No man is an ass and every laughing thing is a man, therefore every laughing thing is an ass."

One further rule should be added for the sake of completeness:

(2.5)   If the conclusion is negative, one premiss must be negative; or, if the premisses are affirmative, the conclusion must be affirmative.[37]

Writers such as Gebwiler and Breitkopf excluded such possibilities as "*AAE*" from consideration, although they were not specifically excluded by the rules already listed. It is possible that logicians accepted (2.5) as a corollary of *dici de omni* and *dici de nullo* which was so obvious that it did not need to be stated.

After the general rules, came the specific rules for each figure:

(3.1)   If the minor premiss of a mode belonging to the first figure is negative, nothing follows.

If the minor premiss is negative, the major premiss must be affirmative, and the major term will not be distributed. If one premiss is negative, the conclusion must be negative. Thus, the major term will be distributed in the conclusion although it was not distributed in a premiss.

(3.2)   If the major premiss of a mode belonging to the first figure is particular, nothing follows.

If the major premiss is particular and the minor premiss is affirmative (by 3.1) the middle term will not be distributed.

(3.3)   If the major premiss of a mode belonging to the second figure is particular, nothing follows.

The major term will not be distributed in the major premiss, but it will be distributed in the conclusion since (by 3.4) the conclusion must be negative.

(3.4)   If the premisses of a mode belonging to the second figure are affirmative, nothing follows.

If both premisses are affirmative, the middle term is not distributed.

(3.5)   If the minor premiss of a mode in the third figure is negative, nothing follows. Cf. (3.1).

(3.6)   The conclusion of a mode in the third figure must be particular.

If the conclusion is not particular, there will be a term which is distributed in the conclusion but which is not distributed in the premisses. If the conclusion is a universal negative proposition, both terms will be distributed, but since the minor premiss is affirmative (by 3.5) the minor term will not have been distributed in a premiss. If the conclusion is a universal affirmative proposition, the minor term will be distributed, but since both the premisses will be affirmative, only the middle term will have been distributed in the premisses.

Normally no special rules were offered for the fourth figure, but the following analogues of (3.1) and (3.2) could be used:

(3.7)   If the major premiss of a mode in the fourth figure is negative, nothing follows.

(3.8)   If the minor premiss of a mode in the fourth figure is particular, nothing follows.

Given these rules, it was possible to pick out all the valid modes of the syllogism. Some people gave just fourteen, but the most usual number was nineteen, four in the first figure, five in the second, five in the third, and either five indirect modes of the first figure or (rarely) five direct modes of the fourth figure. There are, of course, twenty four valid direct modes and it is the five subalternate modes that are missing. The existence of the two subalternate modes of the first figure, *Barbari* and *Celaro*, was noted, but it was argued that they were included in *Barbara* and *Celarent* because they were deducible from them, and hence that they need not be given separately.[38] Marsh and Wallis gave two subalternate modes from the second figure, and Aldrich, who recognized the fourth figure, listed all five of the possible subalternate modes.[39] Even Aldrich was not completely happy with his list, however, for he said that twenty four modes were possible, only nineteen were tolerable, and only fourteen were probable.[40]

An analysis of the rules which were offered, and of the kind of justification which they were given, makes it plain that only four rules are in fact necessary for the task of picking out all the valid modes of the syllogism. The four in question are: (1) the middle term must be distributed at least once; (2) no term should be distributed in the conclusion unless it has been distributed in a premiss; (3) nothing follows from two negative premisses; (4) the conclusion is negative if and only if one premiss is negative. The first and second of these rules were included in a list of subsidiary rules by Bartholomaeus de Usingen and Gebwiler, and they were given a more prominent position by some scholastic authors, as well as by Arnauld and Aldrich.[41] The third rule was listed by everyone; and the fourth was rarely given in its complete form except by Arnauld and Aldrich [see above]. However, I know of no logician who contented himself with such an austere set of rules. Aldrich, whose account of the syllogism is the best available, combined these four rules with a number of others in such a way that he was able to pick out all the valid modes with an economy of effort and an accuracy that no one else displayed.[42] He began with the sixty four possible combinations of *A*, *E*, *I* and *O* propositions. He excluded sixteen of these because they violated the rule that nothing follows from two negative premisses. Twelve were excluded because they violated the rule that nothing follows from two particular premisses. Twelve were excluded by the rule that if a premiss is negative, the conclusion must be negative. Eight were excluded by the rule that if a premiss is particular the conclusion must be particular. Four were excluded because the conclusion was negative but neither premiss was. He then investigated the remaining twelve possibilities in the light of the four possible figures. In each case, six of the possibilities were excluded because the middle term was undistributed or because a term distributed in the conclusion was not distributed in a premiss. Thus twenty four modes were shown to be valid, six modes for each of the four figures.

Using Aldrich and Clichtoveus as my sources, I will now give a complete list of all the valid modes together with their mnemonic names. Indirect modes are included for all except the five subalternate modes.

(1.11)	$MaP . SaM \rightarrow SaP$	Barbara
(1.12)	$MeP . SaM \rightarrow SeP$	Celarent
(1.13)	$MaP . SiM \rightarrow SiP$	Darii
(1.14)	$MeP . SiM \rightarrow SoP$	Ferio
(1.15)	$MaP . SaM \rightarrow SiP$	Barbari [subalternate]
(1.16)	$MeP . SaM \rightarrow SoP$	Celaront [subalternate]
(1.21)	$MaP . SaM \rightarrow PiS$	Baralipton
(1.22)	$MeP . SaM \rightarrow PeS$	Celantes
(1.23)	$MaP . SiM \rightarrow PiS$	Dabitis
(1.24)	$MaP . SeM \rightarrow PoS$	Fapesmo
(2.11)	$PeM . SaM \rightarrow SeP$	Cesare
(2.12)	$PaM . SeM \rightarrow SeP$	Camestres
(2.13)	$PeM . SiM \rightarrow SoP$	Festino
(2.14)	$PaM . SoM \rightarrow SoP$	Baroco
(2.15)	$PeM . SaM \rightarrow SoP$	Cesaro [subalternate]
(2.16)	$PaM . SeM \rightarrow SoP$	Camestrop [subalternate]
(2.21)	$PaM . SeM \rightarrow PeS$	Casere (Faresmo)
(2.22)	$PeM . SaM \rightarrow PeS$	Cesmatres
(2.23)	$PiM . SeM \rightarrow PoS$	Firesmo
(2.24)	$PoM . SaM \rightarrow PoS$	Boraco
(3.11)	$MaP . MaS \rightarrow SiP$	Darapti
(3.12)	$MiP . MaS \rightarrow SiP$	Disamis
(3.13)	$MaP . MiS \rightarrow SiP$	Datisi
(3.14)	$MeP . MaS \rightarrow SoP$	Felapton

(3.15)	$MoP . MaS \rightarrow SoP$	*Bocardo*
(3.16)	$MeP . MiS \rightarrow SoP$	*Ferison*
(3.21)	$MaP . MaS \rightarrow PiS$	*Daprati*
(3.22)	$MaP . MeS \rightarrow PoS$	*Fapleton (Fapemo)*
(3.23)	$MaP . MiS \rightarrow PiS$	*Damisis*
(3.24)	$MiP . MaS \rightarrow PiS$	*Disati*
(3.25)	$MaP . MoS \rightarrow PoS$	*Bacordo*
(3.26)	$MiP . MeS \rightarrow PoS$	*Fiseron (Fipemo)*
(4.11)	$PaM . MaS \rightarrow SiP$	*Bamalipton (Bramantip)*
(4.12)	$PaM . MeS \rightarrow SeP$	*Camentes (Camenes)*
(4.13)	$PiM . MaS \rightarrow SiP$	*Dimatis (Dimaris)*
(4.14)	$PeM . MaS \rightarrow SoP$	*Fempasmo (Fesapo)*
(4.15)	$PeM . MiS \rightarrow SoP$	*Fremsismo (Fresison)*
(4.16)	$PaM . MeS \rightarrow SoP$	*Camenop* [subalternate]
(4.21)	$PaM . MaS \rightarrow PaS$	*Bambara*
(4.22)	$PaM . MeS \rightarrow PeS$	*Camerent*
(4.23)	$PiM . MaS \rightarrow PiS$	*Dimari*
(4.24)	$PiM . MeS \rightarrow PoS$	*Fimero*

3. Proof by reduction

The second method of picking out the valid modes of the syllogism is that of proof by axioms and rules. The theory of reduction provides a close approximation to this method, for it involves taking the four so-called perfect modes and using them as axioms in the proof of all the imperfect modes. The word 'reduction' is misleading, for it suggests that the imperfect modes are somehow transformed into perfect modes, and many of the later sources strengthen this impression.[43] The earlier sources, however, make it quite clear what was involved. The reductive principle, said Bartholomaeus de Usingen, is a principle by virtue of which the validity of one syllogism which is less well known is shown through the validity of another syllogism which is more well known.[44] There were said to be three kinds of reduction, ostensive reduction, reduction *per impossibile*, and reduction by exposition. Obviously the process of proof involved the use of non-syllogistic rules, and the earlier sources offered two alternative sets of rules for ostensive reduction. The most elaborate set is the following:[45]

(1.11) $AeB = BeA$
(1.12) $AiB = BiA$ Simple Conversion
(1.21) $AaB \rightarrow BiA$
(1.22) $AeB \rightarrow BoA$ Conversion *per accidens*

These principles were not explicitly included in the set of reductive principles, but I am restating them here for ease of reference.

The formula on the left is the *conversa*, or P, and the formula on the right is the *convertens*, or $\check{P}$.

(2.1) $P.Q \rightarrow R \vdash P.Q \rightarrow \check{R}$

"Whatever premisses imply the *conversa*, also imply the *convertens*."

This principle is supported by valid consequence (3.61): whatever precedes the antecedent of a valid consequence, precedes the consequent.

(2.21) $P.\check{Q} \rightarrow R \vdash P.Q \rightarrow R$
(2.22) $\check{P}.Q \rightarrow R \vdash P.Q \rightarrow R$

"Whatever conclusion follows validly from some propositions also follows validly from the conjunction of one of them in its proper form with the *conversa* of the other."

This principle is supported by valid consequence (3.62): Whatever follows the consequent of a valid consequence follows the antecedent.

(2.23) $\check{P}.\check{Q} \rightarrow R \vdash P.Q \rightarrow R$

"Whatever conclusion follows validly from some propositions also follows from their *conversae*."

(3) $P.Q \rightarrow R \vdash Q.P \rightarrow R$

"Whatever premisses imply a conclusion directly imply the same conclusion indirectly when they are transposed."

This principle is supported by the fact that transposition does not change truth or falsity. All it changes is the nomenclature of the terms when the major and minor terms are defined according to their order of appearance.

Finally, one may list the four perfect modes of the syllogism as axioms:

(4.1) $MaP.SaM \rightarrow SaP$ *Barbara*

(4.2) $MeP \cdot SaM \rightarrow SeP$ *Celarent*
(4.3) $MaP \cdot SiM \rightarrow SiP$ *Darii*
(4.4) $MeP \cdot SiM \rightarrow SoP$ *Ferio*

Given these rules, some imperfect modes could be given a one line proof, as follows:

Cesare: $MeP \cdot SaM \rightarrow SeP \vdash PeM \cdot SaM \rightarrow SeP$
              (4.2), (1.11), (2.22)

Baralipton: $MaP \cdot SaM \rightarrow SaP \vdash MaP \cdot SaM \rightarrow PiS$
              (4.1), (1.21), (2.1)

Others require a more elaborate procedure:

Camestres: $AeB \cdot CaA \rightarrow CeB \vdash CaA \cdot AeB \rightarrow CeB$ (4.2), (3)
              $CaA \cdot AeB \rightarrow CeB \vdash CaA \cdot BeA \rightarrow CeB$ (1.11), (2.21)
              $CaA \cdot BeA \rightarrow CeB \vdash CaA \cdot BeA \rightarrow BeC$ (1.11), (2.1)
              $AeB \cdot CaA \rightarrow CeB \vdash CaA \cdot BeA \rightarrow BeC$ First to last.

The other set of rules included the same rules of conversion and the same four axioms, but offered the following variants on (2) and (3):[46]

(2.1) $P \cdot Q \rightarrow P \cdot \breve{Q}$
(2.2) $P \cdot Q \rightarrow \breve{P} \cdot Q$
(2.3) $P \cdot Q \rightarrow \breve{P} \cdot \breve{Q}$

"From premisses which are *conversae* follow the *convertentes*."

(3) $P \cdot Q \rightarrow Q \cdot P$

"From any premisses follow the same premisses transposed."
Camestres can now be proved like this:[47]

$CaA \cdot BeA \rightarrow BeA \cdot CaA$ (3)
$BeA \cdot CaA \rightarrow AeB \cdot CaA$ (2.2)
$AeB \cdot CaA \rightarrow CeB$ (4.2)
$CeB \rightarrow BeC$ (1.1)
$CaA \cdot BeA \rightarrow BeC$ First to last

There were two ways of setting out a proof:

A. *Celantes*

$AeB \cdot CaA \rightarrow CeB$ (4.2)
$CeB \rightarrow BeC$ (1.11)
$AeB \cdot CaA \rightarrow BeC$

"From a universal negative major and a universal affirmative minor is made a universal negative first figure syllogism which concludes indirectly, e.g. No animal is a stone and every man is an animal, therefore no stone is a man." This is so, for by the second conclusion [*Celarent*] it follows: "No animal is a stone and every man is an animal therefore no man is a stone." And further it follows: "No man is a stone therefore no stone is a man." Therefore from first to last it follows: "No animal is a stone and every man is an animal therefore no stone is a man"...[48]

B. *Celantes*

$$AeB.CaA \rightarrow AeB.CaA$$
$$AeB.CaA \rightarrow CeB \qquad (4.2)$$
$$CeB \rightarrow BeC \qquad (1.11)$$
$$AeB.CaA \rightarrow BeC \qquad \text{First to last}$$

"*Celantes* is reduced to *Celarent* by simple conversion of the conclusion of *Celarent* not because *Celarent* is made from *Celantes*, for in the same way *Celantes* can be made from *Celarent*, but because *Celantes* is proved to be a formal consequence through *Celarent*, and this involves the simple conversion of the conclusion of *Celarent*. It is done in this manner: From the premisses of *Celantes* follow the premisses of *Celarent*: and from the premisses of *Celarent* follows the conclusion of *Celarent*: and from the conclusion of *Celarent* follows the conclusion of *Celantes* by simple conversion: therefore this conclusion also follows from the premisses of *Celantes*, because whatever follows the consequent of a valid consequence follows its antecedent."[49]

Some authors, notably Clichtoveus, went through each of the imperfect modes and offered a detailed reductive proof, but this was not strictly necessary, owing to the information hidden in the name of each mode. The vowels indicated the order and type of propositions; the initial letter indicated which perfect mode was to be used in reduction; S following a vowel showed that the proposition in question was to be converted simply; P following a vowel showed that the proposition in question was to be converted *per accidens*; and M showed that the premisses were to be transposed. This information in conjunction with the rules listed above offers a mechanical way of constructing an ostensive proof for nearly all of the modes which are already known to be valid.

The two exceptions are *Baroco* and *Bocardo* which, as the *C* indicates, can only be proved by means of *reductio per impossibile*, which involves an extra rule.

$$(5.111) \quad P.Q \to R \vdash -R.P \to -Q$$
$$(5.112) \quad P.Q \to R \vdash P.-R \to -Q$$
$$(5.121) \quad P.Q \to R \vdash -R.Q \to -P$$
$$(5.122) \quad P.Q \to R \vdash Q.-R \to -P$$

"From the contradictory of the conclusion of any syllogism together with one of the premisses necessarily follows the opposite of the other premiss."[50]

An alternative version was:

$$(5.211) \quad -R.P \to -Q \vdash P.Q \to R$$
$$(5.212) \quad P.-R \to -Q \vdash P.Q \to R$$
$$(5.221) \quad -R.Q \to -P \vdash P.Q \to R$$
$$(5.222) \quad Q.-R \to -P \vdash P.Q \to R$$

"Wherever from the contradictory of a conclusion together with one premiss in its proper form the contradictory or contrary of the other premiss is validly inferred, the first consequence is always valid."[51]

With this rule in hand together with the rules dealing with contraries and contradictories, we can obtain the following kind of proof:

Baroco $BaA.CaB \to CaA$ (4.1)
$-(CaB) = CoB$ Equipollence   (2.11)
$-(CaA) = CoA$ Equipollence   (2.11)
$BaA.CoA \to CoB$ (5.112), Replacement

"A universal affirmative major and a particular negative minor make a syllogism of the second figure with a particular direct conclusion: e.g. "Every man is an animal and some stone is not an animal, therefore some stone is not a man." This is so, for by the first conclusion [*Barbara*] it follows: "Every man is an animal and every stone is a man, therefore every stone is an animal." Therefore by the third rule from the contradictory of the conclusion, i.e. "Some stone is not an animal", taken as a minor with the same major, i.e. "Every man is an animal", the contradictory of the other premiss, i.e. "Some stone is not a man", necessarily follows in this way: "Every man is an animal and some stone is not an animal, therefore some stone is not a man."[52]

Jungius offered an interesting alternative to reduction *per impossibile* for *Baroco* and *Bocardo* when he suggested that contraposition should be used instead.[53] He offered the following proof of *Bocardo*:

Bo	Some element is not visible	A
car	Every element is a body	B
do	Therefore some body is not visible	C
Da	Every element is a body	B
ri	Something not-visible is an element	D, from A by contraposition
i	Therefore something not-visible is a body	E, from B and D by first figure syllogism
	Therefore some body is not-visible	F, from E by simple conversion
	Therefore some body is not visible	C, from B by equipollence.

It is obvious from an examination of his proof that he has in mind the mistaken notion of reduction as a process for transforming an imperfect syllogism into a perfect syllogism, for it is *Bocardo*, not *Darii*, that he takes as a premiss. However, one could set out a proof of *Bocardo* using *Darii* as a premiss, and employing the same rules that Jungius appealed to:

(1)	$AoB . AaC \rightarrow AaC . AoB$	Transposition
(2)	$AoB = Ai\bar{B}$	Obversion, (5.12)
(3)	$AoB . AaC \rightarrow AaC . Ai\bar{B}$	(1), (2) Replacement
(4)	$Ai\bar{B} = \bar{B}iA$	Simple conversion
(5)	$AoB . AaC \rightarrow AaC . \bar{B}iA$	(3), (4) Replacement
(6)	$AaC . \bar{B}iA \rightarrow \bar{B}iC$	*Darii*
(7)	$\bar{B}iC = Ci\bar{B}$	Simple conversion
(8)	$Ci\bar{B} \rightarrow CoB$	Obversion
(9)	$AoB . AaC \rightarrow CoB$	(5)–(8), First to last

The proof that Jungius offered for *Baroco* was much simpler. He took a syllogism in *Baroco* and transformed it into a syllogism in *Ferio* by applying a rule of partial contraposition to the first premiss, and a rule of obversion to the second premiss. This proof can also be rewritten in such a way as to bring out its correct formal structure:

(1)	$AaB \cdot CoB \to AaB$	Conjunction, (4.11)
(2)	$AaB \to \bar{B}eA$	Partial contraposition, (4.31)
(3)	$AaB \cdot CoB \to \bar{B}eA$	(1), (2) First to last
(4)	$AaB \cdot CoB \to CoB$	Conjunction, (4.12)
(5)	$CoB = Ci\bar{B}$	Obversion, (5.12)
(6)	$AaB \cdot CoB \to Ci\bar{B}$	(4), (5) First to last
(7)	$AaB \cdot CoB \to \bar{B}eA \cdot Ci\bar{B}$	(3), (6) Valid consequence, (3.91)
(8)	$\bar{B}eA \cdot Ci\bar{B} \to CoA$	Ferio
(9)	$AaB \cdot CoB \to CoA$	(7), (8) First to last

Some authors noted that reduction *per impossibile* could be applied to any imperfect mode, since rule (5) was sufficiently general in nature to apply to all syllogisms. Some simple instructions were given so that proofs could be found with the minimum of effort.[54] When the indirect modes of the first figure are to be reduced *per impossibile*, the contradictory of the conclusion is put in place of the major premiss, the major premiss becomes minor, and the contrary of the minor premiss is inferred, except in the case of *Celantes*, where the contradictory of the conclusion is put in place of the minor premiss which now becomes the major premiss, and it is the contradictory of the major premiss that is inferred. In the second figure the contradictory of the conclusion becomes the minor premiss and the major remains the same; in the third figure the contradictory of the conclusion becomes the major premiss, and the minor premiss remains the same. The mnemonic sentence "*Nesciebatis odiebam levare romanis*" showed which perfect mode was to be used in the reduction.[55] The syllables represent the conclusions of the relevant perfect modes, and they are ordered according to the ordering of the five indirect modes of the first figure, the direct modes of the second figure, and the direct modes of the third figure. Thus, the 'e' in the first syllable, 'Nes', shows that *Baralipton* is to be proved by means of *Celarent*, and the 'i' in the seventh syllable, 'di', shows that *Camestres* is to be proved by means of *Darii*. Had the fourth figure been mentioned, the whole account of reduction *per impossibile* would have had to be revised, since one mode of the fourth figure can only be proved *per impossibile* by appeal to another mode of the same figure.

A few authors mentioned a third kind of reduction, reduction by exposition, which applied to syllogisms of the third figure and involved proof by means of an expository syllogism.[56] Trutvetter offered the following example: "This is a syllogism in *Bocardo*: Some *a* is not *b* and every *a* is *c*, therefore some *c* is not *b*. If the premisses are true it follows that there is an *a* which is *c* and which is not *b*: let this be *f*. It then follows validly: *f* is not *b* and the same *f* is *c*, therefore some *c* is not *b*. Since therefore the conclusion follows formally (in an expository syllogism of the third figure) from premisses which follow formally from the premisses of *Bocardo* and since whatever follows the consequent of a valid consequence also follows the antecedent, the result is that if the expository syllogism is a valid formal consequence, the syllogism in *Bocardo* is a valid formal consequence."[57] Fonseca, however, pointed out that the proof could not be carried out in this fashion, since particular propositions do not imply singular propositions,[58] as will become clear if one looks at the rules for suppositional descent and ascent. In the case of a syllogism with two universal premisses, such as *Darapti*, one can indeed produce a formal proof:

$$MaP \cdot MaS \rightarrow x = P \cdot x = S \qquad \text{Descent}$$
$$x = P \cdot x = S \rightarrow SiP \qquad \text{Expository syllogism}$$
$$MaP \cdot MaS \rightarrow SiP \qquad \text{First to last}$$

However, in cases such as *Bocardo* and *Disamis* one has to rely on an informal argument. Such an argument could look like this: if both premisses of a syllogism in *Disamis* are true, then every member of class *M* is identical with a member of class *S*, and at least one member of class *M* is identical with a member of class *P*. There is no way of identifying this member formally, since particular propositions are equivalent to disjunctions, and no inference can be made from a disjunction to one of its parts. However, one can arbitrarily name an individual, *x*, and say that *x* is a member of both *S* and *P*. If this is admitted, then the particular conclusion follows. Thus anyone who doubts that the conclusion of *Disamis* follows from the premisses, can be shown that accepting the premisses of *Disamis* as true implies an acceptance of the conclusion by virtue of the kind of interpretation which can be given to those premisses.

4. SYLLOGISMS WITH SINGULAR TERMS

It was noted earlier that propositions containing singular terms were admitted to the system, and a careful reading of the sources reveals a number of interesting theorems about such propositions. The reader should be reminded that any proposition whose subject was singular was called a singular proposition, whether the predicate was singular or not, but that any proposition whose predicate was singular was treated as if it were of a standard form. From section (I.4) of this chapter, we obtain the following rules:

(1.1) $x=y .=. y=x$ Conversion (3.311)
(1.2) $x\neq y .=. y\neq x$ Conversion (3.322)
(2.1) $x=A .=. Aix$ Conversion (3.321) and (3.332)
(2.2) $x\neq A .=. Aex$ Conversion (3.322) and (3.333)
(3.1) $Aax \rightarrow x=A$ Conversion (3.331)
(3.2) $x\neq A \rightarrow Aox$ Conversion (3.323)

These rules can be explained and justified in the light of the rules for personal supposition which were discussed in Section II.1 of this chapter. It was laid down there that a singular term has discrete supposition, the subjects of A and E propositions have distributive supposition, and the subjects of I and O propositions have determinate supposition. The predicate of a singular affirmative proposition has determinate supposition, and the predicate of a singular negative proposition has distributive supposition. Thus we can obtain the following translations:

(2.1) $x=A_1 \lor x=A_2 \lor \ldots \lor x=A_n .=. A_1=x \lor A_2=x \lor \ldots \lor A_n=x$
(2.2) $x\neq A_1 . x\neq A_2 \ldots . x\neq A_n .=. A_1 \neq x . A_2 \neq x \ldots . A_n \neq x$
(3.1) $A_1=x . A_2=x \ldots . A_n=x \rightarrow x=A_1 \lor x=A_2 \lor \ldots \lor x=A_n$
(3.2) $x\neq A_1 . x\neq A_2 \ldots . x\neq A_n \rightarrow A_1 \neq x \lor A_2 \neq x \lor \ldots \lor A_n=x$

There were two ways of justifying the use of propositions with singular terms in the syllogism. The first way involved an appeal to regulative principles which could be viewed as supplementary to *dici de omni* and *dici de nullo*.[59] Hieronymus of St. Mark gave a clear account of these.[60] There are, he said, two relevant metaphysical principles: When two things are the same as a third, they are the same as each other, and when of two things, one is the same as a third and one is not, they are not the same as each other. So far as logic is concerned, he said, the force of these principles is captured in the following rules: (1) Terms which are verified of the same univocal singular term are verified of each other; (2) when there are two terms of which one is verified of a univocal singular term and one is negated of that term, the two terms are negated of each other.

The second way, which was sometimes combined with the first, involved the interpretation of singular propositions as having a standard form. Some authors obviously took it that singular propositions were equivalent to particular propositions, since they gave examples of such modes as *Darii* with one universal and two singular propositions;[61] but those who discussed the matter decided that a singular proposition must be treated as if it were universal, since whatever is predicated of the singular term is predicated of the whole.[62] Thus, "All believers are justified, Peter is a believer, therefore Peter is justified" is not an example of *Darii* but of *Barbara*, said Wallis. This interpretation fits in to some extent with what has already been said. If '$x = P$' is equivalent to 'xaP' then by conversion we may obtain 'Pix', but not 'Pax'. On the other hand, double quantification will have to be used to explain why '$x = y$' converts to '$y = x$'. That is, we want not just "All x is y" but "All x is all y".

The most commonly given example of the syllogism with singular terms was the so-called expository syllogism, in which the middle term was singular. The third figure was taken to be the perfect one, since it was governed directly by the two regulative principles,[63] but most people admitted examples from the first and second figures as well.[64] Fonseca added four extra affirmative modes to the second figure which, he said, were reducible to the first figure by conversion of the major premiss.[65] He was relying on rules (2.1) and (3.1). We thus obtain the following list of expository syllogisms:

(1.1)	$x = P . Sax \rightarrow SaP$	*(Barbara)*
(1.2)	$x \neq P . Sax \rightarrow SeP$	*(Celarent)*
(1.3)	$x = P . Six \rightarrow SiP$	*(Darii)*
(1.4)	$x \neq P . Six \rightarrow SoP$	*(Ferio)*
(2.1)	$Pex . Sax \rightarrow SeP$	*(Cesare)*
(2.2)	$Pax . Sex \rightarrow SeP$	*(Camestres)*

(2.3)	$Pex . Six \rightarrow SoP$	(*Festino*)
(2.4)	$Pax . Sox \rightarrow SoP$	(*Baroco*)
(2.5)	$Pax . Sax \rightarrow SaP$	(Reduced to *Barbara*)
(2.6)	$Pax . Six \rightarrow SiP$	(Reduced to *Darii*)
(2.7)	$Pix . Sax \rightarrow SaP$	(Reduced to *Barbara*)
(2.8)	$Pix . Six \rightarrow SiP$	(Reduced to *Darii*)
(3.1)	$x = P . x = S \rightarrow SiP$	(*Darapti, Disamis, Datisi*)
(3.2)	$x \neq P . x = S \rightarrow SoP$	(*Felapton, Bocardo, Ferison*)

A great many combinations of premisses with singular terms are possible, for not only the middle term but also the major and minor terms may be singular. Ramus gave two groups of examples which were frequently used by subsequent authors.[66] One group consisted of what he called special syllogisms, in which the major premiss was general and the minor premiss and conclusion were singular. The other group consisted of what he called proper syllogisms, in which all the propositions were singular. Ramus divided each group into two types of which the first corresponded to Aristotle's second figure, and the second to Aristotle's first figure. There was no apparent reason for this re-ordering, and I shall ignore it, as did most of Ramus's successors.

Special Syllogisms:

(1.1)	$MaP . x = M \rightarrow x = P$
(1.2)	$MeP . x = M \rightarrow x \neq P$
(2.1)	$PeM . x = M \rightarrow x \neq P$
(2.2)	$PaM . x \neq M \rightarrow x \neq P$

Proper Syllogisms:

(1.1)	$x = P . y = x \rightarrow y = P$
(1.2)	$x \neq P . y = x \rightarrow y \neq P$
(2.1)	$x \neq M . y = M \rightarrow y \neq x$
(2.2)	$x = M . y \neq M \rightarrow y \neq x$

Fonseca added the following to the second and third figures:[67]

(2.3)	$x = y . z = y \rightarrow z = x$
(2.4)	$x \neq y . z = y \rightarrow z \neq x$
(3.1)	$x = P . x = y \rightarrow y = P$
(3.2)	$x \neq P . x = y \rightarrow y \neq P$

NOTES

¹ Major, *Introductorium*, cxlvi. Cf. Eckius, *Summulae*, ci^{vo}.

² Peter of Spain, *Summulae*: Bocheński, 4.03, 36f., de Rijk, 44. Cf. Gebwiler; Clichtoveus: Le Fèvre, 82^{vo}f.

³ E.g. Isendoorn, 586; Heereboord, 203; Jungius, 125; Wendelin, 210.

⁴ Fonseca I, 364; Marsh, 127; Du Trieu, 124.

⁵ Burgersdijck, 251; Zabarella, *De Quarta Syllogismorum Figura in Opera*, 124.

⁶ Arnauld, 202.

⁷ Clichtoveus: Le Fèvre, 86. Cf. Pardo, cxxxix^{vo}. In the seventeenth century Wallis (177) noted that there is an indirect mode for every direct mode.

⁸ Wallis, 180–183. Arnauld (202) noted the relationship between the indirect modes of the first figure and the direct modes of the fourth.

⁹ Clichtoveus: Le Fèvre, 86.

¹⁰ Marsh, 134.

¹¹ Burgersdijck, 262; Ormazius, 60vo.

¹² Eckius, *Summulae*, xlviii^{vo}; Mainz; Gebwiler; Bartholomaeus de Usingen. See also John of St. Thomas, *Cursus*, 203.

¹³ Trutvetter, *Summule*; Bartholomaeus de Usingen; Gebwiler; Mainz. Although Clichtoveus listed nine similar modes he denied that they involved a fourth figure: Clichtoveus: Le Fèvre, 86, 84.

¹⁴ Otto, xxiiii. Cf. Pardo, cxxxix^{vo}; Willichius, 182f.; Gorscius, 890f.

¹⁵ Campanella, 391.

¹⁶ Derodon, 606. Isendoorn, 610f., discussed the point, and said that if the premisses are transposed, one will get an indirect conclusion.

¹⁷ Cardano, *Dialectica*, 296f.; Scheibler, *Tractatus*, 94; Arnauld, 188; Aldrich, 17.

¹⁸ Crakanthorpe, 274; Wallis, 182; Arnauld, 188.

¹⁹ Averroes, *Priorum Resolutiorum Liber Primus in Opera* I, 63vo.

²⁰ Niphus, *Libros priorum*, 26vo.

²¹ Jungius, 188.

²² Dietericus, 296.

²³ For further discussion, see Ashworth².

²⁴ Alsted, *Systema*, 394; Bertius, 134; Crellius, 178; Keckermann, *Systema*, 417; Wallis, 150; Zabarella, *Opera*, 130f.

²⁵ Alsted, *Systema*, 394; Keckermann, *Systema*, 417; Du Moulin, *Introductio*, 47.

²⁶ Versor, 121vo.

²⁷ Burgersdijck, 269. Cf. Alsted, *Systema*, 394; Horstius, 268; C. Martinus, *Commentarii*, 313.

²⁸ E.g. Bartholomaeus de Usingen; Eckius, *Summulae*, liiii^{vo}; Mainz; Ormazius, 60; Trutvetter, *Summule*; Gebwiler. For a later source, see Isendoorn, 589.

²⁹ Marsh, 147; Aldrich, 16; Arnauld, 187.

³⁰ Maiolus; Crellius, 186 f.; Alsted, *Systema*, 396.

³¹ For discussion of divine terms see e.g. Celaya, *In libros Prior*, and Sbarroya, *Expositio quarti*. Both these books contain tracts on divine terms.

³² Sbarroya, *Expositio quarti*, vi. For the text, see appendix.

³³ Cf. Breitkopf, *Compendium*; Trutvetter, *Summule*; Eckius, *Summulae*, xlvi^{vo}; Mainz.

³⁴ Clichtoveus: Le Fèvre, 88f.

³⁵ The rules, together with an explanation, can be found in late fifteenth and early sixteenth century sources such as Gebwiler, Bartholomaeus de Usingen, Mainz and Breitkopf,

Compendium. For earlier sources, see Peter of Spain, *Summulae*: Bocheński, 4.05, 37; de Rijk, 44f.; and Dorp. For later sources, see e.g. Du Trieu, 135–140; Burgersdijk, 266–272; Ormazius, 61–62; Jungius, 137f.; Fonseca I 382–386. In the later sources, the rules usually appeared without comment.

[36] For a very clear explanation, see Aldrich, 15:
"Praemissis particularibus nihil probatur. Nam praemissarum altera affirmat: Ergo in illa medium non distribuitur: Ergo distribui debet in reliqua: Ergo illa est negativa in qua medium praedicatur. Ergo conclusio negativa: Ergo praedicatum ejus distribuitur, quod in praemissis non est distributum; Fuit enim vel affirmativae terminus alter, vel subjectum negativae; horum vero nullus distribuitur."

[37] See Aldrich, 15; Arnauld, 183f.

[38] Gebwiler; Bartholomaeus de Usingen; Pardo, cxxxvii[vo].

[39] Marsh, 149f.; Wallis, 192; Aldrich, 18f.

[40] Aldrich, 28.

[41] E.g. Alcalá, 30; Stierius, 21; Arnauld, 181f.; Aldrich, 15.

[42] Aldrich, 17f. Cf. Arnauld (187ff.) who used the same sort of procedure, but excluded the five subalternate modes.

[43] E.g. Burgersdijck, 276ff.

[44] Cf. Gebwiler; Eckius, *Summulae*, liii[vo].

[45] Trutvetter, *Summule*. See also Bartholomaeus de Usingen; Gebwiler. For texts, see appendix.

[46] Otto, xxii[vo]; Clichtoveus: Le Fèvre, 85vo.

[47] Clichtoveus: Le Fèvre, 89vo.

[48] Clichtoveus: Le Fèvre, 89.

[49] Tartaretus, *Expositio*, 27. Cf. Pardo, cxxxvii; Hieronymus of St. Mark. Tartaretus wrote: "…celantes… reducitur ad celarent per conversionem simplicem conclusionis de celarent / non quod de celantes fiat celarent: quia eodem modo de celarent fieret celantes: sed est probare celantes esse formalem consequentiam per celarent: et hoc per conversionem simplicem conclusionis de celarent: et fit hoc modo: Nam ad premissas de celantes sequuntur premisse de celarent: et ad premissas de celarent sequitur conclusio de celarent: et ad conclusionem de celarent / sequitur conclusio de celantes per conversionem simplicem: ergo talis conclusio etiam sequitur ad premissas de celantes: quia quicquid sequitur ad consequens bone consequentie / sequitur ad eius antecedens."

[50] Clichtoveus: Le Fèvre, 85vo.

[51] Trutvetter, *Summule*.

[52] Clichtoveus: Le Fèvre, 89[vo]f.

[53] Jungius, 141f.

[54] E.g. Du Trieu, 148ff.; Eckius, *Summulae*, liiii; John of St. Thomas, *Formal Logic*, 118f.

[55] For early sources, see Trutvetter, *Summule*; Eckius, *Summulae*, liiii. For later sources, see Alcalá, 37; Derodon, 649; R. Sanderson, 138–141; Ormazius, 66vo. Some gave an alternative: *"Phoebifer axis obit terras sphaeram (or aethram)-que quotannis."* See Fonseca I, 414; Du Trieu, 149f.; John of St. Thomas, *Formal Logic*, 119.

[56] Tartaretus, *Expositio*, 28; Fonseca, I 414–420; Du Trieu, 148; Jungius, 148; Burgersdijck, 283.

[57] Trutvetter, *Summule*. Trutvetter wrote: "ille est syllogismus in bocardo: aliquod *a* non est *b*: et omne *a* est *c*: igitur aliquod *c* non est *b*: ad cuius premissas esse veras sequitur quod dabile sit aliquod *a* quod sit *c* et non sit *b*: sit ergo illud *f*. tunc bene sequitur *f* non est *b*: et idem *f* est *c*. ergo aliquod *c* non est *b*. Quom ergo hec conclusio formaliter sequitur (quia expositorie in tercia figura) ad premissas sequentes formaliter ad premissas in bocardo:

et quicquid sequitur ad consequens bone consequentie etiam sequitur ad antecedens consectarium est si syllogismus expositorius est bona et formalis consequentia : syllogismum in bocardo esse bonam et formalem consequentiam."

[58] Fonseca, I 416–418.

[59] See Mainz; Bartholomaeus de Usingen; Gebwiler; Clichtoveus: Le Fèvre, 93vo. For later sources see Scheibler, *Tractatus*, 78; Crakanthorpe, 294; Derodon, 641f.; Du Trieu, 147; John of St. Thomas, *Formal Logic*, 122; Burgersdijck, 265; Aldrich, 14; Fonseca, I 400–402.

[60] Hieronymus of St. Mark wrote: "Et probantur esse boni per duo principia metaphysicalia quorum unum est. quecunque sunt eadem uni tercio inter se sunt eadem. quod principium logicaliter sic exponitur. quicunque termini verificantur de aliquo termino univoce et singulariter tento verificantur de se invicem.... Aliud est principium metaphysicum virtute cuius syllogismi expositorii negativi tenent. Scilicet quorumcunque unum est idem alicui cuius reliquum non est idem. illa inter se non sunt eadem. Hoc principium logicaliter sic exponitur. Si sint duo termini quorum unus verificetur de uno termino singulariter et univoce tento et alter vere negetur de illo. illi vere negabuntur de se invicem."

[61] Gorscius, 891; Willichius, 177; Jungius, 130.

[62] Wallis, 185f., 267. Cf. Aldrich, 22; Scheibler, *Tractatus*, 73.

[63] Bartholomaeus de Usingen; Gebwiler.

[64] E.g. Hieronymus of St. Mark; Scheibler, *Tractatus*, 75; and many others.

[65] Fonseca, I 400.

[66] Ramus, *Dialectica*, 59–67. For special syllogisms see, e.g., Jungius, 131ff. For proper syllogisms, see, e.g., Abraham of Guise, 25vo; Wallis, 187f.; Burgersdijck, 260.

[67] Fonseca, I 396–398.

APPENDIX

LATIN TEXTS

Chapter Two, Part II, Section 1, note 7

Dolz, *Termini*, vi[vo]

... terminus captus logice novem modis diffinitur ibi non curamus de acceptione phisica secundum quam concedimus quod finis urbis parisiensis est terminus: quia illo modo terminus nihil aliud est quam finis alicuius rei.

Primo enim diffinitur sic. Terminus est in quem resoluitur propositio: et hec est diffinitio philosophi primo priorum.

Secundo sic. Terminus est pars propinqua propositionis. et hec est diffinitio Guillermi ochan in principio sue logice.

Tertio sic. Terminus est orationis constitutivum: ut aliqui volunt.

Quarto modo sic. Terminus est quo nectitur propositio: et hec est diffinitio boetii.

Quinto modo sic. Terminus est signum propositionale.

Sexto sic. Terminus est signum ponibile in propositione consueta.

Septimo sic. Terminus est signum quod ex impositione quam actu habet aliquid vel aliqua vel aliqualiter representare natum est potentie cognitive.

Octavo sic. Terminus est signum significans aliquid vel aliqua vel aliqualiter pro quo in propositione taliter poni potest.

Ultimo sic. Terminus est signum ponibile in propositione tanquam subiectum vel predicatum vel tanquam exercens officium que diffinitiones dantur a plerisque. sed si bene respiciantur: licet differant verbis: non autem ratione et sententia. Ideo quamlibet pro libito sustentare poteris: tamen quia ultima videtur clarior: illam in sequentibus tenebimus.

Pro cuius intellectione est advertendum quod ly terminus potest capi quattuor modis.

Primo modo pro omni quod significat se: sive significet aliud a se sive non. et isto modo quelibet res mundi est terminus. Nam quelibet res mundi significat se. et si dicatur pari forma sequitur quod quelibet res mundi esset propositio. Nam quelibet res mundi ad minus in potentia propinqua significat se esse qui est modus significandi propositionalis: concedo sequelam.

Secundo modo: capitur pro omni illo quod significat aliud a se et a suo simili: et a suo prolatore: et a suis partibus: sive pro illo sit ponibilis in propositione sive non. Et isto modo circulus pendens ante tabernam est terminus. similiter et campana collegii.

Tertio modo: capitur pro omni illo quod significat aliud [a] se et a suo simili: et a suo prolatore: et a suis partibus. et cum hoc pro tali est ponibilis in propositione pro tali significato: et isto modo ly homo est terminus.

Quarto modo: capitur ly terminus pro omni illo qui est ponibilis in propositione tanquam subiectum vel predicatum: vel exercens aliquod officium sive talis significet aliud a se et a suo simili: et a suo prolatore: et a suis partibus sive non: et isto modo ly buf est terminus. similiter et quelibet littera alphabeti: et isto modo capitur in proposito et proportionabiliter ly signum potest capi quattuor modis iuxta acceptiones de ly terminus.

Chapter Two, Part II, Section 1, note 9

Major, *Opera*, ii

Terminus accipitur dupliciter. Uno modo phisice ut convenit rebus ad extra quemadmodum dicimus de termino a quo et de termino ad quem. Secundo modo ut convenit dicibilibus: et hoc quintupliciter. Primo modo capite extenso termino quod large vulgo dicimus pro omni signo ponibili in propositione. Secundo modo capitur minus large pro omni signo significative sumpto ponibili in propositione sive fuerit complexum sive non. Tertio modo capitur proprie pro omni signo incomplexo significative sumpto propositione ponibili. Quarto modo propriissime pro omni illo quod significative sumptum potest esse extremum propositionis respectu verbi personalis modi finiti. Quinto modo strictissime pro incomplexo quod potest esse extremum significative sumptum etc.

Chapter Two, Part II, Section 1, note 13

Celaya, *Dial. Introd.*

...ly significare sic solet diffiniri. Significare est representare potentie cognitive aliquid vel aliqua vel aliqualiter. Dicitur notanter potentie cognitive et non intellective: quia aliqui termini bene representant brutis tamen bruta non habent potentiam intellectivam sed cognitivam. Dicitur notanter aliquid propter terminos singularis numeri non collectivos ut sunt isti sortes homo et sic de aliis. Dicitur aliqua propter terminos collectivos et propter terminos pluralis numeri ut sunt isti populus homines et sic de aliis. Dicitur aliqualiter propter sincathegoreumata ut sunt ista omnis non: et sic de aliis.

Circa istam distinctionem dubitatur primo quid sit representare ad hoc respondetur quod representare est facere cognoscere aliquid vel aliqua vel aliqualiter et pro elucidatione huius materie est advertendum quod quadriffariam dicitur aliquid representare. Uno modo obiective et nihil aliud est quam esse obiectum quo mediante causatur noticia vel actus intelligendi et isto modo quodlibet ens mundi dicitur representare quia quodlibet ens mundi potest esse obiectum ad productionem noticie suiipsius. Secundo modo dicitur aliquid representare affective et nihil aliud est quam esse causam efficientem noticie vel actus intelligendi et isto modo anima nostra dicitur representare effective. Tertio modo dicitur aliquid representare formaliter et est esse noticiam vel actum intelligendi: et isto modo termini mentales dicuntur representare. Quarto modo dicitur aliquid representare instrumentaliter: et est esse instrumentum quo mediante causatur noticia vel actus intelligendi: et iste modo dicuntur representare termini vocales et scripti in omnibus istis diffinitionibus. Posui illam particulam noticia propter cathegoreumata et illam particulam actus intelligendi propter sincathegoreumata. Nec posui illam particulam actus intelligendi superfluam in diffinitione de ly representare obiective: nam ly homo et ly animal sunt obiecta in ista omnis homo est animal mediantibus quibus causatur actus intelligendi de ly omnis et de ly est secundum enim omnes logicos et inferius declarabitur sincathegoreumata habent cathegoreumata pro obiectis hoc dixerim propter aliquem modernum parum in artibus excitatum qui in suis importatis asseruit illam particulam superfluam positam a me. Idem etiam modernus credit quod quomodo diffinitur aliquis terminus quicquid illic ponitur est diffinitio vel pars diffinitionis aut diffinitum et ideo dicit quod ly nihil aliud quod posui est superfluum et si istud argumentum valeret sequeretur quod ly est ponitur superflue quomodo dicimus homo est animal rationale: quia non est pars diffinitionis aut diffiniti sed danda est illi venia quia nunc incipit gustare logicalia et verba dicunt aptitudinem in potentia propinqua non solum in istis diffinitionibus sed in omnibus aliis dandis.

Dubitatur secundo quid est significare aliqualiter ad hoc dubium respondet aliquis in suis terminis quod significare aliqualiter est exercere aliquod officium supra aliquem terminum scilicet confundere distribuere et sic de aliis: sed hec diffinitio non valet: quia propositio de significatione totali significat aliqualiter secundum ipsum et etiam secundum communem modum tamen non exercet aliquod officium supra aliquem terminum ut patet intuenti igitur multis aliis modis possem impugnare illam diffinitionem sed pro nunc brevitatis causa missa faciemus. Quidam in suis progymnasmatibus dupliciter nititur salvare talem diffini-tionem. Dicit primo quod solum diffiniebat modum significandi aliqualiter simplicem ut dicit patere ex suis dictis: sed potius oppositum patet ex dictis eius postquam tractat in eodem capite tam de significatione complexa quam incomplexa neque aliam diffinitionem posuit. Dicit secundo quod est dubium aut propositio significat aliqualiter: sed hoc non erat dubium suo preceptori qui expresse illud tenet neque alicui alteri debet esse dubium cum ex opposita opinionem quam postea dicet fuisse Hieronimi pardo sequatur aliquem terminum significare aliqua pro quibus non potest supponere et non est defectus ex parte connotationis quod apud omnes logicos inconvenit. Ideo aliter ad dubium respondetur diffiniendo ly significare aliqualiter sic est denotare rem vel res taliter se habere vel rem vel res non taliter se habere. Prima particula ponitur propter sincathegoreumata incomplexa et propter propositiones affirmativas. Secunda particula ponitur propter propositiones negativas. Nec ex ista diffinitione sequitur quemlibet terminum significantem aliqualiter esse propositionem (ut ille inquit) quia modus significandi propositionis longe diversus est a quolibet. Alio modo significandi aliquali cum modus significandi propositionis sit com-plexus et consurgens ex significationibus partium (et ut verbis philosophie utar in primo capite primi periarmenias) quelibet talis significatio est compositiva vel divisiva significatio vero aliorum sincathegoreumatum est simplex et incomplexa: et hec est differentia quam progymnasmator ille non vidit. Et est advertendum quod significare capitur dupliciter. Uno modo large et isto modo capitur in diffinitione data. Alio modo capitur stricte et tunc solet sic diffiniri. Significare est representare potentie cognitive aliquid vel aliqua vel aliqualiter aliud a se et a sibi simili et a suo prolatore....

Chapter Two, Part II, Section 3, note 61

Raulin

Dubitatur primo, utrum voces significent idem re existente et non existente. Arguitur primo quod non quia ista vox ens non significat idem re existente et non existente quia non existente re nulla res esset et sic ista vox non esset et per consequens nichil significaret.

Secundo ista vox conceptus non significat idem re existente et non existente igitur. antecedens patet quia si nulla res significata per illam vocem existeret tunc conceptus cui subordinatur in significando non esset quia ista vox significavit conceptum cui subordinatur in significando sed sine tali conceptu illa vox nichil potest significare igitur.

Tertio signum et signatum correlative dicuntur ergo omnia relativa sunt simul natura et dicuntur ad convertentiam sequitur quod ista consequentia est bona signum est ergo im-possibile est signum aliquid significare nisi signatum sit ergo vox nichil significat nisi res per eam significata existat et per consequens non significat idem ultimate.

Quarto sic sorte existente hec vox sortes significat ens et eo non existente significat non ens quia significat aliquid quod non est et non ens non est idem enti ergo ista vox sortes non significat idem sorte existente et sorte non existente.

Quinto sic sorte mortuo conceptus sortis non manet in intellectu ergo tunc ista vox sortes significat sortem. consequentia tenet. quia ista vox sortes non significat sortem et antecedens patet. quia conceptus est naturalis similitudo rei significate per ipsum sed non enti non est aliqua similitudo cum nichil sit non enti simile igitur.

In oppositum arguitur quia voces non cadunt a suis significatis et tamen non idem significarent re existente et non existente ergo caderent a suis significatis quia post destructionem rei significate non amplius significarent sua significata.

Secundo sic nisi voces idem significarent re existente et non existente sequeretur quod omnes historie de preteritis gestis essent false quid est contra approbatos auctores et contra sacrum canonem biblie quia tunc non possemus vere loqui de preteritis ut quando dicimus quod hector fuit filius priami vel illi termini hector et priamus nobis significant eosdem homines quos significebant viventibus hectore et priamo vel non si sic habetur intentum. Si non vel ergo nichil omnio significant quid est absurdum dicere vel alio nomine significant et sic non possemus vere loqui de hectore et priamo pro solutione advertendum est.

Sciendum est primo quod significatio nichil aliud est quam noticia intellectus que principaliter est causata ab intellectu et instrumentaliter a voce significativa ita licet significatio sit actus vocis tanquam cause instrumentalis est tamen actus interior anime tanquam cause principalis. Et sic patet quod istud verbum significo ampliat actum ab eo rectum ad presentia preterita futura etc.

Secundo sequitur quod non valet ista consequentia ly antichristus significat hominem ergo significatur hominem qui est quia antecedens est verum et consequens falsum ut satis constat.

Tertio sequitur quod hec consequentia non valet ly antichristus significat antichristum et antichristus nichil est ergo nichil significat quia in prima consequentia arguitur a magis amplo ad minus amplum sine distributione magis ampli sed in secunda nuper capta arguitur a minus amplo ad magis amplum cum distributione magis ampli immo utrobique est fallacia consequentis et licet ly significo faciat terminum se sequentem appellare suam rationem determinatam: tamen de hoc hic non est curandum eo quod presens difficultas non consistit in ista appellatione.

Conclusio prima non omnis vox significativa significat idem re existente et non existente. Patet per duas rationes ante oppositum.

Conclusio secunda omnis vox significativa per impositionem actualem ad cuius significatorum curruptionem sequitur corruptio huius vocis vel conceptus cui subordinatur in significando significat idem re existente et non existente et ex his patet solutio ad primam et secundam rationes in prima conclusione. Ad tertiam dicitur quod consequentia subsistendi non convertitur in terminis relativis quorum alterum est ampliativum sicut est de ly signatum ideo consequentia ista non valet signum est ergo signatum est. Ad quartam negatur minor quia sensus eius est sorte non existente ly sortes significat non ens. i. significat aliquid quod non est nec fuit nec erit nec potest esse nec potest ymaginari esse et ratio est quia terminus cui additur negatio infinitans distribuitur et cum hoc ampliatur per istud verbum significat ut in hoc nomine non ens ly ens distribuitur et ampliatur. Ad quintam negatur antecedens quod conceptus non dicitur naturalis similitudo rei cuius est quia sic omnes res essent similes essentialiter vel accidentaliter cum alia quia conceptus hominis et homo non habent inter se talem convenientiam sed ex eo dicitur naturalis similitudo rei sicut effigies vel ymago alterius rei representativa rei cuius est ymago licet differenter quia ymago representat rem obiective cuius est ymago et conceptus representat formaliter et actu aliter dicitur naturalis quia conceptus naturaliter representat id est de sua natura et non impositione representat rem cuius est immo non enti bene est talis similitudo naturalis et argumentum procedit ex similitudine que est convenientia unius rei cum alia.

Chapter Two, Part II, Section 8, note 120

Derodon, 552

Dices, si horâ primâ fiat propositio formalis affirmans Petrum currere, Petro realiter currente horâ primâ, est vera; si verò horâ secundâ fiat eadem propositio formalis affirmans Petrum currere, Petro non currente horâ secundâ, est falsa: Ergo haec propositio formalis affirmans Petrum currere de verâ mutatur in falsam. Verùm respondetur propositionem formalem horâ primâ affirmantem Petrum currere, aequipollere propositioni formali affirmanti Petrum nunc currere, seu Petrum currere horâ primâ; propositionem verò formalem horâ secundâ affirmantem Petrum currere, aequipollere propositioni formali affirmanti Petrum currere horâ secundâ: Ergo non est eadem propositio, cùm non sit idem praedicatum; currere enim horâ prima, & currere horâ secunda sunt praedicata diversa. Quare propositio quae affirmat rem esse pro eo tempore quo res est, non potest esse falsa: & quae rem negat pro eo tempore quo res est, non potest esse vera; siquidem ex eo quòd res est vel non est tempore adsignificato, propositio id adsignificans vera vel falsa est.

Chapter Two, Part II, Section 9, notes 138 and 139

Cologne, c^{vo}

… supposito quod sortes non sit adhuc hec est vera sortes est animal quod tamen moderni negant dicentes quod hoc verbum est semper importat existentiam. et sic sensus illius propositionis est sortes est animal i. sortes existit animal. hoc autem est falsum quia in propositionibus de est tercio adiacente hoc verbum est non importat existentiam sed conformitatem estremorum ad invicem. et quia res concepte subiiciuntur et predicantur in enunciationibus et non res ad extra. et ergo sive sortes sit sive non sit semper est animal et etiam homo.

Cologne, cvii^{vo}

… esse capitur tripliciter. uno modo pro esse essentie. et sic diffinitio dicit esse i. essentiam et naturam rei. Alio modo ut dicit esse actualis existentie. et sic capitur in propositionibus de est secundo adiacente gratia principii in eo inclusi. ut cum dicitur sortes est. sensus est sortes est existens a parte rei. et istud antiqui concedunt cum modernis. Tercio capitur esse pro esse compositionis extremorum. et sic capitur in propositionibus de est tercio adiacente de materia naturali et sic capitur esse cum dicitur adam est animal: sortes est risibilis: que sunt vere. etiam subiectis non existentibus. quia sensus est illa predicata animal et risibile non repugnant sorti concepto. aut ade concepto. quod est verum. Ratio huius est. quia compositio est quoddam accidens rationis conveniens rebus conceptis. et non rebus extra animam existentibus. ergo homo conceptus potest predicari de adam concepto vere. licet adam non existat ad extra.

Chapter Three, Part II, Section 2, note 28

Hieronymus of Hangest, *Exponibilia*

Hic supponendum est quod ad veritatem ypothetice conditionalis promissive non requiritur impleri promissio vel conditio promissionis sed requiritur et sufficit quod posito ita esse sicut per antecedens significatur ita esset sicut per consequens non distinguendo esse contra fuisse vel fore secundum exigentiam propositionum unde ly si illo modo captum denotat quandam cum comitantiam consequentis ad antecedens non quidem necessariam scilicet quod non possit ita esse sicut per antecedens significatur quin ita sit sicut per consequens sed concomitantiam de facto scilicet quod talis sit habitudo quod posito uno poneretur reliquum et talis ypothetica rectius vocaretur concomitativa quam promissiva quoniam dato quod nulla talis propositio sit iuramento voto vel promissione firmata eadem manet in ea denotatio scilicet concomitantie unius ab alterum sunt enim varie entium habitudines et alique tales quod licet absolute non necessario uno posito ponatur reliquum tamen posito uno reliquum de facto concomittatur ideo cuiuslibet temporis formari potest propositio hypothetica in qua ly si talem denotet concomitantiam ut si amas me do tibi istam tunicam / si amasti me dedi tibi hanc tunicam / si amabis me dabo tibi hoc / si amas me dabo tibi hoc vel dedi tibi hoc / si amasti me dabo tibi hoc.

Ex istis sequuntur correlaria: primum quelibet copulativa affirmativa infert ypotheticam conditionalem concomitativam seu promissivam sed non e contra quare omnis promissiva affirmativa cuius antecedens et consequens sunt vera est vera licet non requiratur illud quare supposito quod cras dabo tibi equum non curo qua causa / iste sunt vere si adam fuit dabo tibi equum / si celum est dabo tibi equum / si antichristus erit dabo tibi equum / si dabo tibi equum antichristus damnabitur / si dabo tibi equum adam peccavit / si paulus peccavit ipse salvabitur / si ipse fuit in gratia fuit in peccato: et e contra cuiuslibet illarum patet veritas cum correlario nam posito ita esse sicut per antecedens significatur ita esset sicut per consequens ymo posito ita esse sicut per antecedens ponitur de facto ita esse sicut significatur per consequens quare talis est concomitantia qualis illic denotatur.

Secundum correlarium quilibet ypothetica illativa infert concomitativam seu promissivam sed non e contra quare omnis promissiva affirmativa cuius antecedens est impossibile vel consequens necessarium est vera: ut si chimera veniet ad me dabo ei equum / si dabo tibi equum tu non eris equus.

Tertium correlarium omnis copulativa composita ex antecedente et opposito consequentis promissive affirmative infert promissivam negativam illi contradicentem ut venies ad me et non dabo tibi equum ergo non si venies ad me dabo tibi equum: quare ad falsitatem promissive affirmative sufficit quod oppositum consequentis stet in veritate cum antecedente sed illud non requiritur patet igitur quod licet non oporteat oppositum consequentis repugnare antecedenti tamen promissiva repugnat copulative composite ex suo antecedente et opposito consequentis verbi gratia iste repugnant si venies ad me dabo tibi equum et venies ad me et non dabo tibi equum in quo fit ut a promissiva affirmativa cum positione antecedentis ad positionem consequentis et etiam ab ea cum destructione consequentis ad destructionem antecedentis valet consequentia: ut si venies ad me dabo tibi equum sed venies ad me ergo dabo tibi equum si veneris ad me dabo tibi equum sed non dabo tibi equum non venies ad me: utraque istarum consequentiarum probatur oppositum consequentis repugnat antecedenti.

Chapter Three, Part III, Section 1, note 1

Caubraith

Rules for Conditionals. lxx–lxx^{vo}.

1. arguendo a tota conditionali affirmativa in sensu quo est conditionalis cum positione antecedentis ad positionem consequentis est formalis consequentia.
2. a tota conditionali affirmativa cum destructione consequentis ad destructionem antecedentis formaliter valet argumentum….
3. a tota conditionali affirmativa ad unam disiunctivam compositam ex contradictorio

antecedentis et consequente est bona et formalis consequentia. ...sed non oportet consequentiam e contrario valere nisi quando partes illius disiunctive formaliter contradicunt vel participant legem contradictoriarum....

4. arguendo a conditionali affirmativa ad alteram conditionalem affirmativam que sic se habet quod antecedens conditionalis que est consequens infert antecedens conditionalis que est antecedens et consequens conditionalis que est antecedens infert consequens conditionalis que est consequens est bona consequentia.

5. arguendo a conditionali affirmativa vel negativa posita eius existentia stante priori significatione ad unam modalem compositam in qua tota conditionalis determinatur ab isto modo necessario: consequentia est bona.

6. arguendo a tota conditionali affirmativa vel negativa cum positione consequentis ad positionem antecedentis non oportet consequentiam valere. ...Dicitur non oportet. quia aliquando sequitur gratia forme: et ubi antecedens est formaliter impossibile vel consequens formaliter necessarium: sequitur etiam aliquando gratia materie: ut ubi antecedens est materialiter impossibile: vel consequens materialiter necessarium: vel antecedens possibile cum consequente convertibile....

7. a tota conditionali cum destructione antecedentis ad destructionem consequentis non oportet consequentiam valere. ...dicitur non oportet propter casus circa precedentem regulam positos in quibus contingit talem modum arguendi valere....

Rules for Conjunctions. lxxxii.

1. a tota copulativa affirmativa in sensu quo est copulativa ad quamlibet eius partem principalem est formalis consequentia.

2. a tota copulativa affirmativa ad unam disiunctivam et solum mutato in vel est formalis consequentia. ...et ratio huius est quia arguitur a propositione habente pauciores causas veritatis ad propositionem habentem plures.

Ex qua regula infertur primo quod arguendo a tota copulativa affirmativa ad copulativam negativam cuius prima pars principalis contradicit prime parti copulative affirmative et secunda secunde est formalis consequentia....

secundo infertur quod arguendo a tota disiunctiva negativa ad copulativam affirmativam dummodo componantur ex partibus principalibus contradicentibus est formalis consequentia.

Tertio infertur quod quicquid sequitur materialiter ad partem copulative sequitur materialiter ad totam copulativam et quicquid sequitur formaliter ad partem copulative sequitur formaliter ad totam.

3. arguendo a parte principali copulative affirmative ad totam copulativam non oportet consequentiam valere: quandoque tamen tenet: sed hoc solum ut in paucioribus aliquando materialiter ut sic arguendo sortes currit ergo sortes currit et deus est. ubi prima pars copulative que est consequens primam partem eiusdem formaliter infert. Secundam vero materialiter et ex consequenti totam copulativam materialiter inferre debet. Aliquando tenet formaliter ut puta ubi una pars utramque infert formaliter sicut hic sortes currit ergo sortes currit et sortes currit vel non currit.

Correlarie sequitur quando una pars copulative infert utramque partem copulative materialiter vel unam materialiter et aliam formaliter illa pars totam copulativam materialiter infert: et si una pars copulative utramque formaliter inferat eadem totam copulativam formaliter infert et non alias quare hec de priori particula.

Rules for Disjunctions. cvii^{vo}–cviii.

1. a parte disiunctive affirmative ad totam disiunctivam affirmativam est formalis consequentia.

2. arguendo a tota disiunctiva affirmativa cum destructione unius partis ad positionem alterius est formalis consequentia....
3. arguendo a disiunctiva affirmativa ad alteram partem principalem eiusdem non oportet consequentiam valere....

Dicebatur non oportet consequentiam valere: quia aliquando gratia materia valet. et etiam gratia forme: exemplum primi sortes currit vel homo est asinus: ergo sortes currit. exemplum secundi sortes currit et sortes non currit vel plato disputat: ergo plato disputat capiendo ly vel pro copula principali: quando partes disiunctive sunt synonime non est questio quin sequatur formaliter.

Et si petas quando valet consequentia a tota disiunctiva ad alteram partem et quando non pro illo ponitur tale documentum.

Quando una pars disiunctive ex utraque infertur in bona consequentia a disiunctiva ad illam partem est bona consequentia et non alias. Et si illa pars ex una parte disiunctive inferatur materialiter et ex altera formaliter: consequentia materialis erit. et si ex utraque inferatur formaliter consequentia formalis erit. formaliter sequitur sortes currit et sortes non currit vel plato disputat: ergo Plato disputat: quoniam illud consequens formaliter sequitur ad secundam partem disiunctive. arguendo a synonimo ad synonimum ad primam propter formalem impossibilitatem antecedentis....

correlaria: (1) arguendo a disiunctiva affirmativa composita ex inferiore et superiore altero extremo manente eodem in utraque suarum cathegoricarum ad partem in qua ponitur terminus superior est bona consequentia bene etiam sequitur sortes currit vel sortes movetur ergo sortes movetur.

(2) si sit aliqua disiunctiva affirmativa: cuius una pars est impossibilis et altera contingens ab illa disiunctiva ad partem contingentem est bona consequentia. Et si pars impossibilis sit materialiter impossibilis consequentia materialis erit et si formaliter impossibilis consequentia formalis erit.

(3) si sit una disiunctiva: cuius una pars est contingens et altera necessaria: ad partem necessariam est bona consequentia et formalis si talis pars sit formaliter necessaria et materialis si materialiter fuerit necessaria.

(4) si sit una disiunctiva: cuius partes sunt convertibiles illa infert utramque partem bene enim sequitur sortes est homo vel sortes est risibilis: ergo sortes est risibilis. sequitur etiam inferendo sortes est homo.

4. arguendo a disiunctiva affirmativa ad copulativam negativam compositam ex partibus contradicentibus partibus illius disiunctive est formalis consequentia. ... Ex isto patet quod arguendo a copulativa ad disiunctivam negativam compositam ex partibus contradicentibus partibus talis copulative est formalis consequentia.

Chapter Three, Part III, Section 1, note 2

Celaya, *Suppositiones*

Prima est ista ex vero nil nisi verum et sub aliis verbis ponitur sic in omni bona consequentia si antecedens est verum et consequens est verum.

Secunda regula est ista: in omni bona consequentia si consequens est falsum antecedens est falsum: oportet intelligere istas regulas cum correlariis que sequuntur extra insolubilia: quia in illis non inconvenit quod aliqua sit bona consequentia in qua antecedens est verum et consequens falsum ut aliqualiter visum est. similiter non inconvenit quod aliqua sit bona consequentia in qua antecedens significet ita esse sicut est: et consequens significet aliter esse quam est.

Ex istis regulis sequuntur duo correlaria. Primum quod si in aliqua bona consequentia antecedens significet ita esse sicut est consequens significabit ita esse sicut est.

Sequitur secundo quod si in aliqua bona consequentia: consequens significet aliter esse quam est antecedens significabit aliter esse quam est.

Tertia regula est: in omni bona consequentia si antecedens est possibile consequens est possibile.

Quarta regula principalis est ista: in omni bona consequentia si consequens est impossibile antecedens est impossibile. Ex istis duabus regulis sequuntur duo correlaria. Primum est quod si in aliqua bona consequentia possibiliter ita est sicut significatur per antecedens possibiliter ita erit sicut significatur per consequens. Sequitur secundo quod si in aliqua bona consequentia impossibiliter ita est sicut significatur per consequens: impossibiliter ita erit sicut significatur per antecedens.

Quinta regula principalis est ista: in omni bona consequentia si antecedens est necessarium: consequens est necessarium.

Sexta regula principalis est ista: in omni bona consequentia si consequens est contingens: antecedens non est necessarium.

Septima regula principalis est ista: ex impossibili sequitur quodlibet i. omnis consequentia cuius antecedens est impossibile est bona.

Octava regula principalis est ista: necessarium sequitur ad quodlibet id est omnis consequentia cuius consequens est necessarium est bona.

Nona regula principalis est ista: in omni bona consequentia si consequens est negandum antecedens est negandum.

Decima regula est ista: si aliqua consequentia scitur esse bona: et antecedens est scitum: consequens est scitum ista regulam ponit philosophus sub aliis verbis in primo capitulo primi posteriorum. scilicet cognitis maiore et minore simul tempore cognoscitur conclusio.

Undecima regula est ista in omni bona consequentia ex opposito consequentis infertur oppositum antecedentis.

Ex ista regula sequitur: quod si aliqua est bona consequentia: et antecedens est una copulativa ex opposito consequentis cum una parte illius copulative infertur oppositum alterius partis.

Sequitur secundo quod si aliqua consequentia est bona quicquid repugnat consequenti repugnat et antecedenti: et sub aliis verbis dicitur sic: in omni bona consequentia oppositum consequentis non potest stare cum antecedente.
Duodecima regula est ista: in omni bona consequentia si consequens est dubitandum antecedens non est concedendum.

Decimatertia regula est ista: quicquid antecedit ad antecedens alicuius consequentie antecedit ad eius consequens: et sub aliis verbis ponitur sic. quicquid sequitur ad consequens bone consequentie sequitur ad eius antecedens. Et ista regula potest intelligi tam de materia quam de forma: sed non de forma acceptionis terminorum ut videbitur in exponibilibus prima causa favente: ut ista consequentia est bona homo currit ergo animal currit et ista sortes currit antecedit seu potest esse antecedens in bona consequentia respectu illius scilicet animal currit. Similiter illa animal currit: sequitur ex illa sortes currit: et iste modus arguendi vocatur modus arguendi de primo ad ultimum. ut arguendo sortes currit. ergo homo currit. homo currit: ergo animal currit: ergo de primo ad ultimum bene sequitur sortes currit: ergo animal currit. Ad hoc quod iste modus arguendi valeat oportet servare duas conditiones quarum Prima est ista quod omnes consequentie intermedie sint bone* vel si non sit nisi una intermedia quod illa sit bona: quia alias modus arguendi non valeret. Secunda conditio est ista: quod pro antecedente secunde consequentie capiatur precise illud quod erat consequens in prima: et sic consequenter de aliis.

Decima quarta regula est ista: a propositione habente pauciores causas veritatis ad
propositionem habentum plures. consequentia est bona. dummodo ille pauciores inclu-
dantur in aliis.

* Text: 'bene'.

Chapter Three, Part III, Section 1, note 3

Celaya, *Expositio*

Rules for Conditionals

...aliqui assignant quinque / et aliqui octo / et aliqui quatuor: sed nos medium tenentes
sex dumtaxat: ex quibus alie facile valent elici ponemus.

Prima est ista: arguendo a tota conditionali cum positione antecedentis ad positionem
consequentis: consequentia est formalis id est arguendo ab una copulativa cuius una pars
principalis est conditionalis et alia pars principalis est antecedens illius conditionalis ad
consequens eiusdem conditionalis: consequentia formalis est....

Secunda regula est ista: arguendo a tota conditionali cum destructione consequentis ad
destructionem antecedentis consequentia est valida i. arguendo a copulativa est una cuius
una pars principalis conditionalis et altera pars principalis est contradictorium consequentis
illius conditionalis ad contradictorium antecedentis eiusdem conditionalis: consequentia
est infallibilis....

Tertia regula est ista: arguendo a tota conditionali ad disiunctivam cuius una pars
principalis est contradictorium antecedentis illius conditionalis et alia pars principalis est
consequens eiusdem conditionalis: consequentia est bona....

Quarta regula est ista arguendo a tota conditionali ad unam cathegoricam de ly
necessario cadente supra totam illam conditionalem: consequentia est bona....

Quinta regula est ista: arguendo a tota conditionali cum positione consequentis ad
positionem antecedentis consequentia raro vel nunquam valet: ...Dicitur in regula raro
vel nunquam: quia si consequens esset impossibile de forma acceptionis terminorum vel
sinonimorum cum antecedente tunc* bene valeret modus arguendi sed non esset ratio: quia
arguitur a tota conditionali cum positione consequentis ad positionem antecedentis: sed
virtute alterius regule bene sequitur / si sortes currit sortes est et non est animal / et sortes
est et non est animal: ergo sortes currit. Similiter bene sequitur / si homo currit homo currit
et homo currit: ergo homo currit.

Sexta regula est ista: arguendo a tota conditionali cum destructione antecedentis ad
destructionem consequentis: consequentia raro vel nunquam valet.... Quare ponatur illa
particula raro vel nunquam: ex precedenti regula lucet.

* Text: 'tuus'.

Rules for Conjunctions

1. A tota copulativa ad quamlibet eius partem principalem. consequentia est formalis.
2. A parte copulative ad totam copulativam consequentia non valet.
3. A tota copulativa affirmativa ad disiunctivam negativam compositam ex partibus
   contradicentibus partibus illius copulative consequentia est formalis... et mutua.

Rules for Disjunctions

1. Arguendo a parte principali disiunctive ad totam disiunctivam consequentia est formalis.
2. A tota disiunctiva: cum destructione unius partis principalis ad alteram partem principalem consequentia est valida.
3. Arguendo a disiunctiva cuius una pars est impossibilis ad alteram partem principalem consequentia valet universaliter: sed non est formalis: ut bene sequitur de materia universaliter sortes est homo: vel sortes est asinus. Ergo Sortes est homo.
4. Arguendo a tota disiunctiva ad alteram eius partem principalem consequentia raro valet....

Chapter Three, Part III, Section 1, note 4

Clichtoveus: Le Fèvre, 70vo–74vo

1. Ab universali ad suam particularem est formalis consequentia.
2. Ab equivalenti ad suam equivalentem est formalis consequentia.
3. A conversa ad convertentem est formalis consequentia.
4. Si ad antecedens sequitur consequens: ad oppositum consequentis sequitur oppositum antecedentis.
5. Si ad oppositum consequentis sequitur oppositum antecedentis: ad antecedens sequitur consequens.
6. Quicquid sequitur ad consequens bone consequentie sequitur ad eius antecedens.
7. Ad impossibile sequitur quodlibet. Necessarium ex quolibet....

Commentary

Septima regula duas habet partes. Prima est ad antecedens impossibile sequitur quodlibet consequens, ut bene sequitur: homo est lapis ergo baculus stat in angulo. Que sic probatur. Sit a est / propositio impossibilis. Dico ad eam sequi quodcunque consequens ut propositionem b est. Patet. quia si non sequatur a est ergo b est. sit gratia discipline antecedens verum et consequens falsum. Cum antecedens a est sit verum per hypothesim: ipsum potest esse verum: et per positum est propositio impossibilis: igitur propositio impossibilis potest esse vera. quod est sue diffinitionis oppositum.

Secunda pars est. Consequens necessarium ex quolibet antecedente sequitur.... Que sic ostenditur. Sit b est propositio necessaria. Dico eam sequi ex quolibet antecedente ut ex isto: a est. Patet: quia si non sequatur a est / ergo b est. sit per diffinitionem male consequentie antecedens verum et consequens falsum. Cum per hypothesin consequens sit falsum: ipsum potest esse falsum. Et positum est esse necessarium: igitur propositio necessaria potest esse falsa quod est contra ipsius diffinitionem. Et he due regule non habent applicationem in disciplinis: quod nullam habeant probandi efficaciam.

8. A tota conditionali cum positione antecedentis ad positionem consequentis: est formalis consequentia.
9. A tota conditionali cum destructione consequentis ad destructionem antecedens: est formalis consequentia....
10. Ad omnem conditionalem sequitur alia conditionalis eiusdem consequentis: cuius antecedens antecedit ad antecedens prime.
11. Ad omnem conditionalem sequitur alia conditionalis cuius antecedens est oppositum consequentis prime / et consequens oppositum antecedentis prime.

12. A tota conditionali cum positione consequentis ad positionem antecedentis: non est necessaria consequentia.

13. A tota conditionali cum destructione antecedentis ad destructionem consequentis: similiter non est firma consequentia.

Commentary

Octave regule exemplum. ut si omnis homo est animal: aliquis homo est animal. sed omnis homo est animal / ergo aliquis homo est animal. Que sic ostenditur. Sit data conditionalis: si a est / b est. Dico ab ea cum positione antecedentis ad positionem consequentis necessariam esse consequentiam / et formaliter sequi: si a est / b est. sed a est / ergo b est. Patet. nam posito antecedente vero: necesse est consequens esse verum. Si enim per hypotesin antecedens si a est / b est sed a est / verum cum ipsum sit propositio copulativa: eius utraque pars per diffinitionem copulative vere / est vera. quare a est / eius secunda pars est vera: et si a est / b est: eius prima pars itidem vera. et ea ipsa est conditionalis: ergo per diffinitionem conditionalis vere impossibile est antecedens eius esse verum consequente existente falso. Atqui antecedens a est / ostensum est esse verum: ergo et consequens b est / est verum. Et idem est consequens totius consequentie date: igitur totius consequentie consequens est verum: quare data consequentia est bona. Et cum datis quibuscunque aliis terminis consimilis argumentandi sit forma: data consequentia est formalis: quod est propositum. Posset eadem regula probari per impossibile posito toto antecedente vero et consequente falso / eodem ferme procedendi modo.

14. Si ad aliquam copulativam sequitur aliquod consequens: ad oppositum consequentis cum alterutra partium copulative sequitur oppositum alterius partis.

15. A tota copulativa ad alteram eius partem est formalis consequentia.

16. A destructione partis copulative: ad destructionem totius est formalis consequentia.

17. A parte copulative ad totam copulativam / non necessaria est consequentia.

18. A destructione totius copulative: ad destructionem partis eius simili modo non valet consequentia.

19. A parte disiunctive ad totam disiunctivam est formalis consequentia.

20. A destructione totius disiunctive ad destructionem partis eius est formalis consequentia.

21. A tota disiunctiva cum destructione unius partis ad positionem alterius est formalis consequentia.

22. A destructione unius partis disiunctive ad destructionem antecedentis: cuius contradictoria alterius partis pars una fuerit / est formalis consequentia.

Commentary

Decimenone regule exemplum. ut bene sequitur homo est animal. ergo homo est animal vel homo est lapis. Que sic demonstratur. Sit data disiunctiva a est vel b est. Dico necessario sequi a est ergo a est vel b est. Patet quia si antecedens est verum necesse est consequens simul esse verum. Sit enim antecedens a est / verum: ipsum est una pars ipsius disiunctive que est consequens: igitur una pars illius disiunctive est vera: quare per diffinitionem tota disiunctiva est vera. et ipsa est consequens: igitur data consequentia est bona quod est propositum......

Vicesima secunda regula hoc declaratur exemplo. bene sequitur non homo est animal: ergo non homo est animal vel homo est lapis et nullus homo est lapis. Fit enim hec argumentatio a destructione unius partis disiunctive ad destructionem totius antecedentis constituti ex tota disiunctiva et contradictorio alterius partis eiusdem disiunctive. Et hec regula procedit ex opposito regule precedentis sicque demonstratur. Sit data disiunctiva a est vel b est: dico necessario sequi non est b / ergo non a est / vel b est / et non est a. Patet. nam formaliter sequitur per regulam precedentem: a est vel b est. Atqui non est a ergo b est: igitur ex opposito per quartam regulam consequentiarum formaliter sequitur non b est: ergo non a est vel b est et non est a: quod est propositum.

23. A tota copulativa ad disiunctivam ex eisdem partibus constitutam est formalis consequentia / at non e contra.
24. A copulativa negativa ad disiunctivam de partibus contradicentibus est formalis consequentia.
    Copulativa negativa equipollet disiunctive affirmative de partibus contradicentibus.
25. A disiunctiva negativa ad copulativam de partibus contradicentibus est formalis consequentia.
26. A disiunctiva ad copulativam negativam de partibus contradicentibus est formalis consequentia.
27. Disiunctiva negativa equipollet copulative de partibus contradicentibus.
28. Ad omnem disiunctivam cuius altera partium est possibilis et altera impossibilis / partem possibilem sequi necesse est.
29. A tota disiunctiva cum positione unius partis ad positionem alterius non est necessaria consequentia.
30. A tota disiunctiva cum destructione unius partis: ad destructionem alterius itidem firma consequentia non est.

Commentary

Vicesime octave regule exemplum. ut bene sequitur: homo est sedens vel homo est lapis / ergo homo est sedens. Et hic antecedens est disiunctiva cuius prima pars est possibilis et secunda pars impossibilis. Consequens vero est illius disiunctive pars possibilis: que sic ostenditur. Sit a est / propositio possibilis: et b est propositio impossibilis. dico recte sequi a est vel b est / ergo a est. Si enim antecedens sit verum: cum ipsum sit una disiunctiva altera eius pars per diffinitionem est vera. At secunda pars b est non est vera: cum sit posita impossibilis: ergo prima eius pars a est / est vera: et illa est date consequentie consequens: igitur si antecedens est verum et consequens verum esse necesse est. quare per diffinitionem data consequentia est bona. quod est propositum. Consimili modo ostendatur quod ad omnem propositionem sequitur copulativa: ex ipsa propositione data et altera parte propositione necessaria constituta ut bene sequitur: homo sedet ergo homo sedet et homo est animal. cum posito antecedente vero oporteat consequens esse verum.

Chapter Three, Part III, Section 1, note 5

Dolz, *Disceptationes*

Rules for Conditionals

Superest iam videre regulas generales in quibus fundantur modi arguendi in conditionalibus que intelliguntur extra insolubilia.
    Prima: omnis conditionalis cuius antecedens est impossibile est vera.
    Secunda: omnis conditionalis cuius consequens est necessarium est vera.
    Tertia: arguendo a tota conditionali cum positione antecedentis ad positionem consequentis consequentia est bona.
    Quarta arguendo a tota conditionali cum destructione consequentis ad destructionem antecedentis consequentia est bona ...
    Quinta arguendo a tota conditionali cuius antecedens est una copulativa et destructione

consequentis cum positione unius partis talis copulative ad destructionem alterius partis consequentis est bona ....

Sexta arguendo a tota conditionali cuius consequens est una disiunctiva et positione antecedentis et destructione unius partis talis disiunctive ad postionem alterius consequentia est bona ....

Septima arguendo a tota conditionali cuius antecedens est una copulativa et consequens etiam cum destructione unius partis copulative consequentis cum positione unius partis copulative antecedentis ad destructionem alterius consequentia est bona ....

Octava: a tota conditionali ad unam disiunctivam compositam ex contradictorio ante-Septima arguendo a tota conditionali cuius antecedens est una copulativa et consequens cedentis pro una parte et consequente pro alia consequentia est bona .... e contra tamen non oportet quod valeat nisi forte talis disiunctiva esset necessaria.

Nona arguendo ab una conditionali ad aliam cuius antecedens infert antecedens et consequens consequens consequentia est bona / ita quod antecedens conditionalis que est consequens inferat antecedens conditionalis que est antecedens et consequens consequens ....

Decima: a tota conditionali ad unam de necessario ubi ly necessario cadit in ita esse talis conditionalis consequentia est bona ut bene sequitur si homo currit animal currit ergo necesse ita est quod si homo currat animal currat: si tamen necesse caderet in existentiam conditionalis sive eius significationis non valeret nisi presuppositis illorum constantiis.

Undecima regula modus arguendi a tota conditionali cum positione consequentis ad positionem antecedentis non oportet quod valeat regula est clara.

Duodecima regula: modus arguendi a tota conditionali cum destructione antecedentis ad destructionem consequentis non oportet quod valeat. multe alie regule possent poni sed iste communiter ponuntur.

Rules for Conjunctions

Ad veritatem copulative requiritur utramque partem principalem esse veram. Ad falsitatem copulative sufficit unam partem principalem esse falsam. Ad possibilitatem eius requiritur quamlibet partem esse possibilem et nullam alteri incompossibilem. ... Ex quo infertur quod aliqua est copulativa impossibilis cuius quelibet pars principalis est possibilis. Ad impossibilitatem copulative sufficit unam partem principalem esse impossibilem: vel unam alteri incompossibilem .... Ad contingentiam vero sufficit unam partem esse contingentem dummodo altera non sit sibi incompossibilis. Ad necessitatem vero requiritur quamlibet partem esse necessariam.

Ad arguendum in copulativis solent poni alique regule.

Prima regula: a tota copulativa ad quamlibet eius partem principalem consequentia tenet de forma acceptionis terminorum.

Secunda regula: a tota copulativa ad disiunctivam negativam cuius una pars contradicit uni parti et altera alteri. consequentia tenet ut prius. Et ex hoc inferuntur multe alie regule: videlicet arguendo a copulativa negativa ad disiunctivam affirmativam compositam ex partibus contradicentibus. consequentia tenet ut prius. Arguendo etiam a tota copulativa ad unam aliam copulativam cuius una pars infertur ex una illius et altera ex alia. consequentia tenet ut prius. Similiter a tota copulativa ad disiunctivam eiusdem qualitatis ex eisdem partibus compositam. consequentia tenet ut prius. Ex quibus infertur quod quicquid sequitur formaliter ex aliqua parte copulative sequitur et ex tota: et quicquid materialiter et materialiter similiter de forma acceptionis terminorum.

Alia regula: ab una propositione de necessario ubi ly necessario dicit necessitatem totius copulative ad unam propositionem ubi ly necessario dicit necessitatem alicuius partis eius consequentia tenet ut prius.

Alia regula: si ex aliqua copulativa sequatur aliqua propositio ex opposito talis cum una parte principali illius copulative infertur ut prius oppositum alterius partis principalis.

Ultima regula a parte copulative ad totam copulativam similiter arguendo opposito modo in multis modis arguendi istarum regularum non oportet semper consequentiam valere....

Rules for Disjunctions

...ad veritatem disiunctive requiritur et sufficit quod una pars principalis sit vera non tollit illam esse veram quod utraque pars sit vera   ad falsitatem disiunctive requiritur et sufficit utriusque partis falsitas semper ibi loquimur de disiunctiva affirmativa que est quando ly vel affirmatur ad possibilitatem eius requiritur et sufficit possibilitas unius partis non tollet etiam illam esse impossibilem utriusque partis possibilitatem ad impossibilitatem vero requiritur impossibilitas utriusque partis ad necessitatem requiritur et sufficit quod una pars sit necessaria vel ille partes repugnent in falsitate vel quo ad aliter esse   Additur secunda pars nam non sufficeret quia datur aliqua disiunctiva necessaria cuius nulla pars est necessaria hoc patet de ista sortes currit vel sortes non currit et dicitur illomodo in secunda parte et non dicitur vel cuius partes opponuntur contradicta quia datur aliqua disiunctiva necessaria cuius nulla pars est necessaria nec etiam partes opponuntur contradictorie hoc patet de ista disiunctiva nullum animal currit vel homo currit dicitur vel quo ad aliter esse quia datur aliqua disiunctiva non necessaria cuius partes repugnent in falsitate hoc patet de hac aliqua propositio est particularis vel aliqua propositio est affirmativa et sic possunt poni ibi due regule.

Prima omnis disiunctiva composita ex partibus contradicentibus est necessaria. Secunda omnis disiunctiva cuius partes repugnent quo ad aliter esse est necessaria....

Ad contingentiam disiunctive requiritur et sufficit quod utraque pars sit contingens et quod nulla pars alteri repugnet vel quod una pars sit impossibilis et altera contingens et non repugnans alteri ibi non capitur repugnans pro propositione repugnante aliqua oppositione....

Prima regula arguendo a parte disiunctive ad totam disiunctivam consequentia est formalis et tenens de forma acceptionis terminorum....

Secunda regula a tota disiunctiva cum destructione unius partis principalis ad positionem alterius consequentia tenet formaliter de forma acceptionis terminorum.... ex qua regula sequitur correlarie quod aliquando arguendo a tota disiunctiva cum destructione partis principalis ad positionem alterius etiam arguitur a tota disiunctiva cum positione unius partis ad destructionem alterius ut patet in hoc modo arguendi sortes currit vel sortes non currit et sortes non currit ergo* sortes non currit. Et si dicas ergo modus talis arguendi ultimus valebit verum est aliquando non tamen universaliter quando valeat et quando non etiam gratia forme acceptionis terminorum satis patet ex dictis.

Alia regula arguendo a tota disiunctiva cuius una pars est impossibilis consequentia est bona ad alteram partem principalem et si talis sit impossibilis gratia materie valebit consequentia de materia et si gratia forme de forma etc.

Alia regula non semper valet arguendo a tota disiunctiva ad quamlibet partem principalem nec etiam a tota disiunctiva cum positione unius partis ad positionem alterius multotiens tamen tales modi arguendi valent ut patet satis ex copulativis....

* Text: 'et'.

Chapter Three, Part III, Section 1, note 6

Enzinas, *Primus Tractatus*, xx–xxii

Rules for Conditionals

1. A tota conditionali **affi**rmativa cum positione antecedentis ad positionem consequentis est formalis consequentia. ...
2. A tota conditionali **affirmativa** cum destructione consequentis ad destructionem antecedentis formalis est consequentia. ...
3. Ab una conditionali ad conditionalem que composita sit ex opposito consequentis prioris pro antececente et opposito antecedentis pro consequente consequentia est mutua.... Hec fundatur in hac regula: si aliqua consequentia est bona contradictorium consequentis infert contradictorium antecedentis. Quam regulam sic ostendo: sit ab a ad b consequentia bona: et contradictorium a sit c et b sit d. aio d inferre c quoniam si non: poterit ergo d esse verum et c falsum: ponatur ergo ita inesse et arguitur sic. d est verum ergo b eius contradictorium est falsum: et quum c est datum falsum: sequitur ergo a eius contradictorium est verum: ergo a est verum et b falsum quare a non infert b quod est contra hypothesim.
4. A conditionali ad unam disiunctivam compositam ex consequente et opposito antecedentis consequentia est formalis.... Ratio huius est quia si aliqua consequentia est bona oppositum antecedentis et consequens componunt disiunctivam necessariam....
5. A conditionali affirmativa ad alteram conditionalem que sic se habet quod antecedens conditionalis que est consequens infert antecedens valet consequentia ceteris paribus: aut si consequens conditionalis que est antecedens infert consequens conditionalis que est consequens....

Et hi sunt modi arguendi que in conditionalibus contingunt: quibus posses addere omnes modos arguendi et omnes regulas que in consequentiis solent poni: quas apud omne sophistarum vulgus poteris invenire. ut gratia exempli. Si aliqua consequentia est bona et antecedens est possibile consequens non est impossibile: et si antecedens est necessarium consequens est necessarium. Si consequens est falsum antecedens est falsum. Si aliquid stat cum antecedente stat cum consequente. Si aliquid repugnat consequenti repugnat antecedenti. Si aliquid sequitur ex consequente sequitur ex antecedente: non tamen e contrario. Si consequentia est concessa bona et concedas antecedens debes concedere consequens si negas consequens debes negare antecedens bene respondendo. Si consequentia est scita bona et antecedens est scitum consequens est scitum: et si consequens est nescitum antecedens est nescitum. Et si consequens dubitatum antecedens non est scitum si antecedens dubitatum: consequens non est negandum. Et si assentis consequentie et assentis antecedenti oportet assentire consequenti. Et si dissentis consequenti oportet dissentire antecedenti. Et si antecedens est impossibile aut consequens necessarium consequentia est bona.

On Conjunctions and Disjunctions

Ad veritatem copulative non requiritur quamlibet cathegoricam esse veram: sed requiritur et sufficit utramque eius partem principalem esse veram ....

Ad falsitatem autem eius sufficit alteram partem esse falsam....

Ad possibilitatem copulative sufficit et requiritur quod quelibet eius pars principalis sit possibilis: dummodo non sint inter se partes incompossibliles.

Ad impossibilitatem sufficit et requiritur quod aliqua pars principalis sit impossibilis vel quod alique partes principales repugnent inter se: et cum impossibile cuilibet repugnet sit ut cuiuslibet copulative impossibilis partes sibi invicem repugnent.

Ad necessitatem copulative requiritur et sufficit quamlibet partem esse necessariam....

Ad contingentiam vero requiritur et sufficit quod una pars principalis sit contingens: dummodo nulli alteri repugnet.

Ad hoc autem quod aliqua copulativa sit dubia sufficit et requiritur: quod quelibet pars sit dubia vel una dubia et altera scita: dummodo una non repugnet alteri: nec ex tota copulativa sciatur falsum sequi in potentia propinqua. Id ultimum est additum propter hanc omnis rex sedet et hic est rex casu quo per ly hic demonstretur homo quem sciam non sedere: et dubitem an sit rex et dubitem etiam an omnis rex sedeat. Hinc patet quum copulativa sequatur debiliorem partem si uni parti copulative assentiamus et alteram ignoremus totam ignoremus et si uni dissentiam toti dissentiamus.

Et per hoc facile potest patere quid de disiunctiva dicendum est quum sequatur fortiorem partem.

Ad veritatem disiunctive affirmative requiritur et sufficit alteram partem principalem esse veram: et ad falsitatem utramque esse falsam: et ad possibilitatem alteram esse possibilem.

Ad necessitatem alteram esse necessariam vel quod partes repugnent in falsitate... quo sit ut sicut omnis copulativa composita ex contrariis et contradictoriis est impossibilis: sic omnis disiunctiva composita ex contradictoriis vel subcontrariis vel ex consequente et opposito antecedentis bone consequentie est necessaria.

Ad contingentiam sufficit et requiritur quod una pars sit contingens et altera impossibilis: vel quod utraque sit contingens dummodo partes non repugnent. Et ad hoc quod assentiamus disiunctive sufficit quod altera pars sit scita vel quod sciatur partes repugnare in falsitate: vel quod sciatur illam disiunctivam sequi in bona consequentia ex aliquo scito. Et ad hoc quod disiunctiva sit dubitanda quod una pars sit dubia et altera scita falsa: vel quod utraque sit dubia dummodo partes non repugnent in falsitate: et dummodo non sciatur illa sequi ex scito.

1. A tota copulativa ad quamlibet eius partem principalem consequentia est bona....
2. A parte principali copulative affirmative ad totam copulativam non oportet consequentiam valere: quandoque tamen tenet: sed hoc solum in paucioribus. ut homo currit ergo homo currit et deus est: et tunc tenet consequentia materialiter quando pars que est antecedens quamlibet partem copulative infert materialiter: et tunc tenet formaliter quando pars que est antecedens infert quamlibet partem formaliter: ut formaliter sequitur omnis homo est animal ergo omnis homo est animal et homo est animal.
3. A copulativa affirmativa in sensu in quo est copulativa ad disiunctivam consequentia est formalis. ex quo patet a disiunctiva **negativa** ad copulativam negativam consequentiam esse bonam.
4. A copulativa negativa ad disiunctivam affirmativam compositam ex partibus contradicentibus partibus illius copulative consequentia est mutua: et etiam a disiunctiva negativa ad copulativam affirmativam compositam ex partibus [contradicentibus] illius disiunctive consequentia est mutua. Ratio horum est: quia antecedens et contradictorium consequentis contradicunt ut statim videbitur.

1. A parte disiunctive affirmative ad totam disiunctivam consequentia est formalis....
2. A tota disiunctiva ad aliquam partem non oportet consequentiam valere et si quandoque valeat materialiter: tunc videlicet cum utraque pars disiunctive principalis infert partem que est consequens materialiter... quandoque tenet formaliter et hoc cum utraque pars disiunctive infert partem que est consequens formaliter....
3. A tota disiunctiva cum destructione unius partis ad positionem alterius consequentia est formalis....

4. Arguendo a disiunctiva affirmativa ad copulativam negativam compositam ex partibus contradicentibus consequentia est mutua. Ista regula iam posita est et patebit ex statim dicendis.

Chapter Three, Part III, Section 1, note 7

Major, *Consequentie*

Sequuntur regule generales consequentiarum prima est ex vero falsum extra se falsificantes non ponendo propositionem plures est impossibile. sed ex vero potest sequi falsum et falsum sequi ex vero in* insolubilia et propositionem plures contingit. Ex qua regula infertur quod hic bene arguitur hec consequentia est bona et consequens est falsum ergo et antecedens. Probatur detur per adversarium consequentia bona et b consequens falsum et c antecedens non falsum. et sequitur quod c antecedens est verum ergo ex c antecedente vero sequitur b consequens falsum contra diffinitionem bone consequentie.

Secundo sequitur quod bene arguitur hec consequentia est bona et consequens est negandum ergo et antecedens. Similiter hec consequentia est bona et antecedens est concedendum ergo et consequens. Eodemmodo hic hec consequentia est bona et consequens est negandum ergo antecedens non est dubitandum.

Tertio sequitur quod ex impossibili sequitur quodlibet quia omnis consequentia cuius antecedens non potest esse verum consequente existente falso est bona. et omnis consequentia cuius antecedens est impossibile est huiusmodi.

Quarto sequitur quod omnis consequentia cuius consequens est necessarium est bona. Probatur omnis consequentia cuius antecedens non potest esse verum consequente existente falso est bona. Sed omnis consequentia cuius consequens est necessarium est huiusmodi igitur.

Quinto. sequitur quod hec consequentia est bona hec consequentia est bona et consequens impossibile ergo et antecedens.

Sexto patet quod ex possibili non sequitur impossibile.

Septimo sequitur quod bene valet hic modus arguendi hec consequentia est bona et antecedens** est necessarium ergo et consequens.***

Octavo patet quod hic modus bene valet hec consequentia est bona et consequens est contingens ergo antecedens est contingens vel impossibile.

Secunda regula est si aliqua consequentia est bona scita esse bona et antecedens est ab aliquo scitum consequens est scitum dummodo non repugnet consequenti sciri.

Tertia regula est si aliqua consequentia est bona ex opposito contradictorio consequentis sequitur oppositum contradictorium antecedentis, et si sit mala non sequitur ex opposito oppositum.

Quarta regula ex cuiuslibet consequentie formalis opposito consequentis formaliter sequitur oppositum antecedentis.

Quinta regula ex cuiuslibet consequentie syllogistice opposito consequentis cum una premissarum sequitur oppositum alterius premisse. Ex opposito conclusionis cum maiore sequitur oppositum minoris et ex opposito conclusionis cum minore sequitur oppositum maioris.

Sexta regula cuiuslibet bone consequentie contradictorium consequentis repugnat antecedenti. sed nullus male oppositum consequentis interemit antecedens. Ex illo sequitur quod idem repugnat sibiipsi. Bene sequitur per primam regulam homo est asinus ergo nullus homo est asinus ergo oppositum consequentis interimit antecedens per hanc regulam sed antecedens contradixit consequentem igitur. repugnare nihil aliud est quam constituere copulativam impossibilem impossibile cuiuslibet propositioni repugnat sed necessarium nulli non impossibili repugnat non necessario nec contingenti aliquod contingens alicui contingenti repugnat verum vero non.

Septima regula quicquid antecedit ad antecedens antecedit ad consequens. Ex qua sequitur quod quicquid sequitur ad consequens sequitur ad antecedens. Ex quibus sequitur quod arguendo a primo ad ultimum est bona consequentia et hoc dummodo consequentie intermedie sint bone....

Octava regula quicquid repugnat consequenti repugnat antecedenti. sed non quicquid repugnat antecedenti repugnat consequenti. sed quicquid stat cum consequente stare necesse est.

Nona regula arguendo a propositione habente pauciores causas veritas ad propositionem habentem plures consequentia est bona.

* Text: 'extra'.
** Text: 'consequens'.
*** Text: 'antecedens'.

Chapter Three, Part III, Section 1, note 8

Pardo, xi–xxiiii

Prima regula ex vero non potest sequi falsum.

Secunda regula. Ex antecedente possibili nunquam in bona consequentia sequitur consequens impossibile ....

Tertia regula ad impossibile id est ad propositionem impossibilem sequitur quodlibet id est quelibet propositio in bona consequentia.

Quarta regula ex propositione necessaria nunquam in bona consequentia infertur propositio contingens.

Quinta regula. propositio necessaria sequitur ad quamlibet: patet ex probatione tertie regule.

Sexta regula si aliqua consequentia est bona oppositum consequentis scilicet contradictorium consequentis debet repugnare totali antecedenti.

Septima regula. Quicquid sequitur ad consequens bone consequentie sequitur ad eius antecedens. Et ista consequentia solet appellari de primo ad ultimum. Et huic regule annexa est alia regula. Quicquid antecedit ad antecedens bone consequentie antecedit ad consequens et declaratio unius regule est declaratio alterius. Hec regula probatur. quia si ad a sequitur b. et ad b. sequitur c. et tamen ad a. non sequitur c. ergo possibile est quod ita sit sicut significatur per a absque hoc quod ita sit sicut significatur per c. ponatur ergo quod ita sit sicut significatur per a: absque hoc quod ita sit sicut significatur per c. tunc sic ad a. sequitur b. per te et ita est sicut significatur per a. ergo ita est sicut significatur per b. et per consequens male dixisti quod ad b sequitur c quia ita est sicut significatur per b et non ita est sicut significatur per c quod est contra diffinitionem bone consequentie.

octava regula. quicquid repugnat consequenti bone consequentie etiam repugnat totali antecedenti.

Hec regula probatur ex septima regula: nam quicquid sequitur ad antecedens sequitur ad consequens et cum in consequentia bona contradictorium consequentis debet repugnare antecedenti secundum sextam regulam: ergo quicquid repugnat consequenti repugnat antecedenti.

Nona regula que sequitur ex precedentibus. si aliqua consequentia est bona et aliquid stat cum antecedente illud idem non repugnat sed stat cum consequente....

Decima regula si aliqua consequentia est bona ex contradictorio consequentis in bona consequentia infertur contradictorium antecedentis.... Isti regule est alia annexa que talis est si ex aliquibus premissis sequatur aliqua conclusio ex contradictorio consequentis cum altera premissarum infertur contradictorium alterius premisse.

Undecima regula. si ad aliquam propositionem cum aliqua necessaria vel cum aliquibus necessariis sequatur aliquod consequens ad eandem propositionem sine appositione illius necessarie vel illarum necessariarum sequitur idem consequens ista regula probatur. quia vel illa propositio que apponitur illis necessariis est contingens vel impossibilis. si impossibilis totale antecedens erit impossibile et cum ad impossibile sequatur quodlibet tunc illa consequentia erit bona. Si est contingens et tunc quero vel consequens est impossibile et hoc clarum est quod non quia tunc ex possibili sequeretur impossibile aut consequens est necessarium et tunc ad illam contingentem sequitur illud consequens necessarium. quia propositio necessaria sequitur ad quamlibet aut consequens est contingens. et tunc clarum est quod illud consequens non sequitur ex illo antecedente ratione propositionum necessariarum sed ratione propositionum vel propositionis contingentis ergo ad illam propositionem contingentem sine appositione illarum necessariarum non minus sequitur consequens contingens quam cum appositione illarum necessariarum.

Duodecima regula. omnes propositiones sic se habentes quod habent penitus easdem causas veritatis in numero inferunt seinvicem in bona consequentia et non solum hoc immo dico ulterius quod a propositione habente pauciores causas veritatis ad propositiones habentes plures causas veritatis est bona consequentia et non contra. ista regula est nota videndo quid est propositionem habere causam veritatis unde dico quod per causam veritatis intelligitur omnis illa propositio ad cuius ita esse sequitur ita esse sicut per aliam propositionem significatur.

Chapter Three, Part III, Section 1, note 9

Pardo, xl^{vo}–lxiii^{vo}

Prima regula si aliqua conditionalis est vera et necessaria et ita est sicut significatur per antecedens ita est sicut significatur per consequens....

secunda regula est a tota conditionali cum positione antecedentis ad positionem consequentis bene valet consequentia. sed non e contra.

Tertia regula a tota conditionali cum destructione consequentis ad destructionem antecedentis est bona consequentia: sed non e contra. ...et ex hac regula sequitur alia regula. Ad omnem conditionalem sequitur alia conditionalis cuius antecedens est oppositum consequentis prime et hoc loquendo de opposito contradictorio et consequens est oppositum antecedentis prime scilicet oppositum contradictorium.

Quarta regula ad omnem conditionalem sequitur alia conditionalis eiusdem consequentis cuius antecedens antecedit ad antecedens prime.

Quinta regula a veritate totius copulative ad veritatem cuiuslibet partis principalis et non e contra est bona consequentia.

Sexta regula si ad aliquam copulativam affirmativam sequatur aliquod consequens ad oppositum consequentis cum altera partium copulative sequitur oppositum alterius....

Septima regula a necessitate copulative affirmative ad necessitatem cuiuslibet partis principalis et e contra est bona consequentia. Unde ad necessitatem copulative sufficit et requiritur necessitas cuiuslibet partis principalis....

Octava regula a possibilitate copulative ad possibilitatem cuiuslibet partis principalis et compossibilitatem earundem ad invicem est bona consequentia et e contra.... Ex istis sequitur talis regula generalis quandocunque ad aliqua antecedentia sequuntur aliqua consequentia et antecedentia [sic] repugnant etiam consequentia [sic] repugnant probatur quia si ad aliqua antecedentia sequantur aliqua consequentia ad copulativam compositam ex antecedentibus sequitur copulativa composita ex illis consequentibus et cum partes copulative consequentis repugnent consequens dicitur impossibile et si partes illius antecedentis non repugnant igitur antecedens est possibile: et sic ex possibili sequitur impossibile sed contra istam regulam sic intellectam.... Quarta conclusio ad possibilitatem copulative sufficit et requiritur quod quelibet eius pars principalis sit possibilis et una alteri compossibilis seu quod ambe partes principales sint compossibiles.

Nona regula. si alicuius copulative affirmative una pars principalis est contingens et alteri parti principali non repugnat copulativa est contingens et e contra....

Decima regula a parte disiunctive affirmative ad totam disiunctivam affirmativam cuius ipsa est pars est bona consequentia et non e contra....

Undecima regula a tota disiunctiva affirmativa cum destructione unius partis principalis ad positionem alterius est bona consequentia.

Duodecima regula. si alicuius disiunctive una pars principalis est necessaria aut ambe partes principales contradicunt aut contradictorie partium repugnant tota disiunctiva est necessaria.... Ex isto sequitur correlarium quod ad arguendum disiunctivam esse contingentem sic debet argui quelibet pars huius disiunctive est contingens et una pars non repugnat alteri neque contradictorie partium ad adinvicem repugnant. ergo disiunctiva est contingens.

Decima tertia regula. si alicuius disiunctive affirmative una pars principalis est possibilis tota disiunctiva est possibilis hec regula satis est nota. nam si una pars principalis est possibilis possibile est ita esse sicut per eam significatur. Si autem possibile est ita esse sicut per eam significatur possibile est ita esse sicut significatur per disiunctivam. et per consequens disiunctiva est possibilis.

Decima quarta regula in qua ostenditur de veritate copulative negative et similiter de veritate disiunctive negative de copulativa ergo negativa talis est regula. Omnis copulativa negativa in qua negatio adverbialis neganter capta preponitur toti propositioni et hoc si negatio in totum sequens feratur equivalet in inferendo disiunctive affirmative composite ex partibus contradicentibus partibus copulative affirmative cuius talis copulativa negativa est contradictoria....

Omnis disiunctiva negativa in qua negatio adverbialis preponitur toti disiunctive equivalet in inferendo copulative affirmative de partibus contradicentibus partibus disiunctive affirmative cuius talis disiunctiva negativa est contradictoria.

Chapter Three, Part III, Section 2, note 10

Hieronymus of St. Mark

1. Ex vero non potest sequi falsum.
2. Ex antecedente possibili nunquam in bona consequentia sequitur consequens impossibile.
3. Ad impossibile sequitur quodlibet i. ad propositionem impossibilem sequitur quelibet propositio in bona consequentia.
4. Ex propositione necessaria nunquam in bona consequentia infertur propositio contingens.
5. Propositio necessaria sequitur ad quamlibet.
6. Si aliqua consequentia est bona, oppositum consequentis scilicet contradictorium consequentis debet repugnare totali antecedenti.

7. Quandocunque ad aliqua antecedentia sequuntur aliqua consequentia. Si consequentia repugnant et antecedentia repugnabunt. ...Probatur regula. Si ad aliqua antecedentia sequantur aliqua consequentia ad copulativam compositam ex antecedentibus sequitur copulativa composita ex consequentibus illis. et cum partes copulative repugnent consequens dicitur impossibile et partes illius antecedentis non repugnant. igitur Antecedens est possibile et sic ex possibili sequitur impossibile.

8. Quicquid sequitur ad consequens bone consequentie sequitur ad eius antecedens. ...Et ista consequentia solet appellari de primo ad ultimum. Et huic regule annexa est alia regula talis. Quicquid antecedit ad antecedens bone consequentie antecedit ad consequens.

9. Quicquid repugnat consequenti bone consequentie etiam repugnat totali antecedenti. Hec regula probatur. Nam quicquid sequitur ad antecedens sequitur ad consequens et cum in consequentia bona contradictorium consequentis debet repugnare antecedenti secundum sextam regulam ergo quicquid repugnat consequenti repugnat antecedenti.

10. qui sequitur ex precedentibus. Si aliqua consequentia est bona et aliquid stat cum antecedente illud idem non repugnat sed stat cum consequente.

11. Si aliqua consequentia est bona ex contradictorio consequentis in bona consequentia infertur contradictorium antecedentis.... Isti regule est alia regula annexa que talis est. Si ex aliquibus premissis sequatur aliqua conclusio ex contradictorio consequentis cum altera premissarum infertur contradictorium alterius premisse.

12. Si ad aliqua propositionem cum aliqua necessaria vel cum aliquibus necessariis sequatur aliquod consequens ad eandem propositionem sine appositione illius necessarie vel illarum necessariarum sequitur idem consequens. Ista regula probatur quia vel illa propositio que apponitur illis necessariis est contingens vel impossibilis. Si impossibilis totale antecedens erit impossibile et cum ad impossibile sequatur quodlibet tunc illa consequentia erit bona. Si est contingens tunc quero vel consequens est impossibile. et hoc clarum est quod non quia tunc ex possibili sequeretur impossibile. Aut consequens est necessarium et tunc ad illam contingentem sequitur illud consequens necessarium, quia propositio necessaria sequitur ad quamlibet. Aut consequens est contingens et tunc clarum est quod illud consequens non sequitur ex illo antecedente ratione propositionum necessariarium sed ratione propositionum vel propositionis contingentis ergo ad illam propositionem contingentem sine appositione illarum necessariarium non minus sequitur consequens contingens quam cum appositione illarum necessariarium.

13. Omnes propositiones sic se habentes quod habent penitus easdem causas veritatis in numero inferunt se invicem in bona consequentia. et non solum hoc. immo dico ulterius quod a propositione habente pauciores causas veritatis ad propositiones habentes plures causas veritatis est bona consequentia et non e contra.

14. Si aliqua consequentia est bona et scita a te esse bona et antecedens est a te scitum consequens similiter est a te scitum dummodo non repugnet consequenti sciri.

15. Si aliqua consequentia est bona et a te scita esse bona et antecedens est concedendum et consequens similiter est concedendum.

16. Si aliqua consequentia est bona et scita esse bona et antecedens est volitum et consequens est volitum.

1. A tota conditionali cum positione antecedentis ad positionem consequentis est bona consequentia. sed non e contra.

2. ...cuius ignorantia multos facit errare. A tota conditionali cum positione consequentis ad positionem antecedentis consequentia non valet universaliter. ...Dicitur notanter in regula quod non sequitur universaliter. quia interdum bene valet argumentum sic arguendo. si homo est asinus homo est rudibilis. sed homo est rudibilis ergo homo est asinus quia antecedens est impossibile.

3. A tota conditionali cum destructione consequentis ad destructione antecedentis est bona consequentia. sed non e contra.

4. Ad omnem conditionalem sequitur alia conditionalis eiusdem consequentis cuius antecedens antecedit ad antecedens prime.

5. A veritate totius copulative ad veritatem cuiuslibet partis principalis est bona consequentia.... Ex quo patet quod a tota copulativa ad quamlibet eius partem principalem est bona consequentia sed non e contra.

6. Si ad aliquam copulativam affirmativam sequitur aliquid antecedens ad oppositum consequentis cum altera partim copulative sequitur oppositum alterius.

7. A necessitate copulative affirmative ad necessitatem cuiuslibet partis et e contra est bona consequentia.

8. A possibilitate copulative ad possibilitatem cuiuslibet partis principalis et compossibilitatem earundem ad invicem est bona consequentia et e contra.

9 & 10 deal with conjoint terms.

11. A parte disiunctive affirmative ad totam disiunctivam affirmativam cuius ipsa est pars est bona consequentia et non e contra.

12. A tota disiunctiva affirmativa cum destructione unius partis principalis ad positionem alterius est bona consequentia.

13. A rationali affirmativa ad unam copulativam cuius una pars est conditionalis eiusdem antecedentis et consequentis et alia pars est copulativa composita ex eodem antecedente et consequente est bona consequentia.

Chapter Three, Part III, Section 2, note 11

Lib. Soph. Oxon.

Rules for Conjunctions

Prima regula est ista. Si una pars copulative est falsa. tota copulativa est falsa. et si utraque pars copulative est vera. tota copulativa est vera.

Alia regula est ita arguendo a tota copulativa ad alteram* eius partem est consequentia bona et formalis....

Alia regula est. A parte copulative ad totam copulativam non valet consequentia de forma. Sed quinque modis tenet de materia. Primo modo quando copulativa fit ex parte inferiori et superiori: tunc arguendo a parte inferiori ad totam copulativam est consequentia bona: ut vos estis homo: ergo vos estis animal. Secundo modo quando copulativa fit ex parte contingenti / et ex parte necessaria: tunc arguendo a parte contingenti ad totam copulativam est consequentia bona ut vos curritis: ergo vos curritis / et deus est. Tertio modo quando copulativa fit ex propositione** possibili / et ex propositione impossibili. tunc arguendo a parte copulative que est impossibilis ad totam copulativam est consequentia bona. ut vos estis asimus: ergo vos estis asinus / et vos curritis. Quarto quando copulativa fit ex partibus convertibilibus. tunc arguendo a parte copulative ad totam copulativam est consequentia bona. ut vos estis homo. ergo vos estis homo / et vos estis animal rationale. Quinto quando copulativa est facta ex duabus partibus quarum una non potest esse vera sine altera: tunc arguendo ab illa parte copulative que non potest esse vera sine altera: ad totam copulativam est consequentia bona: ut vos sedetis ergo vos sedetis et vos estis homo....

Alia regula / oppositum copulative est una disiunctiva facta ex oppositis partium copulative illius....

Rules for Disjunctions

Prima regula est hec. Si una pars disiunctive sit vera / tota disiunctiva est vera / et si ambe partes sint false / illa disiunctiva est falsa....

Alia regula est hec: arguendo a parte disiunctive ad totam disiunctivam est consequentia bona....

Alia regula est ista. a tota disiunctiva ad alteram eius partem non valet consequentia de forma.... Sed quinque modis tenet gratia terminorum. Primo modo quando est aliqua disiunctiva facta ex parte inferiori / et ex parte superiori: tunc arguendo a tota disiunctiva ad partem superiorem est consequentia bona: ut vos estis homo vel vos estis animal: ergo vos estis animal. Secundo modo quando disiunctiva fit ex parte contingenti et ex parte necessaria. tunc arguendo a tota disiunctiva ad partem necessariam consequentia bona ut vos curritis vel deus est ergo deus est. Tertio modo quando disiunctiva fit ex parte impossibili. et ex parte possibili. tunc arguendo a tota disiunctiva ad partem possibilem est consequentia bona: ut vos sedetis / vel vos estis asinus ergo vos sedetis. Quarto modo quando disiunctiva est facta ex terminis convertibilibus: tunc est consequentia bona: ut vos estis risibilis / vel vos estis homo: ergo vos estis risibilis. Quinto modo quando disiunctiva fit ex duabus partibus: quarum una non potest esse vera nisi altera sit vera: tunc arguendo a tota disiunctiva ad illam partem sine que altera non potest esse vera est consequentia bona ut vos estis movens / vel vos estis currens ergo vos estis movens.

Alia regula est hec. arguendo a tota disiunctiva / ad alteram eius partem cum opposito unius partis: ita quod oppositum consequentis non sumitur in minore est consequentia bona....

* Text: 'ulteram'.
** Text: 'probatione'.

Chapter Three, Part III, Section 3, note 12

Eckius, *Summulae*, ci

Proba bonae consequentiae.
Prima proba. Cuiusque bonae consequentiae: oppositum contradictorium vel contrarium consequentis: repugnat antecedenti....

Ex ista proba sequuntur duae regulae.
Prima. Ad impossibile nata est sequi quaelibet propositio....
Corollarium. In bona consequentia potest inferri contradictorium antecedentis....
Secunda regula. Propositio necessaria sequitur ad quodlibet....
Secunda proba.

Quicquid repugnat consequenti alicuius consequentiae: etiam repugnat antecedenti: et quicquid stat cum antecedente bonae consequentiae: stat etiam cum consequente.

Corollarium. Hinc oritur illa regula: ex opposito consequentis contrario vel contradictorio: sequitur oppositum antecedentis....
Tertia proba.

Quicquid antecedit antecedens alicuius bonae consequentiae: antecedit consequens eiusdem: et quicquid sequitur consequens alicuius consequentiae: etiam sequitur antecedens illius:...

Regula corollaria. A primo antecedente ad ultimum consequens pluribus concatenatis est bona consequentia....

Chapter Three, Part III, Section 3, note 13

Eckius, *Summulae*, cii

1. Argumentando a tota copulativa affirmativa ad alteram eius partem principalem et materialem est bona consequentia....
2. A parte principali et materiali disiunctivae ad totam est bona consequentia....
3. A tota disiunctiva affirmativa cum contradictorio unius partis principalis ad aliam partem est bona argumentatio....
4. A tota conditionali cum positione antecedentis ad positionem consequentis est bona consequentia. Similiter cum destructione consequentis ad destructionem antecedentis est bona consequentia....

Chapter Three, Part III, Section 4, note 14

Domingo de Soto, lxxiii^{vo}

Prima. Ex vero non sequitur nisi verum i. si consequentia est bona, et antecedens est verum, consequens est verum. Hec, quam Aristoteles 2 priorum asserit, ex ipsa diffinitione bone consequentie palam sequitur.

Secunda que sequitur ex prima. Falsum non sequitur nisi ex falso. i. si consequentia est bona et consequens est falsum, antecedens est falsum. Hec patet, quia data opposito, antecedens asset verum et consequens falsum.

Tertia. Ex possibili non sequitur nisi possibile. i. si consequentia est bona et antecedens est possibile, consequens est possibile. Hec patet, nam si antecedens est possibile, potest esse verum, et si consequens non esset possibile, nunquam posset esse verum, posset igitur antecedens esse verum consequente existente falso. Eadem regula potest constitui de contingenti, quod videlicet ex illo non sequatur impossibile, et eodem modo probatur.

Quarta que sequitur ex tertia. Impossibile non sequitur nisi ex impossibili. i. si consequentia est bona et consequens est impossibile, antecedens est impossibile. Hec patet, nam si consequens est impossibile, non potest esse verum, et si antecedens esset possibile, posset esse verum, possetque subinde antecedens esse verum consequente existente falso.

Quinta. Ex necessario non sequitur nisi necessarium i. si consequentia est bona et antecedens est necessarium, consequens est necessarium. Hec patet, nam si antecedens est necessarium, semper erit verum, et si consequens non esset necessarium, posset aliquando esse falsum, possetque subinde antecedens esse verum consequente existente falso.

Sexta que sequitur ex quinta. Contingens non sequitur ex necessario. i. si consequentia est bona et consequens est contingens, antecedens non est necessarium. Hec patet, nam si consequens est contingens, potest quandoque esse falsum, et si antecedens esset necessarium semper esset verum, igitur posset antecedens esse verum et consequens falsum.

Septima. Ex impossibili sequitur quodlibet, signo pro generibus singulorum distribuente. i. si consequentia est bona et antecedens est impossibile, consequens potest esse impossibile, contingens, et necessarium....

Octava. Necessarium sequitur ex quolibet, signo pro generibus singulorum distribuente i. si consequentia est bona et consequens est necessarium, antecedens potest esse necessarium, impossibile et contingens....

His octo regulis annectuntur alie due.

Nona. Quicquid sequitur ad consequens bone consequentie sequitur ad eius antecedens.... Qui quidem locus arguendi solet vocari de primo ad ultimum. Et probatur sic. Detur oppositum quod videlicet b. infertur ex a. et c. ex b. et tamen c. non sequatur ex a.

Tunc potest dari a. verum et c. falsum, et cum b. sequatur ex a. eodem casu b. erit verum, et cum c. sit falsum, quod est eius consequens, dabitur in bona consequentia, antecedens verum et consequens falsum. Pari ratione probabis quod quicquid antecedit ad antecedens alicuius bone consequentie antecedit ad eius consequens i. data aliqua bona consequentia, ex quocunque infertur antecedens infertur et eius consequens.

Decima. Que sequitur ex nona. Quicquid repugnat consequenti alicuius bone consequentie repugnat et eius antecedenti. Nam detur oppositum quod videlicet a. repugnat consequenti alicuius bone consequentie et non repugnat antecedenti, tunc sic. A non repugnat antecedenti, ergo potest a. esse verum simul cum tali antecedenti, rursus a. repugnat consequenti, ergo eodem casu quo videlicet a. erat verum consequens dicte consequente erat falsum, ac subinde daretur in bona consequentia antecedens verum et consequens falsum. Eadem arte probabis quod quicquid stat cum antecedenti alicuius bone consequentie stat cum eius consequenti. Sunt et alie regule videlicet quod si aliqua consequentia est bona scita esse bona et antecedens est scitum consequens est scitum, et si consequens est nescitum antecedens est nescitum, et alie de credito, oppinato, et dubitato. He autem posterioristice sunt.

Chapter Three, Part III, Section 4, note 15

Domingo de Soto, lxxiiii

Rules for Conditionals

1. A tota condicionali cum positione antecedentis ad positionem consequentis est formalis consequentia....
2. Secunda, que sequitur ex prima. A tota condicionali cum destructione consequentis ad destructionem antecedentis est formalis consequentia....
3. A conditionali ad disiunctivam compositam ex consequenti et contradictorio antecedentis consequentia est bona....
4. A condicionali ad alteram condicionalem cuius antecedens est contradictorium consequentis prioris, et consequens contradictorium antecedentis, formaliter sequitur....

Chapter Three, Part III, Section 5, note 16

Fonseca, I, 342–348

1. Ex vero non nisi verum, verum autem tum ex vero, tum ex falso colligitur....
2. Ex falso et falsum et verum, falsum autem non nisi ex falso concluditur....
3. Ex necessario non nisi necessarium, necessarium autem ex quolibet (ut aiunt) id est, et ex necessario, et ex contingenti, et ex impossibili colligitur....
4. Ex contingenti nunquam colligitur impossibile, sed vel necessarium, vel contingens: contingens autem nunquam ex necessario, sed vel ex contingenti, vel impossibili, concluditur....
5. Ex impossibili sequitur quodlibet, id est, tum necessarium, tum contingens, tum impossibile: impossibile autem non nisi ex impossibili colligitur....
6. Quicquid stat cum antecedente stat cum consequente: non tamen quicquid stat cum consequente stat cum antecedente....
7. Quicquid repugnat consequenti repugnat antecedenti: non tamen quicquid repugnat antecedenti repugnat consequenti....
8. Ex quocumque sequitur antecedens, sequitur consequens: et quicquid sequitur ex consequente sequitur ex antecedente....

Chapter Three, Part III, Section 5, note 17

Fonseca, I, 432–438

De Syllogismis coniunctis sive hypotheticis

Conditionalium duplex figura esse dicitur. Prior est, cum ponitur antecedens propositionis, ut ponatur consequens. Posterior, cum tollitur consequens, ut tollatur antecedens.

Copulativi autem affirmativi, hoc est, in quibus copulativa coniunctio non negatur, nulli sunt.... In negativis autem una tantum figura esse videtur, in qua nimirum altera pars propositionis ponitur, ut altera tollatur.

In disiunctivis denique affirmativis, hoc est, in quibus disiunctiva particula non negatur... duplex est figura, si modo disiunctio sit ex repugnantibus, quo pacto veteres de disiunctione locuti sunt. Prior ponit alteram partem, ut alteram tollat, posterior tollit alteram, ut alteram ponat.... Cum autem disiunctio non est ex repugnantibus... sola posterior figura apta est.

Chapter Three, Part III, Section 6, note 18

Kesler, 22–29

1. Ex vero non nisi verum: verum autem tum ex vero tum ex falso colligitur.
2. Ex falso falsum et verum, falsum autem non nisi ex falso concludatur.
3. Ex necessario non nisi necessarium, necessarium autem ex quolibet scilicet necessario, contingenti, vel impossibili.
4. Ex contingenti nunquam colligitur impossibile, sed vel necessarium vel contingens: contingens autem nunquam ex necessario, sed vel ex contingenti vel impossibili concluditur.
5. Ex impossibili sequitur quodlibet, hoc est, necessarium, contingens et impossibile. Impossibile autem non nisi ex impossibili colligitur.
6. Quicquid stat cum antecedente, stat etiam cum consequente, non contra.
7. Quicquid repugnat consequenti, repugnat etiam antecedenti, non tamen contra.
8. Ex quo antecedens, ex eo etiam consequens, et quicquid sequitur ex consequente, sequitur etiam ex antecedente.

Chapter Three, Part III, Section 6, note 19

Kesler, 86

1. A totâ copulativâ affirmatâ ad partem ejus datur consequentia.
2. A totâ copulativâ negatâ ad disiunctivam et contrà, valet consequentia, sub extremis negatis.
3. A parte propositionis disiunctivae ad totam valet consequentia, non contra.
4. Ab hypotheticâ ad simplicem, in quâ fundatur, valet consequentia et contra, ut: Si est homo, est animal. Ergo. Omnis homo est animal.

Chapter Four, Part I, Section 5, note 52

Caubraith, lvii[vo]

...quod autem isti modi arguendi sint formales probatur supponendo duas regulas quas ponit Aristoteles secundo perihermenias: quarum Prima est. Arguendo a negativa ad affirmativam predicato variato penes finitum et infinitum posita constantia subiecti negative est bona consequentia. Secunda. ab affirmativa ad negativam sine constantia subiecti predicato variato penes finitum et infinitum est bona consequentia. Quibus suppositis: quod primus modus arguendi sit efficax probatur. bene sequitur. homo non est animal et homo est. ergo homo non est animal: per primam regulam allegatam: et ultra sequitur. homo est non animal. ergo non animal est homo: per conversionem simplicem et ex consequenti infertur. non animal non est non homo: per secundam regulam allegatam: ergo de primo ad ultimum sequitur homo non est animal et homo est: ergo non animal non est non homo: Quia quicquid sequitur ad consequens bone consequentie sequitur ad eius antecedens: sed omnes consequentie intermedie sunt formales (ut communiter tenetur) ergo et ultima. Eodem modo in similibus negativis practicandum est. Quod autem secundus modus arguendi sit validus probatur. bene sequitur. omnis homo est animal et non animal est: ergo omnis homo non est non animal et non animal est: tenet consequentia: quoniam prima pars antecedentis infert primam partem consequentis per secundam regulam. et secunda secundam arguendo a synonimo ad synonimum: ergo totum antecedens infert totum consequens: et ultra sequitur: omnis homo non est non animal et non animal est: ergo omne non animal non est homo et non animal est. consequentia patet ex eo quod prima pars antecedentis infert primam partem consequentis per conversionem simplicem et secunda secundam synonime: et ultra sequitur: omne non animal non est homo et non animal est: ergo omne non animal est non homo: per primam regulam prius allegatam: ergo de primo ad ultimum sequitur. omnis homo est animal et non animal est: ergo omne non animal est non homo tenet consequentia per regulam generalem nunc allegatam. Quicquid sequitur ad consequens bone consequentie sequitur ad eius antecedens: et per consequens ad primum antecedens sequitur ultimum consequens.

Chapter Four, Part III, Section 2, note 32

Sbarroya, *Expositio Quarti*, vi.

Tertia: quod non arguatur a non distributo ad distributum. unde non valet / omne rationale est homo: omne risibile est rationale: ergo omne risibile omnis homo est. Ubi vides in maiori verificationem fieri pro eisdem suppositis: sed uno modo tantum: scilicet quia cuilibet rationali correspondet unum suppositum illius termini homo: sed in consequente requiritur illud et ultra quod cuilibet rationali correspondeat illud idem suppositum et omne aliud ab eo. Si vero dicam sic / omnis homo est animal: nullus equus est homo: ergo nullus equus est animal: posito casu quod tantum sint decem animalia in mundo scilicet 5 homines et 5 equi / antecedens est verum et consequens falsum. Ubi vides / li animal / in maiori verificari cum medio pro 5 suppositis ipsis extremitatis: et pro illis solum fuit facta divisio in minori propositione: quia talis supposita erant inclusa in medio: et ad veritatem conclusionis exigitur verificatio pro decem suppositis ipsiusmet extremitatis: ac proinde requirit divisionem extremitatum in consequente fieri pro pluribus quam facta fuerit in antecedente. Quo fit ut si in maiori diceretur sic / omnis homo omne animal est: Aut in conclusione sic / omnis equus animal non est: consequentia esset bona. Et propter hoc dixit Petrus Hispanus in textu conclusionem debere esse particularem: si aliqua praemissarum fuisset particularis. Unde quando predictum inconveniens cavetur non erit necesse hanc regulam servare.

[I have been unable to check my transcription against the original text.]

Chapter Four, Part III, Section 4, note 45

Trutvetter, *Summule*

Quecunque premisse inferunt conversam etiam inferunt convertentem: vel sic: ad quascunque premissas sequitur conversa in bona consequentia ad easdem sequitur sua convertens.

Quecunque premissarum cum convertente infert conclusionem infert eandem cum conversa: vel: quecunque conclusio sequitur ad aliquas propositiones in bona consequentia etiam sequitur ad aliquas propositiones in bona consequentia etiam sequitur ad unam earum in propria forma cum alterius conversa.

Quamcunque conclusionem inferunt alique propositiones eandem inferre possunt earundem converse: vel sic: quecunque conclusio sequitur ad aliquas propositiones in bona consequentia etiam sequitur ad illarum conversas.

Quamcunque conclusionem premisse alique inferunt directe eandem eedem transposite inferunt indirecte: vel sic: Eadem conclusio que ex aliquibus premissis infertur directe ex ipsis transpositis infertur indirecte.

Quandocunque ex contradictorio conclusionis cum altera premissarum servata in propria forma: infertur contradictorium vel contrarium alterius premisse in bona consequentia semper prior consequentia fuit bona.

Chapter Four, Part III, Section 4, note 45

Bartholomaeus de Usingen

Reducere non est aliud quam bonitatem unius minus notam per bonitatem alterius magis nota ostendere....

Quecunque premissa cum convertente infert aliquam conclusionem: etiam infert eandem cum eius conversa: quia / Quicquid sequitur ad consequens / etiam sequitur ad antecedens. Ex virtute illius cesare reducitur ostensive ad celarent.

Quecunque premisse inferunt conversam: etiam inferunt eius convertentem: quia / Quicquid antecedit antecedens: etiam antecedit consequens. Et virtute illius baralipton reducitur ostensive ad barbara.

Transpositio premissarum significat illam propositionem: Quecunque premisse inferunt aliquam conclusionem directe transposite inferunt eandem indirecte et e converso. Ex virtute illius quarta figura reducitur ad primam.

Syllogisatio per impossibile significat illam propositionem: Quandocunque ex opposito contradictorio conclusionis cum altera premissarum infertur oppositum alterius premisse: tunc prior consequentia fuit bona. Ex virtute illius baroco et bocardo reducitur ad barbara per impossibile.

Et valent iste reductiones ad probationem syllogismorum imperfectorum quia sint bonae consequentiae et formales.

BIBLIOGRAPHY

1. PRIMARY SOURCES

Abrahamus, Nicolaus Guisianus, *Logica Institutio*, Parisiis 1586.

Acerbus, Emilius, *Logicarum Quaestionum Libri Quattuor*, Venetiis 1596.

Agricola, Rudolph, *De Inventione Dialectica libri tres*, Coloniae 1538.

Airay, Christopher, *Fasciculus Praeceptorum Logicorum in gratiam iuventutis Academicae compositus*, Oxford 1628.

Albert of Saxony, *Perutilis Logica*, Venetiis 1522.

Alcalá de Henares, *Collegii Complutensis Sancti Cyrilli discalceatorum F. F. Ordinis B. Mariae de Monte Carmeli Disputationes in Aristotelis Dialecticam et Phylosophiam naturalem iuxta… Thomae doctrinam*, Lugduni 1668.

Aldrich, Henry, *Artis Logicae Compendium*, Oxonii 1691.

Almain, Jacobus, *Consequentie*. Parrhisiis 1508. [No pagination].

Alsted, Johannes Henricus, *Logicae Systema Harmonicum*, Herbornae Nassoviorum 1614. [*Systema*].

Alsted, Johannes Henricus, *Compendium logicae harmonicae*, Herbornae Nassoviorum 1615.

Alsted, Johannes Henricus, *Clavis artis Lullianae et verae logices duos in libellos*, Argentorati 1633.

Angelus, Joannes, *Speculum et radix totius logices ac veritatis*, Bononia 1509.

Argall, John, *Ad Artem Dialecticam Introductio brevis et perspicua, salibus et facetiis undique aspersa, pro tyronibus et novitiis elaborata*, London 1605.

Arnauld, A., *The Art of Thinking: Port-Royal Logic*, translated with an introduction by J. Dickoff and P. James, Library of Liberal Arts, 1964.

Averroes, *Aristotelis… Omnia quae extant Opera… Averrois in ea… omnes… commentarii*, Venetiis 1552.

Balduinus, Hieronymus, *Quesita Logicalia*, Neapoli 1561.

Balduinus, Hieronymus, *Quesita duo Logicalia*, Neapoli 1561.

Bañes, Domingo, *Instituciones minoris Dialecticae quas sumulas vocant*, Salamanca 1599.

Bartholin, Caspar, *Logica major locupletata*, Hafniae 1625.

Bertius, Petrus, *Logicae Peripateticae libri sex*, Lugduni Batavorum 1604.

Blanchellus Faventinus, Menghus, *Subtilissime expositiones questionesque super Summulis magistri Pauli Veneti una cum argutissimis additionibus Jacobi Ritii Aretini et Manfredi de Medicis. Ejusdem Menghi Logica per viam resolutionis facta: Tractatus magnus de primo et ultimo instanti: De primis et secundis intentionibus: De vero et falso: De scire et dubitare: De primo et ultimo instanti tractatus parvus: De maximo et minimo: De tribus praedicamentis. Que omnia cum aliis quampluribus questionibus annexis ab eodem Mengho dum in humanis esset: recognita emendatissima in lucem prodeunt*, Venetiis 1542.

Blundeville, Thomas, *The Art of Logike*, London 1599.

Breitkopf, Gregorius, [Bredekopf, Breytkopff, Laticephalus] *Parvorum logicalium opusculum de suppositione scilicet Ampliatione, Restrictione, et Appellatione, Insuper de Expositione et Consequentiis*, Liptzigk 1507. [No pagination] [*Parv. Log.*]

Breitkopf, Gregorius, *Compendium sive Parvulus antiquorum totam pene complectens logicen*, Lipsick 1513. [No pagination] [*Compendium*]

Brerewood, Edward, *Elementa Logicae*, Londini 1619.

Bricot, Thomas, *Tractatus insolubilium*, Parisiis 1492. [No pagination] [*Insolubilia*]

Bricot, Thomas, *Logicales questiones subtiles ac ingeniose super duobus libris posteriorum Aristotelis dyalecticam*, Parisiis 1504.

Bricot, Thomas: See George of Brussels.

Burana, Johannes Franciscus, *Aristotelis Priora Resolutoria*, Parisiis 1539.

Burgersdijck, Franco, *Institutionum Logicarum libri duo*. Lugduni Batavorum 1634.

Buridan, John, *Summula de dialectica:* The end page says: *Et sic finit totus summularum liber eruditissimi magistri Jo. Dorp veri nominalium opinionum recitatoris interpretis et expositoris textus Buridani...*, [Lyon] 1487. [No pagination]

Buridan, John, *Sophisms on Meaning and Truth*, translated and with an introduction by T. K. Scott, New York 1966. [*Sophisms*]

Buscher, Heizo, *Harmoniae Logicae Philipporameae*, Hannoverensis 1595.

Byrseus, Franciscus, *Dialecticarum Praeceptionum libri duo*, Coloniae 1565.

Caesarius, Johannes, *Dialectica*, Coloniae 1559. [No pagination]

Cajetan of Thiene: See Strode.

Campanella, Thomas, *Logicorum libri tres* in *Philosophiae Rationalis partes quinque*, Parisiis 1638.

Caramuel Lobkowitz, Johannes, *Rationalis et realis philosophia*, Lovanii 1642. [*Philosophia*]

Caramuel Lobkowitz, Johannes, *Praecursor Logicus complectens Grammaticam Audacem*, Francofurti 1654. [*Praecursor*]

Caramuel Lobkowitz, Johannes, *Herculis Logici labores tres sive Praecursoris Logici pars altera*, Francofurti 1655.

Carbo, Ludovicus, *Introductionis in Logicam*, Venetiis 1597.

Cardano, Girolamo, *Dialectica* in *Opera I*, Lugduni 1663. [*Dialectica*]

Cardano, Girolamo, *Contradictiones Logicae* in *Opera I*, Lugduni 1663.

Carpentarius, Jacobus, *Compendium in Universam Dialecticam*, Parisiis 1551.

Carvisius, Stephanus, *Catena aurea in totam logicam*, Venetiis 1561.

Case, John, *Summa veterum interpretum in universam dialecticam Aristotelis*, Londini 1584.

Castro, Bartolus de, *Questiones magistri Bartoli castrensis habitae pro totius logice prohemio. Questiones eiusdem in predicamenta Aristotelis disputatae secundum opinionem Thome Scoti et Ocham textu ex translatione Argiropili inferto. Canones triumphi numerorum ab eodem Bartolo castrense primitus ad iuventi cum carmini chartarum*, Toleti 1513.

Caubraith, Robert, *Quadrupertitum in oppositiones, conversiones, hypotheticas et modales...*, [Paris] 1510.

Celaya, Johannes de, *Expositio in primum tractatum Summularum Magistri Petri hispani*, Parrhisiis [1515?] [No pagination] [*Expositio*]

Celaya, Johannes de, *Expositio magistri Johannis de Celaya Valentini in librum predicabilium porphirii cum questionibus eiusdem secundam triplicam viam beati Thome realium et nominalium*, Parrhisiis 1516.

Celaya, Johannes de, *Expositio in libros Priorum Aristotelis, cum ejusdem terminorum divinorum tractatu*, Parisiis [1516?] [*In libros prior.*]

Celaya, Johannes de, *Expositio Magistri Johannis de Celaya, Valentini, in libros Posteriorum Aristotelis cum quaestionibus eiusdem secundum varias doctorum sententias beati Thomae, Scoti, Ocham, Gregorii de Arimino et aliorum doctorum nominalium per eundem nuperrime revisa et acuta*, Parisiis 1517.

Celaya, Johannes de, *Magna exponibilia*, Parrhisiis 1525.

Celaya, Johannes de, *Magne Suppositiones*, Parisiis 1526. [No pagination] [*Suppositiones*]

Celaya, Johannes de, *Dialectice Introductiones*, Aureliacii (1516?]. [No pagination] [*Dial. Introd.*]

Celaya, Johannes de, M. L. Roure, 'Le traité "Des propositions insolubles de Jean de Celaya".' *Archives d'histoire doctrinale et littéraire du moyen âge* **29** (1962) 235–336. This includes the Latin text and a French translation, as well as a long discussion. [*Insolubles*]

Cenali, Robertus de, *Tractatus terminorum*, Parisius 1508. [No pagination] (*Termini*)

Cenali, Robertus de, *Liber prioris posterioris que resolutionibus cum tractatu de futuris contingentibus*, Parisius 1510. The text also contains *Insolubilia* and *De Obligationibus*.

Chabassius Montiliensis, Amandus, *Institutiones Dialecticae*, Parisiis 1549.

Clauberg, Johannes, *Logica Vetus & Nova*, Amstelaedami 1658.

Clichtoveus, Jodocus, *Fundamentum Logicae. Introductio in terminorum cognitionem, in libros logicorum Aristotelis... unà cum Joannis Caesarii commentariis*, Parisiis 1538.

Clichtoveus: Le Fèvre: See Le Fèvre.

Coimbra, *Commentarii Collegii Conimbricensis e Societate Jesu. In universam dialecticam Aristotelis Stagiritae*, Coloniae Agrippinae 1607.

Cologne, *Copulata super omnes tractatus parvorum logicalium Petri hispani ac super tres tractatus modernorum textui pulcerrime annotata in argumentis et replicis denue diligentissime correcta iuxta inviolatum processum magistrorum Colonie bursam montis regentium*, [Cologne] 1493.

Commentum emendatum et correctum in primum et quartum tractatus Petri Hyspani. Et super tractatibus Marsilii de Suppositionibus: ampliationibus: appellationibus et consequentiis, Hagennaw 1495. [No pagination]

Cornerus, Christophorus, *Methodus inveniendi medium terminum in omni genere syllogismorum, tradita ab Aristotele*, Basileae [1556].

Coronel, Antonius, *Questiones logice, secundum viam realium et nominalium, una cum textus [Porphyrii] explanatione*, Parisiis 1509.

Coronel, Antonius, *Expositio super libros posteriorum Aristotelis*, Parisiis 1510.

Coronel, Antonius, *Duplex Tractatus Terminorum*, Parrhisii 1511. [No pagination] [*Termini*]

Coronel, Antonius, *Prima pars Rosarii... in qua De propositione multa notanda. De materiis propositionum. De contradictoriis in obliquis. De conditionatis et conversionibus ex libro consequentiarum eiusdem assumptis. De modalibus. De propositionibus de futuro contingenti et de modo arguendi ab affirmativa ad negativam*, Parisiis 1512. [No pagination] [*Prima Pars Rosarii*]

Coronel, Antonius, *Secunda pars Rosarii logices... continens septem capitula, primum de suppositionibus, secundum de generibus suppositionum, tertium de relativis, quartum de regulis suppositionum, quintum de ascensu et de descensu, sextum de ampliationibus, septimum de appellationibus*, Parisiis 1512. [Partly paginated]

Coronel, Antonius, *Tractatus Syllogismorum*, [Paris] 1517. [*Tract. Syll.*]

Coronel, Antonius: See Major.

Crab, Gilbert, *Tractatus lucidus terminorum*, Parrhisiis 1524. [No pagination]

Crakanthorpe, Richard, *Logicae libri quinque*, Londini 1622.

Cranston, David, *Tractatus insolubilium et obligationum*, [Paris c. 1512]. [No pagination]

Cranston, William, *Dialecticae compendium*, Parisiis 1540.

Crellius, Fortunatus, *Isagoge Logica*, Neustadii 1590.

Derodon, David, *Logica restituta*, Genevae 1659.

Dialectica, Paris 1545. [No pagination]

Dietericus, Conrad, *Institutiones Dialecticae*, Giessae Hassorum 1655.

Dolz, Juan, *Syllogismi*, Parisius 1512. [No pagination] [*Syllogismi*]

Dolz, Juan, *Termini cum principiis nec non pluribus aliis ipsis dialectices difficultatibus*, Parisius [?]. [*Termini*]

Dolz, Juan, *Disceptationes super primum tractatum summularum cum nonnullis suorum terminorum intellectionibus*, Parisius 1512. [No pagination] [*Disceptationes*]

Dorp, J.: See Buridan.

Ducius, Laurentius, *De inventione medii liber unus*, Lucae 1550.

Du Moulin, Pierre, *Elements de logique*, Sedan 1621.

Du Moulin, Pierre, *Introductio ad logicam* in *Opera philosophica*, Amsterdami 1645.

Duns Scotus, John, *Opera Omnia I*, Lugduni 1639.

Du Trieu, Philip, *Manuductio ad logicam sive dialectica studiosae iuventuti ad logicam praeparandae.... Ab editione Oxoniensi anni 1662 recusa*, Londoni 1826.

Eckius, Johannes, *Bursa Pavonis. Logices exercitamenta appellata parva logicalia a J. Eccio congesta ac examinata*, Argentine 1507. [No pagination]

Eckius, Johannes, *In summulas Petri Hispani extemporaria et succincta*, Augustae Vindelicorum 1516. [*Summulae*]

Eckius, Joh., *Elementarius dialecticae*, Augustae Vindelicorum 1517. [No pag.] [*El. Dial.*]

Enzinas, Ferdinandus de, *Magnorum exponibilium, seu tertium libri oppositionum Ferdinandi de Enzinas compendium...*, Toleti 1523.

Enzinas, Ferdinandus de, *Primus tractatus summularum Fernandi de Enzinas, cum textu Petri Hispani, cui additus est tractatus relativorum*, Compluti 1523. [*Tractatus*]

Enzinas, Ferdinandus de, *Tractatus Sillogismorum*. Lugduni 1528. [*Sillogismi*]

Enzinas, Ferdinandus de, *Tractatus de compositione propositionis mentalis*, Lugduni 1528. [*Prop. Ment.*]

Enzinas, Ferdinandus de, *Oppositionum liber primus*, Lugduni 1528. [*Oppositiones*]

Enzinas, Ferdinandus de, *Termini perutiles et principia Dialectices communia*, Toletani 1533. [No pagination] [*Termini*]

Fantinus, Albertus, *Liber Terminorum*, Parrhisiensi 1499. [No pagination]

Ferebrich: See Strode.

Fonseca, Petrus, *Instituçoes Dialecticas. Institutionum Dialecticarum libri octo*, edited and translated into Portuguese by Joachim Ferreira Gomes. Coimbra 1964.

Fortunatianus, Chirius, *Dialectica*. [Inc.]

Freigius, Johannes Thomas, *Quaestiones logicae et ethicae*, Basileae 1576.

Freigius, Johannes Thomas, *Logica, ad usum rudiorum in epitomen redacta*, 1590.

Gabriel of St. Vincent, *Logica in qua clara methodo resolvuntur non solum difficultates, quae communiter tractari solent à logicis, sed etiam aliae plures*, Romae 1669.

Galitius de Carpenedulo, Marcus Antonius, *Summa totius dialecticae ad mentem S. Bonaventurae*, Romae 1634.

Gassendi, Pierre, *De logicae origine et varietate* in *Opera I*, Lugduni 1658.

Gassendi, Pierre, *Institutio Logica* in *Opera I*, Lugduni 1658. [*Institutio*]

Gebwiler, Johannes, *Magistralis totium Parvuli artis Logices compilatio*, Basileorum urbe 1511. [No pagination]

George of Brussels, *Expositio Georgii super summulis magistri Petri hyspani*, Parisius 1491. [*Super Summulis*] [No pagination]

George of Brussels, *Interpretatio Georgii Bruxcellensis in summulas magistri Petri hispani una cum magistri Thome Bricot questionibus de novo in cuiusvis fine tractatus additis. Textu quoque suppositionum de novo readdito*. [?, ?] [*Interpretatio*]

George of Brussels, *Cursus optimarum questionum super totam logicam: cum interpretatione textus: secundum viam modernorum: ac secundum cursum magistri Georgii: Per Magistrum Thomam Bricot... emendate*. [– – – 1496?] [No pagination] [*Cursus*]

George of Brussels, *Expositio magistri Georgii Bruxellensis in logicam Aristotelis una cum magistri Thomae Bricot textu de novo inserto necnon cum eiusdem quaestionibus...*, Lugduni 1504. [*Expositio*]

George of Trebizond, *Dialectica brevis*, Coloniae 1526. [No pagination]

Gerardus Harderwickensis, *Commentarii in omnes tractatus parvorum logicalium Petri hispani iunctis nonnullis modernorum processum burse laurentiane in universitate Coloniensis continentes incipiunt feliciter. commentarii in omnes tractatus petri hispani et non nullos modernorum... ex divi Alberti magni commentariis per... magistrum Gerardum harderwickensem... elaborati et emendati*, Coloniae 1493. [No pagination]

Geulincx, A., *Opera Philosophica*, edited by J. P. N. Land, in 3 volumes. The Hague 1891–1893.

Goclenius, Rudolph, *Partitionum dialecticarum ex Platone et aliis, libri II*, Francofurti 1595.

Goclenius, Rudolph, *Praxis logica*, Francofurti 1595.

Goclenius, Rudolph, *Institutionum logicarum de inventione liber unus*, Marpurgi 1598. [*Institutiones*]

Gorscius, Jacobus, *Commentariorum Artis Dialecticae libri decem*, Lipsiae 1563.

Gothutius, F. Augustinus, *Gymnasium speculativum*, Paris 1605.

Granger, Thomas, *Syntagma Logicum or the Divine Logike serving especially for the use of Divines in the practise of preaching etc.*, London 1620.

Greve, Henricus, *Parva logicalia nuper disputata*. [Leipzig 149–.]

Gutkius, Georgius, *Logicae divinae seu peripateticae... libro duo*, Coloniae 1629.

Heereboord, Adrian, *Hermeneia Logica seu Synopseos Logicae Burgersdicanae explicatio*, Londini 1658.

Hegendorff, Christian, *Dragmata in dialecticam Petri Hispani*, Basileae 1520.

Hieronymus of Hangest, *Problemata exponibilium*, Parisius 1515. [No pagination] [*Exponibilia*]

Hieronymus of Hangest, *Problemata logicalia*, Parrhisiis 1516. [No pagination]

Hieronymus of St. Mark, *Compendium preclarum quod parva logica seu summule dicitur ad introductionem juvenum in facultate logices*, Coloniensi 1507. [No pagination]

Hilden, Wilhelm, *Quaestiones et commentarii in Organon Aristotelis*, Berlini 1585.

Horneius, Conrad, *Compendium dialecticae*, Helmaestadi 1623.

Horstius, Gregor, *Institutionum logicarum libri duo*, Witebergae 1608.

Hospinianus Steinanus, Johannes, *Non esse tantum triginta sex bonos malosque categorici syllogismi modos, ut Aristoteles cum interpretibus docuisse videtur, sed quingentos et duodecim, quorum quidem probentur triginta sex...*, Basileae 1560.

Hotman, Franciscus, *Dialecticae Institutionis libri IIII*, – – – 1573.

Hundeshagen, Johannes Christophorus, *Logica tabulis succinctis inclusa*, Jenae 1674.

Hundt, Magnus, *Compendium totius logices*, Lyptzk 1507.

Hunnaeus, Augustinus, *Prodidagmata de dialecticis vocum affectionibus et proprietatibus*, Antverpiae 1584. [*Prodidagmata*]

Hunnaeus, Augustinus, *Dialectica seu generalia logices praecepta omnia*, Antverpiae 1585. [*Dialectica*]

Insolubilia. [Southwark 1527?] [No pagination]

Isendoorn, Gisbert ab, *Cursus logicus systematicus et agonisticus*, Oxonii 1658.

Javellus, Chrysostom, *Logicae Compendium*, Venetiis 1572.

Johannes de Magistris, *Dicta circa summulas*. [Preface dated: Moguntie 1490] [No pagination]

John of Glogovia, *Exercitium super omnes tractatus parvorum logicalium Petri Hispani*, Argentine 1517.

John of St. Thomas [Juan Poinsot], *Cursus Philosophicus. I. Ars Logica*, Turin 1930. [*Cursus*]

John of St. Thomas, *The Material Logic of John of St. Thomas*, translated by Y. R. Simon, J. J. Glanville, G. D. Hollenhorst. Chicago 1955. [*Material Logic*]

John of St. Thomas, *Outlines of Formal Logic*, translated by F. C. Wade, Milwaukee 1955. [*Formal Logic*]

Jungius, Joachim, *Logica Hamburgensis*, edited and translated into German by R. W. Meyer, Hamburg 1957.

Keckermann, Bartholomaeus, *Systema Logicae*, Hanoviae 1606. [*Systema*]

Keckermann, Bartholomaeus, *Praecognitorum Logicorum Tractatus III*, Hanoviae 1606. [*Praecogniti*]

Kesler, Andreas, *De Consequentia Tractatus Logicus*, Wittebergae 1623.

Lax, Gaspar, *Tractatus de oppositionibus propositionum cathegoricarum in speciali: et de earum equipollentiis*, Parisius 1512.

Lax, Gaspar, *Exponibilia*, Parisius 1512.

Lax, Gaspar, *Termini, secundo revisi*, Parisiensis [1512?]. [*Termini*]

Lax, Gaspar, *Insolubilia*, Parisius 1512. [*Insolubilia*]

Lax, Gaspar, *Obligationes*, Parisius 1512.

Lax, Gaspar, *Impositiones*, Parisius 1513.

Lax, Gaspar, *Tractatus syllogismorum... una cum tractatu de arte inveniendi medium nomen*, Parisius 1514.

Le Fèvre d'Etaples, Jacques, *Jacobi Fabri Stapulensis artificiales nonnulle introductiones per Judocum Clichtoveum in unum diligenter collecte*, Parisiis 1520.

Lemosius, Ludovicus, *Paradoxorum Dialecticorum*, Salmanticae 1558.

Libavius, Andreas, *Dialectica Phillippo-Rameae ex descriptionibus et commentariis P. Melancthonis et P. Rami aliorumque logicorum etc.*, Francofurti ad Moenum 1608.

Libellus Sophistarum. [London 1501–1502] [No pagination] [*Lib. Soph.*]

Libellus Sophistarum ad usum Oxoniensium. [London c. 1525] [No pagination] [*Lib. Soph. Oxon.*]

Listrius, Gerardus, *Commentarioli Listrii in Dialecticen*, [*Petri Hispani*]. [Zwoll 1520] [No pagination]

Lokert, George, *Sillogismi*, Parisiis [1522].

Lokert, George, *Tractatus Exponibilium*, Parrhisius [1522].

Mainz: Universitas Moguntina: Collegium Maius, *Modernorum summulae logicales cum notabilibus topicorum ac disputatis elenchorum librorum ex Aristotele, boetio, beato augustino, marsilio et ab aliis subtilioribus sententiis viris doctissimis fideliter enucleate*. [1489?] [No pagination]

Maiolus, Laurentius, *Epiphyllides in dialecticis*, Venetiis 1497. [No pagination]

Major, John, *Consequentie inchoate perfecte ab Anthonio Coronel*. [Paris c. 1503] [No pagination] [*Consequentie*]

Major, John, *Parva logicalia*, Parisii 1503. [No pagination] [*Logicalia*]

Major, John, *Obligationes maioris*. [Paris c. 1508] [No pagination]

Major, John, *Abbreviationes parvorum logicalium*. [Paris c. 1508] [No pagination] [*Abbreviationes*]

Major, John, *Termini magistri Johannes Maioris*, Parisius [c. 1510]. [No pagination] [*Termini*]

Major, John, *Opera Logicalia*, Lugduni 1516. [*Opera*]

Major, John, *Introductorium perutile in Aristotelicam Dialecticen, duos Terminorum Tractatus, ac Quinque Libros Summularum complectens, M. Ioannis Majoris Philosophi ac Theologi Parisiensis...*. [Paris] 1527. [*Introductorium*]

Major, John, *Quaestiōnes Logicales... cum eiusdem literali expositione succincta in veterem Aristotelis Dialecticen*, Parisiis 1528.

Manderston, William, *Tripartitum epithoma Doctrinale et compendiosum in totius dialectices artis principia*, ––– 1530. [No pagination]

Margalho, Pedro, *Escólios em ambas as Lógicas à Doutrina de S. Tomás, do subtil Duns Escoto e dos nominalistas. Reprodução facsimilada da edição de Salamanca, 1520.* Tradução de Miguel Pinto de Meneses. Introdução pelo Professor Wilhelm Risse. Lisboa 1965. The Latin title is: *Margallea logices utriusque scholia in divi Thome subtilisque duns doctrina ac nominalium.*

Marsh, Narcissus, *Institutiones logicae. In usum Juventutis Academicae Dubliniensis,* Dublini 1681.

Marsilius of Inghen, *Compendiarius Parvorum logicalium liber continens perutiles Petri Hispani tractatus priores sex et clarissimi philosophi Marsilii dialectices documenta...,* Vienne Austrie 1512.

Martinez Siliceo, Juan, *Siliceus in eius primam Alfonseam sectionem in qua primaria dyalectices elementa comperiuntur argutissime disputata,* Salamantice 1517.

Martinus, Cornelius, *De analysi logica tractatus,* Helmstadii 1619.

Martinus, Cornelius, *Commentariorum logicorum adversus Ramistas,* Helmaestadi 1623. [*Commentarii*]

Martinus de Magistris, *Tractatus Consequentiarum magistri martini magistri.* [Paris 1501] [No pagination]

Melanchthon, Philip, *De Dialectica libri quator,* Witebergae 1531.

Melanchthon, Philip, *Dialectices libri tres,* Lugduni 1534. [*Dialectica*]

Melanchthon, Philip, *Erotemata Dialectices* in Volume 13 of *Opera quae supersunt omnia,* edited by C. G. Bretschneider and H. E. Bindseil. 28 volumes. Halle and Braunschwig 1834–1860.

Mercado, Thomas de, *Commentarii lucidissimi in textum Petri Hispani,* Hispali 1571. [Commentarii]

Mercado, Thomas de, *In logicam magnam Aristotelis commentarii, cum nova translatione textus,* Hispali 1571.

Mercarius, Petrus, *Magistri Petri mercarii normanni Tractatus de argumentatione et partibus eius remotis atque de earum proprietatibus et passionibus,* ––– 1500. [No pagination]

Molenfelt, Martinus, *Tractatus obligatoriorum:* See Tartaretus *Expositio.*

Murner, Thomas, *Logica memorativa. Chartiludium logice/sive totius dialectice memoria: et novis Petri hyspani textus emendatus,* Argentine 1509.

Naveros, Jacobus de, *Preparatio dialectica,* Compluti 1542.

Newton, John, *An Introduction to the art of Logick,* London 1671.

Nihusius, Bartoldus, *Commentarius logicus novus de enuntiationibus et syllogismis modalibus,* Jenae 1618.

Niphus, Augustinus, *Expositiones in libros de sophisticis elenchis Aristotelis,* Parisiis 1540.

Niphus, Augustinus, *Super libros priorum Aristotelis,* Venetiis 1554. [*Libros priorum*]

Ockham, William, *Summa totius logicae,* Oxoniae 1675.

Oddus, Illuminatus, *Logica peripatetica ad mentem Scoti,* Panormi 1664.

Oliver, Thomas, *De Sophismatum Praestigiis Cavendis Admonitio,* Cantabrigiae 1604.

Oña, Pedro de, *Dialecticae introductio quam vulgo Summulas vocant, cum argumentis,* Panormi 1621.

Ormazius, Matthaeus Doniensis, *De instrumento instrumentorum sive de dialectica libri sex,* Venetiis 1569.

Ortiz, Didacus, *Logicae brevis explicatio,* Brixiae 1650.

Otto, Leonard Dietrich, *Summule magistri Leonardi Dieterici Ottonici...,* Argentinensis 1516.

Pardo, Hieronymus, *Medulla dyalectices,* Parisius 1505.

Paul of Pergula: Boh, I., 'Paul of Pergula on Supposition and Consequences', [English translation] *Franciscan Studies* **25** (1965) 30–89.

Paul of Pergula, *Logica and Tractatus de Sensu Composito et Diviso*, edited by Sister Mary Anthony Brown. St. Bonaventure, N.Y., Louvain, Paderborn, 1961. [*Logica*]

Paul of Pergula: See Strode.

Paul of Venice, *Logica Magna*, Venetiis 1499. [*Logica Magna*]

Paul of Venice, *Logica*, Venetiis 1565. [*Logica parva*]

Perionius, Joachimus, *De dialectica libri III*, Basileae 1549.

Peter of Ailly, *Conceptus et insolubilia*, Parisius 1498. [No pagination]

Peter of Mantua, *Logica*, Venetiis 1492. [No pagination]

Peter of Spain, *Summulae Logicales*, edited by I. M. Bocheński. Torino 1947. [*Summulae*]

Peter of Spain, *Tractatus, Called Afterwards Summule Logicales*, edited by L. M. de Rijk. Assen 1972.

Peter of Spain, *Tractatus Syncategorematum and Selected Anonymous Treatises*, translated by J. P. Mullally. Milwaukee, Wis. 1964. [*Syncategoremata*]

Petrella, Bernardinus, *Quaestiones logicae*, Patavii 1571.

Piccolomineus, Franciscus, *Discursus ad Universam Logicam attinens*, Marpurgi 1606.

Piscator, Johannes, *Animadversiones in Dialecticam P. Rami*, Londini 1581.

Polanus, Amandus, *Logicae libri duo*, Basileae 1599.

Prideaux, John, *Tyrocinium ad syllogismum legitimum contexendum et captiosum dissuendum expeditissimum*, Oxoniae 1629. [No pagination]

Priero, Silvester de, *Compendium dialecticae*, Venetiis 1496. [No pagination]

Principia dialecticae... in quaestiones redacta, Posnaniae? [No pagination]

Pseudo-Scotus: See Duns Scotus.

Ramus, Petrus, *Dialectique de Pierre de la Ramee*, Paris 1555. [*Dialectique*¹]

Ramus, Petrus, *Dialecticae libri duo*, Lutetiae 1574. [*Dialectica*]

Ramus, Petrus, *La Dialectique de M. Pierre de La Ramee Professeur du Roy, comprise en deux livres selon la derniere edition...*, Paris 1576. [*Dialectique*²]

Raulin, Johannes, *In Logicam Aristotelis Commentarius*, Paris 1500. [No pagination]

Regius, Johannes, *Commentariorum ac disputationum logicarum libri V*, Witebergae 1605.

Regius, Johannes, *Commentariorum ac disputationum logicarum libri IV*, Witebergae 1608. [*Libri IV*]

Rhodolphus, Chasparus, *Dialectica*, Moguntiae 1550.

Robertis, Honoratus de, *Commentariorum in universam Aristotelis logicam pars prima*, Venetiis 1598. [*Pars prima*]

Robertis, Honoratus de, *Commentariorum in universam Aristotelis logicam pars secunda*, Venetiis 1599.

Rubius, Antonius, *Logica Mexicana, sive commentarii in universam Aristotelis logicam*, Coloniae Agrippinae 1605.

Rudimenta Logicae Peripateticae pro captu Scholae Lubecensis, Lubecae 1620.

Sánchez Ciruelo, Pedro, *Prima pars logices ad veriores sensus textus Aristotelis*, Compluti 1519.

Sanderson, John, *Institutionum dialecticarum libri quator*, Oxoniae 1602.

Sanderson, Robert, *Logicae Artis Compendium*, Oxoniae 1618.

Santolaria, Martinus, *In Dialecticam integram perfecta quaedam institutio*, Oscae 1583.

Sarcerius, Erasmus, *Dialectica multis et variis exemplis illustrata*, Lipsiae 1539.

Savonarola, Hieronymus, *Compendium logice*, Florentie 1497. [No pagination]

Sbarroya, Augustinus, *Dialectice introductiones trium viarum placitam Thomistarum videlicet ac scotistarum necnon nominalium complectentes*, Hispali 1533 [or 1535]. [*Dial. introd.*]

Sbarroya, Augustinus, *Expositio primi tractatus Summularum Magistri Petri Hispani*, Hispali 1533. [*Expositio primi*]

Sbarroya, Augustinus, *Expositio quarti tractatus Magistri Petri Hispani*. [?, ?] [*Expositio quarti*]. The work also contains: *Opusculum terminorum divinorum*.

Scharfius, Johannes, *Exegeseos Logicae Peripateticae*, Wittebergae 1624. [No pagination]

Scharfius, Johannes, *Institutiones logicae*, Wittenbergae 1632. [*Institutiones*]

Scheibler, Christophorus, *Introductio logicae*, Giessae Hessorum 1618.

Scheibler, Christophorus, *Tractatus logicus de syllogismis et methodis*, Giessae 1619. [*Tractatus*]

Scheibler, Christophorus, *Epitome logica*, Gissae 1624.

Sermonete, Alexander: See Strode.

Seton, John, *Dialectica… annotationibus Petri Carteri*, Cantabrigiae 1631. [No pagination]

Smiglecius, Martinus, *Logica*, Ingolstadii 1618.

Smith, Samuel, *Aditus ad logicam*, Londini 1627. [No pagination]

Soto, Domingo de, *Introductiones dialectice*, Burgis 1529. [Unless otherwise specified, all references are to this text]

Soto, Domingo de, *Aeditio secunda Summularum nunc denuo ab innumeris mendis diligenter purgata*, Salmanticae 1547.

Soto, Domingo de, *In Dialecticam Aristotelis Commentarii*, Salmanticae 1571. [*Commentarii*]

Stanyhurst, Richard, *Harmonia seu catena dialectica in Porphyrianas institutiones*, Londini 1570.

Stephanus de Monte, *Ars Sophistica*. [Paris 1490?] [No pagination]

Stierius, Joannis, *Praecepta doctrinae logicae*, Londini 1671.

Strode, Ralph, *Consequentie Strodi cum commento Alexandri Sermonete. Declarationes Gaetani in easdem Consequentias. Dubia magistri Pauli pergulensis. Obligationes eiusdem Strodi. Consequentie Ricardi de Ferabrich. Expositio Gaetani super easdem. Consequentie subtiles Hentisbari. Questiones in Consequentias Strodi perutiles eximii artium doctoris domini Antonii Frachantiani Vicentini*, Venetiis 1517.

Sturm, Johann, *Partitionum dialecticarum libri quator*, Argentorati 1582.

Tartaretus, Petrus, *Expositio magistri Petri Tatareti in Summulas Petri Hispani… Additus est tractatus insolubilium eiusdem et obligatoriorum magistri Martini Molenfelt ex Livonia*. [1514?] [*Expositio*]

Tartaretus, Petrus, *Commentarii in Isagogas Porphyrii et libros logicorum Aristotelis*. [Basle 1515?] [*Commentarii*]

Tartaretus, Petrus, *In Universam Philosophiam Opera Omnia*, Venetiis 1622. [*Insolubilia*]

Thomas Aquinas, *Logica*, Venetiis 1496. [No pagination]

Timplerus, Clemens, *Logicae Systema methodicum*, Hanoviae 1612.

Titelmanus, Franciscus, *Dialecticae Consyderationis libri sex. Aristotelici organi summam, hoc est, totius Dialectices ab Aristotele tractatae complectentes…*, Lugduni 1569.

Toletus, Franciscus, *Introductio in dialecticam Aristotelis*, Romae 1601. [*Introductio*]

Toletus, Franciscus, *Commentaria, una cum quaestionibus in universam Aristotelis logicam*, Coloniae Agrippinae 1607.

Trutvetter, Jodocus, [Isenachensis] *Breviarium dialecticum*, Erphordie 1500. [No pagination] [*Breviarium*]

Trutvetter, Jodocus, *Summule totius logice*, Erphurdie 1501. [No pagination] [*Summule*]

Usingen, Bartholomaeus de, *Summa compendiaria totius logice*, Basileae 1507. [No pagination]

Valentia, Petrus, *Academia sive de judicio*, Londini 1740.

Valerius, Cornelius, *Tabulae totius dialectices*, Venetiis 1564.

Valla, Laurentius, *Dialectice libri tres ... ubi multa adversus Aristotelem: Boetium: Porphy-rium*, [Paris] 1509.

Verdu a Sans, Blasius, *Eius Quaestiones an detur quarta figura decisio*, Coloniae Agrippinae 1627.

Versor, Johannes, *Petri Hispani Summulae Logicales cum Versorii Parisiensis Clarissima expositione*, Venetiis 1583.

Villalpandeus, Gasparus Cardillus, *Traduccion a las Sumulas del Doctor Villalpando ...*, Madrid 1615. [Contains Latin text of *Summa Summae Summularum*]

Vincentius, M. Petrus, *Compendium Dialectices*, Wratislaviae 1597.

Vives, Johannes Ludovicus, *In Pseudo Dialecticos*, in *Opera Omnia III*, Valencia 1782/ London 1964. [Facsimile edition]

Wallis, John, *Institutio Logicae, ad communes usus accommodata*, Editio Quarta. Oxonii 1715.

Wasius, David, *Rudimenta Dialecticae*, Swinfurti 1608.

Wendelin, Marcus Friedrich, *Logicae institutiones tironum adolescentium captui ita accom-modatae*, Amstelrodami 1654.

Willichius, Jodocus, *Erotematum Dialectices libri tres*, Argentorati 1540.

Zabarella, Jacobus, *Opera Logica*, Francoforti 1623.

2. SECONDARY SOURCES ON THE HISTORY OF LOGIC 1400–1650

A. *Books*

Crescini, A., *Le origini del metodo analitico. Il Cinquecento*, Udine 1965.

Del Torre, M. A., *Studi su Cesare Cremonini: cosmologia e logica nel tardo aristotelismo padovano*, Padova 1968.

Gilbert, N. W., *Renaissance Concepts of Method*, New York 1960.

Howell, W. S., *Logic and Rhetoric in England. 1500–1700*, Princeton 1956.

Kenney, W. H., *John Locke and the Oxford Training in Logic and Metaphysics*, Saint Louis University 1959. Unpublished dissertation.

Miller, P., *The New England Mind: The Seventeenth Century*, New York 1939.

Muñoz Delgado, V., *Lógica formal y filosofia en Domingo de Soto 1494–1560*, Madrid 1964. [Muñoz Delgado[A]]

Muñoz Delgado, V., *La lógica Nominalista en la Universidad de Salamanca (1510–1530)*. Madrid 1964 [Muñoz Delgado[B]]

Muñoz Delgado, V., *La obra lógica de Pedro de la Serna 1583–1642*, Madrid, 1966.

Muñoz Delgado, V., *Lógica Hispano-Portuguesa hasta 1600*, Salamanca 1972.

Nelson, N. E., *Peter Ramus and the Confusion of Logic, Rhetoric and Poetry*, University of Michigan Contributions in Modern Philology, No. 2, 1947.

Ong, W. J., *Ramus: Method and the Decay of Dialogue*, Cambridge, Mass. 1958. [Ong[A]]

Ong, W. J., *Ramus and Talon Inventory*, Cambridge, Mass. 1958.

Papuli, G., *Girolamo Balduino. Richerche sulla logica della scuola di Padova nel Rinasci-mento*, Bari 1967.

Prantl, C., *Geschichte der Logik im Abendlande. IV.*, Leipzig 1870; Graz, Austria 1955.

Randall, J. H., *The School of Padua and the Emergence of Modern Science*, Padua 1961.

Renaudet, A., *Préréforme et Humanisme à Paris pendant les premières guerres d'Italie 1494–1517*, Paris 1916.

Risse, W., *Die Logik der Neuzeit. Band I. 1500–1640*, Stuttgart-Bad Cannstatt 1964. [Risse[A]]

Risse, W., *Bibliographia Logica I. 1472–1800*, Hildesheim 1965.
Rossi, P., *Clavis Universalis. Arti mnemoniche e logica combinatoria da Lullo a Leibniz*, Milano-Napoli 1960. [Rossi^A]
Schüling, H., *Bibliographie der im 17.Jahrhundert in Deutschland erschienenen logischen Schriften*, Giessen 1963.
Silvestro da Valsanzibio, P., *Vita e dottrina di Gaetano di Thiene, filosofo dello studio di Padova, 1387–1465*, 2nd edition. Padua: Studio filosofico dei Fratrum Minorum Cappuccini, 1949.
Uedelhofen, M., *Die Logik Petrus Fonsecas*. In *Renaissance und Philosophie. Beiträge zur Geschichte der Philosophie*, edited by Adolf Dyroff. Vol. XIII. Bonn 1916.
Vasoli, C., *La dialettica e la retorica dell'umanesimo: 'Invenzione' e 'Metodo' nella cultura del XV e XVI secolo*, Milano 1968. [Vasoli^A]
Villoslada, R. G., *La Universidad de Paris durante los estudios de Francisco de Vitoria O.P. 1507–1522. Analecta Gregoriana, XIV*. Rome 1938.
Waddington, C., *Ramus, sa vie, ses écrits et ses opinions*, Paris 1855.

B. *Articles*

Abranches, C., 'Pedro da Fonseca. Valor e projecçao da sua obra', *Revista portuguesa de filosofia* **16** (1960) 117–123.
Angelelli, I., 'The Techniques of Disputation in the History of Logic', *Journal of Philosophy* **67** (1970) 800–815.
Ashworth, E. J., 'Joachim Jungius (1587–1657) and the Logic of Relations', *Archiv für Geschichte der Philosophie* **49** (1967) 72–85.
Ashworth, E. J., 'Propositional Logic in the Sixteenth and Early Seventeenth Centuries', *Notre Dame Journal of Formal Logic* **9** (1968) 179–192.
Ashworth, E. J., 'Petrus Fonseca and Material Implication', *Notre Dame Journal of Formal Logic* **9** (1968) 227–228.
Ashworth, E. J., 'The Doctrine of Supposition in the Sixteenth and Seventeenth Centuries', *Archiv für Geschichte der Philosophie* **51** (1969) 260–285. [Ashworth 1]
Ashworth, E. J., 'Some Notes on Syllogistic in the Sixteenth and Seventeenth Centuries', *Notre Dame Journal of Formal Logic* **11** (1970) 17–33. [Ashworth 2]
Ashworth, E. J., 'The Treatment of Semantic Paradoxes from 1400 to 1700', *Notre Dame Journal of Formal Logic* **13** (1972) 34–52. [Ashworth 3]
Ashworth, E. J., 'Strict and Material Implication in the Early Sixteenth Century', *Notre Dame Journal of Formal Logic* **13** (1972) 556–560.
Ashworth, E. J., 'The Theory of Consequence in the Late Fifteenth and Early Sixteenth Centuries', *Notre Dame Journal of Formal Logic* **14** (1973) 289–315.
Ashworth, E. J., 'Andreas Kesler and the Later Theory of Consequence', *Notre Dame Journal of Formal Logic* **14** (1973) 205–214.
Ashworth, E. J., 'Are There Really Two Logics?' *Dialogue* **12** (1973) 100–109.
Ashworth, E. J., 'Existential Assumptions in Late Medieval Logic', *American Philosophical Quarterly* **10** (1973) 141–147.
Ashworth, E. J., 'Some Additions to Risse's *Bibliographia Logica*', *Journal of the History of Philosophy:* forthcoming.
Ashworth, E. J., 'Priority of Analysis and Merely Confused Supposition', *Franciscan Studies:* forthcoming.
Ashworth, E. J., 'The Doctrine of *Exponibilia* in the Fifteenth and Sixteenth Centuries', *Vivarium:* forthcoming. [Ashworth 4]
Bocheński, I. M., 'Duae 'Consequentiae' Stephani de Monte', *Angelicum* **12** (1935) 397–399.

Bocheński, I. M., 'Formalization of a Scholastic Solution of the Paradox of the 'Liar'',
Logico-Philosophical Studies, edited by A. Menne, 64–66, Dordrecht 1962. [Bocheński[1]]

Boehner, P., 'A Mediaeval Theory of Supposition', *Franciscan Studies* 18 (1958) 240–289.

Boh, I., 'A Fifteenth Century Systematization of Primary Logic', *Memorias del XIII
Congreso Internacional de Filosofía*, Vol. V, 47–57. Mexico 1964.

Boh, I., 'Paul of Pergula on Supposition and Consequences', *Franciscan Studies* 25 (1965)
30–89.

Boh, I., 'Propositional Connectives, Supposition and Consequence in Paul of Pergola',
Notre Dame Journal of Formal Logic 7 (1966) 109–128.

Church, A., 'Review of Francis C. Wade: Translator's Introduction. *John of St Thomas,
Outlines of Formal Logic*', *Journal of Symbolic Logic* 24 (1959) 81–83.

Church, A., 'The History of the Question of Existential Import of Categorical Propositions',
Logic, Methodology and Philosophy of Science, edited by Y. Bar-Hillel, 417–424. Amsterdam 1965.

Corsano, A., 'Per la storia del pensiero del tardo Rinascimento. X. Lo strumentalismo
logico di I. Zabarella', *Giornale critico della filosofia italiana* 16 (1962) 507–517.

Dassonville, M., 'La 'Dialectique' de Pierre de la Ramée', *Université Laval Revue* 7[2]
(1952–1953) 608–616.

Dassonville, M., 'La genèse et les principes de la 'Dialectique' de Petrus Ramus', *Revue
Université Ottawa* (1953) 322–355.

De Pinho Dias, A., 'A *Isagoge* de Porfirio na Logica Conimbricense', *Revista portuguesa
da filosofia* 20 (1964) 108–130.

Doyle, J. J., 'John of St. Thomas and Mathematical Logic', *The New Scholasticism* 27 (1953)
3–38.

Duhamel, P. A., 'The Logic and Rhetoric of Peter Ramus', *Modern Philology* 46 (1949)
163–171.

Durkan, J., 'John Major: After 400 years', *Innes Review* 1 (1950) 131–139.

Edwards, W. F., 'Jacopo Zabarella: A Renaissance Aristotelian's View of Rhetoric and
Poetry and their Relation to Philosophy', *Arts libéraux et philosophie au moyen âge*
843–854. Montréal-Paris 1969.

Elie, H., 'Quelques maîtres de l'université de Paris vers l'an 1500', *Archives d'histoire
doctrinale et littéraire du moyen âge* 18 (1950–1951) 193–243.

Faust, A., 'Die Dialektik Rudolph Agricolas. Ein Beitrag zur Charakteristik des deutschen
Humanismus', *Archiv für Geschichte der Philosophie* 34 (1922) 118–135.

Ferreira Gomez, J., 'Pedro da Fonseca: Sixteenth Century Portuguese Philosopher',
International Philosophical Quarterly 6 (1966) 632–644.

Fisher, P. F., 'Milton's Logic', *Journal of the History of Ideas* 23 (1962) 37–60.

Franceschini, F., 'Osservazioni sulla logica di Jacopo Zabarella, nota per la società italiana
per il progresso delle scienze', *Atti della XXVI riunione della Società Italiana per il progresso delle scienze (Venezia, 12–18 Settembre 1937)* 3 (1938) 371–383.

Glanville, J. J., 'Zabarella and Poinsot on the Object and Nature of Logic', *Readings in
Logic*, edited by R. Houde 204–226. Dubuque, Iowa 1958.

Heath, T., 'Logical Grammar, Grammatical Logic and Humanism in Three German Universities', *Studies in the Renaissance* 18 (1971) 9–64.

Hickman, L., 'Late Scholastic Logics: Another look', *Journal of the History of Philosophy*
9 (1971) 226–234.

Moreno, A., 'Implicacion material en Juan de Santo Tomás', *Sapientia* 14 (1959) 188–191.

Moreno, A., 'Lógica proposicional en Juan de Santo Tomás', *Notre Dame Journal of
Formal Logic* 4 (1963) 113–134.

Moreno, A., 'Lógica proposicional en Juan de Santo Tomás', *Sapientia* 18 (1963) 86–107.

Muñoz Delgado, V., 'La enseñanza de la lógica en Salamanca durante el siglo xvi', *Salmanticensis* 1 (1954) 133–167. [Muñoz Delgado [1]]

Muñoz Delgado, V., 'Las sumulas de lógica del curso de filosofía de Fray Pedro de Oña (1560–1626)', *Estudios* [journal of the Orden de la Merced, Madrid] 17 (1961) 411–436.

Muñoz Delgado, V., 'La exposición sumulista de la doctrina silogistica de Fray Domingo de San Juan de Pie del Puerto (†1540)', *Estudios* 19 (1963) 3–49.

Muñoz Delgado, V., 'Narciso Gregorio y la lógica del humanismo en Salamanca durante la segunda mitad del siglo xvi', *Estudios* 19 (1963) 247–254.

Muñoz Delgado, V., 'Confirmación de la interpretación anterior en la obra lógica de Domingo de Soto', *Estudios* 20 (1964) 179–216.

Muñoz Delgado, V., 'Reflexiones acerca de la naturaleza de la lógica en la obra de Domingo de Soto', *Estudios* 20 (1964) 3–45.

Muñoz Delgado, V., 'Domingo Bañez y las sumulas en Salamanca a fines del siglo xvi', *Estudios* 21 (1965) 3–20.

Muñoz Delgado, V., 'Domingo de San Juan de Pie del Puerto y la su obra lógica acerca de las *oppositiones* entre proposiciones', *Estudios* 21 (1965) 161–186.

Muñoz Delgado, V., 'La lógica como 'scientia sermocinalis' en la obra de Pedro Sanchez Ciruelo', *Estudios* 22 (1966) 23–52.

Muñoz Delgado, V., 'Los commentarios a la lógica de Aristoteles de José de San Marcelino', *Estudios* 22 (1966) 187–204.

Muñoz Delgado, V., 'La lógica en Salamanca durante la primera mitad del siglo xvi', *Salmanticensis* 14 (1967) 171–207. [Muñoz Delgado [2]]

Muñoz Delgado, V., 'Nota sobra Pedro Cijar, Pedro Aymerich y Jacobo Almain', *Estudios* 23 (1967) 109–116.

Muñoz Delgado, V., 'Fuentes impresas de Lógica hispano-portuguesa del siglo xvi', *Reportorio de Historia de las Ciencias Eclesiasticos en España*, Salamanca, 1 (1967) 435–464. [Muñoz Delgado [3]]

Muñoz Delgado, V., 'La lógica en la universidad de Alcalá durante la primera mitad del siglo xvi', *Salmanticensis* 15 (1968) 161–218. [Muñoz Delgado [4]]

Muñoz Delgado, V., 'La obra lógica de los españoles en Paris (1500–1525)', *Estudios* 26 (1970) 209–280. [Muñoz Delgado [5]]

Muñoz Delgado, V., 'Los 'Principia Dialectices' (1519) de Alonso de Córdoba', *La Ciudad de Dios* 185 (1971) 44–72.

Muñoz Delgado, V., 'El compendio de 'Dialectica' (1633) de Martín Cajol, profesor de la Universidad de Huesca', *Estudios* 27 (1971) 207–235.

Muñoz Delgado, V., 'Cardillo de Villalpando y la lógica renacentista en Alcalá', *Estudios* 27 (1971) 511–555.

Muñoz Delgado, V., 'Pedro de Campis (c. 1498) y Juan Hidalgo (c. 1515) dos medicos filosofos', *Cuadernos de Historia de la Medicina Española* 11 (1972) 359–371.

Muñoz Delgado, V., 'La lógica de Bernardo Jordán. Estudio de su 'Explanatio in Petrum Hispanum' (Florencia 1514)', *La Ciudad de Dios* 185 (1972) 339–462.

Muñoz Delgado, V., 'La lógica formal en España (1340–1540)', *Estudios* 29 (1973) 37–52.

Muñoz Delgado, V., 'Juan Hidalgo (1516) comentarista del 'Compendio de lógica' de Pablo de Venecia', *La Ciudad de Dios* 186 (1973) 20–36.

Ong, W. J., 'Petrus Ramus and the Naming of Methodism', *Journal of the History of Ideas* 14 (1953) 235–248.

Ong, W. J., 'Ramist Method and the Commercial Mind', *Studies in the Renaissance* 8 (New York 1961) 155–172.

Pagallo, G. F., 'Note sulla *Logica* di Paolo Veneto: la critica alla dottrina del 'complexe significabile' di Gregorio da Rimini', *Atti del XII congresso internazionale di filosofia*, Vol. 9 (Firenze 1960) 183–191.

Prieto de Rey, M., 'Significacion y sentido ultimado. La nocion de *Suppositio* en la lógica de Juan de Santo Tomás', *Convivium* **15–16** (1963) 33–73; **19–20** (1965) 45–72 [Barcelona.]

Risse, W., 'Die Entwicklung der Dialektik bei Petrus Ramus', *Archiv für Geschichte der Philosophie* **42** (1960) 36–72.

Risse, W., 'Mathematik und Kombinatorik in der Logik der Renaissance', *Archiv für Philosophie* **11** (1962) 187–206.

Risse, W., 'Zur Vorgeschichte der cartesischen Methodenlehre', *Archiv für Geschichte der Philosophie* **45** (1963) 269–291.

Risse, W., 'Averoismo e Alesandrinismo nella logica del Rinascimento', *Filosofia* [Turin] **15** (1964) 15–30. [Risse[1]]

Rossi, P., 'Ramismo, logica, retorica nei secoli xvi e xvii', *Rivista critica di storia della filosofia* **12** (1957) 357–365.

Roure, M. L., 'Le traité 'Des propositions insolubles' de Jean de Celaya', *Archives d'histoire doctrinale et littéraire du moyen âge* **37** (1962) 235–336.

Thomas, I., 'Material Implication in John of St Thomas', *Dominican Studies* **3** (1950) 180.

Thomas, I., 'Mediaeval Aftermath: Oxford Logic and Logicians of the Seventeenth Century', in: *Oxford Studies Presented to Daniel Callus, Oxford Historical Society New Series* **16** (1964) 297–311.

Thomas, I., 'The Written Liar and Thomas Oliver', *Notre Dame Journal of Formal Logic* **6** (1965) 201–208.

Thomas, I., 'The Later History of the *Pons Asinorum*' in *Contributions to Logic and Methodology in Honor of I. M. Bocheński*, edited by A. T. Tymieniecka in collaboration with C. Parsons, 142–150, Amsterdam 1965.

Thomas, I., 'Interregnum' under 'Logic, History of' in *The Encyclopedia of Philosophy* **4** (New York-London 1967) 534–537.

Vasoli, C., 'Retorica e dialettica in Pietro Ramo', *Archivio di filosofia* **3** (1953) 93–134.

Vasoli, C., 'Dialettica e Retorica in Rodolfo Agricola', *Atti dell' Accademia toscana di scienze e lettere 'La Colombaria'* **22** (NS 8) (1957–1958) 307–355. [Vasoli[1]]

Vasoli, C., 'Il Poliziano maestro di dialettica', *Il Poliziano e il suo tempo. Atti del IV congresso internazionale di studi sul Rinascimento* (Firenze 1957) 161–172. [Vasoli[2]]

Vasoli, C., 'Le *dialecticae disputationes* di Lorenzo Valla e la critica umanistica della logica aristotelica', *Rivista critica di storia della filosofia*. I: **12** (1957) 412–434; II: **13** (1958) 27–46. [Vasoli[3]]

Vasoli, C., 'J. Lefèvre d'Etaples e le origini del 'Fabrismo'', *Rinascimento* **10** (1959) 221–254, [Vasoli[4]]

Vasoli, C., 'Su una 'Dialettica' attribuita all' Argiropulo', *Rinascimento* **10** (1959) 157–164.

Vasoli, C., 'La dialectica di Giorgio Trapazunzio', *Atti e memorie dell' Accademia toscana di scienze e lettere 'La Colombaria'* **24** (NS 10) (1959–1960) 299–327. [Vasoli[5]]

Vasoli, C., 'Ricerche sulle 'Dialettiche' quattrocentesche', *Rivista critica di storia della filosofia* **15** (1960) 265–287. [Vasoli[6]]

Vasoli, C., 'Juan Luis Vives e un programma umanistico di riforma della logica', *Atti dell' Accademia toscana di scienze e lettere 'La Colombaria'* **25** (NS 11) (1960–1961) 219–263. [Vasoli[7]]

Vasoli, C., 'Il Giovanni Ludovico Vives e la polemica antiscolastica nello *In pseudodialecticos*', *Miscelânea de Estudos a Joaquim de Carvalho* **7** (1961) 679–687.

Vasoli, C., 'Ricerche sulle 'Dialettiche' del cinquecento', *Rivista critica di storia della filosofia* I: **20** (1965) 115–150; II: **20** (1965) 451–480; III: **21** (1966) 123–140. [Vasoli[8]]

INDEX OF NAMES

SYNTHESE HISTORICAL LIBRARY

Texts and Studies
in the History of Logic and Philosophy

Editors:

N. KRETZMANN (Cornell University)
G. NUCHELMANS (University of Leyden)
L. M. DE RIJK (University of Leyden)

1. M. T. BEONIO-BROCCHIERI FUMAGALLI, *The Logic of Abelard.* Translated from the Italian. 1969, IX + 101 pp.
2. GOTTFRIED WILHELM LEIBNITZ, *Philosophical Papers and Letters.* A selection translated and edited, with an introduction by Leroy E. Loemker. 1969, XII + 736 pp.
3. ERNST MALLY, *Logische Schriften* (ed. by Karl Wolf and Paul Weingartner). 1971, X + 340 pp.
4. LEWIS WHITE BECK (ed.), *Proceedings of the Third International Kant Congress.* 1972, XI + 718 pp.
5. BERNARD BOLZANO, *Theory of Science* (ed. by Jan Berg). 1973, XV + 398 pp.
6. J. M. E. MORAVCSIK (ed.), *Patterns in Plato's Thought. Papers arising out of the 1971 West Coast Greek Philosophy Conference*, 1973, VIII + 212 pp.
7. NABIL SHEHABY, *The Propositional Logic of Avicenna: A Translation from al-Shifā': al-Qiyās*, with Introduction, Commentary and Glossary. 1973, XIII + 296 pp.
8. DESMOND PAUL HENRY, *Commentary on De Grammatico: The Historical-Logical Dimensions of a Dialogue of St. Anselm's.* 1974, IX + 345 pp.
9. JOHN CORCORAN, *Ancient Logic and Its Modern Interpretations.* 1974, X + 208 pp.

SYNTHESE LIBRARY

Monographs on Epistemology, Logic, Methodology,
Philosophy of Science, Sociology of Science and of Knowledge, and on the
Mathematical Methods of Social and Behavioral Sciences

Editors:

DONALD DAVIDSON (The Rockefeller University and Princeton University)
JAAKKO HINTIKKA (Academy of Finland and Stanford University)
GABRIËL NUCHELMANS (University of Leyden)
WESLEY C. SALMON (University of Arizona)

1. J. M. BOCHEŃSKI, *A Precis of Mathematical Logic.* 1959, X + 100 pp.
2. P. L. GUIRAUD, *Problèmes et méthodes de la statistique linguistique.* 1960, VI + 146 pp.
3. HANS FREUDENTHAL (ed.), *The Concept and the Role of the Model in Mathematics and Natural and Social Sciences. Proceedings of a Colloquium held at Utrecht, The Netherlands, January 1960.* 1961, VI + 194 pp.
4. EVERT W. BETH, *Formal Methods. An Introduction to Symbolic Logic and the Study of Effective Operations in Arithmetic and Logic.* 1962, XIV + 170 pp.
5. B. H. KAZEMIER and D. VUYSJE (eds.), *Logic and Language. Studies dedicated to Professor Rudolf Carnap on the Occasion of his Seventieth Birthday.* 1962, VI + 256 pp.
6. MARX W. WARTOFSKY (ed.), *Proceedings of the Boston Colloquium for the Philosophy of Science, 1961–1962,* Boston Studies in the Philosophy of Science (ed. by Robert S. Cohen and Marx W. Wartofsky), Volume I. 1963, VIII + 212 pp.
7. A. A. ZINOV'EV, *Philosophical Problems of Many-Valued Logic.* 1963, XIV + 155 pp.
8. GEORGES GURVITCH, *The Spectrum of Social Time.* 1964, XXVI + 152 pp.
9. PAUL LORENZEN, *Formal Logic.* 1965, VIII + 123 pp.
10. ROBERT S. COHEN and MARX W. WARTOFSKY (eds.), *In Honor of Philipp Frank,* Boston Studies in the Philosophy of Science (ed. by Robert S. Cohen and Marx W. Wartofsky), Volume II. 1965, XXXIV + 475 pp.
11. EVERT W. BETH, *Mathematical Thought. An Introduction to the Philosophy of Mathematics.* 1965, XII + 208 pp.
12. EVERT W. BETH and JEAN PIAGET, *Mathematical Epistemology and Psychology.* 1966, XXII + 326 pp.
13. GUIDO KÜNG, *Ontology and the Logistic Analysis of Language. An Enquiry into the Contemporary Views on Universals.* 1967, XI + 210 pp.
14. ROBERT S. COHEN and MARX W. WARTOFSKY (eds.), *Proceedings of the Boston Colloquium for the Philosophy of Science 1964–1966, in Memory of Norwood Russell Hanson,* Boston Studies in the Philosophy of Science (ed. by Robert S. Cohen and Marx W. Wartofsky), Volume III. 1967, XLIX + 489 pp.
15. C. D. BROAD, *Induction, Probability, and Causation. Selected Papers.* 1968, XI + 296 pp.
16. GÜNTHER PATZIG, *Aristotle's Theory of the Syllogism. A Logical-Philosophical Study of Book A of the Prior Analytics.* 1968, XVII + 215 pp.
17. NICHOLAS RESCHER, *Topics in Philosophical Logic.* 1968, XIV + 347 pp.

18. ROBERT S. COHEN and MARX W. WARTOFSKY (eds.), *Proceedings of the Boston Colloquium for the Philosophy of Science 1966–1968*, Boston Studies in the Philosophy of Science (ed. by Robert S. Cohen and Marx W. Wartofsky), Volume IV. 1969, VIII + 537 pp.

19. ROBERT S. COHEN and MARX W. WARTOFSKY (eds.), *Proceedings of the Boston Colloquium for the Philosophy of Science 1966–1968*, Boston Studies in the Philosophy of Science (ed. by Robert S. Cohen and Marx W. Wartofsky), Volume V. 1969, VIII + 482 pp.

20. J. W. DAVIS, D. J. HOCKNEY, and W. K. WILSON (eds.), *Philosophical Logic*. 1969, VIII + 277 pp.

21. D. DAVIDSON and J. HINTIKKA (eds.), *Words and Objections: Essays on the Work of W. V. Quine*, 1969, VIII + 366 pp.

22. PATRICK SUPPES, *Studies in the Methodology and Foundations of Science. Selected Papers from 1911 to 1969*. 1969, XII + 473 pp.

23. JAAKKO HINTIKKA, *Models for Modalities. Selected Essays*. 1969, IX + 220 pp.

24. NICHOLAS RESCHER et al. (eds.), *Essay in Honor of Carl G. Hempel. A Tribute on the Occasion of his Sixty-Fifth Birthday*. 1969, VII + 272 pp.

25. P. V. TAVANEC (ed.), *Problems of the Logic of Scientific Knowledge*. 1969, XII + 429 pp.

26. MARSHALL SWAIN (ed.), *Induction, Acceptance, and Rational Belief*. 1970, VII + 232 pp.

27. ROBERT S. COHEN and RAYMOND J. SEEGER (eds.), *Ernst Mach: Physicist and Philosopher*, Boston Studies in the Philosophy of Science (ed. by Robert S. Cohen and Marx W. Wartofsky), Volume VI. 1970, VIII + 295 pp.

28. JAAKKO HINTIKKA and PATRICK SUPPES, *Information and Inference*. 1970, X + 336 pp.

29. KAREL LAMBERT, *Philosophical Problems in Logic. Some Recent Developments*. 1970, VII + 176 pp.

30. ROLF A. EBERLE, *Nominalistic Systems*. 1970, IX + 217 pp.

31. PAUL WEINGARTNER and GERHARD ZECHA (eds.), *Induction, Physics, and Ethics, Proceedings and Discussions of the 1968 Salzburg Colloquium in the Philosophy of Science*. 1970, X + 382 pp.

32. EVERT W. BETH, *Aspects of Modern Logic*. 1970, XI + 176 pp.

33. RISTO HILPINEN (ed.), *Deontic Logic: Introductory and Systematic Readings*. 1971, VII + 182 pp.

34. JEAN-LOUIS KRIVINE, *Introduction to Axiomatic Set Theory*. 1971, VII + 98 pp.

35. JOSEPH D. SNEED, *The Logical Structure of Mathematical Physics*. 1971, XV + 311 pp.

36. CARL R. KORDIG, *The Justification of Scientific Change*. 1971, XIV + 119 pp.

37. MILIČ ČAPEK, *Bergson and Modern Physics*, Boston Studies in the Philosophy of Science (ed. by Robert S. Cohen and Marx W. Wartofsky), Volume VII. 1971, XV + 414 pp.

38. NORWOOD RUSSELL HANSON, *What I do not Believe, and other Essays* (ed. by Stephen Toulmin and Harry Woolf). 1971, XII + 390 pp.

39. ROGER C. BUCK and ROBERT S. COHEN (eds.), *PSA 1970. In Memory of Rudolf Carnap*, Boston Studies in the Philosophy of Science (ed. by Robert S. Cohen and Marx W. Wartofsky), Volume VIII. 1971, LXVI + 615 pp. Also available as a paperback.

40. DONALD DAVIDSON and GILBERT HARMAN (eds.), *Semantics of Natural Language*. 1972, X + 769 pp. Also available as a paperback.

41. YEHOSUA BAR-HILLEL (ed.), *Pragmatics of Natural Languages*. 1971, VII + 231 pp.

42. SÖREN STENLUND, *Combinators, λ-Terms and Proof Theory*. 1972, 184 pp.

43. MARTIN STRAUSS, *Modern Physics and Its Philosophy. Selected Papers in the Logic, History, and Philosophy of Science*. 1972, X + 297 pp.

44. MARIO BUNGE, *Method, Model and Matter*. 1973, VII + 196 pp.
45. MARIO BUNGE, *Philosophy of Physics*. 1973, IX + 248 pp.
46. A. A. ZINOV'EV, *Foundations of the Logical Theory of Scientific Knowledge (Complex Logic)*, Boston Studies in the Philosophy of Science (ed. by Robert S. Cohen and Marx W. Wartofsky), Volume IX. Revised and enlarged English edition with an appendix, by G. A. Smirnov, E. A. Sidorenka, A. M. Fedina, and L. A. Bobrova. 1973, XXII + 301 pp. Also available as a paperback.
47. LADISLAV TONDL, *Scientific Procedures*, Boston Studies in the Philosophy of Science (ed. by Robert S. Cohen and Marx W. Wartofsky), Volume X. 1973, XII + 268 pp. Also available as a paperback.
48. NORWOOD RUSSELL HANSON, *Constellations and Conjectures* (ed. by Willard C. Humphreys, Jr.). 1973, X + 282 pp.
49. K. J. J. HINTIKKA, J. M. E. MORAVCSIK, and P. SUPPES (eds.), *Approaches to Natural Language. Proceedings of the 1970 Stanford Workshop on Grammar and Semantics*. 1973, VIII + 526 pp. Also available as a paperback.
50. MARIO BUNGE (ed.), *Exact Philosophy – Problems, Tools, and Goals*. 1973, X + 214 pp.
51. RADU J. BOGDAN and ILKKA NIINILUOTO (eds.), *Logic, Language, and Probability*. A selection of papers contributed to Sections IV, VI, and XI of the Fourth International Congress for Logic, Methodology, and Philosophy of Science, Bucharest, September 1971. 1973, X + 323 pp.
52. GLENN PEARCE and PATRICK MAYNARD (eds.), *Conceptual Change*. 1973, XII + 282 pp.
53. ILKKA NIINILUOTO and RAIMO TUOMELA, *Theoretical Concepts and Hypothetico-Inductive Inference*. 1973, VII + 264 pp.
54. ROLAND FRAÏSSÉ, *Course of Mathematical Logic* – Volume I: *Relation and Logical Formula*. 1973, XVI + 186 pp. Also available as a paperback.
55. ADOLF GRÜNBAUM, *Philosophical Problems of Space and Time*. Second, enlarged edition, Boston Studies in the Philosophy of Science (ed. by Robert S. Cohen and Marx W. Wartofsky), Volume XII. 1973, XXIII + 884 pp. Also available as a paperback.
56. PATRICK SUPPES (ed.), *Space, Time, and Geometry*. 1973, XI + 424 pp.
57. HANS KELSEN, *Essays in Legal and Moral Philosophy*, selected and introduced by Ota Weinberger, 1973, XXVIII + 300 pp.
58. R. J. SEEGER and ROBERT S. COHEN (eds.), *Philosophical Foundations of Science, Proceedings of an AAAS Program, 1969*. Boston Studies in the Philosophy of Science (ed. by Robert S. Cohen and Marx W. Wartofsky), Volume XI. 1974, IX + 545 pp. Also available as paperback.
59. ROBERT S. COHEN and MARX W. WARTOFSKY (eds.), *Logical and Epistemological Studies in Contemporary Physics*, Boston Studies in the Philosophy of Science (ed. by Robert S. Cohen and Marx W. Wartofsky), Volume XIII. 1973, VIII + 462 pp. Also available as a paperback.
60. ROBERT S. COHEN and MARX W. WARTOFSKY (eds.), *Methodological and Historical Essays in the Natural and Social Sciences. Proceedings of the Boston Colloquium for the Philosophy of Science, 1969–1972*, Boston Studies in the Philosophy of Science (ed. by Robert S. Cohen and Marx W. Wartofsky), Volume XIV. 1974, VIII + 405 pp. Also available as a paperback.
63. SÖREN STENLUND (ed.), *Logical Theory and Semantic Analysis. Essays Dedicated to Stig Kanger on His Fiftieth Birthday*. 1974, V + 217 pp.
64. KENNETH SCHAFFNER and ROBERT S. COHEN (eds.), *Proceedings of the 1972 Biennial Meeting, Philosophy of Science Association*, Boston Studies in the Philosophy of Science (ed. by Robert S. Cohen and Marx W. Wartofsky), Volume XX. 1974, VIII + 445 pp. Also available as a paperback.

65. HENRY E. KYBURG, JR., *The Logical Foundations of Statistical Inference.* 1974, IX + 421 pp.
66. MARJORIE GRENE, *The Understanding of Nature: Essays in the Philosophy of Biology,* Boston Studies in the Philosophy of Science (ed. by Robert S. Cohen and Marx W. Wartofsky), Volume XXIII. 1974, XII + 360 pp. Also available as a paperback.

In Preparation

61. ROBERT S. COHEN and MARX W. WARTOFSKY (eds.), *For Dirk Struik. Scientific, Historical, and Political Essays in Honor of Dirk J. Struik,* Boston Studies in the Philosophy of Science (ed. by Robert S. Cohen and Marx W. Wartofsky), Volume XV. Also available as a paperback.
62. KAZIMIERZ AJDUKIEWICZ, *Pragmatic Logic,* transl. from the Polish by Olgierd Wojtasiewicz.
67. JAN M. BROEKMAN, *Structuralism: Moscow, Prague, Paris.*
68. NORMAN GESCHWIND, *Selected Papers on Language and the Brain*, Boston Studies in the Philosophy of Science (ed. by Robert S. Cohen and Marx W. Wartofsky) Volume XVI. Also available as a paperback.
69. ROLAND FRAÏSSÉ, *Course of Mathematical Logic* – Volume II: *Model Theory.*